Photomontage Illustrating PRT Installed in Los Angeles Civic Center

FUNDAMENTALS

OF

PERSONAL

RAPID TRANSIT

Based on a Program of Research, 1968–1976, at
THE AEROSPACE CORPORATION, El Segundo, California

Editor and Principal Author
Jack H. Irving, Ph. D.

Associate Authors
Harry Bernstein
C. L. Olson
Jon Buyan

Lexington Books
D.C. Heath and Company
Lexington, Massachusetts
Toronto

Technical questions relative to the study reported in this book should be directed to the authors. Mssrs. Bernstein, Olson, and Buyan should be contacted at The Aerospace Corporation, 2350 E. El Segundo Boulevard, El Segundo, California (mailing address: Post Office Box 92957, Los Angeles, California 90009). Queries to Dr. Irving should be addressed to Jack H. Irving, 13202 Jonesboro Place, Los Angeles, California 90049.

Library of Congress Cataloging in Publication Data

Irving, Jack H   1920-
      Fundamentals of personal rapid transit.

      Includes index.
      1. Personal rapid transit. I. Aerospace Corporation. II. Title.
TA1207.I782   625.4'4   78-13604
ISBN 0-669-02520-8

Published simultaneously in Canada.

Printed in the United States of America.

International Standard Book Number: 0-669-02520-8

Library of Congress Catalog Card Number: 78-13604

FOREWORD

BY THE EDITOR

This book summarizes the work on Personal Rapid Transit (PRT) carried out at The Aerospace Corporation from 1968 to 1976. It is the intent of the authors that the book be useful to experts in and students of transportation and engineering, but in addition we have tried to make it readable by the interested layman. Our emphasis has been in describing concepts rather than engineering details because we believe that it is the concepts that are important, whereas there may be several alternative engineering implementations of approximately equal merit. The use of mathematics is also minimized and where equations do occur, they can be bypassed without too much loss of meaning.[1]

As a not-for-profit company, The Aerospace Corporation conducts a program of company-sponsored research to apply its talents to solving technical problems of public importance. In 1968 one of my duties as a Vice President of the Company was to recommend such a program of research to the management and Board of Trustees for their approval. It appeared to me that the capabilities of the company could be brought to bear effectively on problems of transportation, and no area of transportation was more critical than urban transportation. There was a tremendous cost in wasted time as people drove to work through congested traffic, and again as they returned home. The automobile was responsible for a disturbing trend in land use, especially in Central Business Districts where up to 70% of the land area was being used for streets, freeways, access lanes, parking lots, and sidewalks. Oil shortages were already apparent and it was clear that alternate sources of energy would soon be needed. In auto-oriented cities, and especially in the Los Angeles area, where The Aerospace Corporation is located, automotive air pollution was becoming a serious problem. Moreover, widespread deployment of

---

[1] We regret that we were not able to use metric units, but the analyses reported here were performed over a number of years in British engineering units (feet, pounds, seconds), often using rounded numbers, and it would seem strained to express those rounded numbers in terms of their metric equivalents.

existing transit modes was not the answer because they did not have the features to attract people out of their automobiles; door-to-door trip times would be substantially longer and comfort and privacy would be sacrificed. Transit modes also were plagued either by high capital costs or high operating costs.

The idea of PRT is not a new one. Basically it is an automated taxicab system — a public transit system of three-to six-passenger vehicles operating automatically on a network of exclusive guideways, separate from street and pedestrian traffic. The traveler and his companions would be assigned a private vehicle, not shared with strangers, to take them on a nonstop no-transfers trip from their origin station to their destination station. In 1966 the U.S. Department of Housing and Urban Development sponsored a study, "Tomorrow's Transportation," by a number of organizations to assess the potential of advanced transportation systems. In particular, the studies of the General Research Corporation and the Stanford Research Institute strongly recommended Personal Rapid Transit as having a potential for a high quality of service that might be competitive with the private automobile. However, there were a number of questions about the technical and economic feasibility of PRT systems. The purpose of The Aerospace Corporation research, then, was to try to find satisfactory answers to these questions.

During the first 18 months of the program, work was confined to paper studies which included system economics, network layout, traffic management, vehicle propulsion and control, and safety. Then, for the next two years, in addition to continuing our paper studies, we embarked on an experimental program to test our ideas on propulsion and control. For this purpose we constructed a one-tenth scale model test track. More recently we have developed a number of digital computer programs for simulating traffic management on large networks and for estimating system patronage; we have also developed models for cost and reliability.

We believe that this work has demonstrated the technical and economic feasibility of PRT. We think that our design approach is a good one, but we make no claim that it is the only way to go. With feasibility established and a good design approach demonstrated, The Aerospace Corporation has successfully completed the original intent of the project and has gone as far as a nonmanufacturing organization of its type should go. It is publishing this book to place its findings before the public with the hope that government agencies and private industry will build upon the foundations laid here. For my part, I have recently left Aerospace and am seeking ways to accelerate the realization of the full potential of PRT.

During the period of the Corporation's PRT project others have not been idle. Most of the work carried on in the United States by manufacturers was on near-cousins to PRT, utilizing larger vehicles in the mode of an automated bus service operating on exclusive guideways. Although there is a good deal of commonality with PRT, there are also important differences. Studies relating to PRT were carried out in the United States at a number of universities, with some of the early important work at the University of Minnesota. In England some very significant studies were carried out on a PRT system called "Cabtrack." But of major significance are three full-scale development and test programs for PRT systems — the "Cabintaxi" system in the Federal Republic of Germany, the "Computer-Controlled Vehicle System" in Japan, and the "Aramis" system in France. Since this book is reporting primarily on the work carried on by The Aerospace Corporation, there will be no comprehensive descriptions of the foreign PRT systems which have recently undergone engineering tests, but there will be occasional references to the technologies utilized in these systems.

It is very encouraging that the Urban Mass Transportation Administration of the U.S. Department of Transportation is now sponsoring a program of Automated Guideway Transit Technology development, which spans the technology of PRT as well as other automated guideway transit modes. The Aerospace Corporation is now conducting additional studies of PRT as a part of that program. Hopefully it will not be too long before the United States will have its own full-scale PRT development and test program.

I am deeply indebted to the management of The Aerospace Corporation, and especially to its President, Dr. Ivan A. Getting, not only for the Company's financial support of the activities reported herein, but also for their continued expression of confidence that we were performing meaningful research in an important area. Although the work was under my general cognizance, specific and devoted leadership came from Mr. Harry Bernstein and his associate, Mr. C. L. Olson. The following is a partial list of the others who made an important contribution to this work:

R. W. Bruce	R. B. Fling
L. R. Bush	G. H. Fuller
J. R. Buyan	F. E. Goroszko
D. J. Cavicchio	J. F. Grundvig
W. K. Clarkson	K. E. Hagen
P. Dergarabedian	W. H. Huber
M. V. Dixon	A. L. Johnson, Jr.
M. Donabedian	J. H. Katz

D. E. Kelley

R. C. LaFrance

V. Larson

R. H. Leatherman

S. E. Levine

G. J. Liopiros

R. A. Mack

S. M. Melzer

S. Miller

A. V. Munson

J. Rossoff

A. Schnitt

B. Siegel

T. H. Silva

A. M. Timmer

B. R. Timmer

T. E. Travis

H. W. Webb

J. D. Wilson

As to this volume, each chapter carries the by-line of its principal author, although there has been a significant interchange of ideas among us.

I would like to thank Mr. Burton Sauer and Mrs. A. R. Pearce for their assistance in editing this book, and Messrs. T. Hamilton and H. Fockler for art and production coordination.

The Editor

July 15, 1977

CONTENTS

xii   *Contents*

FIGURES

TABLES

Chapter 1
SERVICE CONCEPTS

Jack H. Irving

1.1 THE NEED FOR A BETTER SERVICE

Today, in the United States, there is no urban public transit which can be considered a serious competitor with the private automobile — except perhaps in New York City where driving is so difficult and parking costs so prohibitive. According to the 1970 census, the combination of bus[1], streetcar, urban rail, and commuter rail serve only 5.5% of the urban trip miles[2]. During the decade 1960-1970, while urban automobile usage was increasing 74% in passenger-miles traveled, bus dropped 26%, and rail 8½%[2]. Since 1970, with massive infusion of public funds, the downward trend nationally in transit use has been arrested (see Fig. 1-1), but only

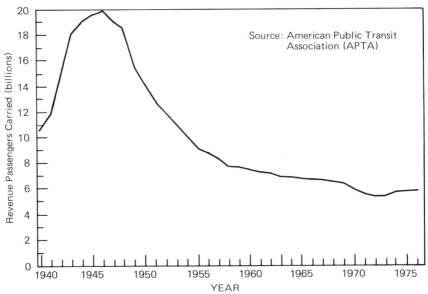

Fig. 1-1. Transit Ridership 1940-1976

[1] Includes trolley-bus but excludes school bus.
[2] 1972 National Transportation Report, U.S. Dept. of Transportation, p. 189.

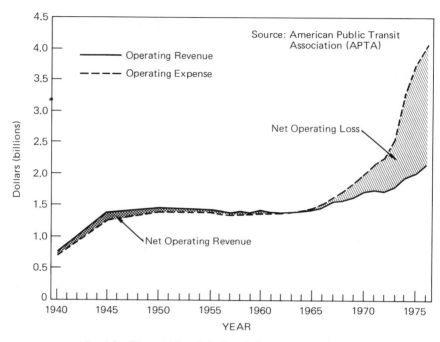

Fig. 1-2. Financial Trends in Transit Operations 1940-1976

with large operating subsidies (see Fig. 1-2). These subsidies are in addition to the very large government subsidies for capital improvement.

The reason for the sad state of public transit is a very basic one — the transit systems just do not offer a service which will attract people away from their automobiles. Consequently, their patronage comes very largely from those who cannot drive, either because they are too young, too old, or because they are too poor to own and operate an automobile. Look at it from the standpoint of a commuter who lives in a suburb and is trying to get to work in the central business district (CBD). If he is going to go by transit, a typical scenario might be the following: he must first walk to the closest bus stop, let us say a five or ten minute walk, and then he may have to wait up to another ten minutes, possibly in inclement weather, for the bus to arrive. When it arrives, he may have to stand unless he is lucky enough to find a seat. The bus will be caught up in street congestion and move slowly, and it will make many stops completely unrelated to his trip objective. The bus may then let him off at a terminal to a suburban train. Again he must wait, and, after boarding the train, again experience a number of stops on the way to the CBD, and possibly again he may have to stand in the aisle. He will get off at the station most convenient to his destination and possibly have to transfer again onto

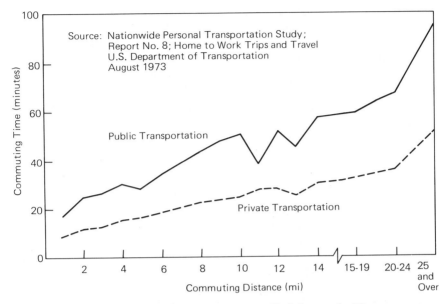

Fig. 1-3. Average Metropolitan Home-to-Work Commuting Time

a distribution system. It is no wonder that in those cities where ample inexpensive parking is available, most of those who can drive do drive.

Quantitatively, the situation is summarized in Fig. 1-3 which compares travel times for the home-to-work trip of those who go by private automobile with those who take public transit. You will note that the transit travel times are almost double those of the automobile. Now, considering that the times for transit given in the figure arose from surveying the relatively few who had chosen transit and not the majority who had rejected transit, we can only imagine what the time ratio would be for the total population.

Of currently available public transit modes, only the taxicab offers a service comparable to that of the private automobile — no transfers are required, one is seated all the way, and the vehicle is not usually shared with strangers. But, one often has to wait for a taxi to arrive and, of course, the taxicab shares with the private automobile the delays of traffic congestion. Unfortunately, from the standpoint of the urban traveler, the taxicab is very expensive because of the high labor component in the operating cost. But, because of its superior service, while transit was falling in the 60's, passenger miles by taxi[3] went up 31% — and with no public subsidy.

What is needed is a transit system which not only will serve the transit captives (the young, old, and poor), and give them a greater

---

[3] See footnote 2.

mobility, but will have the service features necessary to attract a significant number of those who might otherwise drive an automobile. This is especially important during the peak traffic periods when automobile transportation is plagued with problems of congestion and disproportionate air pollution and energy wastage. Areawide personal rapid transit (PRT) has the promise of providing just such a service. Like the automobile, it is convenient, requires no waiting or transfers, and provides privacy. Yet it has low operating costs, is quiet, reduces air pollution, is energy efficient, and relieves dependence on petroleum.

1.2   CATEGORIES OF AUTOMATED GUIDEWAY TRANSIT (AGT)

Historically the term "Personal Rapid Transit" or PRT referred to a system which might be regarded as an automated taxicab system — a system of small three- to six-passenger automated vehicles for the private use of the traveler and his traveling companions, but not shared with strangers; the traveler is carried nonstop and without transfers from his origin station to his destination station. Later "Personal Rapid Transit" was used to refer to any automated guideway system, regardless of the type of service provided or the size of the vehicles, although typically they were much smaller than conventional rail cars.

To clarify this ambiguity in terminology, "Automated Guideway Transit" or AGT has been proposed as the generic term, and "Personal Rapid Transit" or PRT is again restricted to its original historical meaning. This convention, recently adopted by the U.S. Department of Transportation, will be used here.

Automated Guideway Transit (AGT) is thus defined to be any transit system carrying completely automated vehicles on fixed guideways along an exclusive right of way. The guideways may be underground, at ground level, or elevated, but in any event they are grade-separated from street and pedestrian traffic, so that such traffic will not penetrate the exclusive right of way of the automated vehicles. The vehicles can be operated as single units or in trains. Three major categories of AGT systems have been defined:

Shuttle-Loop Transit (SLT)

Group Rapid Transit (GRT)

Personal Rapid Transit (PRT)

Unfortunately there is still not much standardization in the definition of these subcategories, nor are the definitions such that they unambiguously span the entire spectrum of AGT systems. Nevertheless, the definitions are useful in ordering AGT services from the most conventional mass transit services (SLT) to the most personalized (PRT).

The following subsections will define and discuss some of the salient features of these three categories of AGT. In addition, we shall define a promising hybrid of PRT and GRT. In Sec. 1.6 we discuss a related service mode, Dual Mode Transit (DMT), which utilizes vehicles that can travel automatically on an AGT guideway and can also be driven manually on streets and highways.

1.2.1 Shuttle-Loop Transit (SLT)

Shuttle and loop transit systems are the simplest types of AGT systems. The simplest type of shuttle system contains only a single vehicle or a single train of vehicles moving back and forth on a single guideway. There will, of course, be stations at each end of the guideway and there may be intermediate stops as well, as illustrated in Fig. 1-4. This type of system is the horizontal equivalent of an

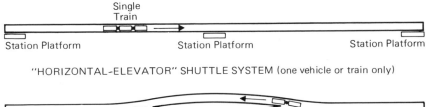

Single Train

Station Platform   Station Platform   Station Platform

"HORIZONTAL-ELEVATOR" SHUTTLE SYSTEM (one vehicle or train only)

SHUTTLE WITH BYPASS (2 vehicles or trains)

Fig. 1-4. Plan View of Two Variations of Shuttle Transit

automatic elevator. A somewhat more complex version could use two or more vehicles or trains with bypasses so that the oppositely-directed vehicles can pass each other. An example of the latter which involves two stations and a single bypass is the Ford Motor Company's ACT (Automatically Controlled Transportation) system for Dearborn, Michigan, and for the airport at Hartford, Connecticut.

In simple loop systems, vehicles or trains of vehicles stop at each station on a guideway loop, as illustrated in Fig. 1-5. A guideway loop is any closed path. An example of a loop system is the Westinghouse Electric system installed at the Seattle-Tacoma Airport.

Because the stations in a loop transit system are on-line and not off on sidings as often employed in the more complex GRT and PRT systems, the headway or time between passage of one vehicle or train and the next is typically 60 sec or greater. This gives time for the first vehicle or train to unload, load, and clear a station area before the next one arrives.

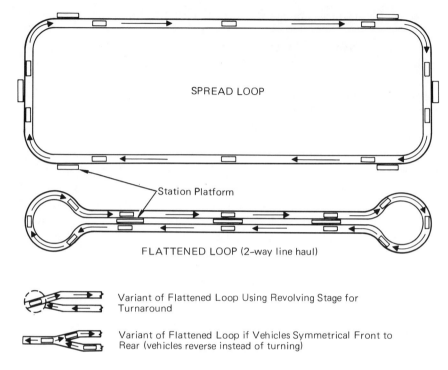

SPREAD LOOP

Station Platform

FLATTENED LOOP (2–way line haul)

Variant of Flattened Loop Using Revolving Stage for Turnaround

Variant of Flattened Loop if Vehicles Symmetrical Front to Rear (vehicles reverse instead of turning)

Fig. 1-5. Several Examples of Loop Systems

There is ambiguity in recent government publications as to whether or not an automated two-way line-haul system is to be regarded as SLT. A line-haul configuration may certainly be viewed as a flattened loop, as illustrated in Fig. 1-5. The figure also shows that instead of the vehicle or train turning by traversing an arc at the end of the line-haul run, variants could use a turntable, or, if the vehicles are symmetrical front to rear, a single spur for reversing the vehicle's or train's motion. One government publication classifies the two-way line-haul as a shuttle with two lines. Still another introduces a fourth category of AGT, Automated Rail Transit (ART), although this term has the unfortunate connotation of implying a rail suspension system, where, of course, any kind of suspension from rubber tires to magnetic suspension might be used.

In any event, the line-haul configuration with on-line stations shares with loop systems the necessity of operating at headways of 60 sec or greater.

Very little more will be said of SLT systems in this volume, although, in discussing the costs and benefits of an area-wide PRT system, conventional line-haul rail will be used as a basis for comparison.

1.2.2 Group Rapid Transit (GRT)

Group Rapid Transit (GRT) systems may be considered as an automated bus or jitney service where a passenger must share a vehicle with others. As with SLT, the vehicles can run alone or in trains, but GRT makes greater use of vehicle switching. Usually stations will be off-line on sidings so that a vehicle or train may stop at selected stations but bypass others. Because most stations are off-line, GRT may use shorter minimum headways than SLT, typically ranging from 3 to 30 sec. Many GRT systems involve branching so that more than one route may be available from the departure station. However, the possibility of a person being required to transfer from one GRT vehicle to another is not precluded. Typical vehicles accommodate from 10 to 70 passengers, some of whom may be standing. Examples of GRT are the Boeing system in Morgantown, West Virginia, and LTV's Airtrans system at the Dallas-Fort Worth Airport.

One common characteristic of all GRT systems is that they require that passengers wait at their origin (departure) station. For the nonstop origin-to-destination service, described below, a traveler arriving at the origin station must wait for a car to be dispatched to his destination station. Such dispatchings must not be too frequent if the vehicle is to have a satisfactory seat loading. If the service involves multiple stops, then a traveler must wait for the right vehicle to come along and pick him up.

Following is a partial listing of the great many possible variations in the type of GRT service.

Service Type A. Nonstop Origin-to-Destination Service

As with PRT, a GRT system may provide a nonstop service between pairs of stations. In GRT, however, the vehicle is shared among strangers. This has the advantage over PRT of decreasing the number of vehicles required. However, for a shared vehicle nonstop origin-to-destination service it is necessary for a patron to wait at his departure station until enough other persons have arrived going to his destination station to warrant the assignment of a vehicle to that trip. Clearly the larger the size of the vehicle[4] being used, the longer the necessary waiting times to realize a sufficient passenger load. An analysis presented in Sec. 1.5 shows that with many stations in a regional system, it may be impossible, regardless of waiting time, to achieve adequate passenger loads. This is not a promising alternative as the principal service in a metropolitan region, but may find some limited use between heavily traveled station pairs or as a part of the

---

[4] As used here the term "vehicle" could mean a single vehicle of a given passenger capacity, or a number of entrained small vehicles to achieve a required passenger capacity.

single transfer service (type E) described below, or in the PRT/GRT hybrid service described in Sec. 1.2.4.

Service Type B. Scheduled Stops Service

This and the next two types of GRT service obtain a satisfactory seat loading by making multiple stops to pick up and/or discharge passengers. In this type of service each vehicle has a predetermined pattern of station stops, although different vehicles may have different scheduled stops. LTV's Airtrans system in the Dallas/Fort Worth Airport is an example of this type of service. Its disadvantage is the inefficiency of making unnecessary stops. A further disadvantage is the inflexibility of the service to accommodate to varying demand or slipped schedules resulting from malfunction. Its advantage relative to certain other GRT services is that it works on a relatively predictable schedule, allowing the passenger to plan his arrival at the departure station just a few minutes ahead of his vehicle's scheduled departure time.

Service Type C. Preassigned Routes and Possible Station Stops with Actual Stops on Demand

In this service concept, a vehicle is assigned a prescribed set of those stations which it will pass on its route, stopping at any station of the set only if a passenger is to be let off or to be picked up for other stations in the prescribed set. (The prescribed set need not be all stations that it passes.) This is more efficient than service type B because of the elimination of unnecessary stops, but does not permit the traveler to plan his arrival at the departure station just ahead of trip departure because of vehicle schedule uncertainties.

Service Type D. Priority Assigned Group-to-Group (or Cycle-to-Cycle) with Stops on Demand

In this service concept a vehicle travels nonstop from a group of origin stations (say, Group X) to a group of destination stations (Group Y). When the vehicle arrives at Group Y, it is then assigned its next destination group (Group Z) on a priority basis. The assign-

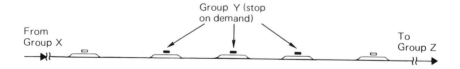

ment could be made in a sequential manner, that is, Group Z could be chosen from a sequence, with each vehicle as it arrives at Group Y being assigned to the next group in the sequence. Alternatively, the stations in Group Y could be polled and the assignment made on the basis of the destination group of the longest waiting passengers, the number of passengers waiting for each group, the cumulative waiting time of passengers destined for each group of stations, or a combination of these factors. The vehicle now would pass every station in Group Y, stopping only to discharge passengers destined for a Group Y station or to pick up passengers going to a Group Z station.

A special type of group, of particular importance in one-way networks, is the cycle of stations. A cycle is a group of stations which can be entered at one of several points, and all stations in the cycle can then be passed without repetition. This is illustrated in Fig. 1-6.

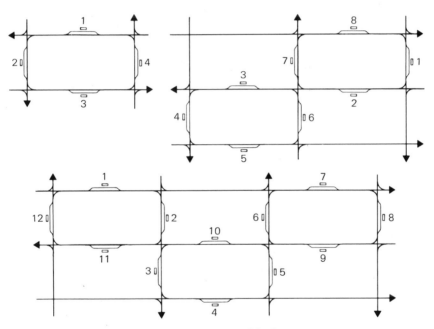

Fig. 1-6. Examples of Cycles

In a group-to-group (or cycle-to-cycle) service, there is no need for all groups (or cycles) to have the same number of stations. A heavily used station, such as might be found at certain work centers, might constitute a group or cycle by itself. A plan was proposed for Gothenburg, Sweden, which, during the evening peak hour, would send shared vehicles from CBD stations — one-station groups — to suburban station groups, each consisting of seven stations. At a CBD station each loading bay was associated with a particular list of suburban station groups, and these groups were sequentially assigned to empty vehicles as they arrived for boarding.

This service scenario and its variants can be used with vehicles of any size. For a given size vehicle there is a trade-off between average service frequency and the number of stops to be made; i.e., the fewer stations in a group or cycle, the longer the service interval required if the operation is to achieve reasonable seat loadings. Of course, the larger the vehicle the more stops or the longer the waiting time will have to be to achieve acceptable seat loadings.

Service Type E. Single Transfer Service — Grid Structure or Intersecting Loops

In its simplest form, this type of service would utilize a grid structure with a number of lines running north-south and others east-west. Vehicles would not transfer but would remain on their assigned lines. In general, a person would have to take one north-south and one east-west vehicle, with a single transfer required. Stations still would be off-line, and generally located at all crossings of east-west and north-south lines.

Since patrons boarding on any line would have only a limited choice of stations (say, 10 or 20), instead of widely scattered stations over the region, shared car service with reasonable seat loadings is easier to arrange. On some lines shared vehicle nonstop service (Service Type A above) from origin to transfer station or from transfer station to destination station might be available. Other lines might employ scheduled stop (Service Type B) or demand stop (Service Type C) service.

A grid system of this type could be configured with crossing two-way lines (if aesthetically acceptable) or with sets of crossing one-way loops. If a two-way line is used, a number of intermediate vehicle-turnaround points should be established to avoid having always to send the vehicles to the end of the line, a procedure which is inefficient because the traffic density requirement is usually highest in the middle.

1.2.3   Personal Rapid Transit (PRT)

PRT vehicles are intended for the private use of a "party" (traveling companions, traveling together by choice, but not including strangers). Typical vehicle designs have maximum capacities of between three and six passengers, all seated. Stations, with few exceptions, are off-line and the network usually includes extensive branching. The vehicles are switched from line to line and carry the passengers from their origin station to their destination station without intermediate stops; no passenger transfers are required.

One variation in PRT service may be worth considering. This variation would allow two or more friends boarding the same vehicle to designate different destination stations, providing they are generally in the same direction; the vehicle would proceed directly to the closest destination and then go on to the others.

In contrast to GRT, where passenger-waiting at the origin station cannot be avoided, there is the possibility in PRT of empty vehicles queued at every station so that passengers can board immediately for departure.

During peak traffic hours the most frequent use of PRT is likely to be the home-to-work and work-to-home trips. Therefore vehicle occupancy should be similar to that experienced in the automobile of today; namely, typical average occupancies ranging from 1.1 to 1.5 persons/vehicle. Somewhat higher occupancies might result if voluntary "PRT pooling" is encouraged by charging a fare by the vehicle rather than by the passenger. Because of the low average occupancy, high capacity per line can only be achieved by operating vehicles at short headways. Therefore, PRT systems are typically designed to have minimum headways[5] of less than 3 sec and possibly as short as ¼ sec.

1.2.4 Hybrid PRT/GRT Service

There may be instances when a hybrid PRT/GRT service is advisable. We are thinking here of a system which is predominantly PRT but where, during the rush hours, vehicle sharing (among strangers) will be required for certain selected regions, such as the CBD. This could come about if, due to capacity limitations, PRT could not handle the traffic into the CBD during the morning rush hours (or the traffic out of the CBD during the evening rush hours) without increasing the number of lines and stations beyond what is aesthetically acceptable. (Such capacity limitations are discussed in Sec. 1.4.) In some historic sections of cities, elevated lines may not be acceptable, requiring that PRT lines be placed underground. Then, for cost reasons, the number of lines and stations will be limited. As a result it may be necessary to limit the number of vehicles entering such underground stations so as to preclude true PRT service and require some mandatory vehicle sharing.

One means of achieving vehicle sharing would be to have vehicles on their way to the CBD in the morning stop to pick up other passengers headed for the same destination station. Unfortunately, this requires that two different procedures be used at each suburban station. There would be immediate boarding for those not going to

---

[5] When headways get this short, it becomes necessary to define the word "headway" quite precisely. Let us define the headway between two vehicles at a particular point on the guideway as the interval of time between the instant when the first vehicle's nose (forwardmost point) passes that particular point and the instant when the nose of the second passes the same point.

the CBD, while those passengers going to the CBD would have to be queued to wait for the right vehicle to come along.

An alternative means for accomplishing the vehicle sharing is to have one "hub" or "transfer" station in each suburb. If a traveler is going to any destination not in the CBD, he will take a PRT vehicle from his local residential station directly to his destination. If his destination is in the CBD, he will take a PRT vehicle to the closest "transfer" station where he will transfer to a vehicle, shared with others, which will travel nonstop to his CBD destination station. Similarly, in the evening the passenger will take a shared vehicle to the transfer station where he will transfer into a PRT vehicle for private service to his home station.

The shared vehicle might be identical to the PRT vehicle (say, with six passengers seating capacity) or it might be two or more such vehicles linked together, or it might be a single longer vehicle but so configured that it was compatible with the PRT guideways and control system. The transfer station might require a branching to separate the PRT vehicles from the vehicles being used for shared service. All stations except the CBD stations and the transfer stations would operate in the much simpler PRT-only mode at all times.

1.3   PRT FOR AREAWIDE URBAN TRANSPORTATION

Although in ensuing chapters we will be discussing the various facets of PRT in some depth, we here present a cursory description of a typical PRT system which may be envisioned as threading throughout a metropolitan area. Our emphasis will be on the service features.

Although a PRT network will of necessity be built in modules over a period of more than a decade, its full benefits will be realized only when it has been extended over a large part of the metropolitan area. Then the PRT service will be easily accessible for almost all trips.

Most lines would be elevated over city streets, because that is the least expensive means of deploying service, but some might be underground and some at ground level. The latter, for instance, might be located in the median strip of a freeway (expressway). We think of lines in residential neighborhoods as being only on the arterial or shopping streets, typically spaced about one-half mile apart, which would mean a maximum walk of two or three city blocks from any point to the closest line. In central business districts (CBD's) or other activity centers, the lines would be much closer, not only for easier access, but also to provide extra line capacity, and especially to provide extra station capacity. (Stations might typically be spaced two blocks apart in CBD's.)

Where lines cross they would be at different elevations to avoid traffic interference[6] but they would be connected by turn ramps to allow a vehicle to turn from one line onto the crossing line. In most areas the guideways would form a one-way network in which any particular arterial street would carry a line only in one direction, say north, and the next parallel arterial would carry a line running south. In this way one minimizes the investment per street, minimizes the visual impact and shadowing, and only two turn ramps are required per intersection, as contrasted with eight ramps at an intersection of a two-way network. Network characteristics are discussed more fully in Chapter 2. The frontispiece is a photomontage of half of a one-way network intersection near Los Angeles City Hall.

Each line in a PRT network has a characteristic speed; all lines do not necessarily operate at the same speed. When a vehicle is to enter a station, it leaves the through-line at line speed and decelerates on the siding, and when it leaves the station it accelerates on the siding before entering the through-line. The higher the line speed, the longer the siding must be.

Turning speeds should be kept low enough to allow a banked turn with a small radius of curvature, permitting the turn ramp to be constructed within existing street intersections without land acquisition. If a vehicle is turning from a high-speed line to a crossing low-speed line, it will decelerate after leaving the high-speed line but before making the turn. Similarly, if a vehicle is turning from a low-speed line to a high-speed line, it will first turn and then accelerate before merging into the high-speed traffic. Turning from one low-speed line to another may require no change in speed, while turning from one high-speed line to another may require deceleration before the turn and then reacceleration before merging.

To achieve sufficient distributed station capacity in a CBD, the stations must be close together. This is difficult to achieve when line speeds are high and station sidings long. Consequently, in most instances CBD line speeds will be restricted to 20 mi/hr or less. At these speeds it usually will be possible to perform the coordinated banked turns without slowing down. In some older cities where the streets are quite narrow, either a lower line speed will be required or slowing at the turns will be mandatory. In suburban areas or along transportation corridors, typical line speeds might range from 30 to 50 mi/hr. Rarely, still higher speeds might be used.

Now let us examine the PRT operation as it might be experienced by a typical user, say a man going from his home to work. He may

---

6 An exception is Japan's Computer-Controlled Vehicle System (CVS) which in crowded areas would have the two crossing lines at the same elevation. This requires that vehicles on the two lines time-share the intersection.

walk about two city blocks to the nearest PRT station. He need not worry if the vehicles leaving that station are going in the wrong direction because the vehicle he boards will be routed automatically onto lines that will carry it to his destination. Assuming that the guideway is elevated in the vicinity of his departure station, he ascends by elevator to the station level. He then takes a plastic card from his pocket, which can be either a PRT credit card or, if he has not established credit with the system, a cash card. The reason for having a travel card which identifies the patron is discussed in Sec. 1.7. He inserts the card into some electronic trip-ordering equipment and pushes buttons indicating the number of his destination station. There are display maps to assist him, or, if he knows the address of his destination but not how to find it on the map, he can be assisted by an information operator accessible by a special telephone. If he has a credit card, the trip will be billed to him automatically (once a month as with telephone bills), but if he has a cash card, he is asked to deposit coins for the amount of the fare. Then, in either case, his card is magnetically encoded with the number of his destination station. (If he is a stranger in town, there is a vending machine at the station from which he may obtain a cash card.)

The traveler then takes his magnetically encoded card and walks to the closest gate on the station platform where a vehicle will be waiting for his use. Dipping the card into a slot next to the gate enables the gate and vehicle door to open simultaneously so that he can enter. (If the vehicle is in the process of pulling up to the gate, the gate will not open until the vehicle has come to a stop.) The magnetic reader at the gate then informs the vehicle of its destination station. After the passenger is seated, the door closes and the vehicle automatically merges into traffic on the through-line. Station operations are discussed at greater length in Chapter 3.

After the passenger has boarded his vehicle and the door has closed, the vehicle is under automatic control until it reaches the platform of the destination station. The automatic controls must include means for controlling vehicles in the station area, on straight sections of guideway, and at intersections and merges. Safe separation from neighboring vehicles is maintained at all times. A number of possible control strategies have been considered and these are discussed in Chapter 4. The question of how to choose routes to minimize travel times consistent with not overloading line capacity is discussed in Chapter 5. (Chapter 5 also considers the question of how to dispatch and route the flow of empty vehicles to ensure that an adequate queue of empty vehicles is maintained at each station.)

Once the passenger arrives at his destination station, the door opens and he alights. He then descends in the elevator to the street level and has less than a block to walk to work. If he works in a major office building or plant, the station may even be integrated into his work facility.

In summary, upon walking to his departure station, the passenger finds a queued empty vehicle waiting for him. He travels nonstop to his destination station at speeds averaging perhaps 30 to 40 mi/hr. After arriving he is only a very short walk from his place of work.

How does the trip compare with going by private automobile? The automobile is more accessible, but in transit it is held up by traffic congestion. Altogether the door-to-door travel times are comparable. Traveling by PRT will be somewhat less costly and the passenger is free to enjoy the view, to read, or to otherwise spend his time productively. Altogether, PRT must be considered a viable competitor with the private automobile.

1.4 LINE CAPACITY

A critical question is whether PRT can achieve the line capacities necessary to carry a significant fraction of urban traffic during the rush hours.

To establish a basis for comparison, let us examine the capacity of a freeway – say one with four lanes in each direction. Maximum throughput of a freeway occurs at about 30 to 40 mi/hr; in that speed range each lane carries one automobile every two seconds – the four lanes carry two each second. If, during rush hours, each automobile is occupied by 1.25 people on average, a four-lane freeway would be carrying 2.5 people/sec or 9000 people/hr.

Now, the actual capacity requirement for any PRT line will depend on the number and spacing of lines, the population density, and the fraction of the population which uses PRT during the rush hours. For most lines the requirement will be less than that of the freeway, but for some lines it may be comparable. If a PRT line were to have the capacity of a four-lane freeway, and if occupied vehicles were to have the same average occupancy as the automobile, then this would require that a PRT line carry two occupied vehicles/sec. There will also be some empty vehicles on the line, although most empty vehicles will be moving in the opposite direction from the prevailing direction of occupied vehicles. Moreover, there must be some available space on the line to accommodate merging from crossing lines. When all of this is considered, minimum headways of 0.3 to 0.4 sec are required if a PRT line were to be fully equivalent to a four-lane freeway.

The minimum headway that can be achieved is

$$H = \frac{L + S}{V},$$ (1.1)

where

> H = minimum headway in seconds,
> V = line speed,
> L = length of vehicle,

and
> S = minimum allowable separation be-
> tween vehicles traveling at a speed V.
> (Depending on the type of control,
> S may be a function of V.)

If L and S are measured in feet, then V must be in ft/sec. (If L and S are in meters, then V must be in m/sec.) The quantity $L + S$ is sometimes called "slot size." It is the length of guideway allocated to each vehicle when vehicles are traveling at minimum separation.

At Aerospace, we have made vehicle layouts which show that L will be about 10 ft. In Chapter 6, covering safety, it is shown that if one vehicle is inadvertently decelerating and the next applies brakes after a 0.2 sec delay and with such force that its deceleration will be 15% above that of the failing vehicle, then, independent of line speed, the vehicles will close on each other by about 4 ft (or less) before they start separating again. With a vehicle separation of about 5 ft, they will not collide. With this separation, the slot length will be about 15 ft. Using this slot length at a line speed of 30 ft/sec (20.455 mi/hr or 9.144 m/sec), the minimum headway will be 0.5 sec. At a line speed of 60 ft/sec (40.909 mi/hr or 18.288 m/sec), the minimum headway will be 0.25 sec.

The total passenger "flow" on a line is given by

$$F = \frac{3600}{H} Dfp,$$ (1.2)

where

> F = passenger flow in passengers/hr,
> H = minimum headway in seconds,
> D = line "density," the ratio of the number
> of vehicles to the number which would
> be carried if all were at minimum
> separation,[7]
> f = fraction of vehicles that are occupied,
> p = average party size; i.e., the average
> occupancy of occupied vehicles.

---

[7] D may also be regarded as the fraction of slots which are occupied by vehicles, although this definition is not easily understandable when a "car follower" type of control system is used (see Chapter 4).

If one wishes to determine the flow during a morning rush hour on a line directed toward the CBD, then f might be estimated at 0.9 or higher because almost all empty vehicles will be traveling in the opposite direction. (The same is true during the evening rush on lines directed out of the CBD.) In Chapter 4 it is shown that the problem of merges is managed easily if D is kept below about 0.8. If we assume that the average party size is 1.25 passengers, then, for a 60 ft/sec line having a minimum headway of 0.25 sec,

$$F = \frac{3600}{0.25} \times 0.8 \times 0.9 \times 1.25 = 12{,}960 \text{ passengers/hr.} \qquad (1.3)$$

This is almost equivalent to the throughput of a six lane freeway.

Thus far we have discussed the minimum achievable headways and the maximum achievable flow rates on PRT lines, and we have compared them with automobile freeways. There is still the question of whether such high rates are really needed. The author is convinced by a study reported in Chapter 5 that such flow rates are indeed desirable. There we consider a scenario appropriate to the 1990's in which it is assumed that 300,000 people work in downtown Los Angeles and that 50% of them take PRT to work, arriving over a two-hour interval. If, due to voluntary "PRT pooling," arrivals average 1.5 passengers/vehicle, then 50,000 vehicles/hr would arrive in downtown Los Angeles during the morning rush hours. With some care we were able to design a network (described in Chapter 2) capable of carrying this load. In this design almost every street in the CBD carries a 30 ft/sec line with minimum headways of 0.5 sec; the corridors radiating from the CBD are 60 ft/sec lines with a minimum headway of 0.25 sec. The purpose of the computer programs discussed in Chapter 5 is to route the traffic of both occupied vehicles and returning empty vehicles so as to avoid capacity overloads. It is the opinion of the author that had the headway requirements been substantially relaxed, it would not have been possible to avoid such overloads without adding still more lines.

The experience with respect to the Los Angeles CBD may be generalized by reference to Fig. 1-7. Assume that a stylized square CBD measures 1.5 mi on a side. With a one-way network spacing of ¼ mi between 30 ft/sec lines, there would be 12 such lines entering the CBD[8] and 12 leaving. Based on the assumptions that went into calculating Eq. (1.3), but changing the headway to 0.5 sec to be compatible with the assumed 30-ft/sec line speeds, the flow on each

---

[8] As described in Chapter 2, the Los Angeles CBD network achieves some extra capacity by running along selected streets two 30-ft/sec lines in the same direction and supported on the same columns. Altogether the network is equivalent to bringing in 16 lines.

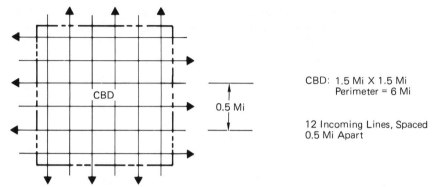

CBD: 1.5 Mi X 1.5 Mi
Perimeter = 6 Mi

12 Incoming Lines, Spaced
0.5 Mi Apart

Fig. 1-7. Stylized Central Business District for Estimating PRT Capacity Requirements

line would be 6,480 passengers/hr. The 12 lines would carry a flow of 77,760 passengers/hr. If the average party size were the assumed 1.5 instead of 1.25 as used in Eq. (1.3), the flow would be 93,312 passengers/hr. In practice this could not be achieved, because the flow to most CBD's tends to be quite nonuniform, and some of the lines would not be carrying a full load.

Clearly, if flow rates in excess of 100,000 passengers/hr are required, it may not be possible to accommodate them all with a pure PRT service. One interesting possibility is the hybrid service described in Sec. 1.2.4.

Although we have just established that for application of PRT to a broad metropolitan region there will be a requirement for headways of less than one second, it should be understood that on most lines (for example, in suburban areas) the actual average headways will tend to be much larger. When PRT is applied to a smaller town with, say, a population of less than 500,000, minimum headway requirements might be several seconds instead of a fraction of a second.

At Aerospace, as described in Appendix B, we have operated a one-tenth scale model PRT system at headways of 0.5 sec. In Japan, the CVS (Computer-Controlled Vehicle System) is being operated in the range of one to two seconds minimum headway. In the Federal Republic of Germany, the "Cabintaxi" system has operated at 1.0 sec headway.

Because GRT can achieve high line capacities without using short headways, we shall now digress from our discussion of PRT to evaluate GRT for areawide urban transportation. Before returning to other aspects of PRT we will also briefly consider Dual Mode Transit (DMT).

1.5   PROBLEMS WITH GRT FOR AREAWIDE URBAN TRANSPORTATION

In the previous section we illustrated how PRT applied to areawide urban transportation must use headways of less than one second to achieve sufficient line capacity. In contrast, GRT may use significantly longer headways. For example, a GRT carrying 25 passengers/vehicle and operating at 10 sec headway provides a line capacity of 2.5 persons/sec, or alternatively a GRT system carrying 10 passengers/vehicle and operating at 4 sec headway also provides a line capacity of 2.5 persons/sec. The reader will recall that this is the throughput of the four-lane freeway we previously used for comparison. Moreover, it certainly is true that for the same total passenger trips GRT requires many fewer vehicles than PRT. The problem lies in the quality of service that can be provided by GRT operating on a large network with many stations.

If a transit system is to be a viable competitor to the private automobile, capable of attracting people who might otherwise drive, then like the automobile it should be readily accessible. Initially we shall make the assumption that, as with PRT, walking will be the principal access to GRT. At the end of this section we shall reexamine the assumption of walking access and try to define a more likely role for GRT.

Let us consider a metropolitan region having 100 sq mi within its developed area. If the population of this area is 1 million people, then the average population density is 10,000 people/sq mi, or about 16 people/acre. This implies a mixture of single and multiple family dwellings. For reasonable walking access there would need to be 4 stations/sq mi.[9] This GRT system would thus require about 400 stations in residential areas. Adding stations in the CBD and other activity centers, and at industrial sites, might bring the total to 500 stations. For a large metropolitan region with several million people, there could be a requirement for more than 2,000 stations in a mature system.

With 10,000 people/sq mi and 4 stations/sq mi, there will be 2,500 people, on average, within the influence of a given station. Since the work force is about 40% of the population, there will be roughly 1,000 workers. In studying PRT we have estimated that approximately 25 to 30% of the workers will go to work by PRT. The others will drive. Certainly the modal split for GRT will be lower, in part due to a door-to-door total travel time which is substantially greater than that of PRT, and in part due to the lack of the privacy which is provided by PRT. But, for purposes of this calculation we shall give GRT a modal split of 25%. Using 25%, we find that 250 workers will take the GRT to work, departing over a 2 hr period. Let us assume that

[9] In Sec. 2.1 (Fig. 2-2) it is shown that with an ideal arrangement of 4 stations/sq mi, there is a maximum walking distance of 3/8 mi and an average walking distance of just under 1/4 mi.

50% or 125 of these trips are destined for 50 stations, with the other 125 to the remaining 450 stations.

First we consider the feasibility of a nonstop origin-to-destination service (Service Type A). There clearly is no feasibility of nonstop ride-sharing for the 125 workers going to some of the 450 scattered destination stations. As to the 125 workers going to the 50 more frequently used destination stations, some 2.5, on average, are going to each station, but only rarely could they share rides because their departure times span a 2 hr period. On those rare occasions when two travelers arrive at the departure station at the same time, it is not wise to require them to share a vehicle. There may be safety in numbers, but here we have only two passengers, which may lead to a security problem. Even if there is no security problem, the ride may be an unpleasant experience for one of the two passengers, which may impel that passenger to return to the privacy of his or her automobile. (On the other hand, if only PRT service is offered, and if two persons note that they usually arrive at the departure station at the same time and that they get off at the same destination station, there is nothing to keep them from voluntarily choosing to travel together as a single party. Such voluntary PRT "pooling" could be encouraged by charging a fare by the vehicle rather than by the passenger.)

Thus, to obtain sufficient seat loading it is necessary to make multiple stops to pick up and/or to discharge passengers.

We have analyzed GRT for vehicles carrying 10 passengers on average and operating in the cycle-to-cycle stop-on-demand service mode identified as Service Type D in Sec. 1.2.2. Door-to-door travel times were compared with those for PRT and the personal automobile, which are very nearly equal. The GRT door-to-door time to one of the more frequently used destination stations will vary from the same time as PRT or auto to double that time, with an average multiplier of 1.5. To one of the less frequently used stations, the GRT door-to-door travel time will vary from the time for PRT or auto to triple that time, with an average multiplier of 2.0.

We have also considered scheduled GRT service and found some decrease in the average waiting time but with time lost in unnecessary stops.

The author feels that for a large metropolitan area, if GRT with walking access were to be used, some service improvement would result by having a grid of intersecting two-way lines with a single transfer required (Service Type E). However, not many cities are so regular in their street systems as to be treated effectively by this kind of grid structure. Moreover, there are serious aesthetic questions which must be raised with respect to the two-way lines, requiring up to four lines with sidings, and with respect to two-level stations at intersections.

In summary, it would appear that for a large network with stations spaced for walking access:

a. A nonstop origin-to-destination service (Service Type A) cannot provide significant ride sharing. In those rare instances where a passenger could share, he must not be forced to share because even one unpleasant experience could lose his patronage. (Voluntary sharing on a PRT service should be encouraged, of course.)

b. Cycle-to-cycle, demand-stop, shared vehicles (Service Type D) can achieve seat loadings of around 10 persons per vehicle. However, average door-to-door travel times can be as much as double those for PRT and the automobile, depending on the frequency of use of the destination station.

c. Other types of GRT service may allow modest improvements in these figures, but each such service introduces a new set of problems.

For these reasons, those who have suggested widely deploying GRT over a broad metropolitan area have not thought of it as a serious competitor to the automobile but rather as an improvement over conventional rail systems. When thought of in this way the network may be thought of as a variation of line-haul with some additional branching. Stations are not within walking access of most of the population, which must depend on access by bus or by automobile (kiss-and-ride or park-and-ride). The principal advantage over conventional rail is that, per mile of guideway, GRT is lower cost, which permits greater coverage at the same investment. Thus, GRT service will be improved over conventional rail, both because of more ready access and because fewer intermediate stops are required.

A still more accepted role for GRT (and SLT) is for circulation in certain activity centers such as CBD's, airports, college campuses, large medical centers, and shopping centers. These applications are quite sensible if a city does not have PRT, or as an interim measure until it has PRT. For example, at an airport GRT can take travelers from a parking lot to a terminal or from one terminal to another. Once PRT is operating in a city, a PRT vehicle could perform not only these functions but also it could take a traveler from his airport terminal directly to his hotel in the CBD. Looking forward to the day when areawide PRT service is in effect, the planners of an airport circulation system might do well to consider the idea of building it so that it could be readily retrofitted to become a part of an areawide PRT system when one becomes available.

1.6   DUAL-MODE TRANSIT (DMT)

"Dual-Mode Transit" is the generic name for any system in which vehicles can travel under automatic control on a guideway and also can be operated manually on the city streets. Although DMT is not strictly a category of AGT, no discussion of AGT service concepts would be complete without a comparison with Dual Mode Transit.

We might distinguish broadly between two categories of DMT according to the size of the vehicle and the nature of the service provided. The first category might be called "Group Dual-Mode Transit" (GDMT) and would use vehicles whose size might be anywhere in the range from a minibus to that of a large bus; they would be operated on the city streets by a bus driver. The other category might be called "Personal Dual-Mode Transit" (PDMT) and would use small three- to six-passenger vehicles, automatically controlled on the guideway and privately driven on the city streets.

In the typical use of GDMT, the bus driver would circulate the vehicle around a particular suburb, picking up passengers going to the CBD. He then would drive the vehicle onto an on-ramp of the automated guideway where he would leave it and board another vehicle to make another collection trip throughout the suburb. The vehicle which he had left at the automated guideway would be taken under automatic control into the CBD, possibly making automatic stops at other stations en route. In the CBD the vehicle would circulate to let off passengers and pick up others, all automatically. It would then return to an off-ramp in a suburb where a bus driver would take over manual control.

An alternative approach, which in most cases would be almost the equivalent of GDMT in its quality of service, and certainly would be simpler, would be to use a manual-only bus or minibus to perform the collection in the suburb and then to take the passengers to a transfer station in the suburb where they could board an SLT or GRT going into the CBD. The SLT or GRT would circulate throughout the CBD and no further transfers would be required. By introducing this single transfer service, there is no necessity to build the more complex vehicle which would operate both manually and automatically. Moreover, because the automated vehicles would weigh less as a result of not requiring an engine and other components for operating on the streets, the SLT or GRT guideway could be lighter than that for GDMT.

Personal Dual-Mode Transit (PDMT) from a service viewpoint is an extremely attractive concept since it combines the automatic features of PRT with the off-guideway flexibility of the private automobile. Some of its proponents have particularly emphasized the appealing concept of owning your own dual-mode vehicle. But there are several serious operational problems that must be solved before PDMT can be realized in a practical system.

There are two approaches to PDMT. One of these approaches uses bimodal vehicles which are equipped to operate under automatic control on the guideway and can also be operated manually on the city streets. The bimodal vehicle could be privately owned or it could be a vehicle owned by the system and rented by the user. One of the problems with the bimodal approach is that there is no assurance that the vehicle will not have been seriously abused by the driver under manual use, and if the vehicle is privately owned, there is no assurance that it will have been properly maintained. As a result there is the threat that it might have a high malfunction rate when operating on the guideway. One possibility is to put each vehicle through an automatic checkout before it is allowed to enter the guideway. Such a procedure clearly represents additional system complexity and cost.

The other approach is to use what is known as a "palletized dual-mode." In this concept, there are flat-bed vehicles or pallets which operate on the guideway just as a PRT vehicle would operate; in fact they might be identical to the pallets used for containerized freight discussed in Sec. 1.8. At a dual-mode on-ramp one would drive a small automobile onto a pallet where it would be secured. Then the pallet would join the stream of automated traffic. In this variation the automobile need have no capability for automated operation and the pallet no capability for manual operation. Unless, however, the automobile were very small, the length of the pallet would need to be considerably greater than that of a typical PRT vehicle, and the weight of the loaded pallet would be so great as to require substantially heavier and more costly guideway structures.

Probably the most serious problem with PDMT, whether palletized or bimodal, is that of the "off-ramp" in a congested area such as the CBD. The vehicles coming down the off-ramp could easily be delayed by the congestion of the city streets. As a result, the off-ramp would become jammed and additional vehicles would not be able to get off. The one thing which must not be allowed is to have the congestion back up onto the automated guideway because then the traffic on the guideway would come to a halt. The solution to this problem is to design the system so that there are no off-ramps in the CBD or other congested areas.

What does this mean for a vehicle which is privately owned? In that event it would be necessary to have the vehicle stop at a station for dual mode vehicles so that the owner and his guests could alight from the vehicle. The vehicle would then automatically proceed to an automatic parking garage. In the evening, when the owner wished to return home, he would have to go to the dual-mode station, request his car, and wait for it to arrive. It has been suggested that he could call from his office ahead of time so as to reduce the wait at the station; but, if he were to arrive at the station after the car had arrived, it is likely that the car would have to be returned to the garage because otherwise it would block traffic at the station. Clearly such a system is very complex and the necessity to wait for one's vehicle at the station is less than ideal.

In our opinion a far more attractive concept of PDMT is to have publicly owned vehicles, probably carried on pallets. Then there is no necessity to take home the same vehicle in the evening that one took to work in the morning. Moreover, the same vehicle can be used by a number of patrons during the day, and this cuts down on the total vehicle fleet. In this concept, on leaving the office one walks to the nearest PDMT station where queued empty vehicles are waiting. After the boarding, the vehicle travels automatically to an off-ramp in the suburb, where the driver drives his small rented automobile off its pallet, down the off-ramp and to his home. In the morning the process is reversed, and the vehicle is relinquished in the CBD so that it is available for others. The fare charged might depend on the mileage and the length of time for which one retained the vehicle, similar to the common practice with automobile rentals today.

Let us compare this type of PDMT with PRT service and the private automobile. Its advantage over PRT is that it can extend service into suburban areas beyond the reach of the guideway system. In addition it might be argued that dual mode transit would permit the network to be designed with a greater spacing between lines because one would be less dependent on walking access. These statements have to be examined rather critically. As to the latter point, the line spacing is determined not only by walking access but also by capacity requirements. In the studies which we have made of the possible use of PRT in Los Angeles, there would have been capacity bottlenecks had substantially larger spacings been used. Moreover, not all patrons can drive; for example, the young, the very old, and those who could not afford the price of overnight rental of the PDMT vehicle. Such patrons may be quite dependent on walking access.

With respect to the point about extending service beyond the region covered by the guideway network, an alternative to having guideway off-ramps at the periphery of the network would be to have parking stations for automobiles. Then one could use one's private automobile for park-and-ride access to PRT. With the PRT stations centered in the middle of the parking lot, there is no reason why more than about two minutes need be lost in the transfer.

Alternatively, one could get to the same peripheral station by being driven (kiss-and-ride), or by scheduled bus or dial-a-ride.[10] As a result the complex on-ramps and off-ramps would be eliminated.

One group of investigators,[11] who initially were strong proponents of this type of dual-mode system, argued convincingly that the patronage of a dual-mode system would substantially exceed that of PRT because, in addition to those who would use walking access, there would be many who otherwise would drive their cars to work but who now would prefer to drive to the automated guideway and use it to save time for a portion of their trip. However, when they tested that hypothesis, using their modal-split model, they found that the customers who gained access by walking, coupled with a few going by dual mode, already unloaded the streets and highways to the point where, with reduced congestion, there was no substantial time saving in going part of the way by dual mode rather than driving all the way by private automobile. Consequently, it was their final conclusion that the total modal split for dual mode would not be substantially increased over that of PRT.

Nonetheless, the whole question of PDMT is so little understood at this time that its service advantages over PRT are very difficult to assess with certainty. It is clear, however, that if PDMT is to become a reality, the problems of safe, reliable, short-headway operation must be solved, and, hence, proceeding with PRT systems is clearly a step on the way to dual mode. Whether the additional benefits will justify going the rest of the way is still open to question.

1.7 SECURITY

We now return to the service features of PRT. From the viewpoint of a traveler, personal security is a very important service feature of any public transportation system. System security, i.e., protection of the system from vandalism, is of less direct concern to the average traveler, except that the steps taken to curb vandalism may impinge on the kind of service offered. This section, then, considers two types of security—passenger security and system security.

---

[10] Dial-a-ride is sometimes called dial-a-bus. The patron telephones a dispatcher and lets him know both the origin and destination of the desired trip, the number of persons in his party, and when they wish to be picked up. The dispatcher, possibly assisted by a computer, will plan the routes to pick up the party as close as possible to the requested time. When there are widely scattered origins and destinations, the service is very costly and wastes much time for the passengers on board. If, however, all passengers have either a common origin or a common destination, such as a PRT or GRT station, somewhat more efficient service can be provided.

[11] William Hamilton and Ben Alexander of General Research Corporation.

PRT is inherently secure for passengers for two basic reasons: (1) a vehicle is not shared with strangers; (2) there is no reason for loitering on the station platform since empty vehicles are queued and waiting for passengers. SLT and GRT are less secure because the vehicles are shared with strangers and because it is necessary to wait on the platform for a vehicle to come along. But the very factors that make PRT secure for the passenger reduce system security through introducing opportunities for vandalism.

In defining equipment and procedures for coping with personal security and the threat of vandalism, there is a delicate balance which must be reached relative to how much invasion of privacy can be tolerated. We will try to define an approach which minimizes the invasion of privacy consistent with exercising what we believe to be acceptable security measures. It should be borne in mind that the solution for one city is not necessarily the best for another.

1.7.1 Passenger Security

We consider the question of passenger security as beginning when the passenger enters the station premises. Clearly the larger security problem is the walk through the city streets on the way to or from the station, but this is beyond the responsibility of the system designer or system operator.

In many cities it will be advisable to have closed circuit television surveillance of the station platform and, perhaps, of the elevators leading to the station platform. As noted above, so long as there is a queue of empty vehicles available at the station, boarding can take place immediately, and the station platform will be occupied only transiently by travelers. Occasionally someone may wish to wait for a friend with whom he will be sharing a vehicle, but because the platform will be nearly empty, the TV surveillance of suspicious loiterers should not be difficult.

It has been suggested that each vehicle should contain closed circuit TV to ensure passenger security, but we believe this to be an unnecessary invasion of privacy. Because of the private use of PRT vehicles, the only threat after boarding a vehicle might come from the forced entry by a potential assailant. The closed circuit TV surveillance of the station platform is a partial protection against forced entry, but we shall shortly describe an additional precaution that might be taken.

Although the operation of the vehicles is entirely automatic, we imagine each vehicle as containing two buttons for the use of the passenger when necessary. One of these buttons, which might be labeled "Next Station," would bring him into the closest station. He might use this button if he suddenly remembers an appointment which had slipped his mind, or if he has to return home to pick up something he had forgotten. At the station he would request another trip and board another vehicle to his new destination.[12] The other button, possibly marked "Emergency Station," would be used to bring the car to one of several stations placed around the network where first aid and police assistance would be available. Once this button was depressed, the vehicle would go nonstop to the closest such Emergency Station, and the "Next Station" button would become inoperative. If a person became ill during the trip, he would push the Emergency Station button. Another use would be protection against forced entry. If a passenger is boarding a vehicle and finds that another person is attempting to force his way into the same vehicle, then by pushing the button the vehicle will be directed to the closest emergency station. Knowing this to be the case, the mere presence of the button will serve as a deterrent to forced entry.

When a vehicle is approaching its destination station, it might be advisable to play a recorded announcement which alerts the passenger that he should prepare to deboard. When the vehicle comes to a stop at the station platform, the vehicle door will open. The vehicle is weighed, and if, after a specified period of time of about 30 to 40 seconds, the passenger has not deboarded, the door will close and the vehicle will proceed to the closest emergency station. Such a procedure would ensure rapid first aid to those in need. It would also ensure that no potential assailant could linger in a car to harass the next occupant(s).

1.7.2 System Security

Because PRT vehicles are not shared with strangers there is a serious threat that vehicles would be vandalized. To deter such action we feel that in many cities it may be necessary to make at least a temporary record of the identity of passengers traveling in each vehicle. For this reason we recommend that each passenger have a travel card which will identify him when he inserts it into the trip-ordering equipment. Those who use a PRT credit card will be billed once a month. Others will use a "cash card" which, nevertheless,

---

[12] Alternatively the passenger could specify a new destination en route without stopping at the next station if each car had trip-ordering equipment into which he could insert his plastic travel card (credit card or cash card) and depress buttons to indicate the number of his new destination station. We do not advocate this alternative because, although it would be an improvement from the service standpoint, it clearly adds a significant cost item to each vehicle. Moreover, it also requires procedures for transferring the billing information, if a credit card were used, or for collecting the cash when a cash card is used.

identifies the passenger.[13]

At each station there should be a special vending machine from which a patron can obtain a cash card. This machine would put him in communication with an operator who would take down the patron's name and address. Possibly, the patron would be required to show some identification which could be inspected by the operator through remote video. Possibly, also the patron's picture could be taken. Then the operator would activate the machine to issue a "cash card" carrying the patron's identification. This identification could be anything from a card number which would serve to identify the patron, to possibly his name and address imprinted on the card. The latter certainly is not necessary to identify the patron, but it may convince him that vandalism could be traced to him.

The problem is how to make at least a temporary record of the identity of passengers on each vehicle with a minimum invasion of privacy. It might be useful to make a comparison with the kind of records that are made of telephone calls. Because most of us are billed monthly for our telephone calls we do not consider that our privacy is being invaded when a record is made of a phone call; in fact, we insist on it to validate the charge. By analogy, the people who are billed monthly for their PRT rides will not consider it an invasion of their privacy that a record is kept on what trips they took and when. On the other hand, there may be times when one would like to make a phone call without a record being made of that call, and this is always possible by going to a nearby pay-station phone. Again, by analogy, if one did not wish a permanent record made of a PRT trip, one should be able to pay cash for the trip instead of charging it.

How, then, does one reconcile the protection of anonymity on at least the PRT trips paid for by cash and the need to identify passengers to deter vandalism? We believe that the compromise may be in keeping only temporary records until the vehicle is inspected nightly.[14] If the vehicle passes inspection and has not been vandalized, all detailed records of who used the vehicle during the day would be erased. If the vehicle is vandalized, the list of users

---

[13] There might be two different ways of using the cash card:
   (1) When the card is inserted into the trip-ordering equipment and buttons are depressed to indicate the number of the destination station, the passenger is notified of the fare, and will need to deposit coins, or
   (2) A patron may deposit his card into a machine and insert coins or bills for advance payment. The balance is magnetically encoded on the cash card, and when he orders a trip the fare is subtracted from the balance.

[14] We believe that every vehicle should be automatically cleaned periodically, possibly nightly. At the same time there would be an automatic checkout to discover any incipient failures, possibly in redundant components whose failure would not have affected the vehicle's operation. At the same time there would be a visual inspection for vandalism.

would have to be kept. Periodically there would be a correlation study to see whether certain types of vandalism were generally associated with the presence of certain passengers. When the evidence mounted that a particular passenger was probably responsible for the vandalism, he would be sent a letter saying that it might be merely a matter of coincidence but that if the vehicles in which he rode continued to be vandalized, it might be necessary to invalidate his travel card. We believe that the very fact that passengers can be identified will serve as an effective deterrent against most vandalism.

Another system security problem has to do with protection against the improper use of invalid PRT credit cards. When a PRT credit card is inserted into the trip-ordering equipment at a station, the card number should be compared with a list of lost and stolen cards. At the same time there could be protection against expired cards or cards canceled for nonpayment or other reasons.

Finally we come to the matter of sabotage. The inaccessibility of elevated guideways (or underground guideways) may be a partial protection against the casual or thoughtless prankster. But, as with any transportation system, there is no feasible way of preventing a well-organized group of terrorists from sabotaging a part of the system. We believe, however, that it is possible to build a system so that there is no "heart of the system" whose loss would paralyze the entire operation.

Quite independent of the question of sabotage is the problem of coping with failures in various system components, including computers and power sources. Here again, to reduce the vulnerability of the operation, it is desirable to use distributed intelligence, redundant components, and backup power. Thus, the very design philosophy which minimizes the impact of natural failures also minimizes the impact of sabotage.

1.8 FREIGHT MOVEMENT

So much of the emphasis on urban transportation is placed upon the movement of people, especially when transit alternatives are being considered, that freight movement often is ignored. Yet freight constitutes a significant portion of street and highway traffic, and is responsible for a disproportionately large share of urban congestion. One need only try to travel across-town in midtown Manhattan to recognize the truth of this statement.

Because conventional transit systems are not used for urban transportation of goods, the problems of freight movement usually are kept quite separate from discussions of transit systems. But, when we are discussing automated guideway transit systems, there is no reason why the guideway cannot also be used for the transport

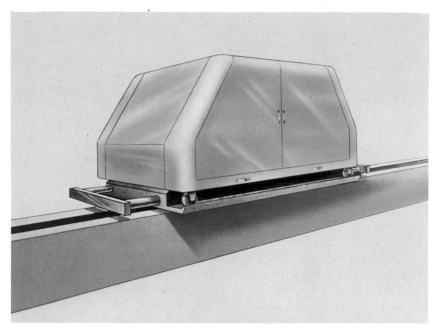

Fig. 1-8. Palletized Movement of Light Freight

of light freight. Clearly there are types of freight movement to which AGT is not well adapted. For example, it could not be used effectively for delivering a load of bricks or sand to a construction site, nor is it well adapted to delivering gasoline to a filling station. However, most of the freight movements within a city are the movements of mail, packages, cartons, crates, and, in general, packaged material with weights of at most a few hundred pounds. This constitutes light freight which could be moved very readily on an automated guideway with an appropriately designed vehicle, e.g., a palletized vehicle such as shown in Fig. 1-8, providing the guideway is readily accessible from both the origin and destination. Freight depots might be on special sidings at such places as branch post offices, warehouses, department stores, and shopping centers. Shipments to neighborhood stores might go to a neighborhood depot where merchandise could be sorted into bins or stalls for each individual store. There could then be periodic deliveries, or else each store could make its own pickups.

AGT also can be used for solid waste movement. The Airtrans system at the Dallas-Ft. Worth Airport is designed to move waste and other material.

Substantial developments have taken place in freight movement as a part of the Computerized Vehicle System (CVS) under development in Japan. On the outskirts of Tokyo they have built a test track consisting of 4.5 km of guideway on which they are testing both passenger and freight vehicles. Their freight vehicles are built to support a removable freight container. They also have built a prototype freight station, different from their passenger station, to automatically handle the containerized freight.

Chapter 2
NETWORK CONFIGURATIONS
Jack H. Irving

2.1 WALKING ACCESS

In Chapter 1 we pointed out that PRT stations should be so placed that they are within a short walking distance of a large fraction of the population. Thus, close station spacing would be used in the more densely populated portions of the city, but, of course, no city could afford to place a large number of closely spaced stations in its sparsely populated areas.

The proximity of stations will depend also upon other factors such as the average income level in a residential neighborhood. For example, it might well be cost effective to have closely spaced stations in a low income area where patrons would depend mainly on walking access; it might not be cost effective to use closely spaced stations in a higher income area. In the higher income area, even if stations were reasonably closely spaced, many patrons might prefer to use their automobiles to gain access to a PRT station because they would save a few minutes of their time, which they value highly. With a limited capital budget, it obviously is a difficult problem to determine where the stations are needed most.

Some cities are laid out in a quite regular gridlike fashion; Salt Lake City is the prime example, but the west side of Los Angeles is also quite gridlike. Other cities have almost randomly oriented streets. Therefore, it is not possible to give a simple formula as to how to place stations to make them most accessible for walking. Nevertheless, it is instructive to consider a segment of regular grid to get a feel for the distribution of walking distances for various patterns of station placement. This is done in Figs. 2-1 and 2-2.

In Fig. 2-1 we consider a PRT system with lines along arterials spaced 1/2 mi apart in both the north-south and east-west directions. It is assumed that the city streets used for walking access within the elementary PRT grid square are also oriented either in the north-south or east-west directions. Two different patterns of station placement are compared. In the upper diagram there are four stations per

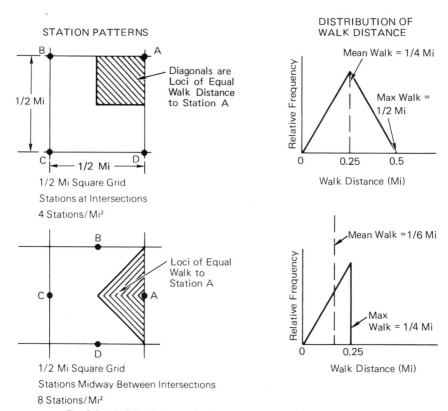

Fig. 2-1. Walking Distance for Various Station Patterns — Square Grid

square mile placed one at each guideway intersection. In the lower diagram there are eight per square mile at the midway points between the intersections. Within the grid square the shaded area is that part which is closer to Station A than to the others. The diagonals within the shaded area represent loci of equal walk distance from Station A and the length of each locus is proportional to the relative area within the elementary grid having the walk distance with which the locus is associated. Under the assumption that there is a uniform population density over the grid square, the relative frequency of any particular walk distance is proportional to the length of the locus associated with that walk distance. For each pattern, the relative frequency is plotted against the walk distance. It is seen that for the upper configuration, with four stations, the distribution function ranges from zero to a maximum walk of 1/2 mi and is symmetrical about the average walk of 1/4 mi. For the lower configuration, with eight stations, the right half of the distribution disappears. We now have 1/4 mi as both the maximum and most probable walking distance, but with a mean walking distance of 1/6 mi.

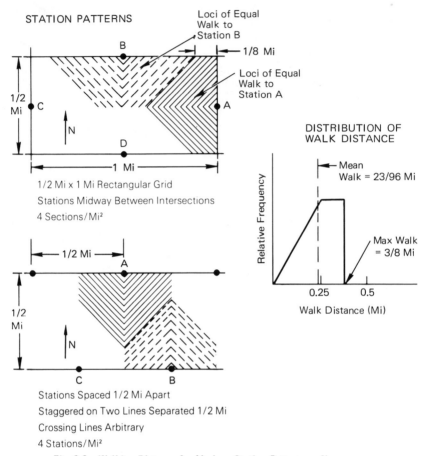

Fig. 2-2. Walking Distance for Various Station Patterns — Nonsquare

Figure 2-2 illustrates that it is not necessary to have lines closely spaced in both directions to achieve short walking distances. We are here assuming that the prevailing direction of traffic flow is in the east-west direction and that lines traveling in these directions are again spaced 1/2 mi apart. The upper diagram illustrates a configuration in which the north-south lines are spaced 1 mi apart and stations are placed midway between the intersections on both east-west and north-south lines. The lower diagram illustrates a configuration in which all stations are on the east-west lines with 1/2 mi spacing between stations, but the stations on the upper line are staggered with the station on the lower line. In this diagram it is immaterial where the north-south lines cross so far as walking distance is concerned. In both diagrams patrons living in the area shaded with solid lines are closest to Station A and those in the area shaded with broken lines are closest to Station B. The relative frequency increases linearly up to a walking distance of 1/4 mi and then is flat out to the maximum distance of 3/8 mi. The mean is 23/96 mi, which is just under 1/4 mi.

In all of the relative frequency plots of Figs. 2-1 and 2-2, it was assumed that the population was uniformly spread over the area covered by a station. In practice, however, multiple family units are more likely to be on the main arterials, where the PRT lines are installed. As a result the average walking distance would be somewhat less than that computed here. To offset this, there will be some irregularity in the patterns of station placement which may have the effect of lengthening the average walk.

2.2 EMPLACEMENT AND ALIGNMENT

Although most PRT guideways will be elevated over city streets, it is also possible to place the guideways underground or at ground level.

2.2.1 Underground Emplacement

Underground emplacement is very costly compared with elevated structures and would tend to be used only where necessary for aesthetic reasons. One example would be that of preserving the architectural integrity of an historic neighborhood. In a study of Automated Guideway Transit for Gothenburg, Sweden, it was felt that the historic walled city should not have elevated guideways, and consequently subways were planned for that sector. The rest of the city has less historic significance and it was felt that elevated guideways would not clash with the prevailing architecture.

We found another example of where underground guideways might be required in our preliminary studies of the Twin Cities of Minneapolis and St. Paul. In the CBD's of those two cities there are a large number of "skyways," which are walking bridges crossing the city streets between the second floors of office buildings and stores. An elevated guideway along one of these streets would have to be installed at the level of the third floor to clear the skyways. Where two such lines intersected, one could dip to the level of the second floor at the intersection, but only if the skyway were not close to the intersection. If skyways cross both streets close to the intersection, then one of the two guideways would have to be elevated to the fourth floor at the point of crossing. To avoid such clumsy configurations it might be necessary in places to use underground guideways. Unfortunately this also means underground stations, and consequently the excavation can be quite costly although considerably cheaper than would be involved with conventional rail.

Another disadvantage with underground emplacement is the relatively long time of construction compared with that required for elevated structures. Construction could involve either tunneling or cut and cover. Although the latter may be cheaper in some instances, it can also be very disruptive during several years of construction. Because of the high cost and likely disruption associated with underground structures, their number should be minimized. Then, to provide sufficient station capacity within the CBD, it probably would be necessary to use shared vehicle service to this area at least during the peak traffic hours. The hybrid system described in Section 1.2.4 would seem particularly attractive under such circumstances.

2.2.2 Ground-Level Emplacement

The problem with ground-level emplacement is the difficulty of separating guideway traffic from automotive and pedestrian traffic. If the guideway is not elevated at least where it crosses streets, then it is necessary to bridge automobile and pedestrian traffic over the guideway. There may be places where such bridging already has occurred and in that event ground-level guideways might be employed. One such example might be at a freeway (or expressway) where the guideway could be built on the median strip or on the shoulder.

Let us consider two cases — the freeway that is in a cut below the city streets, and the freeway that is generally elevated and bridges city streets. For existing freeways installed in cuts below the city streets, the median strip will generally not be satisfactory because it usually will have columns that support the street bridges passing over the freeway. The median strip of an elevated freeway can be quite satisfactory except, of course, any branching from the guideway would require that the branching line become further elevated before turning across the lines of traffic. The elevated freeway poses a difficult problem to elevated guideway lines installed on crossing streets because, when those surface streets go under the freeway, the guideway supporting columns must become much higher to clear the traffic on the freeway.

Another possibility for ground-level guideways would be when two remote communities were connected together by lines requiring very little branching, if any, through the intermediate rural areas. In that event one might afford to elevate the guideway only locally when it passed over crossing highways.

Where ground-level guideways are used, it will be necessary to take special precautions, such as fencing, to minimize access by children at play, by mischief makers, or by domestic animals.

2.2.3 Elevated Guideways—Aesthetics

As indicated earlier, most guideways will be elevated over city streets. For this to be acceptable, a great deal of attention must be placed on aesthetics. The guideway should be as narrow as possible to minimize shadowing and visual intrusion. Because of the importance of this consideration, we at Aerospace have emphasized "monorail-type" support systems rather than flat roadbed types as might be required by a four-wheeled vehicle.

There are two types of monorail, one where the vehicle hangs from the guideway beam in an underhung suspension, and one where the vehicle is supported below in an overriding suspension. In the overriding monorail the bottom of the guideway beam must be about 17 or 18 ft above the street level so that the highest street-driven vehicles will have ample clearance under the guideway. With the underhung configuration, the bottom of the PRT vehicles must be at this height, and the guideway from which they are suspended should be 5 to 6 ft higher. In this configuration the beams are generally supported from above and the supporting column will be at least 8 to 9 ft higher than the columns necessary to support the overriding configuration. Moreover, whereas the columns in the overriding configuration can be centered under the beam, in the case of the underhung configuration, the columns must be to the side, with a cantilevered support of the beam. The overall impact is that the columns must be higher and thicker, and consequently more costly and aesthetically intrusive than columns for the overriding configuration. (Also, as described in Chapter 7, there is greater mechanical complexity when suspending from above, especially at switching sections.) For these reasons we at Aerospace have mainly considered the overriding monorail in our studies of elevated guideway alignment and aesthetics. As a result of design considerations, discussed in Chapter 7, of vehicle suspension and propulsion and of beam stiffness, we have estimated that the beam cross-section would be approximately 3 ft high and 2.5 ft wide.

Another aesthetic consideration is the number of guideways on a given street. With a typical one-way network configuration, there will be only a single through line on any street. Considering also the siding leading into a station, this would mean a maximum of two guideways. In contrast, a two-way system would have traffic in both directions and, including station sidings, there might be as many as four guideways over segments of a street. This is one of several considerations, discussed in Sec. 3.3, for preferring one-way networks for elevated guideways.

Elevated guideways may be aligned either over the curb line or over the center of the street. In either case the guideway may be so designed that, in general, it will require no acquisition of right-of-way. By limiting the speed on turn ramps and using superelevation (banking the turns), it is possible to keep the radius of curvature sufficiently small to accommodate the entire turn ramp without interfering with corner buildings. Station platforms can be narrow structures along station sidings, and again can be installed without requiring land acquisition, in most cases. Alternatively, stations can be integrated into existing building structures and the sidings either brought into or alongside such buildings for easy access.

When aligned over the curb, supporting columns would be imbedded in the sidewalk area. This will cause minimum interference with street traffic, but, if the sidewalk is narrow, the vehicles may be so close to office windows as to create a visual nuisance. We believe it is possible to design the suspension, propulsion, and braking systems to be extremely quiet so that there need be no noise nuisance.

Alternatively the guideway could run down the middle of the street, installed in a center divider about 3 ft wide. Care would have to be taken to protect the columns from being struck by a street-driven vehicle. This type of installation probably is incompatible with a street allocated to one-way traffic because of the difficulties associated with lane changing.

Still a third possible alignment has been suggested by Cerney Associates in a study of Minneapolis.[1] The columns would be installed between the parking lane and the rest of the street. Here the columns do not interfere with through traffic, but they make access to the parking lane more difficult.

One approach to trying to get a better appreciation of aesthetic impact is to prepare photomontages such as that shown in the frontispiece. This shows one of the two turn ramps at a one-way network intersection. The reader will note that of the two intersecting guideways, one is along the curb line and the other is along the center of the street.

Still further appreciation of the visual impact may be obtained by the construction of architectural models. For this reason The Aerospace Corporation sponsored the construction of a 1/160 scale model of several blocks of downtown Los Angeles. We were particularly interested to find out if PRT would fit into this area, with its high buildings, and we were interested to compare the curb-line and street-center alignment options. Photographs of this model are shown in Figs. 2-3 through 2-6. Figures 2-3 and 2-4 show two views of a

[1] Minneapolis People Mover Study, Bechtel, Inc., April 1973.

one-way PRT guideway aligned over the center of Olive Street. Supporting columns are 60 ft apart and are imbedded in the center divider. In the foreground there is a station platform adjacent to the siding. Three empty vehicles are waiting in the input queue just beyond the station platform. The station platform is reached by ascending an elevator in the building shown to the right of Fig. 2-3 and then crossing on a footbridge over to the platform area.

Figure 2-5 shows an alignment over the curb on Grand Avenue. The line to the left is the through line and the one to the right is the station siding. The station platform between the two buildings can be reached either by taking an elevator from the street level or by access from the second floor of the taller office building. In the background one can see the crossing line on 6th Street.

Figure 2-6 shows some details of guideway alignment and support. It is interesting to compare the shadow cast by the PRT guideway with that cast by the buildings, even near noontime, to recognize how little PRT will be responsible for blocking out the sunlight.

Another difficult alignment problem arises when a guideway is to be installed on tree-lined streets. With tree varieties limited in height, the problem would be easily handled, but replanting a street with such varieties might evoke strong reaction regarding preservation of the character of the street and/or the life of existing trees. In some cases, the guideway could be aligned along the centerline of the street, except, of course, where the trees span the street. If located along the centerline, the guideway might be supported by columns embedded in a center divider, or alternatively, supported by arches from the curb-line. In any event, a good deal of ingenuity may be required to find acceptable solutions.

One potential aesthetic benefit of installing a PRT system should be noted — the possibility of modifying and improving the character of selected streets. If, indeed, the transit system is able to attract sufficient patronage, and thus significantly decrease the flow of street traffic, then it may be feasible to eliminate street traffic on certain streets. That would allow the conversion of the street into a walking/shopping mall, or perhaps a linear park with trees, flower beds, and reflecting pools, or perhaps to provide bicycle lanes. If a street cannot be eliminated, it might still be made narrower for street traffic, allowing introduction of bicycle lanes or gardens. Improvements can also be made by incorporating street lighting into the guideway structure, thus eliminating lighting poles.

A significant advantage of elevated PRT is the rapidity and ease with which it can be constructed. Both guideway sections and columns would be prefabricated. After laying the foundation for the columns, the erection of columns and beams can be done very

Fig. 2-3.
Typical Street-Center
Alignment for a
One-Way PRT

Fig. 2-5.
Typical Curb-line
Alignment for
One-Way PRT

Fig. 2-4.
Street-Center
Alignment Viewed
from Below

Fig. 2-6.
Branching Guideways
Showing Typical
Support Details

rapidly. In the Federal Republic of Germany, DEMAG, in erecting the Cabintaxi test track, found that they could erect columns in 60 minutes and a beam in 90 minutes, and they were using beams much longer and heavier than in the design which we have been studying. This ease of construction contrasts notably with the experience for heavy rail systems where, even if above ground, it usually is necessary to create large forms and pour concrete, and, of course, where the track is underground, the times involved in construction are still much longer.

2.3   ONE-WAY VERSUS TWO-WAY NETWORKS

Briefly stated, the advantages of the one-way network may be classified as aesthetics, simplicity of control, and economics. Its disadvantage is that it often is necessary for the vehicle to "circle the block," which lengthens the trip.

In the previous section we pointed out that in a one-way network there will not be more than two guideways on any one street. Away from stations and intersections there will be only one line. In the vicinity of a station there will be two lines, the through line and the station siding. Near an intersection there may be two lines — the through line and portions of the turn ramp.

In contrast, a two-way network will have two through lines, one in each direction, and could have up to two sidings. In addition there could be two station platforms, one on each siding. Consequently, it is clear that on most streets a one-way network will be far less intrusive than a two-way network. The aesthetic difference is even more pronounced at an intersection. As illustrated in Fig. 2-7, a one-way network has only two turn ramps. Where two two-way lines cross, eight ramps are required, if all possible turns are to be allowed. Not only would this be a terribly costly and intrusive structure, but it introduces some very difficult merge problems. In Chapter 4 we discuss the work which Aerospace has done on controlling vehicles at intersections to permit the merging of vehicles from one line on to another. We have restricted our activities to the control problem for one-way intersections, which is difficult enough. The problem of controlling merges with eight connecting ramps would appear to be overwhelming, especially if the system is to degrade gracefully on malfunction.

The economic advantage relates to the fact that for each mile of two-way guideway, one can build over 1-1/2 miles of one-way guideway. This means that to distribute a prescribed number of stations at designated locations, substantial capital cost can be saved by inter-

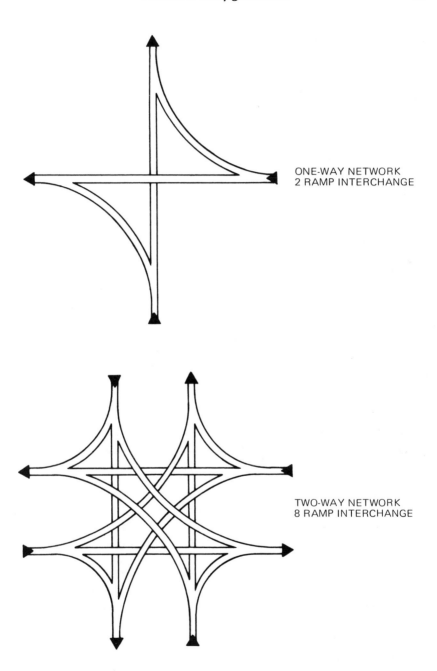

ONE-WAY NETWORK
2 RAMP INTERCHANGE

TWO-WAY NETWORK
8 RAMP INTERCHANGE

Fig. 2-7. Comparisons of Intersections of One-Way and Two-Way Networks

connecting the stations in a one-way network. Alternatively, with a fixed capital budget, a greater portion of a city can be covered.

To estimate the penalty in travel time when using a one-way network in contrast to a two-way network, we shall again idealize to a regular rectangular grid pattern, as indicated in Fig. 2-8. The dots in the figures represent the locations of stations, which are understood to be on sidings. The larger line spacing is "a" and the shorter spacing "b". We consider trips leaving from two different stations — Station A in the middle of one of the longer segments and Station B in the middle of one of the shorter segments. Trip destinations are to 32 different stations, 8 in each quadrant. This number is required to take into account both the direction of the line on which the destination station is located and the direction of the crossing line just upstream of the station. It will be noted that in the analysis we ignore destinations which are near continuations of the lines going through Stations A and B. Although the results can be somewhat anomalous for such stations, such results would not affect the averages significantly because, in a very large network, the anomalous stations would represent only a small portion of the total.

We also consider return trips from the 32 stations to Stations A and B. For each of these 128 trips (2 origins × 32 destinations + 32 origins × 2 destinations), the table in Fig. 2-8 shows the penalty in path length relative to what it would have been had all lines been two-way. It is seen from the grand averages tabulated that the average penalty to or from Station A is $3/4\ a + 5/4\ b$, and the penalty to or from Station B is $1/4\ a + 7/4\ b$, giving a general average of $1/2\ a + 3/2\ b$. Let us consider a numerical example. Assuming that "a" is 1 mi and "b" is 1/2 mi, the general average penalty would be 1.25 mi. At a speed of 30 mi/hr, this would introduce a time penalty of 2.5 minutes.

Actually the time penalty is not as great as this analysis would imply because it assumes that a patron necessarily returns to the same station from which he departed in the morning. Let us imagine that a commuter lived an equal distance from Station A and Station B, and was going to Station 6 in the fourth quadrant. Using our numerical example, if he departed from and returned to Station A, there would be no penalty in the morning, but a penalty of 3.5 mi in the evening. If he departed from and returned to Station B, the penalty would be 1.5 mi in the morning and 1.5 mi in the evening. It would be better to depart from A in the morning and return to B in the evening, with no penalty in the morning and only 1.5 mi in the evening. Similar arguments can be used for any of the 32 stations if one is approximately an equal walk distance from two or more of these.

Since the PRT lines are presumed to be on arterials, the corner

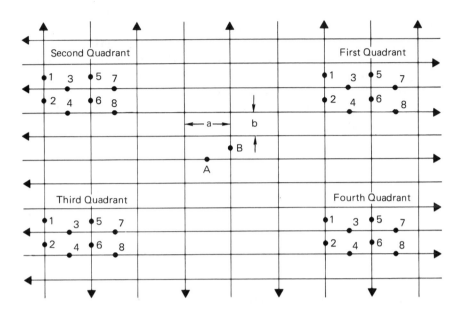

SECOND QUADRANT					FIRST QUADRANT				
Station	From A	To A	From B	To B	Station	From A	To A	From B	To B
1	a	b	0	$2b$	1	0	$a+3b$	0	$6b$
2	a	$3b$	0	$4b$	2	0	$a+b$	0	$4b$
3	a	$a+2b$	0	$a+3b$	3	$a+2b$	a	$a+2b$	$3b$
4	$2a$	0	a	b	4	0	$2a$	0	$a+3b$
5	$a+3b$	0	$3b$	b	5	b	a	b	$3b$
6	$a+b$	0	b	b	6	$3b$	a	$3b$	$3b$
7	a	a	0	$a+b$	7	a	a	a	$3b$
8	$2a+2b$	0	$a+2b$	b	8	0	$2a+2b$	0	$a+5b$
Ave	$\frac{5}{4}a+\frac{3}{4}b$	$\frac{1}{4}a+\frac{3}{4}b$	$\frac{1}{4}a+\frac{3}{4}b$	$\frac{1}{4}a+\frac{7}{4}b$	Ave	$\frac{1}{4}a+\frac{3}{4}b$	$\frac{5}{4}a+\frac{3}{4}b$	$\frac{1}{4}a+\frac{3}{4}b$	$\frac{1}{4}a+\frac{15}{4}b$

THIRD QUADRANT					FOURTH QUADRANT				
1	$a+3b$	0	$2b$	0	1	$3b$	$a+2b$	$6b$	0
2	$a+5b$	0	$4b$	0	2	b	$a+2b$	$4b$	0
3	$a+2b$	a	b	a	3	a	$a+2b$	$a+3b$	0
4	$2a+4b$	0	$a+3b$	0	4	0	$2a+4b$	$3b$	$a+2b$
5	$a+2b$	$3b$	b	$3b$	5	0	$a+3b$	$3b$	b
6	$a+2b$	b	b	b	6	0	$a+5b$	$3b$	$3b$
7	$a+2b$	$a+2b$	b	$a+2b$	7	$a+2b$	$a+2b$	$a+5b$	0
8	$2a+2b$	0	$a+b$	0	8	0	$2a+2b$	$3b$	a
Ave	$\frac{5}{4}a+\frac{11}{4}b$	$\frac{1}{4}a+\frac{3}{4}b$	$\frac{1}{4}a+\frac{7}{4}b$	$\frac{1}{4}a+\frac{3}{4}b$	Ave	$\frac{1}{4}a+\frac{3}{4}b$	$\frac{5}{4}a+\frac{11}{4}b$	$\frac{1}{4}a+\frac{15}{4}b$	$\frac{1}{4}a+\frac{3}{4}b$

GRAND AVERAGES		
From A	$\frac{3}{4}a+\frac{5}{4}b$	From B $\quad \frac{1}{4}a+\frac{7}{4}b$
To A	$\frac{3}{4}a+\frac{5}{4}b$	To B $\quad \frac{1}{4}a+\frac{7}{4}b$
General Ave	$\frac{1}{2}a+\frac{3}{2}b$	

Fig. 2-8. One-Way Network Distance Penalty — Stations Midway Between Intersections

where two such lines cross may be a nucleus of commercial activity. In that event there may be a desire to place a PRT station near the intersection. In a one-way system there is then some merit in splitting the station into two parts, as shown in Fig. 2-9; i.e., a departure platform and an arrival platform. It will be noted that they have been placed so that one can depart along either of the intersecting lines and one can arrive from either also.

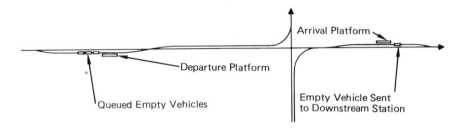

Fig. 2-9. Schematic of Split Station at a One-Way Intersection (not to scale)

Now imagine that we have an entire network of such stations (Fig. 2-10). Again "a" is the larger spacing and "b" the shorter in the rectangular grid. As before we can derive the distance penalty relative to a two-way network. Now we need only consider trips to or from station location A (having two separated platforms) and in each quadrant only four station locations need be considered. The distance penalties are given in the table of Fig. 2-10, where it is seen that the average penalty to or from station location A is "b". If the shorter spacing is 1/2 mi as in our earlier example, then the penalty either way is this amount, and at 30 mi/hr the time penalty is just 1 minute.

This configuration with split stations at intersections (Fig. 2-10) has lower one-way penalties than does the earlier configuration of stations midway between intersections (Fig. 2-8). There are only two station locations per square mile in Fig. 2-10 instead of the four stations per square mile in Fig. 2-8, but each of the station locations will involve almost twice the investment of the nonsplit station (by doubling switches, sidings, platforms, elevators), so that overall costs are comparable. The clear disadvantage is in lengthening the walk distance, as shown in Fig. 2-11. Here, the maximum walk is 3/4 mi and the average walk is 3/8 mi, assuming uniform population density. (These should be compared with the upper diagram in Fig. 2-2.) But, if the population density or, more precisely, the trip activity, is focused very much at the intersection, then the average walk may not have been lengthened and this type of configuration is worth consideration.

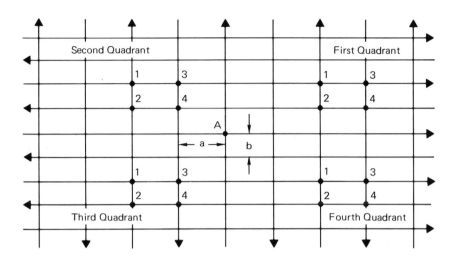

Fig. 2-10. One-Way Network Distance Penalty — Split-Platform Stations at Intersections

It is our opinion that the strong advantages in aesthetics, control simplicity, and economics of one-way networks far outweigh their disadvantage of adding 1 to 3 minutes to the average trip time. There will, of course, be some circumstances where two-way lines will be required. For example, if it is necessary to get from one side of a range of foothills to the other, there may be only a single pass for the guideway, and a two-way guideway will need to be constructed. Under such circumstances, however, branching can generally be minimized in that region.

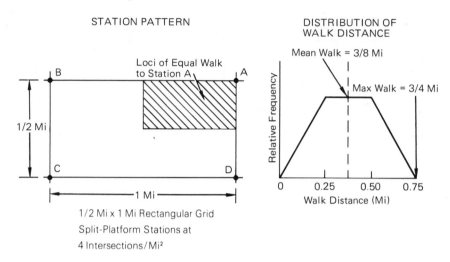

Fig. 2-11. Walking Distances to Split-Platform Stations at Intersections of a Rectangular Grid

2.4   RELATIONSHIP BETWEEN NETWORK CONFIGURATION AND LAND USE

There are two ways in which PRT network configurations interact with land use and transportation needs. One is the requirement placed on the network configuration to meet current and anticipated trip patterns that arise out of existing or planned land use. The other, far more subtle relationship, is the influence that the network configuration and transportation services will have on future growth patterns.

Current trip patterns can, of course, be measured. Anticipated trip patterns can be estimated on the basis of planned land use, as, for example, the location of industry and the corresponding distribution of employee residences. One then hypothesizes a PRT network to carry these trips and performs a modal split analysis which estimates how many of the total trips will be taken on PRT versus those which would go by private automobile or other transit mode. In Chapter 10 we describe The Aerospace Corporation's computing programs by which the modal choices of a large number of travelers are analyzed. Each trip is considered on a door-to-door basis. The choices are based on accessibility of PRT stations, PRT travel times, fare structure, automobile travel times, automobile costs, and the income level of the traveler. These programs provide not only the overall modal split but they estimate as well the activity on each line and at each station. As a result they provide a great deal of insight into which lines and stations are not cost effective, and where additional capacity or accessibility may be required. This allows the planner to redesign his network configuration and station placement to meet the needs of the existing and anticipated trips more effectively.

As for the influence that the network configuration and transportation service will have on future growth patterns, it is important to lay down networks in such a way that they will not foster haphazard and undesired developments nor lead to a dull homogeneity of the metropolitan area. This can be done by differentiating the type of network configurations that are planned for different areas, while still connecting them into one compatible system. For example, in Central Business Districts or other activity centers, good circulation should be provided with short walking distance so as to have good access throughout these areas. Such circulation centers might be interconnected by less-fine-grained networks in transit corridors or by a more skeletal line-haul configuration, depending upon objectives and needs.

In residential areas, PRT lines should only rarely, if at all, be put on single-family residential streets, but rather along the arterials passing through residential areas. Less circulation should be provided in residential areas to discourage their conversion to commercial use (although zoning should continue to be the main control over land use). Lines can generally be somewhat farther apart in residential areas than in activity centers. An example is the treatment of the western section of Los Angeles shown in Fig. 2-12 where better circulation is provided in such activity centers as the Wilshire region, Hollywood, the Miracle Mile, Beverly Hills, Century City, and Westwood, with less circulation in areas which are primarily single family residential.

PRT should bring about the happy medium between the very intense land use brought about by urban rail, and the urban sprawl brought on by complete reliance on the automobile. Urban rail usually brings with it severe congestion. It is well known that if a corridor has already been heavily congested by automobile traffic, building a subway line under that corridor will not relieve the congestion but will intensify it. This occurs because the effect of bringing in the rail encourages additional construction of high-rise buildings for easy access to those who use the rail system. But most people continue to drive their automobiles, and because of the added activity, additional automobiles are brought into the corridor. Because of the advantages to an individual or an industrial or commercial establishment of being within the PRT network area, PRT might be expected to have an inhibiting effect on the city spreading out into rural areas; yet it should not encourage the kind of inefficient, extremely high-density land use that is brought on by installation of urban rail.

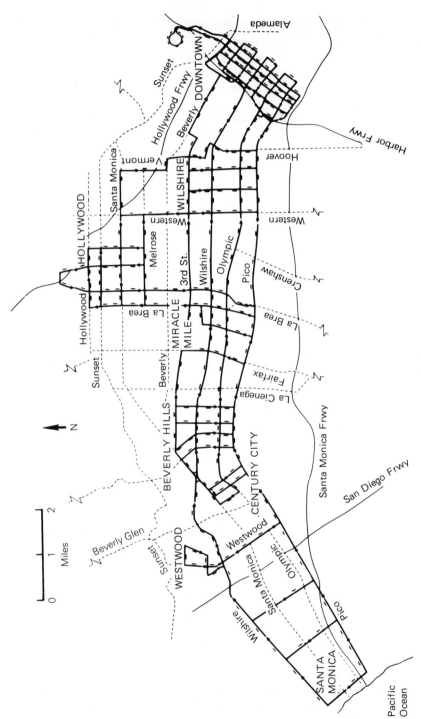

Fig. 2-12. PRT Network for West Los Angeles

2.5   INFLUENCE OF CAPACITY REQUIREMENTS ON NETWORK CONFIGURATION

Requirements in both aggregate line capacity and aggregate station capacity can influence network configuration. For example, we might start the design process by laying out PRT lines and stations along a heavily traveled corridor. Then, on performing a modal-split analysis, we might find that the estimated demand for service along those lines was greater than their capacity. In that event it would be necessary either to increase the capacity of the hypothesized lines by changing speed or vehicle spacing, or to run more lines down the corridor, probably along parallel arterials.

In Central Business Districts line capacity may also be important, especially with line speeds limited. But aggregate station capacity is of even greater importance. The capacity of a simple station with a single platform on a siding depends on the length of the siding, the length of the input queue, the method of operation, and the performance goals. These factors are all discussed in Chapter 3. A simple station of this kind can almost always be installed without land acquisition. One way to increase capacity is to use a number of parallel sidings, each with a platform, but this will require land acquisition and possibly the construction of a large terminal building. Alternatively, one can increase aggregate capacity by having a larger number of the simpler stations. The problem is how to fit enough of them, along with necessary intersections, into a small dense CBD.

We will illustrate the design processes by describing an exercise carried out at The Aerospace Corporation to examine a dense network in downtown Los Angeles. The scenario projected forward to a time in the 1990's when the working force downtown will be approximately 300,000 people. For purposes of the illustration it is assumed that by that time there will be a substantial PRT network throughout the metropolitan Los Angeles area, and that 50% of the downtown workers will arrive by PRT from nine corridors and three outlying parking lots. It is further assumed that they will arrive over a 2 hr period, loaded 1.5 per vehicle. Consequently, during the morning peak period, 50,000 vehicles per hour will arrive downtown. The question is whether it is possible to have sufficient stations and line capacity to handle this flow.

At the outset we obtained data on the number of trips destined to each city block, based on existing and planned office space. This assisted us in distributing the stations to meet the capacity requirements in each subregion of downtown. The assumed speed for the downtown region was 30 ft/sec or about 20 mi/hr. At this speed it is possible to make a coordinated banked turn within the confines of available street widths. With the main line speed and station capacity requirements known in each station, platform and siding lengths can be obtained by the methods described in Chapter 3. The

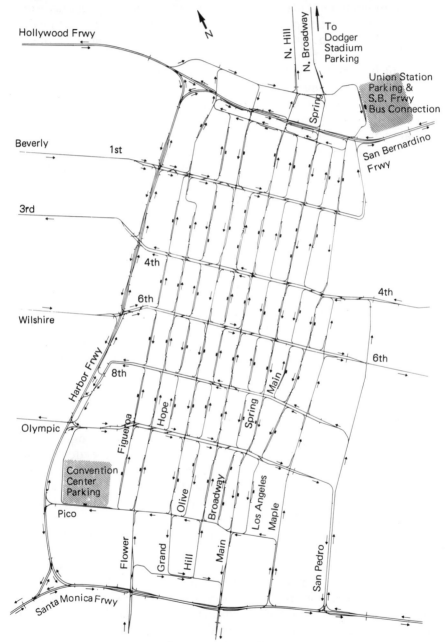

Fig. 2-13. Downtown Los Angeles Network

siding lengths then limit the proximity of neighboring stations. To obtain sufficient distributed capacity, a majority of the downtown streets would need PRT lines.

We next noted that if full grade separation were provided at every intersection of two streets containing PRT lines, the turn ramps (and intersection maneuvering regions on the main lines) would occupy a significant fraction of the linear space and would tend to restrict the space available for station sidings. To avoid this problem we proposed the configuration shown in Fig. 2-13 which is mostly at one level.

PRT stations were placed at three parking lots in the downtown area — at Dodger Stadium, the Convention Center, and Union Station. In addition, there are 58 other downtown stations which, with one exception, are all located along the north-south streets, since these streets have longer blocks. Lines on east-west streets, with short blocks, merely serve as feeder lines to the stations.

On the incoming corridors the line speed is 60 ft/sec (about 40 mi/hr), but each line splits up into two 30 ft/sec lines as it approaches downtown. Each of the utilized east-west streets carries two lines in the same direction, which are presumed to be supported on the same columns, and which have frequent transitions between the two. This is more clearly illustrated in the expanded drawing of Fig. 2-14 where it can be seen that, in principle, the whole network could be constructed at one level without grade-separated crossings. However,

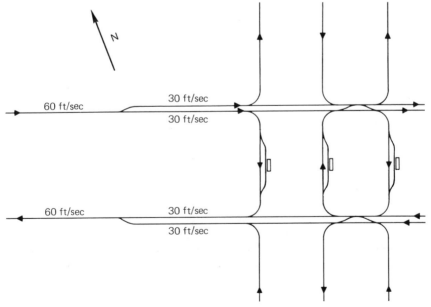

Fig. 2-14. Typical Detail of Downtown Los Angeles Single-Level Network

a north-south through trip would then be quite tortuous. Therefore, we compromised by putting in a few grade-separated intersections to facilitate through north-south traffic. It also will be noted from Fig. 2-13 that the direction of flow on most north-south lines has been chosen to facilitate the flow of occupied vehicles from the west and the return of empty vehicles to the west, because the heaviest traffic corridors lie in that direction.

It might be noted that once a few grade-separated north-south lines have been included, it may not be necessary for all stations to be on sidings. This is illustrated in Fig. 2-15 where Station *A* can be on-line. If Station A were replaced by two sequential stations, then they should both be on sidings.

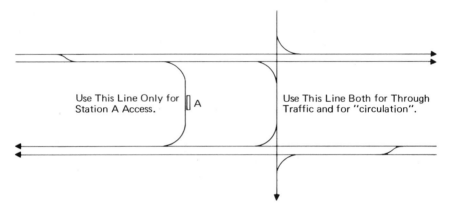

Fig. 2-15. Use of On-Line Station

It is of interest that the network of Fig. 2-13, being largely at one level, was designed to integrate into some planned pedestrian bridges similar to "skyways" of the Twin Cities.

Another approach aimed at working a large number of stations into a small CBD is that taken in Japan's Computer-Controlled Vehicle System (CVS). The designers envision a coarse grid of express lines extending over the metropolitan area. Typical line speeds would be 60 km/hr (about 37 mi/hr). Where these lines cross each other they would be at different elevations, in the usual manner. Within certain coarse grid squares there would be a fine grid, with all lines at one elevation. By using only one elevation it is, of course, necessary for vehicles on crossing lines to time-share an intersection, but the intersections can be made smaller because there is no need to change altitude. It is claimed that the fine grid spacing can be as small as 100 meters (328 ft) and that along any line, stations may be spaced 100 meters apart.

The problem with this approach is that it requires time-sharing the intersections and this introduces the possibility of a broadside collision. When a collision is imminent, it can be averted by warning the oncoming vehicle to apply emergency brakes. In CVS the emergency braking is accomplished by clamping onto a part of the guideway structure; the brake is explosively deployed. The emergency braking deceleration is 2 g. To avoid being thrown out of their seats when this sudden braking occurs, passengers are seated backwards.

Although we think that the CVS design has many clever features (see, for example, Sec. 4.6.7), we cannot endorse line crossings without grade separation because of the risk of broadside collisions. If crossing lines are at different elevations, then emergency braking decelerations can be much lower. Moreover, in contrast with the single-level emergency deceleration used in CVS, we feel that it is important to use a variable emergency deceleration so that no greater deceleration is used in any circumstance than is necessary to cope with the safety threat. This matter is explored further in Chapter 6.

2.6 RELATIONSHIP BETWEEN NETWORK CONFIGURATION AND SERVICE DEPENDABILITY

No matter how carefully the hardware components are chosen, no matter how much redundancy of critical components, and no matter how perfect the maintenance program, there will still be vehicle and other system failures. It is important, however, that when these failures occur they have a minimum effect on service dependability.

One way of protecting service dependability is to have a procedure wherein a failed vehicle is pushed by the vehicle behind it to an emergency siding where the people in the failed vehicle can transfer to a spare vehicle, after which maintenance personnel will pick up the failed vehicle. This procedure would ensure that service is not interrupted; vehicles behind the pushing vehicle lose at most a few seconds, and the parties in the failed and pushing vehicle are delayed by at most a few minutes.

This procedure, however, is not always feasible if the failed vehicle cannot be pushed or if the failure is some sort of blockage of the guideway. In that event, to avoid an accident, succeeding vehicles on the line would have to be brought to a stop and then detoured onto alternate paths to their destination. As soon as possible, the failed vehicle or blockage would have to be removed from the guideway, possibly by using street-driven equipment.

In a PRT network, rich in lines, there are usually many routes for getting from one point in the system to another, and if the operational strategy quickly reroutes the affected vehicles following a line blockage, then a high degree of service dependability can be maintained. In contrast, however, for those areas of a system which are line-haul in nature, a single line blockage could interrupt the entire flow down the corridor in question. There are, however, ways around this problem. Let us consider the example of an alignment along a freeway or other right-of-way on which it is practical to install a two-way guideway system. Now consider a third line being added between the other two. This line could serve as a bypass in the event of failure on either of the other lines. It would, of course, require frequent interchanges between the middle line and the other two. The method of line clearing is illustrated in Fig. 2-16 where four time "snapshots" are presented.

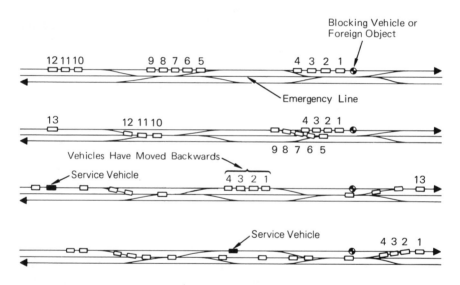

Fig. 2-16.   Elevated, Two-Way Line-Haul Guideway — Sequential Events
during Emergency Operations

The problem is even more severe where there are blockages on subway lines, for here we have not only the problem of arranging for traffic to bypass the blocked area, but there is also the problem of getting access to the blocked area for rescue and repair. For a one-way subway line, it may be advisable to connect the station sidings together, as illustrated in Fig. 2-17, into a continuous through line so that in the event of a failure on the main line the siding can be used as a bypass of the blocked area. At most, one station would have to be shut down to avoid interference with through traffic.

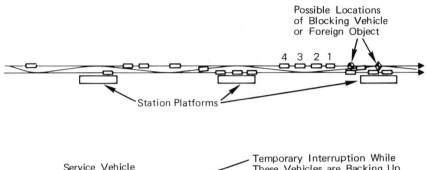

Station Platforms

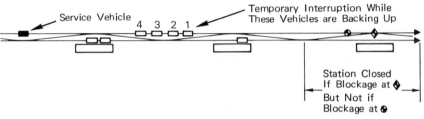

Fig. 2-17. One-Way Subway Line with Continuous Station Off-Line — Sequential Events during Emergency Operations

Chapter 3
STATIONS
Jack H. Irving

3.1 STATION TYPES

In this section we shall examine some of the general station types which are possible with PRT. They will be classified in accordance with the number of platforms, their arrangement on sidings, and whether the vehicles are stationary or moving when they are being deboarded or boarded. The variant known as a "docking" station also will be discussed.

3.1.1 The Single-Platform Station on a Simple Siding

The simplest station type, and one of the most useful, consists of a single platform adjacent to a simple siding. The same platform is used for deboarding and boarding, although in some modes of operation the vehicle, after being deboarded, may move forward before being boarded. The length of the platform depends on the maximum number of vehicles which must be simultaneously accommodated for deboarding and boarding. We refer to each vehicle location as a "berth." The number of platform berths, N_P, may typically vary from 1 to 3 in a residential station, and from 3 to 24 in a CBD station. Each berth should be about 1 ft longer than the vehicles to allow a 1 ft separation. Thus, for a 10 ft long vehicle, the berths would be about 11 ft.

Figure 3-1 is a sketch of the siding for this type of station. From left to right the sections of the siding are:

1. the entrance section, which accommodates branching from the through line onto the siding and accommodates deceleration
2. the input queue section, which provides a number of "input queue slots," the same length as the platform berths, for vehicles waiting to approach the platform
3. the platform section, with its N_P berths
4. the output queue section, where vehicles can be queued awaiting available space on the through line
5. the exit section, a mirror image of the entrance section.

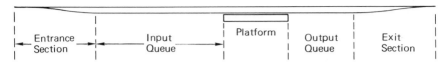

Fig. 3-1. Simple Siding for Single-Platform Station

Figure 3-2 is a plan view of an entrance section for a line speed of 30 ft/sec. It is based on an analysis carried out in Appendix A, Sec. A.3, and on the numerical assumptions listed in Fig. 3-2, which are quite conservative for all passengers seated.

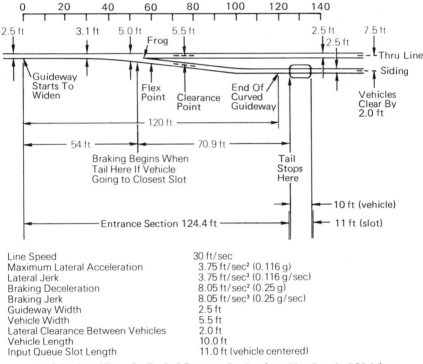

Line Speed	30 ft/sec
Maximum Lateral Acceleration	3.75 ft/sec² (0.116 g)
Lateral Jerk	3.75 ft/sec³ (0.116 g/sec)
Braking Deceleration	8.05 ft/sec² (0.25 g)
Braking Jerk	8.05 ft/sec³ (0.25 g/sec)
Guideway Width	2.5 ft
Vehicle Width	5.5 ft
Lateral Clearance Between Vehicles	2.0 ft
Vehicle Length	10.0 ft
Input Queue Slot Length	11.0 ft (vehicle centered)

Fig. 3-2. Plan View of a Typical Entrance Section for a Line Speed of 30 ft/sec

In addition, it is assumed that a vehicle which is to stop in the closest input queue slot will start braking when its tail is 1.8 sec into the entrance section. As a result of this assumption, when the tail passes the clearance point,[1] the vehicle will be only 0.5 ft behind

---

[1] It will be noted from the figure that although the guideways diverge for 120 ft, vehicles on the two lines would clear once the tail of the one on the siding has passed the "clearance point" which is only 75 ft downstream of the onset of divergence. (The 120 ft is merely the line speed multiplied by 4 sec, the time to carry out a lateral displacement of 7.5 ft. This time depends only on lateral jerk and acceleration, and is independent of line speed.)

where it would have been with no braking. Clearly, this poses no hazard.

By allowing the divergence and braking regions to overlap, the total entrance section is only 124.4 ft long. As the figure shows, had we kept divergence and deceleration as sequential operations, the entrance section would have been 66 ft longer.

As noted, the exit section is just the mirror image of the entrance section, based on the assumption that the longitudinal acceleration and jerk (rate of change of acceleration) used in the exit section are numerically equal to the braking deceleration and jerk.

Figure 3-3 is a plot of the length of the entrance (or exit) section as a function of line speed, with all other assumptions as indicated above (see Eq. (A.14) of Appendix A). For the higher speeds, the quadratic term in the braking (or acceleration) distance dominates and the length grows rapidly with line speed. For line speeds below 27.37 ft/sec, the braking (or acceleration) can all take place within the divergence (or convergence) region, and the curve becomes a straight line, representing the length of this region.

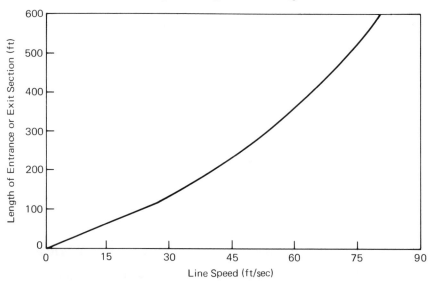

Fig. 3-3. Length of Entrance or Exit Section versus Line Speed

The input queue section of Fig. 3-1 not only provides a temporary storage site for occupied vehicles waiting to approach the platform but it also provides a place to queue empty vehicles. In Sec. 3.2 it is shown that, to obtain good performance of an activity-center station during morning and evening peak traffic periods, the input queue should be approximately twice as long as the platform and the output queue equal in length to the platform.

During peak traffic hours at a busy station there is a continuing flow of vehicles and the station works very well. But when the station is not busy, and especially in a residential area, the configuration of Fig. 3-1 has a substantial weakness. Imagine that it is just before 7:00 a.m. and a number of empty vehicles are queued in the input-queue section awaiting residents of the area on their way to work. Now imagine that one person who works in the residential area or one of its neighborhood stores arrives by PRT. To bring his vehicle to the station platform (assumed small), it would be necessary to advance almost all of the empty vehicles past the platform, and thus "waste" them. One way around this problem will now be discussed.

3.1.2 Single-Platform Station on a Siding with Two Entrances

To avoid wasting empty vehicles when bringing in an occupied vehicle one merely needs to have two entrances to the siding, one for empty vehicles and one for occupied vehicles. This is illustrated in Fig. 3-4. When this type of configuration is used at a residential station, it is possible to keep empty vehicles queued during the morning peak, even though some occupied vehicles might be arriving.

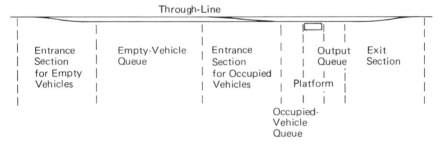

Fig. 3-4. Siding with Two Entrances for a Single-Platform Station

Because of the low arrival rate of occupied vehicles during the morning rush hours, and because they need not be queued for long, the occupied-vehicle input queueing space can be very short, perhaps two or three slots in length. In contrast, the empty-vehicle queueing space must store a significant number of empty vehicles if the queue is not to be depleted with surges in demand. The empty-vehicle queueing space must also be substantially larger than the average length of the empty-vehicle queue if there is to be room for empty vehicles that arrive during periods of a lull in the demand. This is especially true if empty vehicles are not readily accessible from nearby vehicle storage facilities, but, on the other hand, if a storage facility is very near, then the capacity for storing empty vehicles at the station can be reduced.

In Sec. 5.7 we discuss the problem of maintaining an adequate supply of empty vehicles and present the performance of a station of the type shown in Fig. 3-4, when some 3 to 5 parties/minute are departing from the station. This is a particularly heavily used residential station in contrast to the average. The station simulated had a platform length of 3 slots, an occupied-vehicle queuing space of 3 slots, and an empty-vehicle queuing space of 15 slots, although the average number of empty vehicles queued was only half this number.

The same station, operating during the evening, would not require bringing any empty vehicles to the station, but might require a somewhat longer space for the occupied-vehicle input queue. Consequently, the mode of operation during the evening would be to bring the occupied vehicles onto the siding through the first entrance rather than the second. The last few vehicles unloaded at the platform would remain there for any parties wishing to depart or until replaced by new occupied vehicles to be deboarded.

It also may be advisable to use two entrances to the siding of an activity-center station, but with the second entrance being used only during the nonpeak hours for occupied vehicles. This is illustrated in Fig. 3-5. We are assuming that the station platform has been sized to handle peak-hour traffic in accordance with the procedures to be discussed in Sec. 3.2.

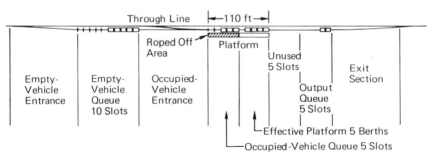

OPERATION DURING NONPEAK HOURS

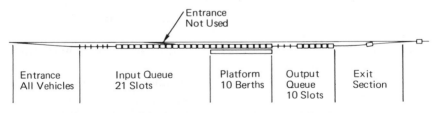

OPERATION DURING PEAK TRAFFIC HOURS

Fig. 3-5. Activity-Center Station with Two Entrance Sections

Let us assume, for purposes of illustration, that the platform has 10 berths. During the nonpeak hours, 5 berths clearly are adequate. Consequently, as indicated in the upper sketch of Fig. 3-5, the last 5 platform gates could be roped off and the berths for these gates could be used to queue occupied vehicles. Just upstream of the platform would be the second entrance section, used for occupied vehicle entrance during the nonpeak hours. With a line speed of 30 ft/sec, the second entrance section would be about 125 ft long. Just upstream of that there would be a queue section with perhaps 10 slots for empty vehicles. During peak hours the second entrance would not be used to admit vehicles and consequently could be used as a part of the input queue, holding about 11 vehicles. When combined with the queuing space that was used for empty vehicles during nonpeak hours, this gives a total input queuing space of 21 slots upstream of the platform. This is ideal for peak-hour operation.

3.1.3 Two-Platform Stations

There are two types of two-platform stations which are worth considering.

One is the kind illustrated in Fig. 2-9 for installation near an intersection of a one-way network. As indicated in that figure, the departure platform is placed so as to allow departure along either outgoing line, and the arrival platform is placed to allow arrival from either incoming line. The departure platform would require an input queue for storing empty vehicles only, and the arrival platform would require a temporary input queue for occupied vehicles waiting to get to the platform. Both platforms would require an output queue for vehicles which have left the platform and are waiting to find available space on the through line. Of course, both platforms would require entrance and exit sections.

The second type of two-platform station is illustrated in Fig. 3-6. It is appropriate for placement midway between two intersections. Both platforms are on a single siding but separated by an empty-vehicle queueing space. Both empty and occupied vehicles come in through the single entrance section, wait only as long as necessary in the input queue, and proceed to the arrival platform. Since no boarding takes place at this platform, all vehicles leaving the plat-

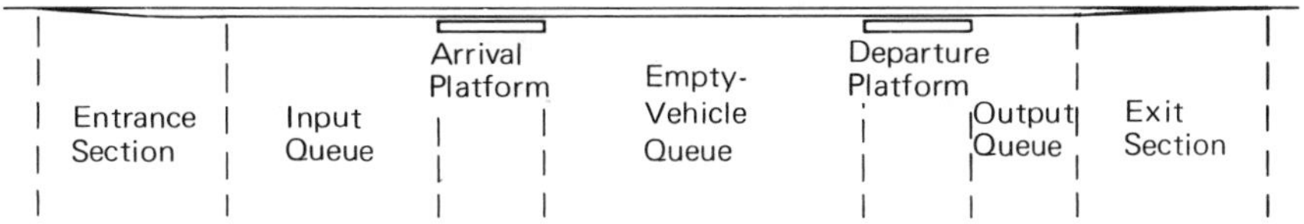

Fig. 3-6. Two-Platform Station on a Single Siding

form are empty and are stored in the empty-vehicle queue. They are called forward to the departure platform, as required, to serve departing parties. As before, the output queue is for temporary storage while awaiting space on the through line. A station of this type requires a somewhat longer siding than the others we have discussed.

Because both of the two-platform stations discussed here require an extra platform and more siding than the stations described in Secs. 3.1.1 and 3.1.2, they clearly will be more costly and therefore would be used only when specially indicated. One of their advantages is that they segregate arriving passengers from departing passengers, which may simplify passenger flow within the station itself. Also, because neither of the platforms has both deboarding and boarding, the average dwell time of vehicles at the platform is somewhat reduced. Consequently, to achieve capacities similar to the one-platform stations, the platforms can be somewhat shorter, i.e., fewer vehicles need to be brought in for a loading or unloading cycle.

A prior Aerospace Corporation paper[2] examined the two-platform station of the type illustrated in Fig. 3-6 as an activity-center station during peak traffic, and concluded that it does not have performance advantages over stations of the type illustrated in Fig. 3-1. However, it is the opinion of the author that the work cannot be considered definitive and there still are some open questions.

3.1.4   The Moving-Belt Station

All of the stations discussed up to now have involved deboarding or boarding a stationary vehicle. Therefore, they have sometimes been called "taxi stations" because the operation is similar to loading a queue of standing taxicabs. In contrast, it is possible to design a station so that people deboard and board slowly moving vehicles from a moving belt whose speed is matched to that of the vehicles.

To illustrate, let us assume as before that the vehicles are 10 ft long and they are spaced 1 ft apart in the station area. If the vehicles and the belt move at 2.2 ft/sec, one vehicle will enter the deboarding/boarding area each 5 sec. The moving belt should be long enough to provide ample time for vehicle deboarding and boarding in all but exceptional cases. Thus it probably is advisable to provide 60 sec for deboarding and subsequent boarding. This would require a belt 132 ft long. In those rare instances where a party had not completed boarding within that period of time, there would need to be sensors

---

[2] K.J. Liopiros, "PRT Station Operational Strategies and Capacities," *Personal Rapid Transit II*, U. of Minnesota (Feb 1974).

that automatically stop the belt and the stream of vehicles until the party had boarded.

The advantage of this type of station is that it provides continuous operation and that each vehicle automatically gets out of the way of the next. However, it has two significant defects. First, it is substantially more expensive because of the cost of the moving belt and the length of platform required. Second, there is a serious safety problem, that of protecting the passenger from falling into the guideway. For the "taxi stations" the passenger is protected by a continuous wall or fence which separates the station platform from the guideway; the vehicles all stop at fixed berths and the passengers enter through "gates" in the wall or fence. But since the vehicles are moving in the moving-belt station, the only way to protect the passenger would be to have a moving wall with openings through which he could enter a vehicle, and this would further complicate the design.

The throughput of such a station is very easy to compute. In our example the throughput would be one vehicle each 5 sec. However, by using platooning techniques, it is possible to exceed such throughputs at fixed platform stations. Consequently, we see no need for further consideration of the moving-belt station.

3.1.5 Docking Stations

A "docking station" is a fixed platform station which uses a guideway design capable not only of moving vehicles forward (and backward) but sideways. In such a design the vehicle can pass by other vehicles at the platform and then move sideways into a chosen platform berth. When the vehicle is loaded and ready to depart it can move sideways and then bypass the vehicles ahead of it without delay. The ability to dock has been cited as one of the advantages of air suspension.

The real domain of docking stations is their use in GRT systems. The reader will recall that in GRT operation there are a number of people waiting on a platform for different vehicles. The order of arrival of these vehicles will depend on what stops they have had to make and how long each stop took. Therefore, without docking it would be difficult to predict far in advance at what berth each vehicle will stop. Thus, as a vehicle approached a station it would be necessary for the people waiting for it to scurry around to the right berth. But with the ability of sideways motion a vehicle can always stop at a prescribed berth, moving forward from the input queue when that berth is available and bypassing other vehicles at the platform.

There is no such requirement for a PRT system since all vehicles are, from the standpoint of the user, identical. It might be argued that docking PRT vehicles is useful because it would allow departing vehicles to bypass a vehicle delayed by a slow boarder. But on the average, this will not help because the dynamics of moving the vehicles sideways and then forward adds enough time to the typical advancement cycle to more than compensate the occasional time savings. Moreover, the docking station, because it requires a wider guideway, and a particular type of guideway, will present greater aesthetic intrusion and will be more costly.

3.2 PERFORMANCE OF AN ACTIVITY-CENTER SINGLE-PLATFORM STATION

This section will address the question of how long the input queue, platform, and output queue need be at a single-platform activity-center station, and how that station should be operated, to provide a specified "throughput" without unduly sacrificing the quality of service. By "throughput" we mean the number of vehicles deboarded each hour during the morning rush hours or boarded each hour during the evening rush hours.

In 1973 The Aerospace Corporation developed two simulation programs[3] — one to study the performance of a single-platform station of the type illustrated in Fig. 3-1, and the other to study a two-platform station of the type illustrated in Fig. 3-6. During the preparation of this book, the former program was reexamined and found to have several significant errors. In addition, it was felt that a more realistic strategy of operation could be employed. As a result, an entirely new program for a single-platform activity-center station (Program "STATION") was written.[4] This program has provided the performance data that will be the topic of this section.

In Sec. 3.2.1 we treat some preliminaries related to boarding and deboarding and the advancement of vehicles in the station area. In Sec. 3.2.2 we discuss operational strategies. Then in Secs. 3.2.3 and 3.2.4 we examine station performance during the morning rush hours and the evening rush hours, respectively. The criteria of satisfactory performance are quite different for those two periods. The results are summarized in Sec. 3.2.5.

3.2.1 Some Preliminaries

To find the number of vehicles that can be processed each hour by a station it is necessary to know how long it takes for parties to deboard and board and how long to move vehicles from the input

---

[3] See footnote 2.
[4] Frank Goroszko and J.H. Irving.

queue into the platform area.

Later we shall be emphasizing platoon operation of a station where a number of vehicles are advanced simultaneously from the input queue to the station platform. Then deboarding and boarding begins. When all vehicles at the platform have completed deboarding and boarding (and certain other events have occurred), they will be advanced into the output queue while a new platoon is brought up to the platform. Clearly, the time to get all vehicles at the platform ready to move is paced by that vehicle which takes the longest to deboard and/or board. During the morning rush hours all vehicles going to an activity-center station will be deboarded but only a few vehicles will be boarded. For some platoons there may be no vehicles to be boarded; in that case the pace will be set by the slowest deboarding party. But, when one or two vehicles of the platoon are boarded, one of these vehicles may set the pace even though the deboarding party is quite average in its time to deboard.

Because deboarding and boarding times vary from party to party, both because of the variation in party size and because of the difference in agility in the individual passengers, we cannot use specified boarding and deboarding times but shall assume them to be distributed. Because it is the slower-to-average parties that determine when the platoon is ready to move, the exact nature of the distributions for the short deboarding/boarding times is not important, but the distribution should have a "tail" for the longer times to properly account for the slower parties, even though they are in the minority.

One mathematical form which would seem to have the right shape is the lognormal distribution which appears in Fig. 3-7. (The logarithm of the deboarding or boarding time is normally distributed.) It will be noted that the distributions have the desired tails for the longer times and even behave reasonably for shorter times. To specify a lognormal distribution, two numbers are required — the mean and the root-mean-square (RMS) deviation, the latter being a measure of the average spread. Altogether the simulation accepts four numbers, two for the deboarding distribution and two for the boarding. The numbers which we used are:

	Deboarding	Boarding
Mean Time	8.0 sec	10.0 sec
RMS Deviation	3.0 sec	4.0 sec

We know of no definitive data that can be used to establish these numbers, although we are aware of an experiment carried out by Messerschmitt-Bölkow-Blohm (MBB) several years ago. A number of automobiles (4-door sedans) were driven up to a marked

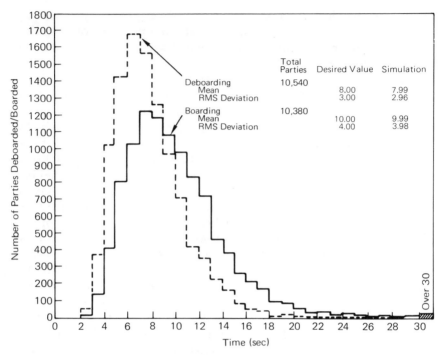

Fig. 3-7. Lognormal Distribution for Vehicle Deboarding/Boarding

area to load into or discharge passengers from the back seat. With an average party size of 1.5, the mean unloading time was 8 sec and the mean loading time was 10 sec. If MBB employees were the subjects of the experiments, it might be argued that they probably were more agile than the representative passenger; but we are dealing here with simulating rush hour traffic at an activity-center station where most of the passengers will be workers on the way to work or on their way home. Of greater importance, it should be far easier to deboard or board a PRT vehicle than the back seat of an automobile. The PRT door would be wider, the vehicle higher, and possibly a portion of the roof will slide away too; crouching should be minimal. Nevertheless, to be on the conservative side we took the MBB means for purposes of our simulation.

Now, we consider the time required to index the platoon forward. Based on limiting acceleration and deceleration to 0.25 g, jerk to 0.25 g/sec, and speed to 22 ft/sec, the time for indexing is plotted in Fig. 3-8 as a function of the number of slots moved.

It will be recalled that we have assumed that input queue slots, station berths, and output queue slots are all 11 ft long. We limited the station speed to 22 ft/sec to keep headway down to 0.5 sec, although this may not be necessary. In addition, we assumed a some-

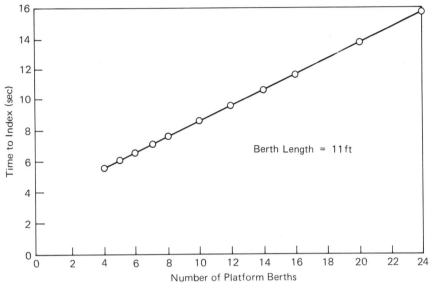

Fig. 3-8. Time to Index

what longer entrance section and exit section than now appears necessary in the light of the discussion of Sec. 3.1.1 and Sec. A.3 of Appendix A. The effect of these conservative assumptions is to slightly underestimate station performance.

3.2.2 Operational Strategies

Most of the early work of Aerospace was based on the strategy of allowing a vehicle to move forward into a station berth whenever one was available. During periods of moderate station usage this means that each vehicle as it arrives would stop in the berth behind the one which was then deboarding or boarding. When the wave of stopping vehicles got to the position of the last berth, the front berths would have been cleared out, but they would not be accessible from the input queue. Consequently, during the deboarding/boarding of the vehicle in the last berth, a short input queue would develop and when the vehicle in that berth moved forward, the input queue would be emptied in a platoon-like movement. This would be followed by another backward-moving wave through the berths. As the traffic rate increases, this kind of operation, which has been referred to as the "trickle operation," approaches that of platooning, and consequently should have a similar performance.

We feel, however, that this type of operation should be ruled out because it may present a safety hazard. Recalling that the vehicles are only 1 ft apart at the station platform, if a vehicle were to overshoot its mark, it could bump another vehicle with a passenger alighting or entering. To avoid this possibility we have restricted our attention to platoon strategies.

In a platoon strategy, entering vehicles also stop in the input queue only 1 ft behind the vehicle ahead, but if they were to overshoot they would strike a vehicle with seated passengers rather than one being boarded or deboarded. At an appropriate time a platoon of vehicles is brought forward from the input queue to the platform as the platoon alongside the platform is advanced to the output queue.

The advancement or "indexing" of the platoons cannot take place, of course, until there is adequate room in the output queue. The process of merging vehicles from the output queue onto the main line is relatively rapid because, in addition to the vacant spaces which were originally on the line, each vehicle which enters the siding creates another vacant space. As a consequence, the time to merge vehicles from the output queue onto the main line is less than the time necessary to bring in an adequate number of vehicles for the next platoon. This being so, the output queue need be no longer than the platform. Only rarely will there be a few seconds wait for the output queue to "clear." (We use "clear" to mean that the last vehicle in the output queue has started its acceleration to merge into the main-line traffic.)

We have considered two different platoon strategies:

Strategy A — index the platoons forward as soon as deboarding and boarding have been completed and the output queue is clear; and

Strategy B — index the platoons forward as soon as deboarding and boarding have been completed, the output queue is clear, and there are sufficient vehicles in the input queue to fill all platform berths.

It will be noted that in Strategy A the average elapsed time ("cycle time") between successive indexings is somewhat less than for Strategy B because it is never necessary to wait for the arrival of vehicles into the input queue. But the platoon brought forward in Strategy B will fill every berth while that of Strategy A is of variable length, depending on the number of vehicles that were available in the input queue at the time of indexing. We reasoned that these should be nearly offsetting factors affecting throughput and therefore the two strategies should lead to about equal throughputs. However, for operation during the evening rush hours, there is a very pragmatic reason for choosing Strategy B.

To understand this reason, imagine that we have a station having 10 berths at its platform and operating under Strategy A. Because of the variable length of the platoon brought in from the input queue there would be no assurance that vehicles would stop at Berths 9 or 10. Especially during periods when there was very little reverse flow, i.e., no arrival of occupied vehicles, the loading process might be completed rapidly and the platoons would be advanced, in accordance with Strategy A, before 10 vehicles were available in the input queue. As a result, there would be a learning process and people would not go to Berths 9 and 10. Then, even when there were adequate vehicles in the input queue to send vehicles to these berths, the vehicles would not be used. (The system could not be designed to wait for people to walk, or even run, from other berths and then insert their travel cards into the cardslots next to Gates 9 and 10 because this would add so much time to the boarding process as to substantially delay the next indexing.) As a consequence, Berths 9 and 10 would fall into disuse and would, in effect, be wasted.

In contrast, when Strategy B is used, all gates can be used equally and there are no preferred gates. One method of operation under Strategy B might be to direct the passenger to a specified gate at the time that he requests his trip. In this way gate usage may be kept evenly distributed.

Although we feel that Strategy B will work better than Strategy A for the evening rush hours, we have no reason to prefer it for the morning rush hours. Indeed, Strategy A may be somewhat better for the morning rush hours, especially during slack periods, because it would not keep people waiting in the input queue as long. But the simulations we have carried out are not directed to slack periods but rather to finding the maximum throughput, and we believe that, when the station is operating near capacity, the two strategies, as remarked earlier, should be nearly equal in their performance for the morning rush. Consequently, because of the pressure of time, we chose Strategy B for our simulation program — both for the evening and morning rush hours.

One other operational aspect is that which was alluded to earlier. People must not be allowed to start boarding after the others at the platform are well along in that process because that would materially delay the next indexing. This means that a person departing from a specified berth must have inserted his travel card into the slot beside the gate and withdrawn it before the vehicle comes to a stop or within a specified short time thereafter; otherwise, the gate and vehicle door will not open.

There are two other elements of strategy which affect only the evening operations. One of these has to do with bringing in an excess supply of empty vehicles to ensure that, even with fluctuations in passenger demand and in empty vehicle arrival, there still will be a supply of empty vehicles adequate to ensure that a long queue of passengers waiting to depart will not develop. As a result of this excess of empty vehicles, there will be many empty vehicles denied access to the input queue because it will be full. This has no serious consequences because the same empty vehicles could then be made available to neighboring stations in the CBD or other activity center to ensure that they, too, have an adequate supply.[5] An unfortunate consequence might be that there would be insufficient room in the input queueing space to accommodate an occupied vehicle that might be arriving during the evening peak traffic. This brings us to the last strategic measure, which is to reserve the last space or two in the input queue for occupied vehicles only.

3.2.3   Operation During the Morning Rush Hours

Operations at an activity-center station during the morning rush hours are much simpler than during the evening rush hours. During the morning all arriving vehicles will be occupied and the only criterion of acceptable service from the traveler's point of view is whether or not his vehicle is allowed to enter the station siding when it comes to the siding entrance. If his vehicle cannot enter the siding because the input queue is full (called a "miss"), the vehicle is required to circle the block and try again.[6] We define "miss rate" as the number of misses divided by the number of vehicles attempting to enter the station siding. The problem, then, of designing a station for morning operations is to find the lowest cost combination of input queue, station platform, and output queue which provides the necessary throughput at an acceptable miss rate.

Although there may be a few parties departing from the activity-center station during the morning rush hours, there are so many vehicles available for them that they will have immediate service. Their need to board, however, will sometimes delay the time when vehicles are ready to be indexed forward, and as a result the station

---

[5]   The excess vehicles serving the CBD or an activity center could be thought of as a circulating reservoir of vehicles for that area during the evening rush hours. Any station requiring one of these vehicles can pull it in off the main line. Because this reservoir of empty vehicles is shared, the number of excess empty vehicles can be a smaller percentage of the total vehicle throughput for the area than would be required without sharing. The number of excess empty vehicles required is proportional to the square root of the demand. Hence, if 16 similar stations shared a common reservoir of empty vehicles, the number of excess empty vehicles routed to that reservoir would only need to be 4 times the number that would have been sent to each individual station without sharing.

[6]   Once a vehicle has circled the block, it would be given priority over any of its neighbors that had not circled.

throughput will be diminished.

Before discussing the real problem of operating within acceptable miss rates, we shall first discuss the station throughput under saturation conditions. During the morning rush hours, saturation conditions are those where a very large number of occupied vehicles are trying to get into a station, so many that most of them cannot be accommodated. "Saturation throughput" is the number of vehicles/hr (or parties/hr) deboarded under these conditions. Although the miss rate under saturation conditions would be entirely unacceptable, the saturation throughput is still a useful concept because it serves as a guide in sizing the station to meet specified throughput requirements.

The saturation throughput is plotted in Fig. 3-9 for three values of reverse flow, as a function of N_P, the number of platform berths. As noted above, when there is reverse flow, i.e., when there are also parties to be boarded, the throughput is diminished. Under saturation conditions the input queue is full or nearly full at the time the deboarding and boarding are completed; consequently, even with Strategy B there is only rarely a need to delay indexing while waiting for vehicles to enter the input queue. Because of this, as long as the input queue is a little longer than the platform, the saturation throughput is almost independent of the length of the input queue.

Each of the circled points in Fig. 3-9 was obtained by a computer simulation run. It is seen that by going to sufficiently long platforms,

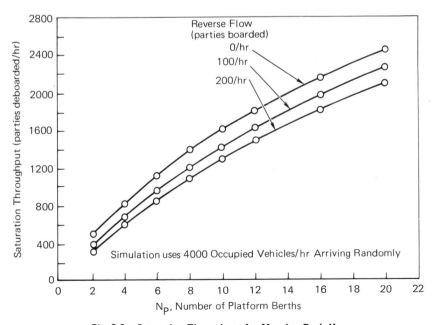

Fig. 3-9. Saturation Throughput for Morning Rush Hours

saturation throughputs can exceed 2000 parties/hr.

Now we turn to the real problem of sizing a station to meet a specified throughput requirement with an acceptable miss rate. Here the length of the input queuing space takes on an important role because the queuing space, if long enough, can store a temporary surge of arriving vehicles and thus lower the miss rate.

We illustrate the design process by considering a throughput requirement of 1000 parties/hr to be deboarded and a reverse flow requirement of 200 parties/hr to be boarded. Referring to Fig. 3-9 we see that there must be 8 platform berths to achieve a saturation throughput of over 1000. (A platform with 7 berths saturates at about 950 parties/hr.) To bring the miss rate down to an acceptable level, it might be expected that a platform with more than 8 berths would be required. Consequently, we investigated platforms with 8, 9, 10, and 12 berths. In addition, to find the impact of using an underdesigned station, we also investigated a station platform of 7 berths. For each of these, we varied the input queue length over a considerable range. The results are plotted in Fig. 3-10. There we plot miss rate versus total station slots.

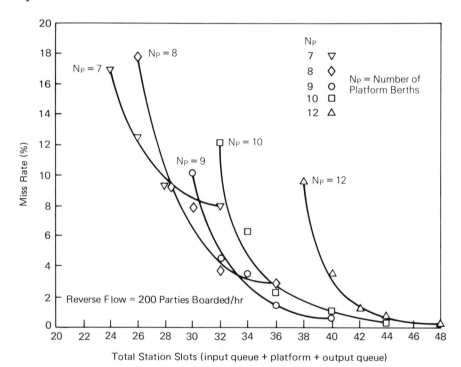

Fig. 3-10. **Miss Rate During Morning Rush Hours for a Throughput of 1000 Parties Deboarded/hr**

Each of the plotted points represents the average of at least four simulations, each representing two hours of activity. For the higher miss rates there is a considerable spread in the data to be averaged, but at the lower miss rates the spread is quite small.

Figure 3-10 shows that if the miss rate is to be brought below 1%, the station platform must be at least 9 berths long. It also shows that for any specified miss rate the station with 9 berths is superior to that with 10 or 12 berths because it is less costly. Not only is the platform shorter, but the siding is reduced because it requires fewer total station slots in the input queue, platform area, and output queue combined. This is not difficult to understand when it is recalled that we are here working with a fixed arrival rate of 1000 vehicles/hr. If a platform of 9 berths with an adequately long input queue is adequate to handle the throughput at a low miss rate, then platforms with 10 or 12 berths are overdesigned, adding unnecessary slots both at the platform and in the output queue.

It might be noted that if the miss rate is to be less than 1% for the 9-berth platform, the input queue should be at least 20 slots long, corresponding to 38 total station slots.

Figure 3-11 presents similar data for three other throughput requirements — 500, 1500, and 2000 vehicles/hr to be deboarded. Corresponding optimum platforms appear to have 5, 16, and 24 berths, respectively. If the miss rate is to be 1%, input queues should have 10, 28, and 39 slots, respectively.

3.2.4 Operation During the Evening Rush Hours

Operation during the evening rush hours is more complex than during the morning rush hours.

There are two criteria of acceptable service. The principal one will be how long parties must wait before they are able to board. A secondary criterion is that there should be an acceptable miss rate for the relatively few people arriving at the activity-center station during the evening peak traffic. As indicated earlier, this miss rate can be kept under control by reserving the last slot or two in the input queue for occupied vehicles only. We carried out most of our simulations with only one slot reserved, and found that this led to a miss rate of about 1 or 2% for occupied vehicles. With two slots reserved, there are virtually no misses.

As previously discussed, we found that it was necessary to bring in an excess of empty vehicles to ensure against the development of a long queue of waiting passengers. We simulated several cases where the planned arrival rate of vehicles was equal to the planned departure rate of parties. In some of these simulations, depending on how the

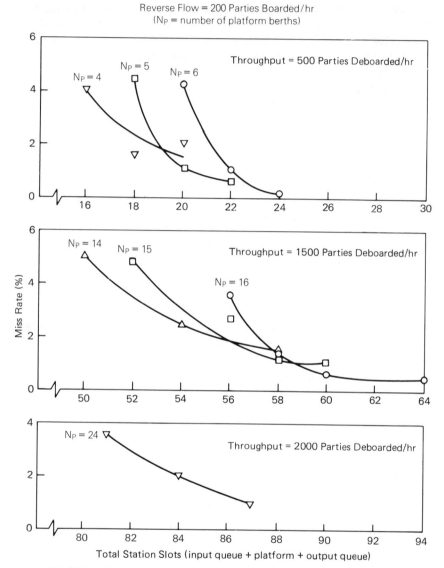

Fig. 3-11. **Miss Rate During Morning Rush Hours for Various Throughputs**

random numbers fell, vehicle arrivals would stay ahead of demand and no significant queues of waiting parties developed. In other cases, where the random numbers were less favorable, vehicle arrivals fell behind, and long queues of waiting passengers resulted. Once a queue has developed as a result of fluctuations in demand and/or vehicle supply, it is difficult to eliminate the queue and it persists for a long time. The only solution, as indicated, is to order an excess of vehicles.

As might be expected, we also confirmed that for the smaller stations where average vehicle arrival rates are lower, fluctuations become relatively more important and a larger percentage of excess vehicles must be ordered.

As during the morning rush hours, it is useful to find saturation throughput for the evening rush hours as a guide to station sizing. "Saturation throughput" here is defined as the number of parties boarded each hour under saturation conditions. For the evening, saturation conditions imply that vehicle indexing is being paced entirely by the time necessary to deboard and board vehicles, and not by the availability of parties wishing to depart or vehicles to serve them. Fig. 3-12 is a plot of saturation throughput versus N_P, the number of berths at the platform. Again, the throughput is given for three levels of reverse flow, i.e., the number of deboarding parties/hr. Comparing Fig. 3-12 to Fig. 3-9, the throughputs are seen to be somewhat smaller because of our assumption that the mean boarding time is 10 sec while the mean deboarding time is only 8 sec. However, as the reverse flow becomes significant, the pacing vehicles are those which are both deboarded and boarded, and the two saturation throughputs should be approximately equal.

To illustrate the design process for the evening rush hours, we consider a throughput requirement of boarding 1000 parties/hr with a reverse flow requirement of deboarding 200 parties/hr. From Fig. 3-12 it is seen that the platform must have at least 8 berths to exceed

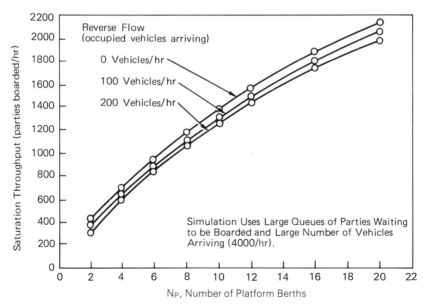

Fig. 3-12. Saturation Throughput for Evening Rush Hours

the throughput and reverse-flow requirement. Consequently we considered stations with platforms having 8, 9, 10, and 12 berths and, as in the morning case, also considered one with 7 berths to find the effect of an underdesigned station. Again, several input queue sizes were investigated for each platform. The results are presented in Fig. 3-13 where the average waiting time is plotted against the total station slots. The waiting time here is defined as the elapsed time from the instant when a person is at the station gate ready to board to the time when his vehicle arrives at the gate. The dashed curves represent simulations in which 5% extra vehicles were ordered, and the solid curves are for 10% extra vehicles.

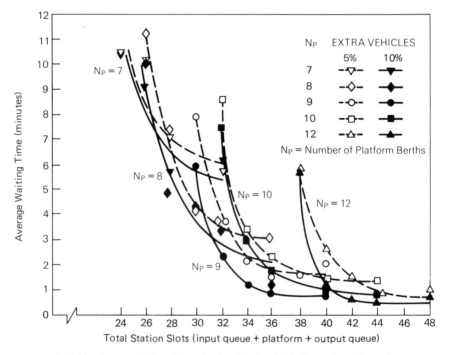

Fig. 3-13. Average Waiting Time During Evening Rush Hours for a Throughput of 1000 Parties to be Boarded/hr

As before, each data point represents the average of at least four 2-hr simulations. There is a very large spread in simulation results when the average waiting time is high. The spread is particularly significant for an 8-berth station, because, depending upon the random numbers, it could either develop a long queue or practically none. With a platform of 9 or more berths, and a reasonable input queue, the data become quite consistent.

Looking at the curves it would appear that 10% extra vehicles are required if waiting times are to be less than 1 minute. One again sees that a station of 9 berths is superior to one of 10 or 12 berths, both in requiring a shorter platform and fewer total slots. The station with 9 platform berths need have only 36 total slots, i.e., 18 slots in the input queue, although there is some improvement for longer queues. (It may be recalled that for the morning rush hours the recommended input queue was 20 slots.)

Figure 3-14 presents similar data for throughput requirements of 500, 1500, and 2000 boarding parties/hr. In all cases the reverse

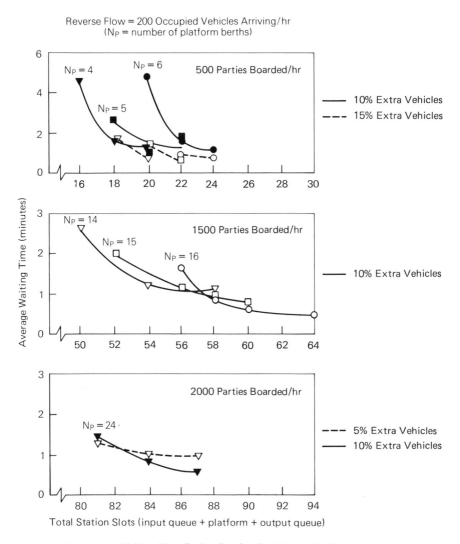

Fig. 3-14. Average Waiting Time During Evening Rush Hours for Various Throughputs

flow was taken as 200 arriving occupied vehicles/hr. It would appear that for a station requiring a throughput of 500 parties/hr, 15% extra vehicles should be brought to the station. A good choice would appear to be a platform having 5 berths (the same as the morning) and an input queue of 12 slots. (The morning required only 10.) At 1500 parties/hr, platforms with 14 or 15 berths appear to be somewhat underdesigned. A good design would appear to be one of 16 berths, with an input queue of 28 slots, which is identical with the morning requirement. For 2000 parties/hr, 24 berths and an input queue of 39 slots appears to be very satisfactory for both morning and evening operations.

3.2.5 Performance Summary

We have presented the results of our simulation of single platform stations in an activity center, both for the morning and evening rush hours. In each case we found the number of platform berths and input queue slots required to achieve specified throughputs without sacrificing the quality of service. For the morning operation we considered a miss rate of less than 1% to represent quality service, and for the evening operation we considered a waiting time of less than 1 minute to be quality service. Remarkably, in spite of the difference of these definitions, we found that the same number of platform slots were required and almost the same size input queues. Taking the larger input queue as being the dominant requirement, the results are summarized in Fig. 3-15.

As has been noted for both the morning and evening rush hours, an underdesigned station will not meet the requirements for quality service but an overdesigned station, though wasteful, will meet the requirements. Consequently, if there is some uncertainty in the throughput requirements at the time a station is being planned for an activity center, it may be wise to slightly overdesign it, to be on the safe side or to allow for growth in demand. If it turns out that the platform is longer than it needs to be, then several of the rear gates could be decommissioned or roped off, and the siding opposite them could be considered as a part of the input queue. Alternatively, since the station platform may be built in modules, with one module per berth, one might not overdesign, but instead add modules as required. This can be done most simply if the siding is sufficiently long from the outset.

3.3 STATION DESIGN CONSIDERATIONS

In Chapter 2 we pointed out that PRT guideways and stations can be underground, at ground level, or elevated. Certainly this will

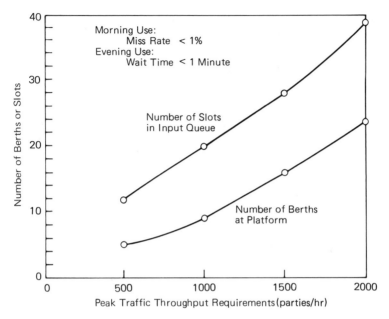

Fig. 3-15. Number of Platform Berths and Input Queue Slots to Achieve a Specified Throughput Without Sacrificing the Quality of Service

be one important factor affecting station design. For the reasons pointed out in that chapter, however, most of the stations will be elevated. Many will be integrated into or adjacent to major facilities such as office buildings, hotels, department stores, schools, sports arenas, or airline terminals. These will be of special design to blend architecturally into the overall facility, but with adequate attention paid to the functional features as well.

The remainder of the stations, and by far the greater number of them, will be elevated stations that stand free from existing structures. There would be significant economy if these were based on modular design and prefabricated parts. The majority of the station structural elements — floor and roof sections, walls, supporting beams, and columns — can be precast or prefabricated and delivered to the construction site in a variety of assembled arrangements to suit the station size and/or available working space conditions.

We have investigated both escalators and elevators as a means to get to or from the elevated structure. Not only are escalators more expensive, but the aged and incapacitated may find them difficult to manage. We much prefer elevators, which can also accommodate wheel chairs, baby carriages, and shopping carts. A single elevator will be adequate for the typical station in the residential areas and the smaller stations in activity centers, but the larger stations in activity centers may require two or more elevators. For the very largest stations an escalator might be used, but one elevator would still be required for those who cannot manage the escalator. In addition, there must be stairs for emergency use.

Figure 3-16 is a sketch of a moderately-sized (6 berths) activity-center station installed over the center of a street. A footbridge carries the passengers from the elevator or stairs to the loading platform. Trip-selection equipment is located on the footbridge. The station

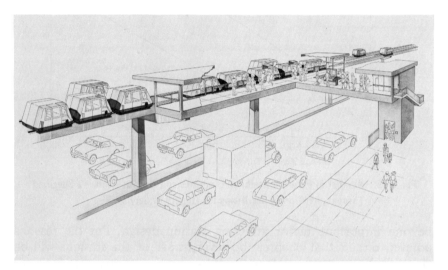

Fig. 3-16. Activity-Center Station Installed Over Center of Street

platform need only be about 8 ft in width. In this design the protective wall comes only to waist height and the sliding gates are indicated in the wall. Figure 3-17 is a design more appropriate to a curbline installation.

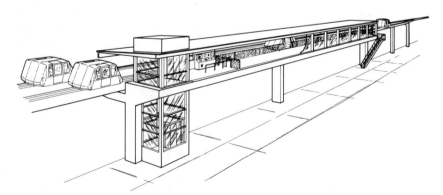

Fig. 3-17. Activity-Center Station Installed Over Curb Line

We have already discussed the functions of much of the electronics equipment to be located at each station, including the trip-selection equipment, the vending machine for "cash travel cards," the closed circuit television for platform surveillance, and the card readers located at each berth to control vehicle access and to inform the vehicle of its destination and other pertinent information. In addition, a station microcomputer would control the movement of vehicles and the assignment of berths to departing parties. The computer would be built with sufficient redundancy to ensure a very high probability of dependable service. For certain types of control systems, one of the functions of the microcomputer would be to dispatch empty vehicles, in the proper ratio, to preassigned destinations. For example, during the morning rush hours a CBD station will send its empty vehicles to a selected set of suburban stations, but later in the morning the empty vehicles will be sent to "car barns" for storage. In addition to diurnal variation of the empty vehicle dispatching instructions, they may be altered from time to time by a central computer.

Chapter 4

CONTROL ALTERNATIVES

Jack H. Irving

4.1 OVERVIEW OF PRT OPERATIONS AND CONTROL

There are many aspects of PRT operations and control.

In this chapter and in Chapter 5 we discuss PRT normal operations and control while in Chapter 6 we consider safety and the emergency operations employed in response to an operational failure or other hazardous condition. But, in comparing the various control options for normal operations, we will need to glimpse ahead to consider their safety, their vulnerability to failure, and the ease with which system operation may continue following a failure, although degraded in quality.

Chapter 5 treats the subjects of vehicle routing and empty vehicle management. To a large extent, those subjects can be treated quite independently of the type of control system used. The routing problem is one of assigning routes for all trips to minimize trip times or trip costs without leading to capacity overloads. It is true that the capacities achievable with different types of control systems may vary, but the routing problem can be solved by treating allowed capacity as an assigned parameter; the methodology does not change. There is further elaboration on this point in Sec. 5.1 after we have defined the control options in Chapter 4.

One aspect of the overall control problem is that of "lateral control." In some AGT designs there are four-wheeled vehicles which are steered much as a street-driven vehicle is steered, but automatically; the control system for the steering is a part of lateral control. We shall not treat steering control further because another approach has been broadly adopted in PRT designs, one which requires no active control system. In those designs the vehicles are physically constrained in their lateral motion by being continuously in contact with the sides of the guideway, although the vehicle usually is shock-mounted through appropriate springs and dampers to partially isolate passengers from being laterally buffeted by irregularities in the guideway wall. In Chapter 7 we will discuss vehicle suspension, including the lateral constraints.

Another facet of lateral control is vehicle switching. In Sec. 4.6.6 we will briefly discuss how switching can be controlled and in Chapter 7 we will discuss the design of switching mechanisms.

Any control concept must include the longitudinal control of vehicles along stretches of guideway, vehicle control at intersections and merges, and station operations and control. We already have covered the subject of station operations and control, so stations will be touched on only lightly in this chapter.

If a PRT system is to achieve the high capacities required in accordance with the arguments of Sec. 1.4, it must operate at very short headways; i.e., with small separations between vehicles. Section 4.2 treats the choice of minimum headway. This choice is not so much dependent on normal operations of the PRT system as it is on the question of passenger safety at the time of a vehicle failure. Thus the minimum allowable headways will depend on the safety policy adopted, the type and frequency of failures that can occur, the response times, the levels of emergency braking available, and on the use made of compressible bumpers and passenger constraints. Questions related to safety are discussed more fully in Chapter 6, but they will be touched on in Sec. 4.2 to show how they affect the choice of minimum headway and its possible dependence on line speed.

Then, in Sec. 4.3 through 4.5 we describe three of the more prevalent control concepts — synchronous, quasi-synchronous, and asynchronous control. Each of these concepts embodies a large number of characteristics. It is often assumed, incorrectly, that the characteristics of each must be grouped together and that a PRT (or GRT) must operate throughout with the same characteristics. Because of this impression, these three concepts have become stereotypes. Now we have come to understand that the characteristics can be admixed to give a very broad spectrum of control systems, and we also understand that the control characteristics can vary from one network element to another. In Sec. 4.6 we will discuss the spectrum of choices available. Nevertheless, it is still useful to first describe the three stereotypes, as a point of departure for the variations and hybrids.

4.2   THE CHOICE OF MINIMUM HEADWAY

It is important that PRT operations be very safe. In this section we shall examine some of the well-known safety criteria affecting the choice of minimum headway. If the adoption of criteria is capricious or based on an unreasoned standing tradition, it may rule out the possibility of short headways and therefore make PRT infeasible for certain applications. Criteria should be based on a realistic analysis of failure modes and other hazardous conditions and of their consequences on passenger safety. Chapter 6 presents such an analysis for some of the more important facets of safety.

One traditional criterion is the so-called "brick wall" approach which assumes that a failing vehicle stops instantaneously and that vehicles must be separated by a distance sufficient to allow the following vehicle to apply brakes and come to a stop before colliding with the disabled vehicle. The ratio of the separation to the stopping distance is known as k. The brick wall criterion corresponds to having k > 1. If the following vehicle, after a delay of 0.2 sec, were to decelerate at 0.7 g (the maximum attainable in standard automobiles), the initial separation would have to be 89 ft to avoid collision at an initial speed of 40 mi/hr.

Fortunately, a vehicle does not stop instantaneously when it malfunctions. Even in the extreme case where all wheels lock, a vehicle will traverse quite a distance while sliding to a stop. For example, at 40 mi/hr and with a 0.7 g deceleration rate, it will slide 77 ft. Even though vehicles do not stop instantaneously, the brick wall criterion has been adopted into regulations for conventional rail in many nations, and is now interpreted in many places as applying to all AGT systems. As a better understanding develops of the real safety issues and as systems are proven out on experimental test tracks, the old regulations will give way to more realistic ones.

Later we will return to a safety criterion which is closely related to the "brick wall" stop. This is where the sudden stop is not caused by a vehicle malfunction but by the striking of a massive object on the guideway. For the moment, however, let us continue our discussion of vehicle failures leading to inadvertent decelerations.

The approach at Aerospace (discussed in Chapter 6) is to have the failing vehicle measure its own inadvertent deceleration and report the measurement, together with other diagnostics, to a local computer which has control jurisdiction in the segment of the network where the failure occurs. (Other normal operational functions of the local computer will be discussed in later sections of this chapter.) If the local computer decides that the failing vehicle can be pushed, then the following vehicle is instructed to make a soft engagement with the failing vehicle, reaccelerate to line speed, and push the disabled vehicle to an emergency siding where a spare vehicle will be available. If the local computer decides that the failing vehicle cannot be pushed, then the following vehicle(s) are brought to a stop. At Aerospace we have chosen the headway to avoid impact during this emergency stop.

In Chapter 6 we shall demonstrate that if the deceleration of the following vehicle is about 15% greater than that of the failing vehicle, and if the onset of its braking is not delayed more than 0.2 sec after the onset of failure in the leading vehicle, then a 5-ft separation is more than adequate to ensure that vehicles do not collide. At first the vehicle separation will decrease, but as the velocity of the following vehicle drops below that of the failing vehicle, the separation reaches a minimum and starts to increase again. The total encroachment (maximum decrease in separation) is less than 4 ft. Had the delay been only 0.1 sec, the encroachment would be less than 1 ft. Only if there were a multiple failure, such as the failure of the second vehicle's brakes simultaneously with the locking of the first vehicle's wheels, would there be a collision. Thus, we have set the headway criterion in the Aerospace design so that no collisions will occur with "single-point" failures.

If the failing vehicle has locked its wheels, its rate of deceleration in g's will be equal to the coefficient of sliding friction between the wheels and guideway. Obviously, if the second vehicle's braking deceleration is to be 15% greater than the failing vehicle's rate of deceleration, then the second vehicle cannot rely on traction brakes. The primary mode for braking in the Aerospace design does not depend on traction; it is a linear motor used both for propulsion and braking. In the Federal Republic of Germany the Cabintaxi design is also independent of traction; it uses a different kind of linear motor for propulsion and uses eddy current braking. The Japanese CVS design uses traction brakes for normal braking and clamps the guideway for high-level 2 g emergency braking.

When braking is not dependent on traction, the guideway and wheels should be designed to minimize the coefficient of sliding friction. This has the effect of lowering the locked-wheel deceleration rate and thereby lowering the braking deceleration rate required in the following vehicle.

For a system that does use traction braking, let us first assume that braking deceleration on the following vehicle is 0.7 g (22.5 ft/sec^2), and that this exactly matches the deceleration of the failing vehicle with locked wheels. After a delay of 0.2 sec, there is a closing speed of 4.5 ft/sec, and subsequently this remains constant until the vehicles collide or the failing vehicle comes to a stop. Thus, an alternate policy to the one Aerospace adopted is to permit a collision velocity of about 4.5 ft/sec (3 mi/hr) for a single-point failure, rather than requiring that there be no collision.[1]

The problem with traction braking occurs when the following

[1] Even in the Aerospace design, if the reason for the inadvertent deceleration is that the leading vehicle has accidentally applied its brakes at their maximum rate of deceleration, then when the following vehicle matches this rate after a 0.2 sec delay, there will be a collision at somewhere around 4 to 5 ft/sec, depending on the maximum braking rate used.

vehicle has smooth tires and cannot develop as large a deceleration as the failing vehicle. If, for example, the following vehicle can only develop a 0.6 g deceleration rate (in contrast to 0.7 g in the failing vehicle), then the closing velocity will increase by 3.2 ft/sec for each additional second before impact. If the vehicles were initially only 5 ft apart, they will impact at a closing speed of 7.0 ft/sec (0.79 sec after the following vehicle applies its brakes). But if the vehicles are initially 30 ft apart and the line speed is at least 75 ft/sec (51.1 mi/hr), they will impact at 14.5 ft/sec (3.11 sec after the following vehicle applies brakes).

Thus far we have pointed out that with 0.2 sec for brake application, with 5 ft separation, and with nontraction brakes, no collision need occur when a single-point failure leads to inadvertent deceleration of a vehicle. (If braking response times can be brought down to around 0.1 sec, still shorter separations could be used.) Alternatively, if traction brakes are used, the impact velocity would normally be only about 4.5 ft/sec (but could be three to four times higher if the following vehicle has smooth tires and the vehicles are further separated). A separation of around 5 ft is more than adequate to manage the merging of vehicles.

Now let us return to the situation where a "brick wall" stop can occur, and that is the rare occasion where a massive object, such as a tree, has fallen across the guideway. Then, if no warning has occurred, the first vehicle that strikes the massive object will strike it at line speed, regardless of the headway. To protect the passengers in that vehicle, there must be such protective devices as compressible bumpers and passenger restraints (e.g., air bags). These are discussed in Chapter 6. As the striking vehicle rapidly decelerates, the following vehicle is warned and starts to brake.

Here is where the safety policy is involved. If the policy is that the second vehicle should avoid hitting the first, then the system must operate with $k > 1$ (i.e., according to the "brick wall" criterion). If the second vehicle is allowed to hit the first, then at what collision velocity may it strike the first? For the Cabintaxi system, operating at a line speed of 10 m/sec (32.8 ft/sec or about 22 mi/hr), the second vehicle was initially allowed to strike the first at 4 m/sec (13.1 ft/sec). The designers have considered increasing the allowed impact velocity up to 8 m/sec when shorter headways are required. At Aerospace our studies, reported in Chapter 6, have shown that with the proper design of the vehicle body structure, bumpers, and passenger constraints, the passengers can be well protected with "brick wall" collisions up to at least 75 ft/sec (about 50 mi/hr).

The minimum separation between vehicles which can be used, corresponding to any allowed impact velocity, is given by

$$S = V\tau + (V^2 - V_c^2)/2a_B, \qquad (4.1)$$

where

S = minimum allowed separation distance,

V = line speed,

V_c = allowed impact velocity between second vehicle and first after first vehicle has been stopped by brick-wall collision with massive object,

a_B = braking acceleration of second vehicle,

τ = effective delay time between collision of first vehicle and the effective[2] onset of braking of second vehicle.

Equation (4.1) is plotted in Fig. 4-1. The solid curves are for an effective delay of 0.2 sec and a braking deceleration of 0.8 g. They are given for values of allowed impact velocity ranging from 0 to 90 ft/sec. The dashed curves are based on limiting braking deceleration to 0.5 g.

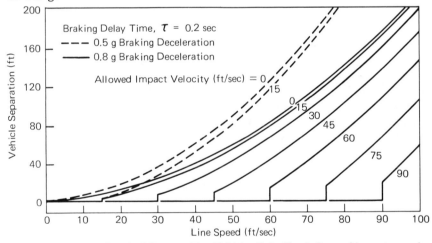

Fig. 4-1. Separation Required Between Two Vehicles if the First is Stopped Instantaneously by Hitting a Massive Object and the Second Brakes to Reduce its Impact Velocity to a Specified Value

To understand the sudden jump that appears in each curve, consider the case of limiting impact velocity to 60 ft/sec. If the line speed is 60.1 ft/sec, and there is a delay of 0.2 sec in braking, then the

[2] If one assumes a delay t_0 before brakes are applied, followed by a jerk duration t_J while the braking acceleration is being brought up to the value a_B, then "the effective onset of braking" is halfway through the jerk period; i.e., $\tau = t_0 + 0.5\, t_J$.

second vehicle will travel 12 ft before braking, and thus the separation must be at least 12 ft. But, if the line speed is only 59.9 ft/sec, no braking is required to keep impact velocity below 60 ft/sec, and the minimum headway could be zero if this were the only safety criterion.

It is not clear how seriously the separation criterion given in Fig. 4-1 should be taken. First, the scenario is predicated on a massive object that can instantaneously stop the first vehicle. With proper design the guideway would be protected from such objects, and even a heavy branch of a tree is not so massive that it would not be pushed some distance. Second, since passengers in the first vehicles have no warning of the foreign object, the danger to which they are exposed is not related in any way to the separation between vehicles. Third, if passengers in the first vehicle are to be adequately protected (by compressible bumpers and passenger constraints), then passengers in the following vehicle(s), will have at least the same protection. Fourth, the maximum exposure to this threat occurs only on the highest speed portions of the network and only when vehicles are following at minimum headway.

For all of these reasons we have not considered the separation criterion of Fig. 4-1 as being of primary significance in our work at The Aerospace Corporation. Rather, we have placed primary emphasis on inadvertent failure and on the ease of merging and therefore have planned on minimum separations of approximately 5 ft. As stated earlier, we believe that the data on passenger safety indicates that a brick wall collision of up to 50 mi/hr will cause no serious injury and consequently the 5-ft separation is quite adequate up to these speeds. To be conservative, one might lengthen the separation on lines with characteristic speeds above 50 mi/hr, but the advisability of doing this would depend on additional study. The determination will require more detailed design considerations, additional data relative to passenger injury at higher speeds, and an evaluation of the frequency of the rare occasions which might require additional separation between vehicles to further protect passengers in the second vehicle.

With the above caveats, Fig. 4-2 shows the minimum headway which would result from accepting the separations of Fig. 4-1, but limiting the minimum separation to be no shorter than 5 ft. The solid curve represents the headway in seconds which corresponds to using a 5-ft separation between vehicles. To illustrate how the figure is used, consider an allowed impact velocity of 60 ft/sec. For line speeds below 60 ft/sec, the minimal headway is that indicated by the solid curve; for line speeds above 60 ft/sec, the minimum headway is that given by the dash-dot curve labeled 60.

If passenger protection has been provided which allows some

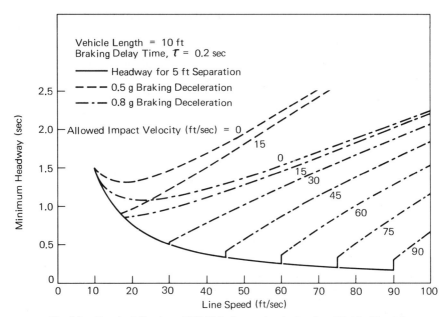

Fig. 4-2. Required Headway if Vehicle Separation is that Specified in Fig. 4-1 but Not Less Than 5 ft

high impact velocity, like 75 or 90 ft/sec, then the system, in general, will operate on the solid curve; i.e., with 5-ft separation. This is the case with the Aerospace Corporation design. In that event, the higher the speed the shorter the headway. But, if the vehicle's protective devices and the adopted safety policy limit the impact speed between second and first vehicles to some low value, like 15 ft/sec, then the system will operate on the appropriate dashed or dash-dot curve and there is a critical trade-off that needs to be made between headway and line speed. It is because of this type of trade-off that the Cabintaxi line speed has been limited to 10 m/sec (about 22 mi/hr).

In summary, we have seen how sensitive the choice of a minimum safe headway can be to the adoption of a suitable safety policy and the response times, the level of emergency braking available, and the impact velocity that can be absorbed without injury to passengers. Because different control systems will be characterized by different response times to inadvertent deceleration, they may vary somewhat in the minimum headways achievable. In addition, capacity is dependent not only on minimum headway but also on the amount of space that must be left vacant on a line to permit the entry of vehicles coming from other lines or station sidings. Since different control systems may have different effectivity in using the available space for the merging, this too will influence the practical capacities attainable. These questions will be treated later in this chapter as a part of our comparison of different control alternatives.

4.3   SYNCHRONOUS CONTROL

Because of its complexity, and a number of other shortcomings to be discussed below, strict synchronous control is not taken very seriously today by most investigators. Yet, as did others, Aerospace started its investigation of PRT control by at first focusing on synchronous control. By discussing it first, we introduce some concepts which carry over to quasi-synchronous control.

Synchronous control is based on the concept of a moving "slot" which is a space of specified length moving along a guideway. Sometimes the "slot" is referred to as a "moving block." Either the slot is vacant or it is occupied by a vehicle centered in it. At a point of merging, the slots on the two merging lines are so synchronized that they exactly coincide on the merged line.

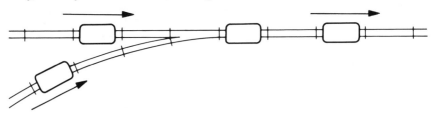

Slots may accelerate, but in doing so they stretch. (Likewise, during deceleration, slots shrink.) To understand this, consider a string of vehicles centered in adjacent slots 15 ft long and traveling at 30 ft/sec. The vehicle headway is 0.5 sec. When the vehicles pass a given point they start to accelerate up to a speed of 60 ft/sec. After reaching this speed, they still have a headway of 0.5 sec, but now the slot surrounding each one is 30 ft long.

It should be made clear that the slot is imaginary, not something physical; it is a useful concept to explain the allowed locations of moving vehicles. An equivalent concept is that of equally spaced points moving along a guideway, with each vehicle with its nose at one of the points, although not all points will have vehicles at them. The longitudinal control problem is to keep each vehicle centered in its slot, or, what is equivalent, following its point. For this reason such longitudinal control systems sometimes are called "point followers," although the term "point followers" would also include following points not equally spaced.

The longitudinal control is accomplished by observing the vehicle's position as a function of time, comparing that position with where it should be, and introducing speed adjustments to correct the position. The measurements and the determination of the correction needed can be made either from the vehicle itself or from the wayside; i.e., by instrumentation mounted on the guideway. These alternatives will be discussed further in Sec. 4.6.7.

The principal challenge for any control system is to avoid conflicts at merges and at stations. A conflict at a station occurs if a vehicle arrives at a station but finds it cannot enter the siding because there is no room for it. A conflict at a merge occurs if two merging vehicles are trying to occupy the same space (i.e., the same slot) on the merged line.

The essential idea for "synchronous control" is to set up a reservation system under the control of a large central computer, and not to allow a passenger to depart from his origin station until reservations for his whole trip are confirmed in advance. Here is how it works in its simplest form. When the passenger requests his trip, the request is transmitted to the central computer. There, the route to the destination station is looked up, and the exact time, measured from the instant of departure, past every merge point en route and to the destination siding is also looked up or computed. These times are very precise because of the synchronous slot motion.

A departure time is postulated, well enough in advance to ensure that the passenger(s) will have completed boarding at that time. Based on the postulated departure time, the time of arrival at the destination station is determined. If, as a result of previously confirmed reservations, the destination station is "booked to capacity," the process will be repeated either with a different route or with a new (later) postulated departure time. When the destination station is found to have available capacity at the calculated time of arrival, the next step is to check the availability of slots on each link of the route.

A "link" is here defined to mean the section of guideway from one merge point to the next. Slot availability is confirmed by checking a table of slot reservations. It is not enough to confirm that a slot is available where the vehicle turns onto a specified line, because that same slot could be reserved for another vehicle which will be merging into the slot as it passes a downstream intersection or as it passes a merge point with a siding from a station. That is why it is necessary to reserve the slot for every link along the way. If slots are not available, a new (and still later) departure time is postulated and the entire process is repeated, including checking both destination station and slot availability en route.

On a busy network it is extremely difficult to find available slots for the entire trip. For this reason, all of those who have worked with synchronous control have introduced a degree of flexibility by allowing the vehicle to move to neighboring slots on the main line and/or by allowing it to maneuver at an intersection to gain access to one of several slots after completion of the turn. One variation which uses slot changing at intersections and also allows flexibility in routing is referred to as "Trans-Synchronous."[3]

In some approaches the slots are thought of as being grouped into larger moving blocks. If the time of passage of a block were equal to the average interval at which the destination station can safely accept vehicles, then one (and only one) vehicle going to that destination station can be assigned to a block, but it could be in any slot of the block. The reservation of slots en route is facilitated by the freedom to move vehicles within the block, even though the order of the vehicles cannot be changed.

When, for some postulated time of departure, both destination station and slots are available, the new reservations are recorded and the ticket might be magnetically encoded with the planned departure time. If that time is some minutes away, the patron is informed that he must wait and he is not allowed to board until shortly before his scheduled departure. Alternatively, he can be allowed to board at once and the vehicle held in a holding area. In either case the station must be so designed as to allow a vehicle to depart precisely on schedule without being held up by others. This might be accomplished by the moving belt station described in Sec. 3.1.4, providing the departing party gets into the right vehicle and providing the belt doesn't need to be stopped for slow boarders. The docking station is another possibility.

The initial appeal of synchronous control is the general principle that the more information that exists on the state of the system and the totality of trips to be processed, the closer the control system can come to achieving some theoretical optimum operation. But in practice, synchronous control has a number of serious shortcomings:

a. The system requires a large computer to process and store reservations. Because failure of the computer would be catastrophic, two or more may be needed for redundancy.

b. The system is dependent on relatively long communication distances which makes communication vulnerable.

c. Destination stations would have to operate well below their capacity to assure that reserved time would be available. Departure areas would have to be designed to assure that departing vehicles could leave on schedule without interference from others. The station must provide a holding space for vehicles and/or an area for passengers waiting to board. Altogether, the station will have grown in size, cost, and complexity.

[3] "The Manhattan Project — A Cost Oriented Control System for a Large Personal Rapid Transit Network," R. Morse Wade, IBM Corporation, published in *Personal Rapid Transit-II*, University of Minnesota, Dec. 1973.

d. Should a vehicle fail, decelerating to a stop, it will cause all of the vehicles behind it to lose synchronization. Then other vehicles scheduled to turn onto that line will not be able to do so and must continue going straight. But the slot in which such a vehicle continues might be reserved after the next crossing, and so a conflict could be created. At the very least, a large number of vehicles would have to be reprogrammed en route with a new route and a new set of reservations, and possibly the desynchronization would propagate throughout the network.

To accommodate such failures more gracefully, it has been suggested that a certain fraction of all slots be left vacant for emergency use only. Then the vehicle forced to move straight ahead because it could not make its turn would adjust its position into one of the emergency slots and thus avoid conflict (except, perhaps, with another which had taken an emergency slot). Although this probably can be made to work, the effect under normal operations of not using emergency slots is to degrade the normal line capacity.

In summary, we do not favor synchronous control.

4.4 QUASI-SYNCHRONOUS CONTROL

Most of the work at The Aerospace Corporation has been devoted to quasi-synchronous control, including some of its variations which are discussed in Sec. 4.6. In Sec. 4.4.1 we describe the general concept of quasi-synchronous control and in 4.4.2 we consider in more detail the design and operation of intersections.

4.4.1 General Description of Quasi-Synchronous Control

As in synchronous control, quasi-synchronous control uses the concept of imaginary slots moving in a synchronous manner along the guideway. Again, on most of the guideway between intersections, either a slot is empty or there is a vehicle centered in it. But, in the vicinity of an intersection, vehicles may be instructed to advance slots or to slip slots to resolve conflicts on merging.

The principal difference between this and synchronous control is that there is no reservation system. When a vehicle is boarded, it moves into an output queue on the siding, as described in Chapter 3. Then vehicles in this queue are merged into slots on the main line as soon as possible.

Conflict resolution at an intersection is under the control of a local microcomputer which, assuming a one-way network, has a jurisdiction extending back along both incoming lines to the first upstream merge points. At the entrance to its jurisdiction area (or even before), there are wayside sensors to determine which slots are empty and which have vehicles in them. A vehicle passing the sensor reports the number of its destination station and whether it is empty or occupied by passengers. Then the local computer refers to a routing table to see whether the nominal route to the destination is one requiring the vehicle to turn or to go straight ahead.

The "nominal route" will usually be the fastest route, although it could be the shortest or the one consuming the least energy, or some "least-cost" combination of these. More important, if all vehicles took the fastest (or least-cost) route, certain parts of the network might become overloaded; i.e., the assigned traffic could exceed the physical capacity. To avoid this situation, not all trips will be assigned fastest (or least-cost) routes, but some will be assigned slightly slower (or more costly) routes to "balance the traffic." In particular, empty vehicles may be sent on slower routes to allow occupied vehicles to be routed the fastest way. Thus, each local computer may have two routing tables, one for occupied vehicles and one for empty. It is also obvious that different routing tables should be used for different times of the day. During the nonpeak traffic, for example, fastest or "least-cost" routes could be used for all trips. How to set up routing tables to minimize trip times or "costs" consistent with avoiding overloads is presented in Chapter 5.

Once the local computer knows for both incoming lines which slots have vehicles and which of these vehicles should turn, it goes through a set of computations (algorithms) to determine which vehicles should maneuver (advance or slip slots).

The location of the maneuvering will depend on the geometry of the intersection. If the maneuvering takes place before the switch point, it is a "single-stream" intersection; if after, it is a "split-stream" intersection. The performance of these two types of intersections is discussed in Sec. 4.4.2 where it is found that for reasonable traffic densities, especially for the split stream, almost all conflicts can be resolved.

Now, occasionally it will be impossible to accomplish all planned turns without slowing down traffic on one of the lines upstream of the computer's jurisdictional region. (This could occur, for example, if all slots within the jurisdiction on one line were occupied, no vehicles were turning off of that line, but some wanted to turn onto it.) To avoid such an occurrence, the local computer has the authority to deny a turn and require the would-be turner to go straight. In giving the local computer this authority, maneuvers can be restricted to a stipulated region entirely within the computer's jurisdictional area, and each computer can act autonomously without interfering with the actions of its neighbors.

The vehicle which is denied its turn will move straight ahead and will be routed to its destination station by the local computers at downstream intersections. This situation is illustrated in Fig. 4-3 where a vehicle leaving Station S_1 is destined for Station S_2. The shortest path requires turns at A, B, and F. But, if there is heavy traffic coming from the north at A and there are many vehicles coming from the west and trying to turn south at A, then the vehicle destined for S_2 may be denied its turn. In that event it would proceed straight. As it approached intersection C, the local computer there would continue it straight ahead. The computer at D would cause it to turn, after which it will proceed south to Station S_2. The distance and time penalty for the "detour" is quite insignificant.

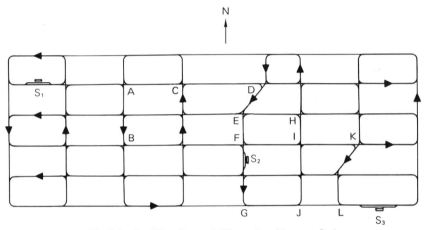

Fig. 4-3. One-Way Network Illustrating Alternate Paths

On the other hand, if the vehicle proceeds along its nominal path ABF and then is denied the turn at F, it will have to circle the block and reach S_2 along the path FIHEFS$_2$. This would add several minutes to its trip. To avoid this rather severe time penalty, the computer at F will choose instead to deny the turn to another vehicle going to S_3, since the path FIKLS$_3$ is only slightly longer than the nominal path FGJLS$_3$. Thus, a priority system is used in denying turns; the vehicles which would be most delayed by the denial will be the last to be denied.

When using quasi-synchronous control, the options for keeping vehicles centered within their assigned slots are the same as those for synchronous control. Measurements of time and position, and hence position error, can be done from the vehicle or the wayside. More-over, if the vehicle is equipped to make the measurements, then, when the intersection computer requires the vehicle to carry out a maneuver to resolve a conflict, the computer need only command the vehicle to advance or slip a prescribed number of slots, beginning at a specified time (or position); the vehicle can program details of the maneuver. This is the approach which we used on our scale model test track. If measurements are made from the wayside, then the wayside computer must control the maneuver. This is the approach used in Japan's Computer-Controlled Vehicle System. Both the Aerospace and CVS measurement techniques are discussed in Sec. 4.6.7.

Switch actuation at a branch point can either be under the control of a local wayside computer or of the vehicle. In the Aerospace design, described in Chapter 7, we utilize electromagnetic switches on the guideway under the control of the local computer. In other designs the switch is on board the vehicle.

In addition to the many local computers, a quasi-synchronous system also employs a large central computer which is used for strategic and administrative functions, but not for the tactical control of individual vehicles. One of its strategic functions is the balancing of network traffic under exceptional circumstances. It accomplishes this by sending to the various intersection microcomputers appropriate tables for traffic routing. If, for example, a section of guideway were blocked, it would send out an emergency set of routing tables which would cause the intersection computers to route traffic around the blocked area. When a large sporting event was about to let out, it would send to the nearby intersection computers routing tables which would cause them to route through-traffic around the stadium area to minimize congestion in that area. It could also send to station computers instructions to dispatch their surplus empty vehicles to the stadium to meet the extraordinary demand.

Among its administrative functions would be validating travel cards when a trip was being ordered to make sure that the card had not expired and had not been reported as lost or stolen. Another would be customer billing. Still another would be sending each vehicle, perhaps once a day, to a facility where it would be automatically cleaned and checked out for incipient malfunctions.

One of the virtues of the quasi-synchronous approach is that it is relatively invulnerable to failure, and when it does fail, it fails gracefully. This subject is discussed at length in Chapter 6, but briefly here are the reasons:

   a. If a vehicle or other object blocks the guideway, the central computer will be notified and new routing tables will be sent out so that little additional traffic will enter the affected area. The local computers will then clear the area, except for the blocking vehicle or other obstruction which must be manually removed.

   b. If a local computer fails, or rather a redundant set of such computers fails, then all intersection switches are set to the "straight ahead" position and there is no danger of collision, but routes will be somewhat longer.

c. Since the central computer is not involved in direct control of traffic, its failure will at most cause a degradation of service because of its unavailability for rebalancing the traffic for special situations. The unbalanced traffic would merely mean that a larger number of vehicles would be detoured by intersection computers. During the outage, all travel cards will be accepted as valid.

4.4.2 Quasi-Synchronous Intersection Control

The first intersection geometry investigated at Aerospace was the "single-stream" intersection.[4] An example is shown in Fig. 4-4 for a line speed of 30 ft/sec. The figure is based on the use of climbing and diving turn ramps, which, of course, must have double curvature. If double curvature is not used, then the divergence section, the climb (or dive), the turn, and the convergence section must all be distinct. This would move each divergence point about 200 ft farther away from the point of guideway crossing. Using a single-stream intersection, maneuvering (i.e., slot changing[5]) is accomplished upstream of the points of divergence to the turn ramps.

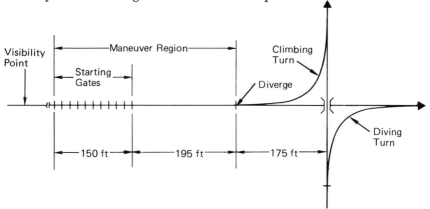

Fig. 4-4. Single-Stream Intersection for a Line Speed of 30 ft/sec

---

4 "Quasi-Synchronous Control of High-Capacity PRT Networks," A.V. Munson, Jr., et al., The Aerospace Corporation, published in *Personal Rapid Transit*, University of Minnesota, 1972.

5 Slot changing can mean either slot slipping or slot advancing. During slot advancing the vehicle temporarily accelerates to a higher speed and then returns to line speed, and during slot slipping it temporarily reduces its speed. The maneuvers assumed are limited both in acceleration (or deceleration) and jerk (rate of change of acceleration), and are discussed in Appendix A, Sec. A.2.

Within the broad framework of completing the maneuvers up-stream of the divergence point, and not allowing traffic to "back up" beyond the jurisdictional area of the local computer, there are still many strategies which could be adopted. No attempt was made to find optimal performance strategies but rather we sought heuristic approaches which would be easy to implement and which would be able to handle the large majority of the tractable cases. The rules that were finally adopted for our simulation studies are the following:

a. At a line speed of 30 ft/sec, all maneuvers are carried out over a distance of 195 ft (thirteen 15-ft slots). This distance is adequate for the vehicle to come to a comfortable stop halfway, wait if necessary, and then accelerate up to line speed over the second half. This permits anywhere from one to an infinite number of slots to be slipped. Moreover, 195 ft is also an adequate distance to comfortably advance one or two slots. Had the distance been less than 180 ft, two-slot advances would not be possible.

    If maneuvers were all based on using the same acceleration or decel-eration and the same jerk, they would take different guideway lengths, depending on the number of slots to be gained or slipped. We reasoned, however, that if the space had to be there anyhow for the more severe maneuvers, one might as well use all of it to make the less extreme maneuvers more comfortable; i.e., to use lower accelerations and jerks for them. Figure 4-5 is a plot of the maximum acceleration and jerks encountered as a function of the number of slots to be advanced or slipped.

b. To resolve an intersection conflict two types of maneuvers are allowed. Either the turning vehicle can advance or slip slots to a point where it can merge into a vacant slot on the other line (forcing others on its line to move if necessary), or a vehicle or string of vehicles on the other line can be advanced or retarded to make a slot available for the turner. Slot advances are preferred over slot slipping and, for each of these, moving the turning vehicle is given preference over moving the vehicle in conflict with it. In no case, however, is a turning vehicle already aligned for merging forced to move out of alignment to ac-commodate a would-be turner not yet aligned. The region upstream of the visibility point is assumed not to have any gaps or turners.

c. When a group of adjacent vehicles must all slip a slot, or several, then they must all start their decelerations simultaneously if they are not to encroach upon one another. Assuming 15-ft slot length, this means that the vehicles will be 15 ft apart when they start their maneuvers. These starting positions are referred to as "gates" and, as Fig. 4-4 illustrates, there might typically be 10 gates, although the number of gates was taken as a variable. If there are insufficient gates to provide starting positions for slipping all vehicles in a string, then the maneuver must not be allowed, and the would-be turner must be denied his turn.

    More generally, the starting gate to be used by any particular vehicle depends upon the number of slots that it is going to slip, the number of slots to be slipped by the vehicle ahead of it, the gate used by the vehicle ahead of it, and the number of vacant slots between the two vehicles. Each vehicle moves as far forward as it safely can before starting its maneuver; this provides more room for the vehicles behind it. Under some circumstances, such as when the vehicle ahead is advancing, the next vehicle may always move forward to the front gate before starting its maneuver.

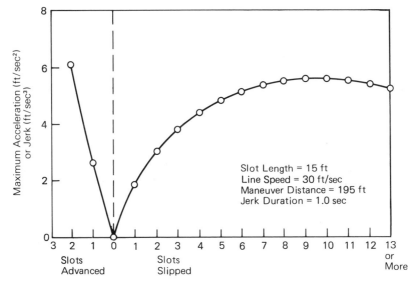

Fig. 4-5. Maximum Acceleration and Jerk for Various Slot Changes

The measure of performance is, of course, to keep the percentage of turns denied as small as possible. The results of the simulation are shown in Fig. 4-6 for 20% and 40% of the vehicles trying to turn. We found that for 60% line density, i.e., with each incoming slot having a 60% chance of being occupied, less than 1% of the turns were denied. However, at line densities over 70 or 75%, the percentage of turns denied increases rapidly with increases in line density. Thus, although the single-stream intersection gives very satisfactory performance at the lower line densities, its performance at the higher densities would tend to limit practical line capacities to less than 3/4 of their theoretical limit.

Minor improvements might be effected by increasing the number of gates or using a more sophisticated strategy for resolving conflicts, but there is a far more basic difficulty. It stems from the mutual interference in the maneuvering region between vehicles that should turn and vehicles that should go straight. A vehicle scheduled to turn may not be able to maneuver without forcing other vehicles to maneuver also. If any of these is scheduled to turn and is already aligned with its target slot, its alignment would be disturbed. A similar situation exists if the vehicle blocking the turn cannot vacate its slot without causing a vehicle turning off of its line to lose alignment.

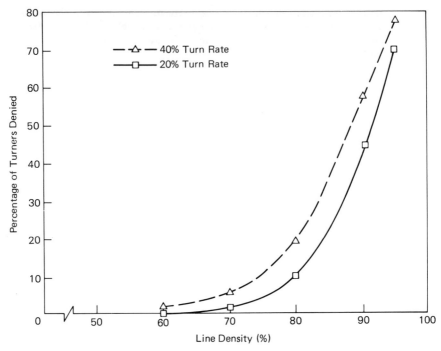

Fig. 4-6. Performance of a Single-Stream Intersection

The solution is to separate the vehicles intending to turn from those intending to go straight before they reach the maneuver zone. This has the effect of creating additional slot vacancies, and hence maneuvering flexibility, in the stream being maneuvered. Additionally, the turning and nonturning streams can now be maneuvered independently.

Therefore, a split-stream intersection geometry was defined (Fig. 4-7). This geometry necessitates additional guideway length on the turn ramp to accommodate the maneuver region between the divergence point and the intersection crossing.[6] For the split-stream intersection, the turning vehicles first go through an altitude change and then a moderately banked turn of small radius. Of course, on the turn, the lateral component of gravity will balance centrifugal force at only one speed; therefore, it was decided for purposes of initial simulation studies that slot changing maneuvers might best be performed only by nonturning vehicles. Again, both position advancing

---

[6] The reason for completing the maneuver before the crossing is related to the safety issue. If, because of malfunction, a vehicle moves into the wrong slot, there may be a conflict on merging. This situation will be detected by wayside sensors at the point of crossing, and there is still sufficient time to stop one or both of the conflicting vehicles before they reach the merge point.

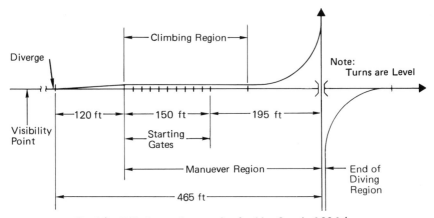

Fig. 4-7. Split-Stream Intersection for Line Speed of 30 ft/sec

and retarding maneuvers are permitted, with preference being given to advancing maneuvers for a maximum of two slots. The rules stated as (a) and (c) for the single-stream intersection still hold for the split-stream.

The results of the split-stream intersection simulation are shown in Fig. 4-8, where for ease of comparison the single-stream results are repeated. Split-stream clearly achieves significant improvement at the higher line densities.

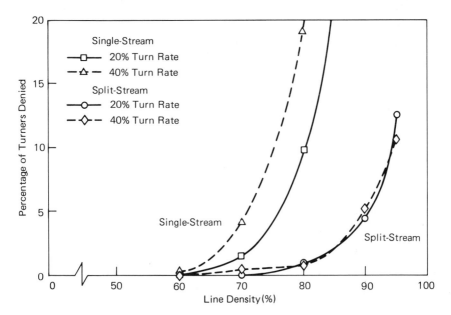

Fig. 4-8. Comparison of Single-Stream and Split-Stream Performance

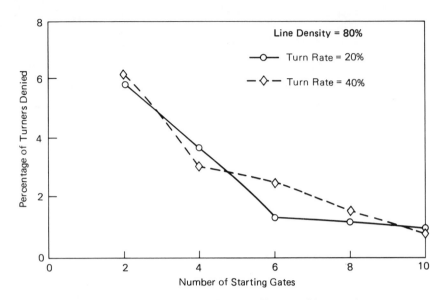

Fig. 4-9. Dependence of Turn Denial on Number of Starting Gates in a Split-Stream Intersection

Figure 4-9 shows how the percentage of turns denied depends on the number of starting gates in the split-stream intersection maneuver zone. It is a bit surprising how few starting gates can be used without serious degradation in performance, and the results are almost independent of turn rate.

When the space for starting gates is limited, further improvement in intersection performance may be achieved by

a. allowing the separation between vehicles in the maneuver region to temporarily fall below the nominal separation (of about 5 ft), especially when the speed of both vehicles is reduced below 30 ft/sec, and/or

b. to allow maneuvers to start at any arbitrary point (not fixed gates), as far forward as possible, consistent with satisfying the minimum separation criterion throughout the maneuver.

We recently wrote a computer program which computes these starting positions, but it has not yet been integrated into the intersection simulation program.

4.5   ASYNCHRONOUS CONTROL

Asynchronous control is not based on a principle of synchronous slot motion along the guideways, but rather on maintaining at least the minimum allowable headway between adjacent vehicles. Often the minimum separation between vehicles is considered a function of speed, with the separation between vehicles shortening at lower speeds as it does with automobiles on a highway. Whether the minimum separation is indeed a function of speed, and, if so, how it varies with speed is dependent on the headway policy adopted (Sec. 4.2). The traditional asynchronous system uses equipment on board the vehicle to measure the separation between it and the vehicle ahead. Thus, in contrast to the "point-follower" systems we have just been discussing, asynchronous systems are usually "car followers."

In the usual car-follower system, to eliminate the need for communication between vehicles, a vehicle knows only the location of the vehicle immediately ahead of it, and nothing about the locations of the vehicles ahead of that one. Thus, a vehicle has no knowledge of the sudden stopping of a downstream vehicle until the one immediately ahead of it has started to brake. As a result, the braking response propagates back along the guideway in a wavelike manner. Moreover, since the usual measurements are of separation and possibly relative velocity, detection of an inadvertent deceleration of the vehicle ahead may be delayed from when it would have been detected had the vehicle reported its own anomalous deceleration. As a result of these two types of delay, minimum headways need to be somewhat longer for the stereotypical asynchronous control than for quasi-synchronous control, although this has less influence on headway than does the safety policy discussed in Sec. 4.2.

Although a definitive comparison of headways for asynchronous and quasi-synchronous control can only be carried out once there is a detailed design of each system, it still will be instructive to illustrate by hypothetical although reasonable numerical examples. First let us compare the two types of system when the headway policy is one of avoiding a collision when the vehicle ahead has inadvertently locked its wheels and is decelerating at 0.7 g (22.5 ft/sec^2). Let us assume further that the vehicles are equipped with brakes capable of producing a deceleration of 0.8 g. For the quasi-synchronous control system, assume that it takes 0.1 sec for the accelerometer aboard the failed vehicle to detect the inadvertent deceleration, for a report to be made to the local computer, and for the local computer to order the succeeding vehicle to apply brakes. Assume further that the succeeding vehicle takes 0.2 sec to build up its braking deceleration to 0.8 g with a constant jerk rate during this build-up. The effective delay, τ, between the onset of inadvertent deceleration and the "effective time of braking" is then 0.2 sec (the delay of 0.1 sec plus one-half the jerk period). The maximum encroachment of the succeeding vehicle on the failed vehicle is 3.6 ft, which implies that an initial vehicle separation of 5 ft would be more than adequate to avoid collision.

For an asynchronous control system in which there is no communication between vehicles, it is highly unlikely that the inadvertent deceleration would be detected in 0.1 sec, for in that time the failing vehicle would have been displaced only 0.1 ft from the position that it would have occupied had there been no failure. Let us assume that the inadvertent deceleration is only detected after 0.2 sec when the displacement is 0.4 ft. The total effective delay, τ, will now be 0.3 sec, including one-half the jerk period. This leads to an encroachment of 8.1 ft, requiring an initial separation of about 10 ft. Thus, with a 10-ft long vehicle the minimum space allocated to a vehicle must be 20 ft, in contrast to 15 ft for the quasi-synchronous control system. As a result, for any characteristic line speed, headways will have to be 33% longer.

The assumption of 0.2-sec jerk time to build braking deceleration is compatible with the use of fast-acting mechanical brakes. However, for the primary braking methodology described in Sec. 7.3 (reversing current in the pulsed dc linear motor used for propulsion), full braking force can be reached in less than 0.002 sec. An asynchronous system would then require only a 5-ft separation to avoid collision, compared with about 1 or 2 ft for quasi-synchronous. But, a separation of, say, 3 ft would be required in any event to manage merging. Thus, slot size for asynchronous would be 15 ft compared with 13 ft for quasi-synchronous, which corresponds to a 15% increase in headway.

Now we consider another numerical example for the case where passengers are not protected by air bags and the headway policy is that indicated in Fig. 4-2. Let us assume that the maximum braking deceleration available is 0.5 g and that the policy is that when one vehicle has struck a large immovable object (such as a fallen tree), the vehicle behind it will be allowed to impact the first vehicle at any speed up to 15 ft/sec. Let us assume a line speed of 60 ft/sec. If, as above, the quasi-synchronous control is characterized by a τ of 0.2 sec, Fig. 4-2 shows that the headway would be 2.1 sec. In considering an asynchronous system with a τ of 0.3 sec, the first term in Eq. (4.1) for vehicle separation would be increased by 6 ft and, as a result, the headway would be increased by 0.1 sec. This represents only a 5% increase in headway.

In summary, when relatively longer headways are being used, the additional delays of a car-follower system detecting an inadvertent deceleration are not significant, but if there is an attempt to maximize capacity with the use of very short headways, then the extra delays can be quite significant, depending on the jerk time for emergency braking. When the extra delay for asynchronous control is significant, it may be possible to avoid that extra delay by having the failed vehicle measure its own inadvertent deceleration and report it directly to the vehicle behind.

The Cabintaxi system under development in the Federal Republic of Germany is an example of a system which uses car-follower techniques. Each vehicle broadcasts a 100-kHz signal into a lossy line; the signal propagates backward along the guideway. The next vehicle back detects this signal and can determine the separation by the amplitude of the received signal. By using two separated transmitters on each vehicle it is possible to cancel out the forward-moving signal and reinforce the backward-moving signal so that the net signal propagates only backwards along the guideway. Also, each vehicle transmits backwards a signal which just cancels the backward-moving signal from the vehicle ahead; this keeps the signals from propagating back to more than one vehicle. Except in the vicinity of a merge, this whole car-follower system is redundant with two lossy lines, one on each side of the guideway.

The difficult problem in asynchronous control is that of merging, because there is no direct way for a vehicle to compare its distance from the merge point with that of a vehicle on the other guideway with which it may be in conflict. As a result, there needs to be some means for letting a vehicle know the location of the potentially conflicting vehicle. In the Cabintaxi system, on each guideway upstream of a merge, the inside lossy line (i.e., the one closer to the merging guideway) is broken into segments. The vehicles no longer transmit into the broken line, but each segment carries a signal brought to it by an electrical connection from the corresponding point on the outside lossy line of the other guideway. Thus, each vehicle measures the separation from the actual vehicle ahead of it on the outside lossy line, and on the inside line it measures the separation to a "ghost" vehicle which is the same distance from the merge point as the real conflicting vehicle on the other guideway. To avoid overreaction to the ghost (jamming on the brakes) when it first appears and there is still a long way to the merge, the signals coming into the first few segments of the broken line are attenuated to make the ghost appear farther away. As the merge point is approached, the amount of attenuation is gradually decreased to zero so that the true distance to the ghost can be measured.

One of the features which distinguishes a stereotype asynchronous system from the stereotype quasi-synchronous system is the response that takes place to conflicts at intersections. We noted above that in quasi-synchronous control a turn is denied rather than forcing traffic to slow down upstream of the jurisdictional area of an intersection computer. This was necessary to provide each local intersection computer with autonomy. In the stereotypical asynchronous system, turns are not denied. Therefore, if conflicts develop, incoming traffic is slowed down and this slowdown can propagate back to upstream intersections and merges, much as automobile traffic "backs up" on a busy highway. In Sec. 4.6.3 we shall show how this stereotypical approach might be improved upon.

As a result of the somewhat larger minimum headway and the less efficient merging which comes from not knowing the make-up of both merging streams, line capacities on an asynchronous system are somewhat lower than on a corresponding quasi-synchronous system. As pointed out, however, these differences are not as significant as those that might arise from differences in safety policy (Sec. 4.2).

Routing on an asynchronous system could be quite similar to that on a quasi-synchronous system where at each intersection there would be a local computer to look up whether the nominal route requires the vehicle to turn. Again, these routing tables could be varied from time to time as necessary to balance the traffic. This function, as before, would be carried out by a central computer.

Asynchronous control shares with quasi-synchronous control the virtue of failing gracefully. Failures of the central computer or the local routing computers have substantially the same impact as their failures on a quasi-synchronous system. If the guideway were blocked, it would be necessary for a local computer to supervise the line-clearing procedures, as indeed was the case with quasi-synchronous control.

Since a car-follower system has no need to depend on a wayside computer or a communications link to maintain separation, it might seem to be safer than a quasi-synchronous control system. However, one should be cautious with such arguments because the maintenance of separation still depends upon the proper functioning of certain equipments. Again taking the Cabintaxi system as an example, the avoidance of collision between two vehicles on the same guideway is dependent on the proper functioning of the transmitters of the vehicle ahead and of the receivers of the following vehicle because a loss of signal would be interpreted as an infinite separation. A loss of signal is especially critical when approaching a merge point because in those regions there is no longer redundancy. At a merge there is also dependence on the transmitters of the conflicting vehicle on the other guideway. Less serious are breaks in the continuity of the lossy line along the vehicle's own guideway or a break in the connection to one of the segments near a merge, because these cause only transient errors. Before one can reach any firm conclusions about relative safety, it is necessary to look very deeply into the design, the degree and kind of redundancy, and the consequences of the failure.

Before leaving the subject of asynchronous control we should briefly describe a novel PRT system, Aramis, under development by Engins Matra in France. In that system, optical ranging is used to keep vehicles traveling 1 ft apart in platoons or "trains," although the trains are separated from each other by headways of about 1 minute. If one of the vehicles in a platoon should decelerate suddenly, the vehicle behind it makes contact so soon that very little relative velocity will have developed.[7]

As a train passes a station siding, some of the vehicles will leave the train and enter the siding. The remaining vehicles will close ranks as soon as possible, again reducing separations to 1 ft. A vehicle leaving a station siding does not try to merge into a train, but rather waits until the train has gone by and merges into the very large space between trains. It then accelerates to catch up to the train ahead and becomes the last vehicle in that train.

The Aramis is very effective in a line-haul configuration but is not intended for use in a network with many closely spaced crossing lines. The problem is in turning from one line to another. Vehicles that need to turn might have to be queued for some time to wait for a train to go by. If there were many vehicles waiting to turn, there might not be adequate space for storing them without building an off-line storage area.

Vehicles arriving at the intersection when a train was not going by would be able to turn without delay, but then it might take them a long time to catch up with the last train to pass. While they were catching up, the train might have passed other intersections and stations. Thus the problem is introduced as to how to merge vehicles from these downstream intersections and stations into the stream of vehicles already trying to catch up with the train. To the best of our knowledge, Engins Matra, the developers of Aramis, have not tackled this problem, since they envision Aramis as a line-haul system.

4.6 THE SPECTRUM OF CONTROL OPTIONS

In Secs. 4.3 through 4.5 we have described synchronous, quasi-synchronous, and asynchronous control. Each had a number of characteristics with similarities in some areas and dissimilarities in others. Now we shall try to get to the root of these characteristics.

The principal characteristics represent the system designer's choice as he makes the critical decisions which will define the control concept for his system. (After the major decisions are made there still are many possible design implementations of any chosen control strategy.) Although there is no unique way to list the critical decisions,

---

[7] For example, if the failing vehicle decelerates at 0.7 g (22.5 ft/sec^2) and the following vehicle does not brake, the impact velocity will be 6.7 ft/sec.

the following may be regarded as a representative list of the questions that need to be addressed:

a. Which control functions should be centralized and which decentralized?

b. What kind of a reservation system should there be, if any?

c. What uses should be made of "wait-to-merge" and "wave-on" strategies for handling excessive traffic at merges and intersections? How does this affect network design?

d. Should sequencing of vehicles at a merge or intersection be under the control of a local computer?

e. Should a car-follower or point-follower system be employed?

f. How should switching be controlled?

g. For a point-follower system, should position and speed be measured by the vehicle or from the wayside? How should the position be controlled?

h. For a point-follower system, should discrete or continuous positions be used? Is systemwide synchronization desirable?

We shall now discuss these critical decision areas and some of the viable control options available.

4.6.1 Centralization versus Decentralization

Which functions should be centralized and which decentralized?

By this time the reader will understand that we believe that those functions which are vital to the continuing operation of the system should be decentralized as much as possible. In particular, the functions of headway maintenance, merging, switching, intersection control, and station control should be decentralized. They may be under the control of small "local computers," working perhaps in cooperation with small computers on board the vehicles. If these functions were centralized, then a failure of the central computer might paralyze the entire network. In contrast, the failure of a local computer might at most disable a single station or cause all turns to be denied at a single intersection.

There are two aspects of routing and empty-vehicle management — the tactical and the strategic aspects. The tactical aspect is how to control the routing of individual vehicles and when and where to dispatch individual empty vehicles. We envision these as decentralized functions. For example, routing may be accomplished by having a local computer at each intersection (or shared by a small group of intersections) interrogate the vehicle to determine its destination and then refer to a table of turn instructions to find out whether the vehicle should turn or not. Dispatching of empty vehicles from any station should be under the control of the station's local computer, which first determines which vehicles are surplus and then refers to a list of stations in need of empty vehicles to determine where the next one should be sent.

The strategic function, which must be carried out centrally to have any meaning, is to modify the intersection local computers' turn instruction tables or the station computers' dispatching lists to better balance the traffic or to serve special needs. A failure of the central computer will, at most, degrade the quality of service; it will not leave the vehicles bereft of turn instructions, and surplus empties will have somewhere to go. The strategic "override" by the central computer must always "pass through channels" and never go directly to the vehicle, for otherwise the vehicle may be receiving conflicting orders and/or the local computer might not know that its orders are being countermanded.

It is also valid to think of the central computer as carrying out certain administrative functions listed in Sec. 4.4.1, which it can carry out efficiently and which are not vital to safety or service dependability.

4.6.2 Reservations

What kind of a reservation system should there be, if any?

In discussing synchronous control we considered the reservation of both stations and slots. Our conclusions were that such a reservation system is unnecessarily complex and does not fail gracefully. Of course, it must be acknowledged that in principle a centrally controlled reservation system could use very sophisticated algorithms to optimize the vehicle flow; but, if a much simpler approach will work almost as well, then there is very little incentive to introduce the full-blown reservation system. Indeed, we have shown that very high line densities are feasible with quasi-synchronous control, and in Chapter 5 we shall show how nominal routes may be chosen to keep average line densities safely within practical limits. Thus slot reservation would certainly seem unnecessary.

There may, however, be some virtue in having a station reservation system or, as an alternative, a "station delay warning" system. Either system could be superimposed on quasi-synchronous control or asynchronous control.

Here is how a station reservation system might work. When a patron inserts his travel card into the trip selection equipment and enters the number of his destination station, the information will be transmitted to the central computer. The central computer predicts the time of arrival at the destination station, assuming that the patron and his party proceed at once to the boarding platform and that their vehicle is routed along its nominal route. The prediction is only within crude tolerances of about ± 1/2 minute at best. The computer then looks up previously confirmed reservations to find the average rate of arrival at the predicted arrival time. If the destination station is not saturated, the reservation is confirmed and the travel card magnetically encoded in the usual way. If the destination station is saturated at the predicted arrival time, the computer searches forward through the record of confirmed reservations until it finds a period when the average arrival rate is below the station's capacity. The patron is then informed of how long he must delay his boarding.

At the same time he is informed of the delay, the patron may be shown a map of his destination area which would display not only his requested station but the neighboring stations as well. Each of these can be marked with the delay, if any, associated with it. After examining the map, the patron either confirms his original selection or he may change his request to one of the neighboring stations. His travel card is appropriately encoded with the number of his requested station, but it also carries encoded information on when he may be allowed to board. He is also informed directly of the time he may board. Until that time his card will not open the boarding gates.

A "station delay warning" system operates in a quite similar manner except the passengers are not delayed in boarding. They are allowed to board at once and the delays refer to how long they will have to "circle the block" around the destination station. Another difference is that, in a reservation system, precedence is given to those who request their trips first; in a delay warning system, precedence is given to those who arrive at the destination station first. If a vehicle has circled the block, it will be given priority in entering the station siding over neighboring vehicles which have not yet circled; one that has circled the block twice will be given priority over one that has circled once, etc.

In a station delay warning system, the central computer estimates the arrival time and predicts the number of vehicles that will then be circling the block with precedence over the new patron's vehicle. It will thus be able to predict the number of circlings for the new patron and hence his delay. In making this prediction it must include all vehicles which will arrive ahead of the patron's vehicle, even vehicles for trips not yet requested from origin stations close to the destination station. The latter can be projected on the basis of normal demand, possibly discounted if very long delays are encountered.

The station delay warning system, as the reservation system, presents the patron a map showing neighboring stations and their delays (projected circling times). This gives him the opportunity to confirm his original request or to change it. Then his travel card is encoded with the number of his selected station, but no delay times are recorded. His party proceeds at once to the boarding platform and boards.

Are the benefits of a station reservation system or station delay warning system worth the cost and added complexity? If all stations were sized properly to meet their demand, such systems would be completely unnecessary. But, if the demand at a station is badly underestimated, or if the demand increases suddenly, then there is a problem. Of course, if the high demand persists, in many cases the station can be enlarged to satisfy and probably exceed the demand. But, until the enlargement is completed, station reservations or delay warning could improve the service. Moreover, there will be occasions when the station cannot be enlarged, either because funds are not available, or because there is no room for a larger station with its longer siding. The latter situation is most likely to occur in a CBD or other activity center where stations are close together. Under those conditions, the patron would find it particularly useful to know that there is a long delay to his requested station but that there is no delay to its nearest neighbor, a block or two away.

It may be argued that, even without a station reservation or delay warning system, the patrons will adjust their requests, through a learning process, to equalize the demand among neighboring stations. Certainly this will occur at the activity-center stations during the evening rush hours because, if patrons see long waiting lines at one station, but not at the next, many of them will walk to the station with the shorter lines. The learning process will be more difficult in the morning if no indication is given at the suburban origin station on delays to be encountered at the activity-center destination station. But, patrons will learn by experimentation and they will learn from friends. As they circle the block they may observe stations whose input queue is not full. Some may even push the "Next Station" button (Sec. 1.7.1) which would bring them into the first station approached with space available.

It is the author's belief that, if either can be justified, a station delay warning system is generally preferable to a station reservation system. As far as the patron is concerned, the two are about equivalent. Each warns him of delays and informs of the availability of neighboring stations. It is of little concern to him whether he is delayed at his origin station or by circling the destination station. The reservation system saves a little energy involved in circling, and a few vehicles, but if almost all stations have been properly sized to meet their demand, the savings would not be significant. The disadvantage of a reservation system, when compared to a delay warning system, is that it requires all stations to have a waiting area and means for keeping a party from boarding before the assigned time. This not only increases station cost but it may complicate the security problem at the station.

An exception may occur when a significant part of the PRT network is in a line-haul configuration, for then, if the station is "missed," there are no blocks to be circled. Under these circumstances, a station reservation system would be preferred. But, if there are only a few stations on the line-haul portion of the network, the best approach may be to overdesign these stations to virtually eliminate the possibility of a vehicle being forced to bypass one of them because the input queue was full; then the reservation system would be unnecessary.

4.6.3   Wait-to-Merge versus Wave-on

What uses should be made of "wait-to-merge" and "wave-on" strategies for handling excessive traffic at merges and intersections? How does this affect network design?

Both quasi-synchronous and asynchronous control systems can involve a certain amount of slowing down or waiting at intersections. In an asynchronous car-follower system, vehicles will slow down to allow merges from the other line, and in a quasi-synchronous system they may slip slots. Where the stereotype asynchronous system differs from the stereotype quasi-synchronous is in the means of handling excessively high traffic densities.

In the stereotypical quasi-synchronous system, maneuvering is confined to two regions within the jurisdictional area of a local computer, one on each of the two lines approaching the intersection. If a would-be turner cannot be accommodated by maneuvering vehicles within these maneuver regions, the would-be turner is "waved-on;" i.e., it is denied its turn. By this means there is no "backing up" of traffic congestion; congestion at one intersection will have no direct influence on upstream intersections.

In contrast, the stereotypical asynchronous system does not use "wave-on" tactics; rather, each vehicle will follow its predestined route no matter how long it must "wait to merge" or what impact this waiting may have on propagating congestion upstream.

Thus, it would appear that excessive traffic at intersections is managed by "wave-on" tactics when using stereotypical quasi-synchronous control and by "wait-to-merge" tactics for stereotypical asynchronous control. We shall now examine these stereotypical approaches to find their implications and we shall explore variations to improve overall system performance. We begin by examining quasi-synchronous control.

"Wave-on" is possible at an intersection because there are alternate routes to the destination. If the vehicle is denied its turn, it can go straight and still reach its destination. At a simple merge there are two incoming lines but only one outgoing line; wave-on has no meaning. Thus, there is an apparent implication that no simple merges can be used in a network under quasi-synchronous control because at a simple merge there is no way of avoiding the backing up of traffic when the traffic flow on the two incoming lines is greater than the capacity of the single outgoing line. One solution is indeed to design a network with no simple merges (except at station sidings), and we shall shortly illustrate how this can be done. But an alternate approach that does allow simple merges is to precede the simple merge by a branch point (point of divergence) under the control of the same local computer which controls the merge. In this way traffic may be diverted to keep from overloading the merge.

First let us illustrate how to design a network without simple merges. One natural location for simple merges is at the borders of a network. Referring to Fig. 4-3, the points G and L are such merge points. However, one way to avoid merges at the edge of a network is to use a "scalloped" network, as indicated in Fig. 4-10. The reader should at first ignore the dotted lines in this figure. The scalloped network consists of four loops indicated by the solid lines of the figure. Three of these loops are simple rectangles; two are predominantly north-south and the other is east-west. The fourth loop is around the perimeter and crosses itself in four places. It will be noted that this network has 24 intersections, but no merges.

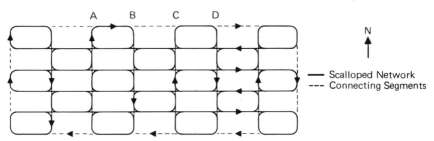

Fig. 4-10. Scalloped Network with Connecting Segments

Now imagine that we add the 10 connecting segments shown by the dotted lines. The network now has 10 merge points, one of which is marked C. Conflicts can be resolved at C by treating the segment BC much like a siding. If the traffic coming from the south at C plus that from the west does not exceed the capacity of the line segment CD, conflicts can be resolved by employing slot advancing and slipping maneuvers. But, if the densities are too high, then traffic coming from the south at C has precedence on the line CD over traffic coming from the dotted segment BC. In short, "wait-to-merge" is employed at merge point C with the waiting done by the vehicles on BC, just as though they were in the output queue on a station siding. Should the line segment BC become completely occupied, the traffic coming from A would be forced to turn south at point B. Thus, even though there might be a backing up of traffic from C, the backing up can go no further than the branch point B. This illustrates how one can manage traffic at a merge point (C) by diverting traffic at an upstream branch point (B).

We have thus shown an example of a network (the scalloped network) which has no merge points (except at station sidings), and we have shown at least one way of using wait-to-merge control at merge points without an uncontrolled backing up of traffic congestion. Another interesting case is provided by the Los Angeles network shown in Fig. 2-13. Although we envisioned the network operating under a control system that might generally be classified as quasi-synchronous, it had many simple merges. Therefore, there would be many line segments, predominantly on north-south lines, that would operate on the wait-to-merge principle.

Now let us consider a PRT system which uses stereotypical asynchronous car-follower control. The performance of the system might be improved by introducing a variation of wave-on at busy intersections. This is especially true if the system is operating with a safety policy which allows the vehicles to operate at minimum separations which cannot be significantly decreased when traffic slows down.[8] When, on the other hand, the separations can be significantly decreased, then slowing down may so *increase* the capacity of the slowed down line as to relieve traffic congestion at upstream merges. In such cases little can be gained by the wave-on variation.

Here is how the wave-on system works. When the average line densities on both outgoing lines at the intersection are within certain specified limits, then no turns are denied; all vehicles follow the turn instructions specified by the routing table for that time of day. (These turn instructions, it may be remembered, do not necessarily direct all vehicles along minimum time paths, but rather along paths as fast as possible, consistent with having the projected average traffic densities less than practical capacities throughout the network.) But,

---

[8] This is the case where passengers are well enough protected so that, in the rare event when the vehicle ahead has been stopped instantaneously by striking a massive object, the following vehicle can be permitted to strike the stopped vehicle at an impact speed higher or nearly as high as the line speed. Referring to Fig. 4-2, the line speed would be to the left of the minimum for the permitted impact speed (i.e., the system would be operating on the solid curve) or, at most, slightly to the right of the minimum.

when one of the outgoing lines would be too crowded for a short period of, say, 30 sec, as a result of an upward fluctuation of the number of vehicles coming in on that line and required to go straight and/or the number of vehicles coming in on the other line and required to turn, then the local computer has the authority to deny turns onto the crowded line. This authority avoids the backing up of traffic congestion which would result from the excessive slowdown of vehicles trying to merge. In determining which vehicles should be denied their turns, the computer must refer to a priority table and deny turns for those vehicles whose trip times will be the least penalized by the denial.

The reader will see that this wave-on strategy is identical in almost every way to that which we discussed under quasi-synchronous control (Sec. 4.4.1). The only difference is that for a car-follower control system the wave-on is called when projected densities averaged over some short period of time are too high, while for quasi-synchronous control the wave-on is invoked when the local computer's conflict resolution algorithms are unable to find a solution that limits maneuvers to prescribed maneuver regions.

In summary, we have seen that both wave-on and wait-to-merge strategies can be employed on a single network, regardless of whether the vehicles are otherwise controlled quasi-synchronously or asynchronously.

4.6.4 Sequencing of Vehicles at a Merge or Intersection

Should sequencing of vehicles at a merge or intersection be under the control of a local computer?

In quasi-synchronous control the sequencing of vehicles at a merge or intersection is a function under the control of a local computer. The local computer knows which vehicles should turn, if possible, and where gaps exist in the incoming traffic streams; it computes how the vehicles should maneuver to effectively use the available space. The maneuvers used can include a vehicle moving forward relative to the stream, or moving backward. Thus a vehicle on one of two merging lines might be closer initially to the merge point than several vehicles on the other line, but after the maneuvers it might be more distant from the merge point than the several. This could occur either by the vehicle dropping back a considerable distance and/or the several advancing. For simplicity we might call this "passing," even though the two merging lines might initially be perpendicular to each other.

In contrast, under typical car-follower control, like that of Cabintaxi (Sec. 4.5), there is no passing. It will be recalled that each vehicle measures the distance not only to the vehicle ahead of it on its own guideway, but to a "ghost" vehicle which is the same distance from the merge point as the conflicting real vehicle on the other line. A vehicle will slow down if it is too close to the ghost. There is never an attempt to accelerate and pass the ghost. Because no advancing maneuvers are used, and because there is no way for a vehicle to drop back to allow vehicles on the other line to pass it (they would only drop back further), there is a less efficient use of available space. To the best of our knowledge there have been no studies to date which have quantized this difference in efficiency.

The reader will note that the essential benefits in using a local computer are that advantage can be taken of a knowledge of the entire stream of vehicles and their longitudinal spacing, that vehicles can be instructed either to advance or fall back, and that vehicle "passing" is permitted. Whether or not the vehicles are nominally constrained to synchronized slots is immaterial to the argument. Nor does it matter how the measurements are carried out so long as they are made known to the local computer. For example, the measurements can be made by the vehicles or by wayside instrumentation. Finally, it does not matter how the maneuvers are controlled as long as there is a high degree of certainty that they will be carried out faithfully.

One reason often given for adopting a car-follower system is to keep the system implementation "simple." It is argued that with the car-follower approach no local computers are required, although some means are required to get information to each vehicle on the location of the conflicting vehicle on the merging line. But, isn't the local computer really needed for other functions, even when using a car-follower approach?

We have described asynchronous control in Sec. 4.5 as including a local computer to look up routing instructions, and in Sec. 4.6.3 we pointed out how with car-follower control, overall system performance might be improved by having the local computer monitor line densities and use the wave-on principle to avoid excessive backing up of traffic congestion. It might be argued that the latter function is not necessary and that the former could have been performed by routing tables at the departure station with turning instructions stored aboard the vehicle. However, there is another important function of the local computer — that of controlling emergency situations. In Chapter 6 we shall discuss car-pushing strategies where one vehicle makes a soft engagement with the vehicle ahead of it which is failing, and pushes that vehicle to an emergency siding. Making such a soft engagement would be contrary to the normal working of a car-follower control system and would have to involve an override from a local computer. If traffic has come to a stop because of guideway blockage, the local computer is required to "clear the lines." This line-clearing procedure may even involve moving some vehicles backward. All in all, the local computers carry out so many functions that it is difficult to see how a well-designed system could do without them. If, indeed, they are there and there are communication links to them, then, in the author's opinion, when line capacity is an important issue the local computers should be used to sequence vehicles at merges and intersections.

4.6.5 Car Follower versus Point Follower

Should a car-follower or point-follower system be employed?

We have already discussed a number of the possible disadvantages in car-follower systems. These will be reviewed briefly and then a few new points touched.

In Sec. 4.5 we pointed out that, because of delays encountered in detecting the inadvertent deceleration of downstream vehicles, car-follower systems require somewhat longer minimum headways, and therefore lower theoretical capacities, than systems under the supervision of a local computer. Under the local computer, the anomalous deceleration is sensed by the failing vehicle and reported to the local computer which warns the following vehicles to start braking at once. Without such a reporting system the sudden deceleration of a vehicle would not be detected by the vehicle immediately behind it until a measurable difference developed in the relative velocity or possibly even in the separation distance. A vehicle further back would not know of the failure until the chain of braking reactions propagated back to the vehicle immediately ahead of it.

This disadvantage of the typical car-follower system could be eliminated if each vehicle reported its anomalous deceleration to the vehicle behind it, and if this information were relayed back along the line. There would also need to be some way to report to vehicles on a merging line. All of this, of course, complicates the system mechanization.

In Sec. 4.6.4 we pointed out that when merges and intersections are under the control of a local computer, higher efficiencies can be achieved than when a car-follower control system is used. The local computer can take advantage of a knowledge of the two streams of incoming vehicles and the location of gaps; with a car-follower, each vehicle has knowledge only of the vehicle immediately ahead and of the conflicting vehicle on the other guideway. With a local computer, vehicles may be ordered to advance or slip back relative to the nominal traffic stream and "passing" vehicles on the other guideway is permitted; with a car-follower, advancing and "passing" are prohibited. When we say that higher efficiencies can be achieved at merges or intersections under the control of a local computer, we mean that the incoming lines can operate at a higher fraction of their theoretical capacity without causing serious overloads at the merges or intersections; i.e., without significant backing up of traffic congestion or, in the case of intersections using wave-on, without excessive detouring of vehicles from their nominal routes.

Thus, we have seen that the theoretical capacity of a car-follower system is somewhat lower than that of a system under the control of a local computer unless it is complicated by the addition of a reporting system which allows a vehicle to report its anomalous deceleration to other vehicles, and we have seen that a car-follower must operate at a lower fraction of its theoretical capacity to keep from overloading merges and intersections. Therefore, the car-follower approach is not indicated when the highest capacities must be achieved. (However, as pointed out earlier, safety policy is of far greater importance in achieving high capacity.)

In addition to the questions of capacity just discussed, there are considerations of emergency operations such as car pushing and line clearing. It would seem that, regardless of the type of normal operations, the supervision of such emergency operations would have to be under the control of a local computer.

Up to this time we have been discussing the term "car follower" in its usual context of meaning a system where vehicle-borne equipment measures the distance to the vehicle ahead and then the following vehicle's speed is adjusted to maintain safe separation. However, there might be a second meaning of the term "car-follower," relating to the motion of one vehicle being adjusted to maintain the separation from the vehicle ahead, regardless of how that separation is measured. For example, if there were continuous or very frequent wayside measurements of the positions of all vehicles, as in the Japanese CVS system (see Sec. 4.6.7), then it might be possible to use control algorithms which adjust a vehicle's speed, not to keep it in a prescribed slot or to follow a designated "point," but rather to adjust its distance from the vehicle ahead. If, indeed, a system operating under these principles were under the control of a local computer, then there is no reason why such a system could not achieve capacities as great as those achievable by quasi-synchronous control. In fact, we alluded to the use of such car-following techniques in Sec. 4.4.2 when we spoke about improving intersection performance by allowing maneuvers to start at arbitrary points, rather than fixed gates, consistent with satisfying a criterion for minimum separation from the vehicle ahead.

4.6.6   Control of Switching

How should switching be controlled?

There are two stages in the control of switching. First, it must be decided which of two branches the vehicle should take. If merges and intersections are under the control of a local computer, the local computer will make that decision. Second, the decision should be communicated either to wayside equipment or to the vehicle so that the switching mechanism may be activated.

The switching cannot involve moving any massive parts of the guideway because if it did, short headways could not be maintained. For example, at a line speed of 75 ft/sec (about 50 mi/hr), if vehicles are separated by 5 ft the time between the passage of the tail of one vehicle and the nose of the next is only 1/15 sec. There are generally two ways of accomplishing switching in such a short time. One way is to have the switching mechanism on board the vehicle. In that event it can be activated well in advance of the vehicle reaching the point where guideways begin to diverge. For example, it could be a set of rollers on the vehicle which "grab" one side of the guideway. Another means for accomplishing switching rapidly is to use electromagnets mounted on the guideway to pull the vehicle onto one branch or the other. This is the approach Aerospace followed in its scale model development (Appendix B).

When the latter method is used, there is no need to communicate any switching instructions to the vehicle and there is no need to rely on proper operation of on-board switching mechanisms. The electromagnetic switching should be designed, however, so that in the event of a power failure the vehicle will automatically lock into one of the diverging lines. At an intersection, any vehicle not yet into its turn at the time of power failure would be locked to whichever side of the guideway would carry it straight through the intersection with no turns. One of our reasons for choosing electromagnets was related to the specific approach we had to propulsion and braking. This relationship is developed in Chapter 7.

4.6.7   Measurement and Longitudinal Control

For a point-follower system, should position and speed be measured by the vehicle or from the wayside? How should the position be controlled?

One approach to position measurement is to have this function performed by wayside equipment. The Japanese CVS design is an example of this approach. In CVS the wayside computer takes a poll of vehicles by addressing each one by its own unique identification code. The vehicle replies by broadcasting a signal through an antenna just a few centimeters away from a number of wire pairs running along the length of the guideway. Some of the pairs are twisted in the vicinity of the antenna and they cannot pick up the signal, but other pairs are separated in that vicinity and they will pick up the signal. The pattern of which wire pairs are twisted and which are separated changes about every 20 cm on the station sidings and somewhat less frequently on the main lines. The vehicle can be located by which of the wire pairs have picked up the signal. By interpolation, positions can be determined quite accurately. To the best of our knowledge, there is no direct wayside speed measurement in CVS. Speed can, of course, be determined quite accurately from successive position measurements, provided that such measurements are frequent and not too "noisy."

If position and speed are determined by very frequent wayside measurements, at most every few feet of travel, there are two generic alternatives for controlling the vehicles:

a. One alternative is to transmit to each vehicle the amount of acceleration or deceleration required to correct its position and speed errors. This commanded acceleration might be corrected to include the acceleration necessary to compensate for gravity when the vehicle is climbing or diving. If the vehicle had an accelerometer on board, it could adjust its motor thrust until the measured acceleration equaled that commanded by the wayside controller. This control method has the advantage of having tight (fast acting) feedback around an "inner loop" which adjusts the motor current promptly in response to gusts which might accelerate or decelerate the vehicle. There is no need to wait for updated position measurements.

b. Alternatively, if the vehicle were not equipped to measure acceleration, the wayside controller would transmit commanded vehicle thrust (or motor current) which should then include not only the thrust required for acceleration and grade, but also an estimate of the thrust required to overcome friction and air drag (including the effects of wind). This approach would depend on a motor calibration so the commanded thrust could be used to adjust motor current. If the estimated thrust (or current) was wrong, the vehicle would temporarily depart from the moving point it was to follow. This would be detected by the wayside position-measurement equipment and the commanded thrust would be altered. This alternative depends solely on feedback from the position-measurement "outer loop."

If vehicles are traveling at very small separations, then, from the safety standpoint, any sudden inadvertent deceleration must be detected on board and reported to the local computer as soon as possible. As discussed in Sec. 4.2, a 5-ft separation requires the following vehicle to effectively apply its braking force within approximately 0.2 sec after an extreme (locked wheels) inadvertent deceleration of the leading vehicle if collision is to be avoided. To be compatible with this figure, the measurement and reporting of the extreme anomalous deceleration might take about 0.1 sec. During that time the speed will have changed by only about 2 ft/sec and the position error by only about 0.1 ft. Thus, the wayside position measurement is of little use in the early detection and measurement of an extreme inadvertent deceleration (unless the position were measured at intervals substantially less than 0.1 sec and with a measurement error substantially less than 0.1 ft). If, indeed, an accelerometer is to be included for safety purposes, then there appears to be no reason for not using control alternative *a*, which, as pointed out earlier, should be more responsive to gusts than alternative *b*.

Since it seems worthwhile to measure acceleration on board, the question might arise as to whether speed too should be measured on board. If speed is measured on board, then wayside position measurements may be made far less frequently, as we shall soon demonstrate. But first we note that if wayside position measurements are infrequent, it becomes difficult, if not impossible, to deduce speed from these measurements because they give average speed between measurement sites, and not instantaneous speed. Therefore, if wayside position measurements are infrequent, then measuring speed on board is highly desirable.

Once the vehicle is at the "moving point" that it is tracking, then, in principle, it would never depart from this point if it could maintain the correct speed at all times. When speed is measured on board, the wayside controller (local computer) will specify desired speed, and the on-board longitudinal controls will attempt to keep the measured speed matching the commanded speed. Of course, there may be wind gusts or other disturbances that prevent the vehicle from maintaining an absolutely correct speed; but if the vehicle could measure precisely the deviation of its speed from that required, it could integrate this deviation to find its position error and subsequently could adjust its speed to eliminate the position error.

No analog measurement of speed is accurate enough to prevent the vehicle from "drifting off" from the moving point it should be following. As a result it is necessary to make a periodic position measurement to eliminate cumulative drift. If, for example, there were a 1% error in measuring speed, and if the vehicle is required to drift no further than 1.0 ft from its "moving point," then there must be an independent position measurement every 100 ft. Such position measurements could be made by wayside sensors, or, as we shall see later, they could be made from the vehicle.

In contrast to the relatively inaccurate analog measurement of speed, certain digital means for measuring speed could, in principle, maintain position indefinitely. This would require that all clocks throughout the system be perfectly synchronized (but not necessarily accurate). This is the approach that was used in The Aerospace Corporation's 1/10-scale model test track; timing pulses were sent to each vehicle from a master clock. Because of the danger that some of these pulses could be lost in transmission, it might be better to have clocks on each vehicle which would be periodically synchronized to a master clock. But even with perfect synchronization there is still a necessity to take some position fixes. For example, there is the problem (discussed below) of initialization after system shutdown. Also, it will be recalled that in our discussion of quasi-synchronous control we suggested a guideway-mounted vehicle sensor at the entrance to the jurisdictional area of each local computer. In Sec. 6.5.1 we will describe how such guideway-mounted sensors might also be used just upstream of a merge point to make certain that no two vehicles approaching the merge are in conflict. If guideway-mounted vehicle sensors are needed for other purposes, it would seem advisable to use them to obtain position fixes, and if this is done, then there is no necessity to synchronize the vehicle clocks with a master clock. For purposes of illustration, assume that a position fix is taken every 0.5 mi and that the vehicle clocks are only accurate to 1 part in 10,000 (about 9 sec per day). The drift would then be only 0.26 ft between position fixes.

Figure 4-11 illustrates how a digital system, depending upon such position fixes, might work. As described above, each vehicle would generate a continuous stream of clock pulses by having an oscillator on board whose frequency was controlled to about 1 part in 10,000. For purposes of illustration let us assume that the pulse rate is 10,800 pulses/sec. Along the guideway there are evenly spaced fiducial marks which, for purposes of illustration, we shall assume to be separated by 1.0 ft. These marks are detected by a fiducial mark sensor aboard the vehicle.

In the Aerospace design the propulsion and primary braking systems (Secs. 7.2 and 7.3) employ evenly spaced guideway-mounted ceramic magnets. Every second magnet has its north pole facing inward toward the vehicle-mounted motor primary, and the alternate magnets have their south poles facing inward. These magnets are 6 inches long and are spaced 6 inches apart full scale. Hall-effect

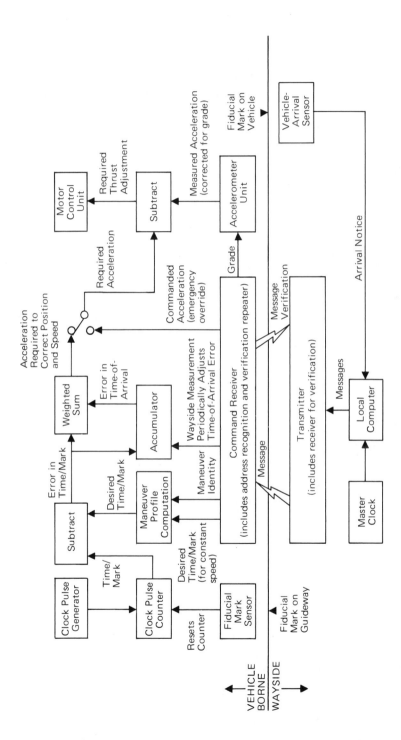

Fig. 4-11. Essentials of The Aerospace Corporation Approach to Longitudinal Control

detectors aboard the vehicle sense the leading edge of the magnets to commutate current among a number of primary coils. (The current in any coil is turned off when it is between magnets. When the current in a coil is on, the direction of the current will depend on the polarity of the magnet adjacent to the coil.) Since the magnet's leading edge must be sensed for purposes of commutating current, this sensing may also be used as the fiducial mark sensing required for speed control. Thus we regard the leading edge of the magnets as being the fiducial marks spaced 1.0 ft apart.

Let us continue our illustrative example. If the vehicle is to travel at a characteristic speed of 60 ft/sec, it is informed by the local computer that it should count 180 clock pulses between successive fiducial mark detections — 10,800 pulses/sec divided by 60 fiducial marks/sec. (In the figure this is shown as "Desired Time/Mark" where the unit of time is the time between successive clock pulses.) If the count is higher than 180, the vehicle is moving too slowly; if the count is lower than 180, it is moving too fast.

We shall now show that for small errors the error in velocity is proportional to the time/mark error. The measured velocity is

$$V_M = \frac{D}{t_M},\qquad(4.2)$$

where D is the distance between fiducial marks and t_M is the measured time to traverse D (i.e., t_M is the measured "time/mark"). The desired velocity, V_D, is related to the desired time/mark, t_D, by the equation:

$$V_D = \frac{D}{t_D}.\qquad(4.3)$$

Therefore, the velocity error is

$$\delta V = V_M - V_D = D\left(\frac{1}{t_M} - \frac{1}{t_D}\right) = -\frac{D}{t_M t_D}(t_M - t_D)$$

$$= -\frac{V_D}{t_M}(t_M - t_D) \approx -\frac{V_D}{t_D}(t_M - t_D).\qquad(4.4)$$

In the last step we have replaced t_M by t_D since the error in time of passage between adjacent marks is assumed small compared with the time itself. Equation (4.4) shows that the error in velocity is proportional (but of the opposite sign) to the time/mark error, $t_M - t_D$.

In addition to determining the time (count) error in passing between successive fiducial marks, the on-board equipment also accumulates the time error. This cumulative time error at the instant of detecting a fiducial mark represents the error in the time of arrival at that fiducial mark. For small errors, the position error, δX, is merely $- V_D$ multiplied by the time-of-arrival error. Thus,

$$\delta X = - V_D \left[\sum_i (t_M - t_D)_i + \delta t_f \right], \qquad (4.5)$$

where $(t_M - t_D)_i$ is the time error in passing the ith spatial interval between marks, starting with the site of the last position fix, and δt_f was the time-of-arrival error at the last position fix.

As the vehicle passes the guideway-mounted vehicle-arrival sensor, a fiducial mark on the vehicle is detected and the arrival event is reported to the wayside computer. This enables that computer to instruct the vehicle to adjust the time-of-arrival error at the output of the accumulator, thus eradicating any drift errors caused by the imperfect clock or due to missed counts or missed wayside fiducial marks.

Both velocity and position errors may be nulled by requiring an acceleration, a_R, given by

$$a_R = -\frac{1}{\tau_1} \left(\delta V + \frac{1}{\tau_2} \delta X \right), \qquad (4.6)$$

where τ_1 and τ_2 are time constants which determine the dynamics with which position and velocity errors are eliminated. Substituting δV from Eq. (4.4) and δX from Eq. (4.5), a_R may be written

$$a_R = \frac{V_D}{\tau_1} \left[\frac{1}{t_D} (t_M - t_D) + \frac{1}{\tau_2} \sum_i (t_M - t_D)_i + \frac{1}{\tau_2} \delta t_f \right] \qquad (4.7)$$

The required[9] acceleration, a_R, is then compared with the measured acceleration, a_M, to find the required thrust change. In finding a_M, grade information is used to correct the accelerometer measurement to compensate for the component of gravity which is measured if the vehicle is climbing or diving.

The digital longitudinal control system we have just described can also be used to control the advancement or slipping of slots (or fractions of slots). By way of illustration, let us assume that the vehicle is to slip back one 15-ft slot or 15 fiducial marks. To slip back it must temporarily reduce its speed and will get a higher than 180 count at the reduced speed. The total number of extra clock-pulse counts during the slot-slipping maneuver is 2,700 (15 fiducial marks x 180 pulses/fiducial mark). Thus, one way to control the slip would be to have the vehicle follow some deceleration profile until 1,350 extra clock pulses were counted and then to accelerate back

---

[9] Under certain emergency situations, as when the vehicle ahead is inadvertently decelerating, the local computer will specify the required acceleration (deceleration) as an override.

to line speed while another 1,350 extra pulses are counted. This can be done either by storing a sequence of the clock-pulse counts (between neighboring pairs of fiducial marks) desired during the maneuver or by using a formula to compute the sequence. For the 1/10-scale model, which only operated at one line speed, we stored a few sequences in the vehicle's digital control electronics, each sequence representing a different maneuver, i.e., a different number of slots gained or slipped. We now believe it might be better to compute the sequences because of the very large number of different maneuver profiles that might be used if the system employs many different line speeds.

Let us now turn to the question of initialization, as might be required during reestablishment of traffic flow following a power failure or line blockage.

We need to distinguish three cases:

a. The first is typified by the situation which might occur following the removal of a line blockage. There would be a string of stopped vehicles but the line ahead would be clear. In that event, the first vehicle of the string would be given an instruction to accelerate to the characteristic line speed; one second later the next vehicle would be so instructed, etc. Some distance after each vehicle had achieved line speed it would pass a wayside sensor[10] which would report its arrival to the local computer. This would allow the local computer to decide what slot should be assigned to the vehicle or what moving point the vehicle should track, and the computer would then transmit a time-of-arrival error to the vehicle. As explained above, this would reset the output of the on-board count-error accumulator which would then lead to a transient adjustment of speed to eliminate the time-of-arrival (or position) error.

In this type of initialization it is not necessary to know the exact position of the stopped vehicles but only their identities and order so that they may be given the start instruction in the proper sequence.

b. The second case is typified by the situation that might occur following reestablishment of power after a systemwide power failure. Consider, for example, a single loop on which all vehicles had stopped. In this event, all vehicles on the main

[10] At the very least, such wayside sensors should be located a little upstream of intersections and merges to provide the local computer with accurate information for resolving potential conflicts.

line would simultaneously be instructed to accelerate up to line speed, using a standard acceleration profile. During the acceleration process and the subsequent cruise at line speed they would hold approximately to their initial spacing. Then, as each passed a wayside sensor, it would be given a time-of-arrival error which would allow it to correct its position.

This initialization approach should be satisfactory following a power failure because the vehicles would probably have received simultaneous instructions to come to a stop at the time of the failure so that their separations when stopped would be approximately equal to their previous running separations. However, to facilitate this type of initialization, wayside sensors should probably be as close as 500 to 1,000 ft, and certainly should be placed upstream of intersections and merges so that a vehicle may correct its position before it attempts to merge.

If the vehicles on the network shown in Fig. 4-10 were brought to a stop, then this method of initialization would be used for vehicles on the solid lines in that figure. It will be recalled that such lines consist of complete loops. Vehicles that had stopped on the dotted lines would not be started up until those on the loops were up to line speed, and they would be handled by initialization method c, discussed below. An exception would be those on the dotted line already committed to the merge. Those vehicles would be started simultaneously with those on the loops, since there clearly is space for them on the loops and otherwise they might block the vehicles on the loops.

c.   The third method of initialization applies to vehicles stopped on a siding or on a main-line segment treated like a siding for merge control. Vehicles on the dotted line segments of Fig. 4-10 are an example of the latter. This method would also apply to certain line-clearing procedures, discussed in Sec. 6.3.1, where vehicles on a blocked line are waiting to merge into the traffic stream on a crossing line.

Here the technique is very similar to that described under a. above, with the vehicles accelerated one at a time. But, instead of starting them up at some regular intervals, they are started at such times as necessary to merge them into available spaces on the main line they are entering. This requires an approximate knowledge of the stopped vehicle's position. One way of obtaining this position is to have the vehicle count the number of fiducial marks it has passed since passing the last wayside sensor.[11] (The vehicle's fiducial mark counter would be reset to zero by an instruction from the local computer when a wayside sensor detects the vehicle's arrival.) When initialization is about to occur, the vehicles would be interrogated as to their fiducial-mark counts.

Thus far we have postulated the use of wayside sensors to take position fixes. An alternative would be to have each vehicle periodically measure its own position in absolute terms. There might be, for example, a number of identifiable master fiducial marks, say, every 1,000 ft. The vehicle could, on reaching such a mark, report the event to the local computer. The computer could then inform the vehicle of its time-of-arrival error which would reset the output of the count accumulator shown in Fig. 4-11, resulting in a position adjustment. This alternative approach for taking position fixes has the disadvantages of depending on each vehicle to correctly determine the identity of master fiducial marks and of requiring additional communication from the vehicle to the local computer. It has the advantage, however, that once the vehicles are equipped to read the identity of master fiducial marks, these marks may be placed closely together at negligible extra cost, and this may facilitate initialization.

The reader will see that there are many different approaches of approximately equal merit for accomplishing longitudinal measurement and control. Let us try to summarize what we have learned:

a. There must be absolute position fixes. This may be accomplished either by a wayside sensor which observes the arrival of each vehicle (or, more precisely, of an identifiable fiducial mark on the vehicle) and reports the event and the vehicle's identity to the local computer, or, alternatively, there can be identifiable master fiducial marks along the guideway and the vehicle can report its arrival at such a mark, together with the mark's identity, to the local computer. In either case, the local computer will become aware of all such events and will use the error in time of arrival to instruct the vehicle.

b. If the absolute position measurements are frequent, at most every few feet, the speed may be derived from the position measurements. Otherwise there must be an independent speed measurement, probably aboard the vehicle. Speed may be measured with considerable precision by using a digital technique to measure the time of passage between closely spaced

---

[11] An alternative would be to start each vehicle creeping along the guideway until it passes a wayside sensor just upstream of the turn or merge, and then, if no space is available for merging, to stop it there until a space comes along into which it can merge.

fiducial marks (fiducial marks not requiring an encoded identity). Because of the position fixes described in a. above, there is no need to have the vehicle clocks synchronized with a master clock.

c. Maneuvers to allow merging should be ordered by the local computer but can be carried out without wayside supervision (or with wayside supervision if the designer prefers).

d. It is desirable to have acceleration measured on board the vehicle, not only to minimize the time for detection of an inadvertent deceleration which might cause a safety hazard, but also to provide quick response to gusts.

e. After a system or partial system shutdown, there are several means for reinitializing traffic flow. These may require somewhat more closely spaced position fixes than would otherwise be necessary, and probably, in any event, will require a position fix just upstream of intersections and merges to enable the local computer to determine the necessary maneuvers for resolving conflicts. If position fixes are not very close together, it may be necessary in some circumstances for the vehicle to report its approximate position to the local computer so that it can be merged into traffic already in progress on a main line. This position could be obtained by counting fiducial marks from the last position fix.

It should be noted that the entire discussion of measurement and control in this section applies to point-follower systems, whether or not slots are used.

4.6.8 Discrete versus Continuous Positions — Synchronization

For a point-follower system, should discrete or continuous positions be used? Is systemwide synchronization desirable?

For both synchronous and quasi-synchronous control (Secs. 4.3 and 4.4), we described a system of moving imaginary slots absolutely synchronized throughout the system. Either a slot would be vacant or a vehicle would be centered in a slot, except near a merge or intersection where vehicles might be changing position from one discrete slot to another. In Sec. 4.6.4 we noted that the arguments for efficient merging and intersection control were dependent on supervision by a local computer but were not dependent on whether incoming and outgoing vehicles were indeed restricted to slot centers. We now reexamine the question more broadly to see whether slots really perform a useful function and whether there is any need to synchronize them throughout the system.

We know that to accomplish merges from station sidings or turn ramps there must be ample space on the main line available for the entering vehicles. Does it matter whether this available space is aggregated into vacant slots or scattered about? To be more specific, if 20% of the capacity of a line is to be left vacant (80% line density), does it matter whether four vehicles are spaced to leave one whole slot vacant, or two 1/2 slots, or three 1/3 slots? If a turning vehicle were aligned with the whole vacant slot it could merge directly into it without requiring any maneuvering of the four vehicles. But, more likely, they would have to shift slots to move the vacant slot into alignment with the merging vehicle. This being the case, it would be about as easy to maneuver to create a slot from the two 1/2 slots or the three 1/3 slots. Thus it would seem that the average line densities that can be used should be about the same whether or not the vehicles are confined to slots, so long as vehicle sequencing is under the control of a local computer with full knowledge of where the vacant space is available.

It will be recalled that in Sec. 4.4.2 we suggested that there not be a discrete set of maneuver starting gates in the maneuvering regions of an intersection. Rather, we recommended a continuum of maneuver starting points where each maneuver is started as far forward as possible consistent with adequate separation from the vehicle ahead being maintained throughout the maneuver. The precise starting point would depend on the maneuver to be performed (i.e., how much distance was to be gained or lost), the maneuver being performed by the vehicle ahead, the point where it started its maneuver, and the initial separation between the two vehicles. Although this prescription was intended for a quasi-synchronous system adhering to a slot-oriented approach, it clearly applies equally well if the vehicles neither start nor end their maneuvers centered in slots.

One argument which might be proposed for adhering to slots is the relative simplicity of implementation, especially if the fine control of maneuvers (not the choice of maneuver) is to be delegated to the vehicles. The local computer would merely instruct the vehicle to "drop back 3 slots" and the velocity profile for the 3-slot slip could be stored in the vehicle's computer. This is how we carried out maneuvers on the 1/10-scale model.[12] But, as pointed out in Sec. 4.6.7, it is probably better to compute the velocity profile because of the large number of possible maneuvers when several line speeds are used. If the maneuver is computed, it can easily be computed for an arbitrary distance to be gained or slipped.

[12] More accurately, we stored profiles of the number of timing pulses that should be counted between the passage of neighboring fiducial marks.

In summary, it would seem that there is no compelling reason for adhering to slots, but also there is no compelling reason for abandoning them, except in the maneuver region of a split-stream intersection where the length of double guideway may be somewhat shortened by using a continuum of maneuver starting points rather than discrete starting gates.

If a system uses the slot principle, there is still the question of whether the slots need to be synchronized throughout the system or only within the jurisdiction of a local computer. The reason for having slots synchronized within at least the area under the jurisdiction of a local computer is so that a vehicle coming in on one line can merge into a slot coming in on another without having to move vehicles fractional slot lengths.

If the synchronization is not universal, then, as vehicles leave one jurisdiction (where they were slot-centered) and enter another, they will no longer be centered in slots. Of course, it is not difficult to instruct them to shift a fraction of a slot to recenter themselves. The instruction must come from the local computer so that a vehicle which must be moved will not be moved into an occupied slot.

Thus, it would seem that systemwide synchronization is not necessary; on the other hand, it is not difficult to achieve. All that is required is that the local clocks be synchronized periodically with a systemwide master clock. When that is done, there is no longer the necessity for position adjustment for vehicles leaving one jurisdiction and entering another. But, if the master clock should fail or the communications to it break down, the operation can continue with each local clock responsible for local synchronization.

Chapter 5

ROUTING AND EMPTY
VEHICLE MANAGEMENT

Jack H. Irving

5.1 LACK OF DEPENDENCE ON TYPE OF CONTROL

As noted in Sec. 4.1, the problems of routing and empty vehicle management can be addressed almost independently of the type of network control system employed.

Let us illustrate by considering the routing strategy. The objective is to minimize vehicle travel times while avoiding line saturation. If lines are not saturated, rerouting at intersections (when using quasi-synchronous control) or the "backing up" of traffic (when using asynchronous control) will be rare events. In that case, the total trip time for any candidate route is highly predictable, and the fastest route for each trip can be determined with a high degree of certainty. The route so determined depends only on network geometry and line speeds and is clearly independent of the type of control system used — synchronous, quasi-synchronous, asynchronous, or any of their variants. If, however, assigning each vehicle to its fastest route should lead to a predictable overloading of certain line segments, then it will be necessary instead to assign some of the trips to somewhat slower routes to avoid such overloading. There can now be a slight dependence on the type of control, because at predicted line densities lines would be unsaturated for one type of control but overloaded for another. Nevertheless, the methodology for balancing the traffic is the same; only the results will be different.

Likewise the empty vehicle management problem is also almost independent of the type of control system. Empty vehicles must be dispatched from stations having a surplus of vehicles to stations where they will be needed. Optimum dispatching patterns utilize that combination of dispatching orders and routes which minimizes the sum of the empty vehicle trip times and thus the number of empty vehicles in transit at any instant of time. For low line densities everywhere, all vehicles can travel along their least-time routes and the dispatching orders would depend only on the surplus or shortage of empty vehicles at all stations, the network geometry, and the line speeds; there would be no dependence on the type of control employed. But, if the combined traffic of occupied and empty vehicles has overloaded certain portions of the network, then some of the empty vehicles will have to take alternate routes, and this in turn could affect dispatching orders. Since different control systems might have different capacities, overloading might occur with one control system but not another; thus the empty vehicle dispatching orders could depend on the type of control system employed. However, the methodology for obtaining optimal routes and dispatching orders does not depend on the type of control; only the results do.

5.2   AN OVERVIEW OF THE DESIGN AND ANALYSIS PROCESS

Chapter 2 outlined many considerations that must go into laying out a candidate network and in placing the stations on it. Once the candidate network has been drawn up, its ability to attract patronage and its ability to effectively handle the resultant traffic flow will have to be analyzed. Aerospace has developed a set of computer programs to accomplish such analyses, even for very large networks.

The first of these, Program NET, discussed in Sec. 5.3, has been designed to accept coded data on the network in terms of points on the network called nodes and how they are connected together. It also accepts internodal distances and times (or speeds), and capacity limitations. NET checks the consistency of the data, issues diagnostic instructions to the designer, and organizes the information for use by other programs.

The information organized by NET is sufficient in itself to enable the least-time route to be determined from any node (including origin stations) to any destination station. If needed, these routes and the associated station-to-station times can be found by Program ROUTE. This program is discussed in Sec. 5.4.

Before it can be determined if the network will be overloaded at any of its nodes, it is first necessary to have an estimated origin-destination (O-D) trip matrix; i.e., a table of how many parties will be traveling per hour from each origin station to every possible destination station. There are two ways this can be done. If data, time, and money are available, the preferred way is to perform a system patronage analysis by the methods described in Chapter 10. This will not only supply the needed O-D trip matrix but it will supply much other useful data for improving the system. If the patronage is not estimated by this full-blown analysis, the alternative is to use Program GENOD (Generate O-D) to obtain a fairly crude estimate of the O-D trip matrix, which may still be quite adequate for initial network planning. Let us briefly describe the two alternative approaches.

Chapter 10 describes the patronage estimation methodology, a

Monte Carlo modal-split simulation program package developed by Aerospace. This package "models" a statistically significant set of travelers to determine their individual modal choice; e.g., which of them drive to work and which go by PRT. The city is divided into zones (usually Traffic Analysis Zones) and, based on data giving the income distribution for residents of each zone, and trip data giving the number of trips from each zone to every other zone, each modeled traveler is randomly assigned an income level and exact door locations for both his origin and destination. The model takes into account driving distances and times, automobile cost factors, and parking costs. It requires information on the PRT fare structure, on station locations, and on travel times between each pair of stations from Program ROUTE. It gives the traveler the option of reaching PRT by several access modes, which may include walking, park-and-ride, kiss-and-ride, scheduled bus, or dial-a-ride, depending on the station. Then, based mostly on out-of-pocket costs, travel times, and the value of time, a modal decision is made for that traveler. By repeating this process for a large number of travelers, statistics may be gathered which not only estimate the patronage but the constituency of that patronage by location and income level. Of importance here, it creates an O-D trip matrix of how many trips will go from each PRT station to any other.

As described, the modal split analysis was based on station-to-station travel times found from least-time routes by Program ROUTE. Subsequently it may be found that certain nodes are overloaded and the traffic may be rerouted with some trips following somewhat slower routes. In principle, the modal-split simulation could be repeated and would show less patronage on the rerouted trips than before; again, the traffic could be balanced with somewhat improved travel times. Although such iterations could be repeated until oscillations settle down, our experience in examining the downtown Los Angeles network indicates that the impact of rerouting to balance traffic is so small on typical travel times that the effect on patronage would be insignificant compared with the effects of other uncertainties in the patronage estimation analysis.

As stated above, an alternative approach to estimating the PRT station-to-station O-D trip matrix is to use the very simple Program GENOD. Once the PRT network is defined, including the station placements, it should be possible to infer from residential and employment densities in the vicinity of stations, from an assumed modal split, and from an assumed passenger loading per vehicle, the number of vehicle trips leaving from and arriving at each station. Program GENOD is then used to pair up these trip ends in proportion to the activity defined for each station. Thus, it assumes that the number of vehicle trips per hour from station i to station j is given by

$$N_{ij} = \frac{D_i A_j}{T} \text{ (rounded)}, \tag{5.1}$$

where

D_i = number of vehicle trips/hr departing from i,

A_j = number of vehicle trips/hr arriving at j,

and T = total number of vehicle trips/hr on the system.

The only tricky part of GENOD is the rounding procedure to preserve the trip totals to and from each station.

After the O-D trip matrix is estimated by one of the two methods described above, this matrix and the network descriptive data from NET are used in Program BALO to balance the traffic of occupied vehicles (Sec. 5.5). BALO, after finding least-time paths (it imbeds a version of ROUTE as a subroutine), modifies these paths as little as possible to achieve at all nodes traffic flows which are less than a stipulated percentage of their theoretical limiting capacities. The stipulated percentage may depend on the type of control system used. It should be chosen to achieve high intersection performance, i.e., a low probability of rerouting where wave-on is used and minimal "backing up" of traffic where wait-to-merge control is used. (See Sec. 4.6.3.)

Then Program FEAS is used to obtain a feasible solution to the empty-vehicle dispatching problem (Sec. 5.6.2). Finally, Program BALE (Sec. 5.6.3) modifies least-time paths of empty vehicles as little as possible to achieve traffic flows which, when superimposed on the flow of occupied vehicles, will not overload the network. With the paths so obtained, and using the feasible dispatching orders from FEAS as an initial guess, BALE optimizes the dispatching orders to minimize the empty-vehicle fleet size.

We will illustrate this total process by returning to the example of the downtown Los Angeles network displayed in Fig. 2-13. It will be recalled that the scenario has 50% of the 300,000 CBD workers arriving over 2 hours, with vehicles carrying 1.5 passengers on average. Thus, 50,000 vehicles/hr arrive at the 58 downtown stations during the morning rush hours. Figure 5-1 shows the 9 corridors and 3 parking lots from which these trips originate.

For purposes of simulation of the traffic flow downtown and in the immediate surrounding area, it is not necessary to detail the location of each of the suburban stations. Consequently, on each corridor we placed one fictitious station which is assumed to generate

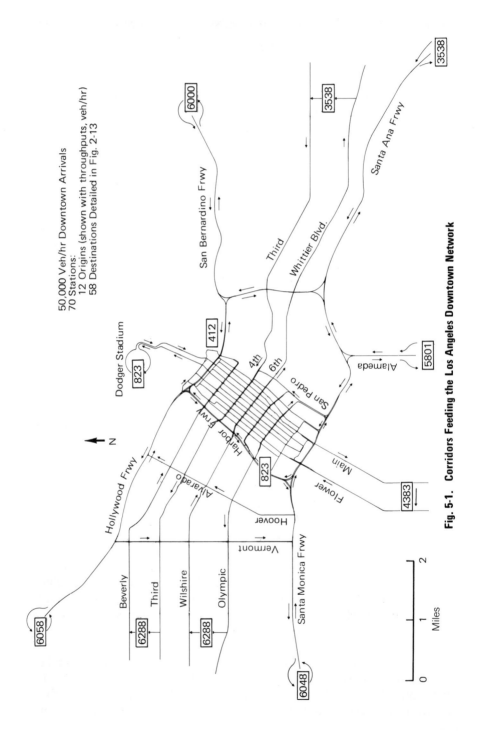

50,000 Veh/hr Downtown Arrivals
70 Stations:
   12 Origins (shown with throughputs, veh/hr)
   58 Destinations Detailed in Fig. 2-13

Fig. 5-1.   Corridors Feeding the Los Angeles Downtown Network

all the trips that, in reality, would come from the totality of all suburban stations along that corridor. Of course, each corridor has an outgoing line to return empty vehicles to these trip-generating stations.

In studying the downtown Los Angeles network, we assumed that the 9 fictitious stations feeding the corridors would generate trips in proportion to current automobile traffic, and we assumed traffic from the 3 outlying parking lots would be proportional to the parking lot sizes. As described earlier, the 58 downtown destination stations were scaled to handle a capacity of 50% of the working force in their area, as determined from existing and planned office space. For this study Program GENOD was used to find the O-D trip matrix.

For the purposes of the study we did not consider reverse flow; i.e., the small amount of traffic going from downtown to the suburbs in the morning. As a result, the size of the "empty-vehicle fleet" will be somewhat exaggerated in proportion to the number of occupied vehicles. Moreover, the trips to downtown would probably represent only a small portion of the total peak hour trips in Los Angeles; the others are likely to be far better balanced, with occupied vehicles flowing in both directions and with much less empty-vehicle dispatching required.

The empty-vehicle dispatching methodology discussed in Sec. 5.6 is based on averages, but at any particular suburban station during the morning rush hours the average need for empty vehicles may have unpredictable variations from one work day to another, and, in addition, on any particular day there will be random fluctuations in the need for empty vehicles during the morning rush hours. These problems are dealt with in Sec. 5.7.

5.3 NETWORK DESCRIPTION (PROGRAM NET)

Once the designer has laid out his candidate network, he must feed a description of the network into the computer so that routes may be determined and traffic analyzed. Program NET accepts the descriptive data, analyzes them for consistency, and organizes them. For purposes of routing, it is not necessary to know network geometry but network topology is essential; that is, it is not necessary to know whether a particular network link is straight or curved, but it is necessary to know to what it is connected.

To begin with, the user must identify and number network nodes, with no node having more than two successor nodes. As a matter of heuristic convenience, and with no implications on actual geometry, we call the two successors the "straight successor" and the "turn successor." The nodes identified must include all stations and certain, but not all, branch points (points of line divergence). Six pages of instruction at the beginning of NET's Fortran listing assist the user in identifying a set of nodes which minimizes the number of nodes. One trick which substantially reduces the number of nodes is to identify both the center point of an off-line station and the corresponding point on the bypass line by the same node number, and then to classify this node number as Class 2. (On-line stations are Class 1, and branch points Class 3.) When it notices the Class 2 classification, the routing program will route through the bypass and only add station incremental times at the beginning and end of the trip. This trick makes it unnecessary to consider the branch point leading to the station siding and the first downstream branch point from the station as nodes, except when there are additional merges upstream of that branch point.

The foregoing will give the reader a rough idea of what nodes must be identified for finding routes, travel times, and distances. But since the user is also interested in capacity constraints, he must identify as Class 4 nodes certain, but not all, main line points where accelerations begin. These are points where the velocity is lower than at the next branch point and could represent capacity bottlenecks.

The user prepares one punch card for each node giving the node number, its class, its capacity in vehicles per hour, its successor node numbers, and the distance and time to each successor node. Alternatively, he may invoke a conversion subroutine which converts planimeter readings to metric or English units, and calculates the times from prescribed speeds.

Since the network design process is iterative, an earlier used node may be deleted. It is not necessary to renumber nodes; the programs are not bothered by missing node numbers. But NET will give the user a list of skipped node numbers so that he can see whether the cards for them were inadvertently left out.

NET also carries out a number of consistency checks on the data submitted, and provides the user with warning diagnostics. It, for example, checks the reasonableness of times and distances. It checks node succession consistency; it checks that every node has at least one predecessor and that no node is its own successor.

Finally, NET numbers the stations, prints out organized data for the user, including a list of each node's predecessor nodes (often more than two), and records the results on tape or disk for the use of subsequent programs used in the analysis of PRT routing and empty vehicle dispatching.

Currently NET and all the other programs operate on a CDC 7600 computer with up to 1,000 stations, 2,000 nodes, and 4,000 links (the paths from a node to one of its successors). The downtown Los Angeles example uses 70 stations (58 downtown, plus the 12 trip-generating stations) and 301 nodes (actually numbered from 1 to 313, with 12 numbers skipped).

5.4 LEAST-TIME ROUTING (PROGRAM ROUTE)

Program ROUTE finds the least-time route from each node to each possible destination station. This is accomplished by a technique known as dynamic programming. Here is how it works.

The program starts with Station 1 and traces paths leading to this station backwards in time. First the predecessor nodes of Station 1 are found. It will be recalled that although a node has at most two successors, it can have any number of predecessors. Each predecessor node is labeled with its time of transit to Station 1. It is also labeled with a turn instruction consisting of a "1" if the station is its straight successor or a "2" if the station is its turn successor. Let us denote as node A the labeled node with the least transit time to Station 1. Next, the predecessors of A are found and labeled with their transit times to Station 1. Each is also marked with a turn instruction — a "1" if A is its straight successor or a "2" if A is its turn successor. If a predecessor of A has already been labeled as a direct predecessor of Station 1, the two transit times are compared — the one for the direct path to Station 1 versus the one for the path passing through A — and the node is labeled with the lesser of the two transit times, together with the corresponding turn instruction. The process continues in this way. At each step, from all labeled nodes whose predecessors have not yet been found, that node is selected which has the least transit time to Station 1. Then the selected node's predecessors are found and labeled with their transit times to Station 1 and turn instructions to the selected node. For any predecessor already labeled, its new transit time is compared with its old and the lesser is chosen for the label, together with the corresponding turn instruction. When the predecessors to all nodes have been found and labeled, the process is complete. Each node has now been labeled with its transit time to Station 1, following a least-time path, and the turn instruction indicates whether the trip starts out by going straight or turning. The entire process is now repeated for each of the other stations.

At first, a standard dynamic programming procedure was used, but later we discovered that we could save at least a factor of 10 in execution time by organizing the intermediate results of the computation to eliminate exhaustive searching procedures. As a result, Program ROUTE requires only two seconds of CDC 7600 computing time to fully analyze the 70 stations and 313 nodes of the downtown Los Angeles network.

Figure 5-2 shows the first portion of a table printed by ROUTE which summarizes these routing instructions, each line presenting instructions from 75 nodes. The first 5 lines of the table are instructions on how to get to Station 1 from each of the 313 nodes of the downtown Los Angeles network. The first line indicates that coming from any node 1 through 11 the vehicle should proceed straight, but from nodes 12, 14, and 15 it should turn to start on the least-time path to Station 1. It will be noted that the third line begins with a zero indicating that node 151 is a missing node; i.e., a node number not used by the planner in laying out his network. It is clear that this table provides the basic information which is required by each intersection control computer to route vehicles toward any destination station. An incidental function of ROUTE is to print a diagnostic message if it finds that the network design is such that no path exists between some node and some station.

LOS ANGELES 70-STATION NETWORK

```
DESTINATION    TURN INSTRUCTIONS
STATN  NODE    0=MISSING NODE, 1=STRAIGHT, 2=TURN
  1      1     11111 11111 12122 12122 11211 21122 11211 22211 22121 12121 12112 21121 21221 12111 11222
                22112 12122 11212 21122 21212 11221 12122 21012 22221 22122 12021 11112 21121 11121 20212
                01122 12221 22221 11211 11211 01112 11220 22221 22122 12021 11112 21121 11121 12021
                21022 11110 11212 12211 11112 12211 11111 11122 22111 11112 11222 11111 22211 11111 11111
  2      2     11111 11111 12122 12121 22121 11122 11211 22012 12111 12121 11211 01211 21121 21121 11221 11122
                22112 12122 11212 21122 11521 11122 21012 21012 22221 22122 12021 11112 21121 11121 20212
                01222 12221 22221 11211 11211 01212 11220 22221 22122 12021 11112 21121 11121 21022
                11111 11111 121
  3      3     11111 11111 12122 12121 22112 22211 11211 22212 12111 12121 12121 21212 21121 12211 21121
                22212 12122 11122 11112 11112 11522 12122 12210 22012 11222 22122 01220 21120 21111 11211 21122
                01121 12221 22222 22211 11112 12211 11111 11122 22111 11112 11112 11111 11111 11111 11111
                11111 11111 121
  4      4     11111 11111 12122 12121 22112 21211 22122 11122 12111 12121 12121 21212 21121 12211 21121
```

Fig. 5-2. Program ROUTE's Table of Routing Instructions

Figure 5-3 shows excerpts of two other tables produced by Program ROUTE. One of these presents the travel time in minutes to each station from any other station when following the least-time route. The other gives the travel distance in miles, assuming the user has selected English units; if he has chosen metric units, the table is given in kilometers.

Up to this time we have spoken of Program ROUTE as though it minimized travel times between any specified node and any specified destination station. To do this it must use the information which the program user supplies to Program NET regarding travel time(s) from each node to its successor(s). Now, if instead the user, in the punch card columns in which he normally enters the time(s), supplies Program NET with information on the energy consumed in traveling from each node to its successor(s), then Program ROUTE will find least-energy paths instead of least-time paths. This idea can be further generalized to obtain "least-cost" paths. Here cost could be considered an appropriately weighted function of time, distance, and energy. Throughout the rest of this chapter, when we discuss procedures for minimizing travel times compatible with not overloading nodes beyond their practical capacities, it should be understood by

LOS ANGELFS 70-STATION NETWORK

```
  DEST      DEST
STATION     NODE        TRAVEL-TIMES (MINUTES) ...

   1          1      10.45  11.78  10.40  14.08  14.57  15.20  15.53  15.20  11.07  12.33
                     10.32  11.72   9.70  11.27  11.78  13.23  11.63  12.06  12.03  11.57
                     10.22  10.97  11.68  10.10  12.13  11.63  11.82  11.18  12.52  10.50
                     10.65  11.43  11.13  12.17  10.13  10.10  10.68  10.62   9.47  11.98
                     12.50   9.13  10.14  10.83   9.22   9.95  10.70   3.32  10.13   3.02
                      9.02  10.80  11.27  11.77   9.93   9.93   9.48   8.82   9.98  10.23
                     11.40   9.80   9.60   8.63   8.60   9.78   8.23   9.40   3.98  11.63

   2          2      12.37  20.33  11.23  14.92  15.42  17.03  17.75  17.12  12.38  14.25
                     12.23  12.55  11.50  11.56  13.92  14.06  13.17  13.85  14.35  13.48
                     13.06  12.80  12.97  13.00  12.02  13.55  13.73  13.02  11.30  13.42
                     12.48  13.27  12.17  12.67  11.05  12.02  11.78  12.52  12.05  13.82
                     13.33  11.05  12.10  12.60  11.05  11.77  11.32  11.65  11.42  10.85
                     10.85  12.23  12.10  11.52  10.43  11.77  11.32  11.65  11.42  12.07
                     12.23  11.72  11.52  10.47  10.43  11.70  10.12  11.23  11.52  12.47
```

LOS ANGELES 70-STATION NETWORK

```
  DEST      DEST
STATION     NODE        TRAVEL-DISTANCES (MILES) ...

   1          1       5.55   7.48   6.52   9.00   9.36   8.81  10.15   9.80   6.98   7.43
                      5.91   7.41   5.87   6.23   6.19   6.82   9.28   6.14   6.36   6.94
                      5.54   5.80   6.02   6.00   7.13   6.96   7.02   5.87   6.43   5.98
                      5.69   5.96   5.94   5.90   6.02   5.84   7.01   5.68   5.28   6.13
                      7.01   5.51   5.87   5.75   5.20   5.45   5.69   5.57   5.34   5.13
                      5.13   5.59   6.77   6.94   4.99   5.77   5.44   5.28   5.06   5.53
                      6.64   5.74   5.65   4.99   5.03   5.59   4.87   5.30   5.45   6.72

   2          2       7.87  12.73   7.10   9.57   9.94  10.07  11.46  11.11   8.29   8.74
                      7.22   7.99   7.18   7.55   7.44   8.81   7.54   7.96   9.67   8.25
                      6.80   7.05   7.82   7.31   8.44   8.27   8.33   7.12   7.69   7.29
                      6.94   7.21   7.09   7.48   7.33   7.15   7.32   7.49   6.54   7.38
                      7.59   6.82   7.18   7.01   6.45   6.70   6.88   6.54   7.15   6.38
                      6.38   6.84   7.34   7.51   7.08   6.69   6.54   6.31   6.71   6.79
                      7.22   7.05   6.96   6.25   6.28   6.90   6.13   6.55   6.70   7.30
```

Fig. 5-3. Program ROUTE's Table of Inter-Station Travel Times and Distances for Least-Time Paths

the reader that we could well have been discussing the minimization of "cost" rather than time.

5.5   BALANCING THE TRAFFIC OF OCCUPIED VEHICLES (PROGRAM BALO)

It is apparent that if all trips were to be routed along their least-time paths, the required flow rate might, at certain nodes, exceed the node's physical capacity. If such an overload condition is anticipated, it will be necessary to balance the traffic by planning the routing of some vehicles along paths other than their least-time paths. This is the procedure undertaken in Program BALO.

The "O" in BALO stands for "occupied." BALO, which at first ignores empty vehicles, attempts to minimize travel times of occupied vehicles, consistent with the constraint that no node shall be overloaded. Program BALE then creates dispatching orders and routing instructions for empty vehicles, taking into account the ambient load of occupied vehicles prescribed by BALO. Clearly, the strategy here is to give precedence to the occupied vehicles; an empty vehicle may be routed along a path of longer duration because of the line congestion caused by occupied vehicles; an occupied vehicle, on the other hand, will not normally be routed along a path of longer duration because of line congestion caused by empty vehicles, even though it might be rerouted as a result of congestion caused by other occupied vehicles. An exception to this rule occurs where a certain number of empty vehicles must pass through a prescribed node to get to a station where they are needed or to leave a station which is a source of empty vehicles. If this irreducible number of empty vehicles, when added to the ambient load of occupied vehicles, exceeds the node's capacity, then the only solution is to rebalance the traffic of occupied vehicles, using the irreducible count of empty vehicles as an ambient load. Under these circumstances, BALO will be repeated after executing BALE.

ROUTE, which we described earlier, is built into BALO as a subroutine. In addition to performing the functions described in Sec. 5.4, this version of ROUTE will also, for any O-D trip matrix, compute the hourly traffic flow requirement (or loading) which would go past every network node if every vehicle followed its least-time path. It also provides histograms of travel times and distances; that is, it indicates how many vehicle trips lie within each time or distance interval. Finally, it computes average times and distances.

Program BALO is an iterative routine. On the first iteration, subroutine ROUTE is provided with true internode travel times and distances. ROUTE then determines the least-time paths and consequent loadings at each node. Then, BALO compares the resultant loadings with the node capacities that were specified to Program NET by the designer. If all nodes are loaded at less than a user-prescribed percentage of the capacity (taken as 80% in the Los Angeles network example), no further iterations are required; the traffic is balanced. But, if certain nodes are overloaded, then for each overloaded node BALO computes a "time penalty" to be ascribed to that node, and this penalty is added to the internode times from that overloaded node to its successor(s). The time penalty is computed as a broken-line function of its loading. There is no penalty for loadings less than a stipulated percentage of capacity (a percentage not necessarily equal to the maximum allowable percentage). For higher loadings, the penalty grows with the load.

When ROUTE is called on the second iteration, it uses these penalized times, and now finds the "least-penalized-time" path from each origin station to each destination station; then it again finds the traffic load at each node.

Let us consider a node, N, somewhat overloaded on the first iteration when true least-time paths were used. Let us say it is given a 10-sec penalty, and, to keep things simple, assume no other node is penalized. Assume that the least-time path from Station A to Station B passes through N; and that the least-time path from Station C to Station D also passes through N. Let P_{AB} be the least-time path from Station A to Station B which does *not* pass through N. If the time on

P_{AB} is only 7 sec longer than the least-time path which does pass through N, then on the second iteration ROUTE will use the P_{AB} path because its penalized time will be 3 sec shorter than that for the least-penalized-time path through N. Let P_{CD} be similarly defined as the least-time path from Station C to Station D which does *not* pass through N, and assume that the time on P_{CD} is 16 sec longer than the least-time path from C to D. On the second iteration, ROUTE will again prescribe the least-time path through N because, even with the 10-sec penalty, its penalized time is 6 sec shorter than that of P_{CD}. Thus, the trip from A to B will be diverted away from N, but the one from C to D will not.

After the second execution of ROUTE, Program BALO again compares the new loadings at each node with the node capacities, and the penalties are increased where necessary. The program continues to iterate in this manner until all nodes reach satisfactory loads, or until a prescribed maximum number of iterations (no larger than 10) has been reached. If, after 10 iterations, the traffic has not been balanced, it may be that the network has a built-in bottleneck. Therefore, the designer examines the results after 10 iterations (or a lesser number if he so prescribes), and in those regions which are persistently or repeatedly overloaded, he may wish to redesign his network. At his option, however, he may continue from where he left off with further iterations.

With each iteration, ROUTE computes new histograms and averages of *actual* (not penalized) times and distances along the paths it has prescribed, which are not necessarily least-time paths. By comparing these from iteration to iteration, the designer can determine whether the balancing procedure is adding significantly to times and distances.

The user of BALO can choose which tables he wants printed after the first iteration, the intermediate iterations, and the last iteration. These choices include the turn instruction table (Fig. 5-2), the true interstation time and/or distance tables (Fig. 5-3), a table giving node loadings, penalties, capacities, and loads going from each node to each of its successor nodes, and a table of histograms and averages for time and distance.

BALO also produces two summary tables shown in Figs. 5-4 and 5-5. Figure 5-4 illustrates portions of a table which gives the node loadings for each of 6 iterations carried out on the downtown Los Angeles network for the morning peak period. It is seen that node 165 (branch node — Class 3) was overloaded on the first iteration and was given a penalty of 11 sec. This penalty was quite sufficient to reduce the traffic through this node to an acceptable level. It dropped from 10,341 to 4,088, which is well below the

LOS ANGELES 70-STATION NETWORK

LOADS AT NODES

NODE	CL	ITER	PEN	CAPAC	O	IN	DEST	THRU	LOADS ORIG	OUT	OUT-S	OUT-T
1	2	1	0	14400		0	0	0	3538	3538	3538	0
		2	0	14400		0	0	0	3538	3538	3538	0
165	3	1	0	7200	*	10341		10341		10341	8761	1580
		2	11	7200		4088		4088		4088	2508	1580
		3	11	7200		4088		4088		4088	2508	1580
		4	11	7200		3976		3976		3976	2396	1580
		5	11	7200		3976		3976		3976	2396	1580
		6	11	7200		4439		4439		4439	2859	1580
166	3	1	0	7200		2545		2545		2545	1067	1478
		2	0	7200	*	7306		7306		7306	5828	1478
		3	5	7200	*	6773		6773		6773	5295	1478
		4	9	7200	*	6279		6279		6279	4801	1478
		5	12	7200	*	5917		5917		5917	4439	1478
		6	15	7200		4967		4967		4967	3489	1478
167	3	1	0	7200		1067		1067		1067	0	1067
		2	0	7200	*	5828		5828		5828	4894	934
		3	2	7200		5295		5295		5295	4361	934
		4	3	7200		4801		4801		4801	4030	771
		5	4	7200		4439		4439		4439	3686	753
		6	5	7200		3489		3489		3489	2912	577
168	3	1	0	7200		1317		1317		1317	0	1317
		2	0	7200		2017		2017		2017	1852	165

Fig. 5-4. Program BALO's Summary Table of Traffic Loadings of Occupied Vehicles

allowed capacity of 5,760 (80% of 7200). But in the course of diverting the traffic, new bottlenecks were created on nodes 166 and 167. On the third iteration, node 166 was given a 5-sec penalty and node 167 a 2-sec penalty, which was sufficient to bring traffic on node 167 to within allowed limits. Node 166 was still overloaded and so the penalty was progressively increased. By the sixth iteration the penalty was 15 sec and this was sufficient to reduce the node loading below 5,760. At the end of 6 iterations, all loads throughout the network were acceptable.

Figure 5-5 illustrates the summary table which, for each iteration, gives averages and histograms for actual times and distances. It will be noted that the balancing of traffic for the downtown Los Angeles network was accomplished by increasing the average trip time from 9.42 minutes to 9.48 minutes; that is, by adding only 3.6 sec to the average trip. (This supports our earlier assertion that in performing modal-split analysis one can usually consider PRT trip times for the least-time trips, without significantly affecting the results.) The average distance was increased by only 0.04 mi. Figure 5-5 also displays the occupied-vehicle fleet size:

$$\text{Fleet size} = \frac{\text{Average trip time (minutes)}}{60} \times \text{total number of trips/hr}$$

Since the travel times and distances were so little affected by the route diversions, it is likely that the Los Angeles network could have carried still higher morning peak traffic loads. However, initial attempts to balance the traffic with 70,000 vehicles per hour (a 40% increase) showed that some network redesign was probably advisable.

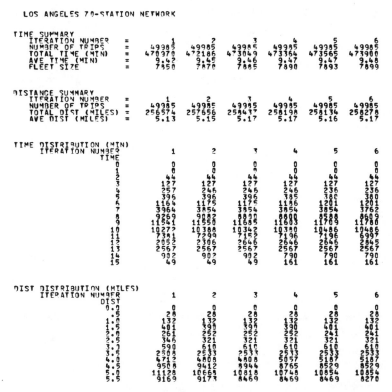

Fig. 5-5. Program BALO's Summary Table of Averages and Histograms
of Trip Times and Distances

For the downtown Los Angeles network, the entire CDC 7600 computing time for BALO, including the six iterations of ROUTE, was only 14.5 sec.

5.6 EMPTY-VEHICLE DISPATCHING AND ROUTING

5.6.1 Definition of the Dispatching Problem

The problem of managing empty vehicles is more complex than that of managing occupied vehicles because one must solve the interacting problems of dispatching and routing.

At the outset, we restrict our study to the steady-state flow which might reasonably characterize the middle portion of the morning or evening peak period. This restriction is not as limited as it might seem. For example, during the early portion of the morning peak, suburban stations will be receiving empty vehicles from car barns instead of downtown. If these car barns are considered as source stations for empty vehicles, the methodology will still apply as long as the rate of flow from these sources is approximately constant.

With this steady-state flow restriction, we may consider N_{ij}, the number of occupied vehicle trips per hour from Station i to Station j, as a constant independent of time. Then, the number of occupied vehicle departures from Station i is

$$D_i = \sum_{j \neq i} N_{ij}, \qquad (5.2)$$

and the number of arrivals is

$$A_i = \sum_{j \neq i} N_{ji}. \qquad (5.3)$$

From this, it follows that

$$\sum_i A_i = \sum_i D_i. \qquad (5.4)$$

Now, if $A_i > D_i$, the ith station will be a source of S_i empty vehicles, where

$$S_i = A_i - D_i. \qquad (5.5)$$

If $D_j > A_j$, the jth station will be a user of U_j empty vehicles, where

$$U_j = D_j - A_j. \qquad (5.6)$$

If a station has precisely the same number of occupied vehicle arrivals and departures, then it is neither a source nor user station. It may be considered as a neutral station and is of no importance so far as empty vehicle management is concerned. From Eqs. (5.4), (5.5), and (5.6), and the definition of a neutral station,

$$0 = \sum_{\substack{all \\ stations}} (A_i - D_i)$$

$$= \sum_{\substack{neutral \\ stations}} (A_i - D_i) + \sum_{\substack{source \\ stations}} (A_i - D_i) - \sum_{\substack{user \\ stations}} (D_j - A_j)$$

$$= \sum_{\substack{source \\ stations}} S_i - \sum_{\substack{user \\ stations}} U_j.$$

Therefore,

$$\sum_{\substack{source \\ stations}} S_i = \sum_{\substack{user \\ stations}} U_j. \qquad (5.7)$$

Let us renumber the stations so that the N_S source stations are numbered 1, 2, . . ., N_S, and the N_U user stations are numbered 1, 2, . . ., N_U. We also redefine S_i as the number of empty vehicles available per hour from the ith source station, and U_j as the number of empty vehicles needed per hour from the jth user station. Then Eq. (5.7) can be written

$$\sum_{i=1}^{N_S} S_i = \sum_{j=1}^{N_U} U_j. \tag{5.7a}$$

Let E_{ij} be the number of empty vehicles dispatched per hour from the ith source station to the jth user station. It must follow that

$$S_i = \sum_{j=1}^{N_U} E_{ij} \quad (i = 1, \ldots, N_S), \tag{5.8a}$$

and

$$U_j = \sum_{i=1}^{N_S} E_{ij} \quad (j = 1, \ldots, N_U). \tag{5.8b}$$

Eq. (5.8a) represents N_S constraints on the E_{ij} and Eq. (5.8b) represents N_U more constraints; but these constraints are not independent because of the restriction represented by (5.7a). Hence, the number of independent constraints is

$$N_C = N_S + N_U - 1. \tag{5.9}$$

Next, let us imagine that we knew precisely the path, and hence the time, for empty vehicle trips from each source station to each user station. Let T_{ij} represent the time (in hours) from the ith source station to the jth user station. Then, the average number of empty vehicles en route from i to j would be $E_{ij} T_{ij}$, and the total empty fleet en route would be

$$F_E = \sum_{i=1}^{N_S} \sum_{j=1}^{N_U} E_{ij} T_{ij} \tag{5.10}$$

Our problem is to find the dispatching orders, E_{ij}, which will minimize the empty vehicle fleet size, F_E, subject to the N_C independent constraints of Eqs. (5.8a) and (5.8b). This is a well-known problem in linear programming known as the Hitchcock or "transportation" problem. The term "transportation" here arises from the application of transporting products from factories to customers.

The classical approach to this problem is to find a "basic feasible" solution first, and then to improve that solution iteratively until an optimal solution is found. A "feasible" solution is any set of E_{ij} which obeys the constraints of Eqs. (5.8a) and (5.8b). A "basic feasible" solution is a feasible solution in which all of the E_{ij} are zero except for a small set, no more than N_C in number. For a large complement of stations, the iterative procedure for changing a basic feasible solution into an optimal solution can be very time-consuming, unless one starts with a very good basic feasible solution. Program FEAS was designed to provide that good basic feasible solution.

5.6.2   The Basic Feasible Solution (Program FEAS)

Program FEAS finds a basic feasible solution to the dispatching problem by a dynamic programming procedure somewhat reminiscent of the method of Program ROUTE. In doing this, it uses true internode transit times provided by Program NET.

Starting from the first source station, FEAS traces all possible paths *forward* in time (not backwards as in ROUTE). Starting at time zero, it finds the time of arrival at the two (or one) successor nodes of the source station, and labels these with their times. Then, choosing the node with the lesser time label, it finds its successor nodes, and labels them with their times of arrival. This process is continued. At each step, from all labeled nodes whose successors have not yet been found, that node is selected which has the least time of arrival from the first source station. The selected node's successors are found and labeled with their times of arrival. If a successor was previously labeled, then the new time of arrival is compared with the old and the lesser is chosen for the label. This is continued until one of the selected least-time nodes is a user station; timewise, this is clearly the closest user station to the first source station.

Let us assume by way of illustration that the source station is supplying 700 vehicles per hour and that the user station just reached needs only 150 vehicles per hour. Then, a dispatching order for sending 150 vehicles to this station is listed, the remaining need of the user station is marked down to zero, and the remaining supply of the source station is marked down to 550. The paths from the source station are now continued until another user station is located. Let us say it needs 400 vehicles per hour. A second dispatching order is now listed, this one for 400 vehicles, and the remaining supply is decreased to 150. Again, the paths are continued, and when a third user station is located, it needs 250 vehicles. The remaining supply is inadequate. But a dispatching order for the remaining supply of 150 vehicles is listed, the remaining supply marked down to zero, and the remaining need of the user station reduced to 100.

Now, one starts a dynamic search *backwards* in time from the unfulfilled user station, to find the closest source station that can supply it. If that source station has 380 vehicles available, then a dispatching order for 100 is listed, the remaining need of the user station is reduced to zero, and the remaining supply of the new source station is reduced to 280. Again, we start tracing *forward* from the new source station. However, if the new source station only had 60 vehicles, the *backwards* tracing would have had to continue in order to meet the unfulfilled need for 40 vehicles.

If in the course of tracing backwards, one comes to a source station whose supply has already been depleted, one ignores that source station and continues backwards to the next. Similarly, if in the course of tracing forward from a source station, one comes to a user station whose need has already been satisfied, one ignores that user station. The alternating forward and backward tracing is continued until all empty vehicles have been dispatched.

Program FEAS then prints out a table of dispatching orders, shown in Fig. 5-6 for the morning peak traffic. In this table each station is again identified by its original station number, assigned earlier by Program NET. Stations 1 through 12 are the suburban and outlying parking lot user stations, and Stations 13 through 70 are the 58 downtown source stations. There are exactly 69 dispatching orders in the basic solution found, since

$$N_C = N_S + N_U - 1 = 58 + 12 - 1 = 69.$$

The table of Fig. 5-6 also shows the transit times for each of the dispatched trips. When these times are multiplied by the number of empty vehicles on each trip and the product is summed over the dispatching orders [see Eq. (5.10)], one obtains the size of the empty vehicle fleet. For the Los Angeles network, during the morning peak, this is seen to be 6,574 vehicles.

The results obtained by FEAS are also written out on tape or

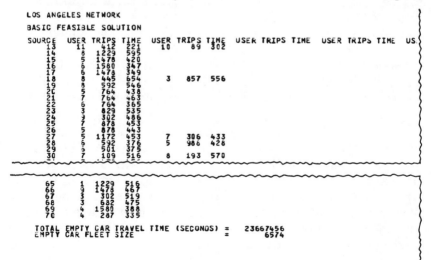

Fig. 5-6. Program FEAS's Table of Dispatching Orders for Empty Vehicles

disk for use in Program BALE. The CDC 7600 computing time for FEAS applied to the Los Angeles network was 0.4 sec.

5.6.3 Optimizing the Dispatching Orders and Balancing the Traffic (Program BALE)

Program BALE is a quite complex program. Its function is to minimize empty vehicle fleet size by finding optimum dispatching orders and a compatible set of routing instructions which avoid traffic overloads. To understand this process, let us consider it on a step-by-step basis.

Step 1. BALE calls on its subroutine RTETIM which is a streamlined version of ROUTE. During its first execution, RTETIM produces a set of turn instructions from every node to each user station, and it computes the matrix T_{ij} of minimum travel times from every source station to every user station.

Step 2. BALE calls on subroutine MINFLT which, starting with the matrix T_{ij} and the basic feasible set of dispatching orders found in Program FEAS, successively improves these orders until an optimal set is obtained. MINFLT employs a technique that is known in the parlance of linear programming as finding "loops." (The reader can find in any standard text on linear programming how this method may be applied to the Hitchcock problem.) Subroutine MINFLT iteratively calls on four subroutines of its own to accomplish the successive improvements. When working on the Los Angeles network, MINFLT went through 31 iterations. Starting with an empty-vehicle fleet size of 6,574 (obtained from FEAS), the first iteration reduced the fleet size to 6,565, the second to 6,555, the third to 6,552. It continued thus until, after the 31st iteration, the fleet was minimized at 6,417 vehicles. (There is no guesswork as to when a minimum is found; the theory provides a simple unambiguous test.)

Step 3. BALE calls on subroutine LOADE, which, using the turn instructions computed by RTETIM and the optimal dispatching orders computed by MINFLT, finds the empty-vehicle traffic load at every node.

Step 4. BALE adds the empty-vehicle traffic loads to the occupied-vehicle loads previously found by Program BALO. These total traffic loads at each node are compared with a user-prescribed percentage (taken as 80% for the Los Angeles network) of the node capacities from NET. If an overload exists at some node, a time penalty is computed for that node, in a manner completely analogous to that used by Program BALO. The time penalty for that node is then added to the internode times from the node to its successor node(s).

Step 5. BALE again calls on RTETIM which, using the penalized internode times, finds least-penalized-time paths from each node to each user station; RTETIM records these paths as turn instructions. It then finds the T_{ij} matrix of true times following these paths. Obviously, some of the T_{ij} will have been increased from their earlier values.

Step 6. BALE again calls on MINFLT which uses the new T_{ij} matrix. But this time MINFLT does not use the original basic feasible set of dispatching orders computed by FEAS. Instead, it uses as its basic feasible set the optimal set of dispatching orders found during the previous execution of MINFLT. Obviously, that set is still feasible because changing the T_{ij} does not change the constraint equations, (5.8a) and (5.8b). This has a profound effect on shortening the execution time of MINFLT. For example, it was earlier stated that, for the Los Angeles network, the first execution of MINFLT required 31 iterations of its four subroutines before an optimum could be obtained; the second execution of MINFLT required only two iterations, i.e., only two cycles of dispatching orders improvement. Of course, with some of the T_{ij} slightly increased, the empty-vehicle fleet size grew, but only from 6,417 to 6,420 vehicles. On the third through fifth executions of MINFLT, there were, respectively, 3, 2, and 3 dispatching orders improvement iterations. The fleet size grew only to 6,421 empty vehicles. During the sixth execution of MINFLT, it was found that, in spite of the empty-vehicle routing changes and the resultant change in T_{ij}, the dispatching orders could not be further improved, i.e., those found in the fifth execution of MINFLT were still optimal. To the nearest integer, the sixth execution of MINFLT again produced a fleet size of 6,421 vehicles.

Step 7. LOADE is again called to find empty-vehicle loadings.

Step 8. BALE again adds on the loadings due to occupied vehicles and compares the totals with capacities. If traffic loads are not acceptable, penalties are increased and the program cycles back to Step 5. If acceptable, it goes on to the summary report printing subroutines.

Like the user of BALO, the user of BALE has a number of printing options. For the first, intermediate, and/or final iterations, he may print tables of turn instructions, a table of travel times between every source and user station, a list showing the progression of fleet size improvements with each internal iteration of MINFLT, a list of optimal dispatching orders found by MINFLT, and a table showing node loadings, which includes separate entries for occupied vehicles, empty vehicles, and total vehicles.

In addition, a summary table provides loadings for each iteration of LOADE (Fig. 5-7). It will be noted that when empty vehicles followed the least-time paths, nodes 141 and 144 were overloaded (exceeded 80% of theoretical capacity). Penalizing those nodes by 4 sec and 2 sec, respectively, was enough to remove the overloads on the second iteration, but overloads now appeared on nodes 142 and 143. When the latter two nodes were penalized on the third iteration, their overloads disappeared but the former two nodes again became overloaded. After six iterations there were no overloaded nodes throughout the network.

When used on the Los Angeles network for the morning rush hours, BALE consumed 5.4 sec of CDC 7600 computing time. Unfortunately, the evening rush hours did not work out as well. First, BALE could not eliminate the overloading at one of the nodes because the irreducible requirement for empty vehicles that had to pass through that node on the way to one of the downtown stations, when added to the ambient loading of occupied vehicles through the

```
LOS ANGELES 70-STATION NETWORK

COMPILATION OF LOADS AT NODES FOR ALL ITERATIONS
NODE  CLASS  ITER  SERVICE  CAPAC  PEN   ---------------------- LOADS ----------------------
                                         IN     DEST    THRU    ORIG    OUT    OUT-S   OUT-T
```

NODE	CLASS	ITER	SERVICE	CAPAC	PEN	IN	DEST	THRU	ORIG	OUT	OUT-S	OUT-T
141	3		OCCUPIED					0		0		0
		1	EMPTY			6644		6644		6644	6644	0
			TOTAL	7200	0 *	6644		6644		6644	6644	0
		2	EMFTY			764		764		764	764	0
			TOTAL	7200	4	764		764		764	764	0
		3	EMPTY	7200	4	5880		5880		5880	2615	3265
			TOTAL	7200		5880		5880		5880	2615	3265
		4	EMPTY	7200	6 *	6221		6221		6221	6221	0
		5	EMFTY	7200	9	2615		2615		2615	2615	0
			TOTAL	7200	9	2615		2615		2615	2615	0
		6	EMPTY	7200	9	4402		4402		4402	2615	1787
			TOTAL	7200		4402		4402		4402	2615	1787
142	3		OCCUPIED			1229		1229		1229		1229
		1	EMPTY			1756		1756		1756	1756	0
			TOTAL	7200	0	2985		2985		2985	1756	1229
		2	EMFTY	7200	0	6872		6872		6872	6872	0
			TOTAL	7200		8101		8101		8101	6872	1229
		3	EMFTY	7200	7 *	1756		1756		1756	1756	0
			TOTAL	7200		2985		2985		2985	1756	1229
		4	EMFTY	7200	7	1756		1756		1756	1756	0
			TOTAL	7200		2985		2985		2985	1756	1229
		5	EMFTY	7200	7	5021		5021		5021	5021	0
			TOTAL	7200	*	6250		6250		6250	5021	1229
		6	EMPTY	7200	10	3234		3234		3234	3234	0
			TOTAL	7200		4463		4463		4463	3234	1229
143	3		OCCUPIED					0		0		1756
		1	EMPTY			1756		1756		1756	0	1756
			TOTAL	7200	0	1756		1756		1756	0	1756
		2	EMFTY	7200	0	6872		6872		6872	5994	878
			TOTAL	7200	*	6872		6872		6872	5994	878
		3	EMPTY	7200	4	5021		5021		5021	5021	0
			TOTAL	7200		5021		5021		5021	5021	0
		4	EMPTY	7200	5	1756		1756		1756	1756	0
			TOTAL	7200		1756		1756		1756	1756	0
		5	EMFTY	7200	5	5021		5021		5021	5021	0
			TOTAL	7200		5021		5021		5021	5021	0
		6	EMPTY	7200	6	5021		5021		5021	5021	0
			TOTAL	7200		5021		5021		5021	5021	0
144	3		OCCUPIED			748		748		748	0	748
		1	EMPTY			5116		5116		5116	5116	0
			TOTAL	7200	0 *	5864		5864		5864	5116	748
		2	EMFTY	7200	2	3638		3638		3638	0	3638
			TOTAL	7200		4386		4386		4386	5116	4386
		3	EMFTY	7200	2	5116		5116		5116	5116	0
			TOTAL	7200	*	5864		5864		5864	5116	748
		4	EMFTY	7200	4	5116		5116		5116	5116	0
			TOTAL	7200	*	5864		5864		5864	5116	748
		5	EMFTY	7200	6	3638		3638		3638	1851	1787
			TOTAL	7200		4386		4386		4386	1851	2535
		6	EMPTY	7200	6	3638		3638		3638	3638	0
			TOTAL	7200		4386		4386		4386	3638	748
145	3		OCCUPIED			866		866		866	481	385
		1	EMPTY			1756		1756		1756	1756	0
			TOTAL	7200	0	2622		2622		2622	2237	385
		2	EMPTY	7200	0	3234		3234		3234	3234	0
			TOTAL	7200		4100		4100		4100	3715	385

Fig. 5-7. Program BALE's Summary Table of Traffic Loadings of Occupied and Empty Vehicles

node, exceeded the node's capacity. This required rerunning Program BALO, while treating the irreducible empty vehicles as an ambient loading. When this was done some of the occupied vehicles were diverted elsewhere and the overloaded condition at that node disappeared. However, even then we were unable to balance the traffic, indicating that the method of selecting time penalties needs refinement.

5.7 CONTROLLING THE SUPPLY OF EMPTY VEHICLES AT RESIDENTIAL STATIONS

The nominal empty-vehicle dispatching plan determined by the methodology discussed in the preceding section is based on average flow rates and does not account for unpredicted variations from one workday to another or for random fluctuations during the rush hours.

We first encountered the impact of fluctuations in Secs. 3.2.2 and 3.2.4 when describing evening rush hour performance at an activity-center station. There we found that to keep passenger waiting times less than 1 minute on average, it was necessary to send approximately 10% excess empty vehicles to each station, the percentage being somewhat dependent on the size of the station. The excess empty vehicles were needed during periods of excessive demand or to make up for downward fluctuation in the normal supply of empty vehicles. But most of the time excess vehicles would be just that, in excess. At such times they could be made available to neighboring stations. Thus we conceived that during the evening peak there would be a circulating reservoir of excess empty vehicles available to any of the stations in the activity center that might need them. Because those stations generally would be clustered, it was practical to think of them as sharing the excess empty vehicle reservoir.[1]

---

[1] Let us describe one of several possible ways in which a circling reservoir might be managed. During the evening rush hours, the nominal dispatching plan would require that a certain fraction of the empty vehicles dispatched to the CBD not be directed to specific stations but to one of several "circulating loops" in the CBD, each labeled with a fictitious station number. As a vehicle so directed approaches each intersection on its route, the local computer at the intersection will look up the fictitious station number, just as though it were a real one, to find out whether the vehicle should go straight or turn. As the vehicle approaches the circulation loop the local computer at the intersection there will turn the vehicle onto the loop. All intersection computers along the loop will keep the vehicle following the loop indefinitely.

Each station computer controls the switch at the entrance to its station siding. Vehicles approaching the switch will be interrogated as to their destination. If they are directed to the station and if space is available in the input queue, the computer will switch them onto the siding. If circulating reservoirs are used, then each station siding will interpret any vehicle carrying a fictitious station number as one available for being switched onto the siding.

At the close of the evening rush hours, the central computer sends new routing tables to all local computers. The new tables will cause vehicles in circulation loops to be routed to designated car barns.

It is more difficult to share empty vehicles among residential stations during morning rush hours because the residential stations are more numerous than CBD stations and more separated, and because they have a lower, and hence less steady, passenger demand rate. Consequently, here we have postulated that each station would have a queue of empty vehicles adequate to average out most of the fluctuations in demand.

At the outset we shall assume that the residential stations are built in the configuration shown in Fig. 3-4 with separate entrance sections for empty and occupied vehicles. An occupied vehicle arriving during the morning rush hours can unload at the station platform without disturbing the queue of empty vehicles.

During the very early morning as the vehicles in the empty-vehicle queue are used, they will be replaced by a preplanned flow of empty vehicles that have been parked in the "car barn" overnight. Somewhat later other empty vehicles will be returning from their first trip(s), according to the nominal dispatching plan, and will arrive at fairly regular intervals. This describes the steady-state situation, but what about fluctuations? It is clear that fluctuations can be handled without excessive waiting times only if a supply of empty vehicles is kept on hand. When the supply starts to dwindle, i.e., when it drops below a predefined minimum level, it is necessary to send for additional empty vehicles. When the supply gets too large, i.e., when the number of empty vehicles available rises beyond a predefined maximum level, then steps should be taken to decrease the normal flow of empty vehicles to the station.

Car barns are distributed throughout the network and, for purposes of simulation, we assumed that when extra empty vehicles are needed they are ordered from one of these car barns (assumed to be 5 minutes away). Also, for purposes of simulation we assumed that when there are too many empty vehicles available, a cancellation order is sent to an empty-vehicle source station in the CBD or other activity center 10 minutes away. The cancellation order causes the source station to dispatch one empty vehicle to the car barn associated with the residential station rather than to the residential station as called for in the nominal dispatching plan. Thus, the effect of a cancellation is not "felt" at the suburban station until 10 minutes later.

The operations which we modeled for the residential station during the morning rush hours differ in some respects from the operations described for activity-center stations in Chapter 3. As in the activity-center station, there is an interval when vehicles are being deboarded and boarded, and there is an interval when vehicles are being advanced; no deboarding or boarding takes place during this latter interval. If during the deboarding/boarding cycle only one party is boarding, that party will board from the front berth; if two, the front two berths, etc. Any vehicle which has been boarded will move forward into the output queue during the next movement cycle; those at the platform that have not been boarded will move forward as far as possible in the platform area. Empty vehicles are not moved into the output queue (ejected) unless this is necessary to make room at the platform for an occupied vehicle. Empty vehicles are moved from the empty-vehicle queue to the platform only when there are an insufficient number of vehicles at the platform and in the occupied-vehicle input queue to serve the passengers waiting to board.

Occupied vehicles are assumed to arrive randomly, with their average rate of arrival being specified as one of the simulation inputs. In contrast, the prescheduled empty vehicles are assumed to arrive at regular intervals. This comes about because of the relatively steady flow through the activity-center station which is the source of these empty vehicles.

Operations were simulated for a larger-than-usual residential station which normally boards 4 parties/minute during the morning rush hours. Two different assumptions were examined regarding vehicle arrivals, one with 2 prescheduled empty vehicles and an average of 2 occupied vehicles arriving each minute, and the other with 4 prescheduled empty vehicles and no occupied vehicles. First we examined the operations during a normal day when an average of 4 parties/minute request service. For this case, the only problems in maintaining an adequate supply of empty vehicles are due to the random fluctuation in the demand for service and the random fluctuation in the arrival of occupied vehicles. But we also examined operations during abnormal days when the average demand is 3 or 5 parties/minute. It is assumed that no means is available for predicting in advance that abnormal demand would occur. Therefore, planned vehicle arrival is still based on the assumption that 4 vehicles/minute are needed. The only way the vehicles can be made to match the demand is to monitor the operation and, based on the observations, to order extra empty vehicles or cancel some of the prescheduled empty vehicles.

The number of berths at the platform and the number of slots in the input queues are specified as inputs to the simulation. After some experimentation we found that 3 berths at the platform, 3 slots in the occupied-vehicle input queue, and 15 slots in the empty-vehicle input queue would be sufficient.

An occupied vehicle that "misses" a station because the occupied vehicle queueing space is full, must "circle the block," which is assumed to take 6 minutes. With 3 slots in the occupied-vehicle input queue, this is an extremely rare event. Any empty vehicles that miss the station, as well as those that are ejected from the platform area to make room for occupied vehicles, are sent to the car barn or to other stations. In any event, it is assumed that each will waste 5 minutes in transit as a result of the miss or ejection.

Basically the type of control used is to compare empty vehicles "available" to the station with the minimum and maximum levels defined earlier. After some trial runs, minimum levels were set at 3 or 4, and maximum levels at 7, 8, or 9. Recalling that cancellations do not take place until the maximum is exceeded, but that the effect of a cancellation is not "felt" at the station for 10 minutes, it is necessary to have the total empty-vehicle queueing space substantially larger than the maximum level if a large number of empty vehicles are not to miss the station because the empty-vehicle queueing space is full. That is why we found it necessary to have about 15 slots in the empty-vehicle queueing space.

In computing the empty vehicles "available," the number of empty vehicles in the input queue should be decreased by the number which will have to be advanced to accommodate parties waiting to board. Adjustments must also be made to take into account the impact of past actions not yet reflected in the size of the empty-vehicle queue; e.g., extra vehicles ordered or cancellations made. If this were not done, the empty-vehicle control system could badly "overshoot" by continuously repeating an already adequate order.

The above procedure is all that is required for the "normal" day when 4 parties/minute wish to board. But, how about the day when 5 parties/minute wish to board? Since in this case it is necessary to order about one extra empty vehicle each minute from the car barn (more or less, depending on fluctuations), and since the car barn is assumed to be 5 minutes away, five of the "available" empty vehicles, as defined above, would be in transit. Therefore, an additional term is subtracted from the "available" vehicles, obtained by multiplying the transit time from the car barn (5 minutes) by the amount that the observed average demand rate for the day exceeds the anticipated demand rate. Likewise, if the observed average demand for the day is less than the anticipated demand, then an additional term is added to the "available" empty vehicles, obtained by multiplying the cancellation propagation time (10 minutes) by the amount that the observed average demand falls short of the anticipated demand.

The "observed average demand" is generally found by dividing the number of parties who have demanded service by the elapsed time. But, if the denominator is too small, the result is very "noisy"; i.e., fluctuations will be mistaken for large changes in average demand. For this reason the denominator is taken to be 30 minutes for the first 30 minutes of operation; after that, it is the total elapsed time.

The important measures of performance are the distribution of passenger waiting times and the increment of empty vehicles required beyond the fleet of empty vehicles, calculated in Sec. 5.6, that would be in transit according to the nominal dispatching plan. This increment consists of empty vehicles at the station and additional empty vehicles in transit. The ones at the station are those in the empty-vehicle input queue and those idle empty vehicles at the platform, the latter occurring when an occupied vehicle has unloaded and there are no passengers to board it. The additional vehicles in transit consist of extra empty vehicles in transit from the car barn to the station and empty vehicles on the way to the car barn after they "missed" the station or were ejected from the platform area.

Possibly the increment of empty vehicles should be reduced by those vehicles which would have been in transit from the activity center empty-vehicle source station in accordance with the nominal dispatching plan, but whose trip has been canceled. However, this would imply that those empty vehicles could effectively be used elsewhere. We have rather taken the more conservative point of view of not taking credit for these cancellations. Instead, we assume that when a cancellation takes place, the vehicle is dispatched to the local car barn. If the car barn is also 10 minutes away from the source station, then the number of vehicles in transit from the source station, whether to the residential station or the car barn, is not changed by cancellation.

The results of the simulation are shown in Fig. 5-8 for the "minimum" and "maximum" set at 3 and 9, respectively. Although these appear to be the best values, the results do not vary much with small changes in these numbers. It will be seen that 90% or more of the parties wait less than 1 minute to board, even when the service request rate is significantly larger than anticipated. Only 1% of the parties need to wait more than 2 minutes.

During normal days about 10 or 11 incremental inactive empty vehicles are required. How does this compare with the number of vehicles involved in revenue trips or returning empty in accordance with the nominal empty vehicle dispatching plan? Assume that during the morning rush the average trip is 10 mi traveled at an average speed of 30 mi/hr. Adding 2 minutes for detours and 1 minute at each station, the total PRT trip lasts 24 minutes. If half of the vehicles must be returned empty to some residential station, not the station they came from but a more convenient one, this brings the total time the average vehicle is involved to about 30 minutes per revenue trip. At 4 parties/minute departing from the residential station and with the average vehicle being involved for 30 minutes,

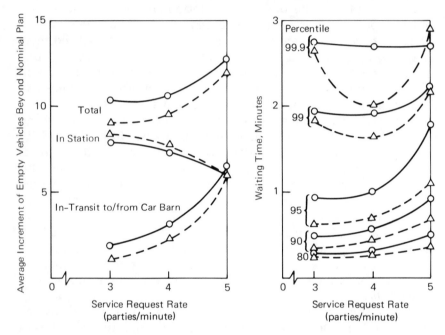

Fig. 5-8. Performance of Residential Station Under Closed-Loop Control of Empty Vehicles

120 vehicles are needed per station. Thus the 10 or 11 incremental vehicles represent an 8% or 9% increase over what would have been required if no attempt had been made to limit waiting times by maintaining an empty vehicle queue by a closed-loop control system.

The percentages would have been somewhat larger for a smaller, more typical, residential station. Offsetting this, it will be recalled that we made two conservative assumptions. First, we assumed that extra empty vehicles come from the car barn and that missed and ejected empty vehicles are sent to the car barn. In reality, the missed and ejected empty vehicles might be sent to a neighboring station so it would not have to order its needed extras from the car barn. Second, no credit was taken for cancellations. In practice the canceled vehicle might be sent directly to another residential station that is short on vehicles rather than first going to the car barn.

As best we can estimate, the cost of having closed-loop control of empty vehicles during the morning rush hours probably is no larger than 10% of the total vehicle fleet. This certainly is higher than the spare empty vehicles needed at activity center stations during the evening rush hours because of the more effective sharing among neighboring stations at that time.

The discussions relative to empty vehicle management are primarily to show that the problems are tractable, that waiting times can be kept very low, and that the cost in extra vehicles is reasonable. Certainly better, more sophisticated methods can be found, but they can only be studied quantitatively with a discrete event simulation of a very large network with many vehicles. Thus far no one has carried out such a simulation. The final system might even involve, in addition to a nominal dispatching plan derived by the methods of Sec. 5.6, a means for pre-emption where any vehicle may be "pulled off" the main line by a station more in need of it than the one to which the vehicle was originally dispatched. Subsequent dispatchings would then be modified to compensate.

Chapter 6
SAFETY AND EMERGENCY OPERATIONS

Harry Bernstein

6.1 INTRODUCTION

Since personal rapid transit could involve a very large number of vehicles operating under automatic control on the guideway network, it is necessary to minimize the probability of operational failure if dependable and safe service is to be provided. High reliability, i.e., a low failure rate, may be achieved by proper design of the PRT equipments and by utilizing carefully regulated checkout and maintenance procedures. In brief, the design and maintenance strategy we recommend is to achieve high reliability in mechanical and electromechanical components by minimizing the use of moving parts (e.g., by using a linear motor), by carefully selecting parts, by using redundancy where possible (e.g., in power shoes), by frequent inspection and preventive maintenance, and by replacing components before they wear out. Reliability in electronics is achieved by careful selection of components, by the ample use of redundancy, and by frequent checkout (probably daily) to replace failed units. Where there is redundancy, the failure of a unit will not lead to an operational failure, because the back-up unit would take over; only in the very rare event of two redundant units both failing in the short time period between equipment checkouts (e.g., in the same day) would there be an operational failure.

With this design and maintenance strategy, very high operational reliabilities can be achieved. Yet, it is impossible to achieve perfect reliability, and there will be operational failures. It is not the purpose of this chapter to discuss further how PRT systems can achieve high reliability or to quantize reliability values; these subjects will be treated in Chapter 8. Rather, this chapter will discuss design approaches and emergency procedures necessary to cope with those rare operational failures when they do occur. In addition there are other safety hazards, unrelated to equipment failure (e.g., a foreign object which falls or is placed on the guideway), which must also be considered in specifying system design and operational procedures. More particularly, we shall try to recommend design approaches and emergency procedures which not only will ensure a high degree of passenger safety but also will minimize service disruption.

Emergency operations and passenger safety issues can best be addressed by first defining the spectrum of hazardous situations and then indicating procedural and design responses thereto. Of course, the delineation of possible hazardous situations must be done in the context of a baseline system design and operating concept. The ensuing discussion presumes a PRT system operating under quasi-synchronous control and incorporating the following features:

a. wheeled support for the vehicles;

b. local computers for determining maneuver instructions to initialize position or to manage traffic at merges and intersections;

c. guideway-mounted electromagnetic switches under the control of the local computers;

d. on-board controls for maintaining position and velocity and for carrying out maneuver instructions; and

e. means for two-way communications between local control computers and the vehicles.

As the hazardous situations are discussed, and possible responses are presented, requirements for additional equipments will be identified as necessary to implement specific emergency strategies.

To create an exhaustive list of the types of failure which might occur it would first be necessary to have a candidate design. Then a failure-mode analysis would be made and the effect on system operations of each failure mode would be determined. The equipment would then be redesigned and the analysis repeated. Some of the more common types of emergency situations which might arise from such failures or from other hazardous conditions are listed in Fig. 6-1 and will be discussed at some length in this chapter.

The hazardous conditions listed in Fig. 6-1 might occur while vehicles are on straight sections of the guideway or on sections of the guideway in the vicinity of intersections, station sidings, or merge points. Some of the failure situations could arise from single-point operational failures, while others would only occur with simultaneous multiple failures (e.g., an inadvertent vehicle deceleration accompanied by the inability of the failed vehicle to communicate with local control computers). Each of these situations and the responses to them will be defined in more detail in succeeding sections of this chapter.

One dominant precept in our approach is to try to have sensing equipment which detects an operational malfunction as soon as possible. The anomalous behavior is reported to the nearest local

Inadvertent Vehicle Deceleration	Failed Vehicle Detects and Communicates	Pushable
		Not Pushable
	Failed Vehicle Uncommunicative	
Vehicle in Motion — Command Links Fail or Command not Properly Executed		
Local Computer, Central Computer, or Switch Fails		
Foreign Objects on Guideway		
Power Outage		

Fig. 6-1. Emergency Situations

computer which assesses the situation and orders the appropriate response. An example, first introduced in Chapter 4, is to have sensing equipment on each vehicle to detect and report anomalous deceleration. Actually, two methods might be used. The first might be to detect a position error or time-of-arrival error[1] larger than could be explained by wind gusts or system noise; this would be particularly useful in detecting the low-level deceleration which might occur as a result of the loss of power or malfunction in the motor or its control unit. A second method might use an accelerometer mounted to measure longitudinal acceleration; this would be particularly useful in rapidly detecting the large decelerations that might occur as a result of locking wheels or striking a foreign object. Because the accelerometer reading would also be affected by grade, some corrective measure would be required, such as feeding the accelerometer reading through a high-pass filter to filter out the slow changes. Alternatively, the effect of grade could be subtracted out.

Anomalous behavior reported to the local computer would probably be communicated by two independent means or at least along two channels to ensure effective communication.

Inadvertent deceleration might be due to a loss of power. Therefore, it is important that the vehicle have enough battery power on board to keep the vehicle's electronic sensing, computing, and communications equipment operating throughout the emergency. We shall see later that it is also advisable to have sufficient battery power for a limited propulsion capability following an extensive power failure.

[1] In the Aerospace design this is the cumulative pulse-count error discussed in Sec. 4.6.7.

6.2 INADVERTENT VEHICLE DECELERATION — FAILED VEHICLE PUSHABLE

The first failure situation listed in Fig. 6-1 is one in which a vehicle is inadvertently decelerating and coasting to a stop, the coasting implying that the failed vehicle is capable of being pushed by the succeeding vehicle if necessary. This situation is generally characterized by small deceleration rates on the part of the failed vehicle, generally less than 0.1 g, the decelerating forces being those of rolling friction and aerodynamic drag. This situation is more likely than one where the vehicle is not pushable, since almost all electrical and electronic failures, as well as many mechanical failures, would leave the vehicle capable of being pushed.

In actual operation the local computer would make the determination as to whether the failed vehicle was pushable. This decision could be made on the basis of the deceleration rate reported by the failing vehicle, accompanied, perhaps, by other diagnostic information such as whether the wheels were still rotating.

6.2.1 Response Strategy

It is, in fact, desirable to have the succeeding vehicle push the failed vehicle after making a soft engagement with it, in order to avoid having to stop traffic on the line and disrupt service. Rather than having the failed vehicle pushed onto a station siding and disrupting service at that station, it may be better to distribute emergency sidings throughout the guideway network, possibly adjacent to some of the station sidings or the vehicle storage facilities. A spare vehicle could be stored at each of these sidings so that any passengers in the failed vehicle could transfer to the spare and continue their trip. Two possible configurations for such an emergency siding are shown in Fig. 6-2.

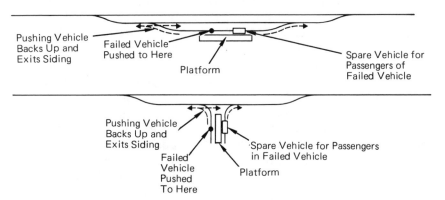

Fig. 6-2. Two Possible Configurations for Emergency Siding

Consider the implementation of such a car-pushing strategy, first assuming that the failed vehicle and succeeding vehicles are in line, i.e., on the same guideway. If the separation of these vehicles is known prior to the failure, and if the magnitude of the failing vehicle's deceleration is known, then it is possible to define a maneuver for the succeeding vehicle to undergo in making a soft engagement with the failed vehicle. After effecting contact, the pushing vehicle will accelerate up to line speed. Since the local computer can predict the distance lost by the pushing vehicle (relative to its continuing at line velocity) in maneuvering for the soft engagement and subsequent reacceleration, the computer can determine what slot-slipping maneuvers must be carried out by vehicles behind the pushing vehicle. Thus, to implement this strategy, the local computer must know not only the deceleration rate of the failing vehicle, but also the location of the upstream vehicles. If a vehicle inadvertently decelerates shortly after it enters the jurisdictional domain of a local computer, that computer must transmit to the computer immediately upstream the data on the action taken by the vehicle just inside its domain, so that the upstream neighbor can decide on the necessary action for the next vehicle.

The situation is further compounded if it is assumed that the inadvertent vehicle deceleration starts to take place when the failed vehicle is approaching a merge point, as shown in Fig. 6-3. Obviously, if the vehicle which would be following the failed vehicle in the soon-to-be-merged stream was coming from the same branch of the merge (Case B), then the situation is similar to the in-line case (Case A); i.e., the following vehicle can push the failed vehicle and succeeding vehicles can be issued slot-slipping instructions as necessary.

If, however, the vehicle which would be following the failed vehicle is coming from the opposite branch of the merge (Case C), then the particular point of failure onset becomes critical in determining failure response. There are three subcases to consider.

In the first subcase (C-1), failure onset is such that the failed vehicle will travel sufficiently far into the merge region to permit its rear bumper to be engaged by the front bumper of the following vehicle, which is coming from the opposite branch of the merge. In this case, the normal pushing strategy may be employed.

In the second subcase (C-2), failure onset is such that the failed vehicle would come to rest upstream and clear of the merge region. Here, vehicles approaching from the opposite branch of the merge may proceed without interruption. When space becomes available, the next vehicle approaching on the same branch of the merge as the failed vehicle may then softly engage the failed vehicle and push it.

In the third subcase (C-3), failure onset is such that the failed

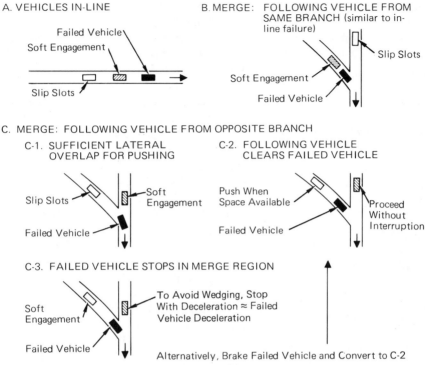

Fig. 6-3. Emergency Strategy — Failed Vehicle Communicative

vehicle would come to rest partially within the merge region. In this case it would be necessary to stop the vehicles approaching from the other branch until a vehicle approaching from the same branch could engage with and push the failed vehicle. Alternatively, it might be possible to apply braking to the failed vehicle, thus increasing its deceleration rate and bringing it to a stop upstream and clear of the merge region. The result now is identical to subcase C-2 described above.

6.2.2 Response Kinematics

The programming of a soft engagement between the pushing and failed vehicles involves several interrelated parameters. For a given initial separation of the vehicles (S) and failed vehicle deceleration (a_F), the amount of braking deceleration to be applied by the pushing vehicle (a_B) in maneuvering to engage is a function of the delay time for brake application (τ) and the permissible relative velocity (ΔV) at the instant of engagement. (For the sake of simplicity, infinite jerk rates will be assumed in this discussion, although in reality a large but finite jerk would be applied. The effect of jerking for a time T_{jerk} is to augment τ by $1/2\, T_{jerk}$.) Thus, for some allowable engagement ΔV (a function of the type of bumpers put on the vehicles), the required braking deceleration of the pushing vehicle becomes a function of the delay time between failure onset and brake applications. There is, of course, a minimum achievable value of this delay time, τ_{min}, which is of the order of 0.1 to 0.2 sec.

First consider what happens when the ΔV allowable equals zero. Figure 6-4 illustrates a spectrum of possible kinematic situations. Each diagram plots the velocity-versus-time history for both the failing and the pushing vehicle. The shaded areas represent the decrease in vehicle separation from the onset of failure. Since the vehicles softly engage ($\Delta V = 0$), the total shaded area in each diagram represents the initial separation distance, S. Examining the diagram for Case A, which assumes that the braking deceleration of the pushing vehicle is equal to the deceleration rate of the failed vehicle, it is clear that engagement cannot take place until the vehicles have come to rest. In this case, if the distance between the vehicles is to be closed, the pushing vehicle must delay the onset of its deceleration until $\tau = S/V_o$; i.e., until it arrives at the point on the guideway where the failed vehicle started its deceleration. Since there is a minimum realizable delay, τ_{min}, there is a minimum separation ($S_{min} = V_o \tau_{min}$) for which $\Delta V = 0$ may be achieved with $a_B = a_F$.

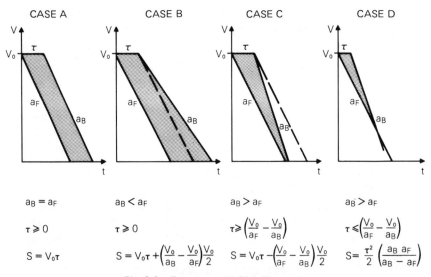

$$a_B = a_F$$
$$\tau \geq 0$$
$$S = V_o \tau$$

$$a_B < a_F$$
$$\tau \geq 0$$
$$S = V_o \tau + \left(\frac{V_o}{a_B} - \frac{V_o}{a_F} \right) \frac{V_o}{2}$$

$$a_B > a_F$$
$$\tau \geq \left(\frac{V_o}{a_F} - \frac{V_o}{a_B} \right)$$
$$S = V_o \tau - \left(\frac{V_o}{a_F} - \frac{V_o}{a_B} \right) \frac{V_o}{2}$$

$$a_B > a_F$$
$$\tau \leq \left(\frac{V_o}{a_F} - \frac{V_o}{a_B} \right)$$
$$S = \frac{\tau^2}{2} \left(\frac{a_B \, a_F}{a_B - a_F} \right)$$

Fig. 6-4. Emergency Braking Kinematics

For values of $S > S_{min}$, it may be desirable to decelerate the pushing vehicle at a lower rate. This would lessen any passenger discomfort in that vehicle, though the distance lost by the vehicle during the engagement maneuver, and hence the number of succeeding vehicles which would have to slip slots, would be increased. To accomplish this, brake application could be made at $t = \tau_{min}$, with $a_B < a_F$, and with a_B appropriately chosen to correspond to the initial separation distance S given by the formula for S appearing under Case B of Fig. 6-4. Again, the failed vehicle will be at rest at the time of the soft engagement.

Where initial separation distances are very short, or where the failing vehicle is decelerating slowly and there is a desire to minimize distance lost by the pushing vehicle, the use of a braking deceleration, a_B, greater than the failed vehicle deceleration, a_F, is indicated (Case C and Case D of Fig. 6-4). For Case C no engagement takes place until the failed vehicle is at rest. Case D corresponds to the engagement taking place before the failed vehicle comes to rest.

One tradeoff has already been identified, namely the choice between earliest possible brake application at lower deceleration values (thus maximizing distance lost), or delayed application of maximum braking to minimize distance lost. The kinematics of this tradeoff are depicted on Fig. 6-5, the diagram therein assuming a

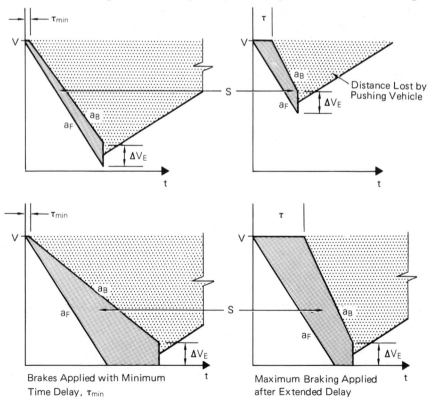

Fig. 6-5. Car-Pushing Strategies

nonzero value of engagement velocity, ΔV_E. It will be noted that just after engagement the two vehicles have a velocity which is the average of their two velocities just before engagement. This assumes that the two vehicles have equal mass. They then reaccelerate together. The upper two diagrams of Fig. 6-5 are drawn for the same initial separation, S (i.e., the same shaded area). They illustrate the much larger distance (the dotted area) lost by the pushing vehicle when braking is not delayed. The lower two diagrams are for a larger value of S where the failing vehicle comes to a complete stop. The effect is the same; less distance is lost by the pushing vehicle when braking is delayed and then maximum braking deceleration is used. The percentage difference in distance lost is less pronounced in this case because the larger part of the distance lost occurs during the reacceleration up to line speed, which is independent of the braking strategy.

The next three figures will quantize the tradeoff illustrated in Fig. 6-5. When the strategy of earliest possible brake application is to be used, the required braking deceleration of the pushing vehicle can be found from Fig. 6-6 for failed vehicle decelerations (a_F) of 0.1 g and 0.25 g. The solid curves are for the engagement velocity $\Delta V_E = 0$ and the dashed curves for $\Delta V_E = 10$ ft/sec. It will be noted that for $\Delta V_E = 0$, the braking deceleration exceeds the deceleration of the failed vehicle only for separation of less than $V_o\tau$ (12 ft in the example). At larger initial separations, the required braking deceleration decreases. Figure 6-6 also shows that still lower braking decel-

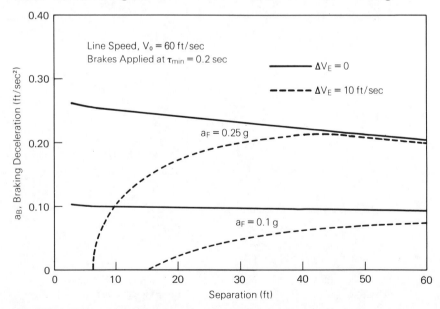

Fig. 6-6. Required Braking Deceleration When Earliest Possible Brake Application is Used

eration can be used if a 10-ft/sec ΔV_E is acceptable for the engagement. In fact, for an initial separation of 5 ft, the brakes need not be applied at all and the vehicles would engage at only 9.0 ft/sec if the failed vehicle decelerates at 0.25 g; they would engage at 5.7 ft/sec with the failed vehicle decelerating at 0.1 g. Altogether, the braking levels indicated by Fig. 6-6 are very low, suggesting that earliest possible brake application is not necessary for comfort.

The effect of braking strategy on distance lost by the pushing vehicle is illustrated in Fig. 6-7 for a failed vehicle deceleration (a_F) of 0.1 g and in Fig. 6-8 for 0.25 g. The figures plot the distance lost as a function of the initial separation between vehicles. The solid curves represent a strategy of starting to brake as soon as possible (assumed to be at τ = 0.2 sec), thereby minimizing the required braking deceleration. The dashed curves represent a strategy of delaying braking and then applying 0.5 g of braking deceleration. Two values of the engagement speed, ΔV_E, are examined — zero and 10 ft/sec.

It will be noted that delaying braking causes a marked reduction of distance lost. For example, referring to Fig. 6-7, for ΔV_E = 0 and with an initial separation of 5 ft, the pushing vehicle will lose 580 ft if it starts to brake after 0.2 sec, but it will lose only 4.4 ft if it delays and then uses a 0.5 g braking level. The reader will, of course,

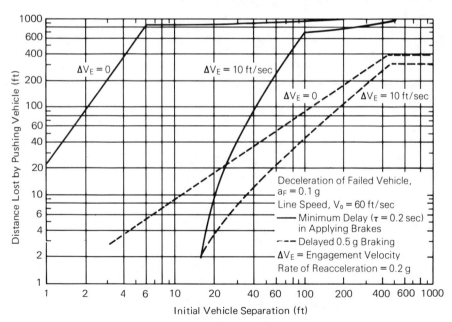

Fig. 6-7. Effects of Braking Strategy and Allowed Engagement Velocity on Distance Lost by Pushing Vehicle When Failed Vehicle Deceleration is 0.1 g

recognize that any strategy between these two extremes may be used to obtain a compromise between low braking deceleration and low values of distance lost.

Figures 6-7 and 6-8 also illustrate the very significant reduction of distance lost which results from allowing a nonzero engagement velocity, ΔV_E. A small engagement velocity is easily absorbed by a compressible bumper at the front of each vehicle. For example, with a 10 ft/sec relative velocity at impact and with a bumper having a 1.25 ft stroke, the passengers would feel only an average 0.62 g deceleration for 0.25 sec during bumper compression[2] (Table 6-1 of Sec. 6.7).

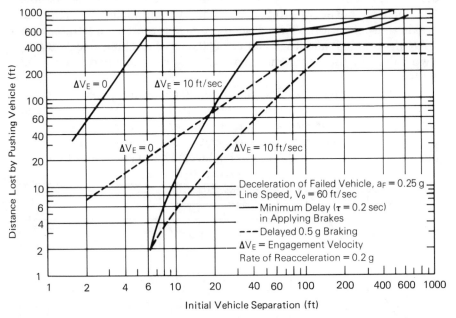

Fig. 6-8. Effects of Braking Strategy and Allowed Engagement Velocity on Distance Lost by Pushing Vehicle When Failed Vehicle Deceleration is 0.25 g

[2] It is convenient to examine the kinematics from the frame of an observer traveling at the average speed of the two vehicles just before they collide (the center-of-gravity frame). With respect to this frame, the vehicles are each traveling at a speed of $1/2 \Delta V_E$ in opposite directions. After collision, each has come to rest in the center-of-gravity frame, the deceleration of each having taken place over a distance equal to one-half the length of the bumper stroke, L_s, assuming only front bumpers are compressible. The acceleration felt at the passenger's seat is then

$$a_s = (1/2 \, \Delta V_E)^2 \, / \, 2 \, (1/2 \, L_s) = (\Delta V_E)^2 \, / 4 \, L_s.$$

Since in the example $\Delta V_E = 10$ ft/sec and $L_s = 1.25$ ft, $a_s = 20$ ft/sec$^2 = 0.62$ g. The duration is the speed lost (in the center-of-gravity frame) divided by the deceleration; i.e., 5.0 ft/sec divided by 20 ft/sec^2.

The distance lost by the pushing vehicle in maneuvering to make the soft engagement and in its subsequent reacceleration to line velocity must be accommodated by the creation of an appropriate number of vacant slots behind the original slot position of the pushing vehicle, if those vacant slots do not already exist in that place. The number (N) of such required vacant slots is simply the distance lost divided by 15, the nominal slot length in feet. The creation of these vacant slots is accomplished by the local computer's issuance of appropriate slot-slipping maneuver commands to succeeding vehicles to shift them rearward and thus effectively bring forward the next N gaps in the vehicle stream. As pointed out earlier, it may be necessary in some circumstances to pass information back to an upstream computer which would control some of the slot-slipping maneuvers.

6.3   INADVERTENT VEHICLE DECELERATION — FAILED VEHICLE NOT PUSHABLE

While highly improbable, some modes of failure would render a vehicle not pushable. For example, an axle could break or the wheel bearings could lock. Such failures would be characterized by higher deceleration rates on the part of the failed vehicle, since the vehicle would essentially be skidding to a stop. The specific deceleration rate would be a function of the type of failure, the types of guideway and wheel surfaces, their condition, and environmental factors (i.e., the presence of rain, snow, or ice). For example, for normal dry concrete guideway surface and rubber tires, a locked-wheel skidding deceleration rate of approximately 0.7 g would be anticipated.

6.3.1   Response Strategy

If the failed vehicle cannot be pushed, succeeding vehicles on the line, including those already on the turn ramps about to enter the affected line, must be brought to a stop. Simultaneously, it might be necessary for the local computers to set intersection switches so that no additional vehicles are allowed onto turn ramps leading to the affected line. To cope with this situation any local computer may have to communicate with computers controlling upstream network elements, since the stoppage will likely propagate beyond the boundaries of a single local computer control zone. The intersection computers would cause as many of the succeeding vehicles as possible to transfer from the affected line to crossing lines so that these vehicles would not have to be stopped. Still, some number of succeeding vehicles will be brought to a stop.

In bringing these vehicles to a stop, the local computer could take advantage of the cumulative separation and gap distances between the failed vehicle and any succeeding vehicles. The result of such an approach would be that vehicles further back in the stream could apply a lesser amount of braking deceleration in coming to a stop. The local computer can determine the required braking deceleration for each succeeding vehicle, given the deceleration rate of the failed vehicle, the number of slots between the failed vehicle and the subject vehicle, the number of those slots which are unoccupied, and the delay time for brake application.

Once the succeeding vehicles have stopped, they will have to be cleared from the affected line by allowing them to start up and transfer onto crossing lines as slot spaces become available. Referring to the network diagram in Fig. 6-9, where a main line is blocked by a failed vehicle (or other obstruction) at A, the following four steps would be involved in clearing the operable vehicles:

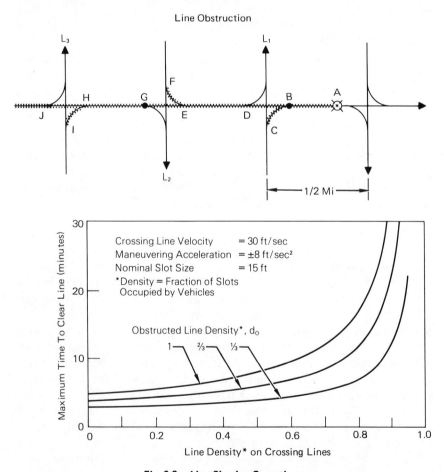

Fig. 6-9. Line Clearing Operations

Step 1. Merge vehicles from *DEG* and turn ramp *FE* onto line L_1, merge vehicles from *GHJ* and turn ramp *HI* onto line L_2, etc.

Step 2. Back-up vehicles from *DBA* on main line so that they are all upstream of point *D*.

Step 3. Advance vehicles from turn ramp *BC*, if possible, or a few at a time, if necessary, and back them up to a point upstream of point *D*. (Can overlap Step 2.)

Step 4. Merge the backed-up vehicles onto line L_1 (or partly onto line L_2, if appropriate).

The graph in Fig. 6-9 presents the time required for line-clearing operations as a function of line densities for an assumed 1/2-mile spacing of the crossing lines. Over the range of reasonable line densities, line-clearing operations would require from 5 to 10 minutes.

The failed vehicle itself must be cleared from the guideway before operations can be reinstated on the affected link. Hopefully the guideway and guideway-mounted equipment will not be damaged, though they also may require some repair. Removal of the failed vehicle may necessitate the use of a street-driven crane (or perhaps a guideway-operable crane vehicle).

6.3.2 Response Kinematics

Assume that the succeeding vehicle is to be stopped just short of bumping the failed vehicle. Figure 6-10 plots the required vehicle separation (tail-to-nose), S, as a function of reaction time (τ_{min}) for brake application in the succeeding vehicle. Plots are presented

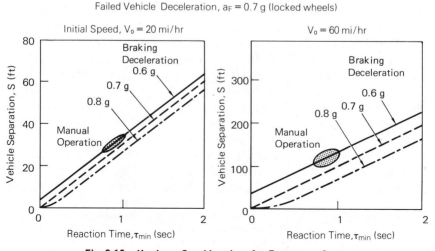

Fig. 6-10. Headway Considerations for Emergency Stop

for line speeds of 20 and 60 mi/hr, both assuming a failed vehicle deceleration of 0.7 g, as might occur if its wheels were locked. Each plot has three curves corresponding to different braking decelerations ranging from 0.6 g (14% lower than the failed vehicle deceleration) to 0.8 g (14% higher).[3]

Imagine for the moment that the vehicles were manually operated, as are automobiles. In this case, reaction times would be on the order of 0.75 to 1 sec. Imagine further that the tires of the succeeding vehicle were slightly worn so that only 0.6 g of braking deceleration could be developed. The shaded areas reflect these assumptions and indicate required separations of 33 ft and 110 ft for speeds of 20 mi/hr and 60 mi/hr, respectively. If one further assumes that these manually-operated vehicles were, in fact, 18-ft-long auto-mobiles, then these required separations equate to approximately one vehicle length for each 10 mi/hr of speed. This is the so-called safe-driving rule for automobiles. Note that it is not predicated on "brick wall" stops of the automobile ahead. Note further that at 60 mi/hr the required separation plus the automobile length yields a headway of 1.45 sec.

Clearly, as seen from Fig. 6-10, the reduced reaction times attainable with automatic control are necessary for achieving emer-gency stopping capabilities commensurate with PRT vehicle separa-tions as small as 5 ft. But reduced reaction times are not in themselves sufficient. Note that for a reaction time of zero, a separation of approximately 40 ft is required for a 0.6-g braking capability and a line speed of 60 mi/hr. However, if small reaction times, on the order of 0.1 to 0.2 sec, can be combined with a braking deceleration slightly (about 10 to 15%) higher than the failed-vehicle deceleration, then separations can be quite small (3.6 ft for τ = 0.2 sec; 0.9 ft for τ = 0.1 sec). The question is how to achieve such braking deceleration if only 0.7 g is attainable through traction.

One possible answer is to make the braking system independent of traction forces. This can be accomplished by using a linear electric motor for both propulsion and braking. The particular type of motor to be used must be capable of rapidly developing the necessary braking forces, and to do so in a reliable and controlled manner. This approach will be discussed further in Chapter 7 where the concept of a pulsed d.c. linear electric motor having some particu-larly appropriate features for a PRT application will be described.

Making the PRT propulsion and braking function independent

---

[3] These curves plot the equations derived in Fig. 6-4. The straight line for 0.7 g braking deceleration is derived under Case A of Fig. 6-4. The straight line for 0.6 g is under Case B. The straight-line portion for 0.8 g is derived under Case C and the parabolic portion for small τ_{min} is derived under Case D.

of traction has an impact on the design of the guideway and wheel surfaces. Since the ability to produce traction forces is no longer a paramount consideration, the significant design parameters become those associated with achieving minimum noise and minimum wear. This suggests a smooth guideway surface and a tire designed with a low coefficient of sliding friction. Then if a vehicle's wheels were locked, it would slide a longer distance and perhaps the braking system could be designed for somewhat less than the nominal 0.8-g emergency braking level indicated by Fig. 6-10 — perhaps no more than 0.5 g would be required.

It is possible to consider other approaches than the use of linear electric motors for propulsion and braking. For example, the necessary braking force could be achieved by clamping the guideway to effectively increase the normal force and hence the friction forces. This is the method used in Japan's CVS for emergency braking, producing a deceleration level of 2 g. However, with this approach, it is not easy to adjust the deceleration to match the needs of any particular situation.

Alternatively, wheel traction could be relied upon with the realization that the succeeding vehicle might bump the failed vehicle and some ΔV would have to be absorbed. Let us assume that after 0.2 sec the succeeding vehicle applies traction brakes to effect a deceleration of 0.7 g, the value previously assumed as the deceleration rate of the failed vehicle with locked wheels. During the delay period the failed vehicle's speed would have decreased by 4.5 ft/sec. This small relative velocity would persist while the two vehicles were decelerating at the same rate, and hence would be the ΔV to be absorbed at impact. But, as pointed out in Sec. 4.2, a problem arises if the succeeding vehicle has smooth tires and can only develop a braking deceleration of 0.6 g. Then, if the line speed is at least 75 ft/sec and the vehicles are 30 ft apart, the impact velocity would be 14.5 ft/sec.

If care were taken to keep tires and brakes in good condition, then relying on traction and the ability to absorb a small ΔV would seem to be a reasonable approach. Thus, this failure situation cannot be construed as demanding a linear motor design. However, the cumulative effect of considering braking controllability, motor wear, reliability, the influence of locally wet or icy guideways, differences in tire wear between vehicles, noise, rate of wheel and guideway surface wear, and other factors indicates that a linear motor is desirable.

6.4 INADVERTENT VEHICLE DECELERATION — FAILED VEHICLE UNCOMMUNICATIVE

It has been postulated in the preceding sections that there be means on board each vehicle for detecting and measuring the magnitude of inadvertent decelerations, and for communicating this information to the local control computer. Earlier we pointed out that, for the enhancement of safety, these means should be redundant. We also suggested that since the cause of inadvertent deceleration could be loss of ability to draw electrical power from the guideway, the vehicle should contain on-board battery power to keep the vehicle's control and communications equipments operational. Thus, in almost all cases, the vehicle will be capable of properly reporting an inadvertent deceleration.

This section deals, however, with a multiple failure situation in which there is loss of the vehicle's sensing and/or communications capability simultaneously with the onset of an inadvertent deceleration.

6.4.1   Response Strategy

There are two possible responses to a multiple failure situation of this type. In the first of these, vehicle sensors can be uniformly spaced along the guideway. When a vehicle is detected by a sensor, the next sensor is alerted to expect that vehicle at a time T later, where T is the time of passage between sensors for vehicles traveling at the characteristic line speed. If that next sensor does not detect the vehicle in a time T plus some small allowable fraction of T, then the vehicle would be presumed to have started to decelerate at some point between the sensor positions.[4] Since it is not known when the deceleration started, there is insufficient information to discriminate between pushable and nonpushable failures; consequently, it must be prudently assumed that the failed vehicle is not pushable (decelerating at approximately 0.7 g) and the succeeding vehicles must be stopped. Since warning of the inadvertent deceleration is delayed in this case from when the warning would have occurred had the failing vehicle been able to communicate, the succeeding vehicle may bump the failed vehicle if, for example, the succeeding vehicle is in the next slot position and the failed vehicle is truly in a skidding deceleration.

The alternative approach is to provide no additional equipment to cope with this failure scenario, but rather to design to minimize the probability of such multiple failures, and in the rare event of their occurrence, to allow the vehicles to collide. With proper design of energy absorption devices and passenger restraints, it will still be possible to avoid passenger injuries, as will be discussed in Sec. 6.7.

---

[4]   In maneuver regions, this simple procedure would be ineffective since different vehicles will be following different velocity-distance profiles in such regions. Hence, within maneuver regions a modified concept for sensor placement and data processing would be necessary, or such regions could be left without these sensors.

The choice between these alternatives must be based on further analyses which consider failure probabilities, the false alarm rate of the guideway-mounted vehicle sensors (and associated unwarranted service disruptions), costs, etc.

6.4.2 Response Kinematics

Assume that the concept of uniformly-spaced guideway-mounted vehicle sensors is to be used. T is the time of passage between sensors for vehicles traveling at the characteristic line speed, V_o.

A sensor will, of course, not sense a whole vehicle but rather some clearly defined fiducial mark on a vehicle. Although the fiducial mark of the vehicle may be expected at a sensor at a particular time, it may appear to be slightly displaced at that time either because of errors in the sensing mechanism or because the vehicle has been affected by wind gusts or other disturbances. Therefore, no action should be taken unless there is a time error greater than some threshold error, ΔT. Alternatively, this may be thought of as a displacement threshold error, $\Delta X = V_o \ \Delta T$.

Figure 6-11 illustrates the sensor positions and indicates a critical point P upstream from sensor B. The position of P depends on the failed vehicle deceleration, a_F. The normal time of transit from P to B is denoted by t_c, which also depends on a_F. Any failures downstream from P, leading to a deceleration a_F, will not be detectable at B because the distance lost would be less than ΔX (i.e., the time lost less than ΔT). Failures upstream of P, leading to a deceleration a_F, would be detectable. For a failure at P, the distance lost in the time t_c would be exactly ΔX; i.e.,

$$\frac{1}{2} a_F \ t_c^2 = \Delta X \ . \tag{6.1}$$

Let us consider a numerical example where the displacement threshold, ΔX, is 0.5 ft. Consider the case where the failure involves locked

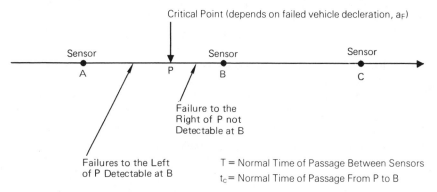

Fig. 6-11. Guideway Sensors for Use When Failing Vehicle Uncommunicative

wheels leading to a skidding deceleration of 0.7 g (22.5 ft/sec^2). Then, from Eq. (6.1), t_c = 0.21 sec.

Clearly, the worst case is where the locked-wheel failure takes place just downstream of P. Then it will not be detected until the vehicle is due at sensor C (Fig. 6-11), a time approximately t_c + T after the locking of wheels. Then the following vehicle is notified to stop, but there is an additional effective delay of τ_{brake} for it to apply its brakes (including one-half the jerk period). The total delay, τ, from the locking of wheels on the failed vehicle to the application of brakes in the succeeding vehicle is given by

$$\tau = t_c + T + \tau_{brake} \qquad (6.2)$$

The velocity lost by the failed vehicle in the time τ is $\Delta V = a_F \tau$ and the distance lost is $1/2\, a_F \tau^2$.

Again let us illustrate by a numerical example. Assume that a_F = 0.7 g (22.5 ft/sec^2), that τ_{brake} = 0.2 sec and, as calculated above, that t_c = 0.21 sec. If we take T = 0.92 sec, then τ = 1.33 sec, ΔV = 30 ft/sec, and the distance lost = 20 ft. Thus, the worst case would occur when 10-ft long vehicles were in 15-ft slots with one vacant slot between them, for they would have a 20-ft separation between them. If the lead vehicle instantaneously locked its wheels just after passing the critical point P in Fig. 6-11, and was also unable to communicate to the local computer, then the vehicles would collide with a relative velocity of 30 ft/sec. The ability to protect passengers under these conditions is discussed in Sec. 6.7.

If in the above example the two vehicles were in adjacent slots, then they would have only a 5-ft separation and the vehicles would collide 0.67 sec ($t = \sqrt{2S/a_F}$) after the onset of the failure (i.e., before being detected by the wayside sensors) and with a relative velocity of 15 ft/sec ($\Delta V = \sqrt{2\, a_F\, S}$).

If, on the other hand, the vehicles are initially separated by more than $1/2\, a_F \tau^2$ (in the example, 20 ft) and if the following vehicle applies a braking deceleration at least as great as the deceleration of the failed vehicle, then the impact velocity cannot get larger than $a_F \tau$ (in the example, 30 ft/sec). If the vehicles have not yet collided when the failed vehicle comes to rest, then the relative velocity at impact is definitely less than $a_F \tau$.

Now let us examine the effect of a 0.92-sec sensor spacing when the failed vehicle decelerates at only 0.1 g (3.2 ft/sec^2), which although rare is certainly more probable than the 0.7 g assumed above. Again taking ΔX = 0.5 ft, Eq. (6.1) yields

$$t_c = \sqrt{\frac{2(\Delta X)}{a_F}} = \sqrt{\frac{2(0.5)}{3.2}} = 0.56 \text{ sec.}$$

The total delay can be as long as

$$\tau = t_c + T + \tau_{brake} = 0.56 \text{ sec} + 0.92 \text{ sec} + 0.2 \text{ sec} = 1.68 \text{ sec}.$$

The maximum relative velocity at collision is then

$$\Delta V = a_F \tau = 3.2 \times 1.68 = 5.4 \text{ ft/sec}.$$

The choice of a 0.92-sec sensor spacing seems reasonable since only in the extremely rare event of a nonpushable failure (skidding deceleration) unreportable by the vehicle could a ΔV of 30 ft/sec at collision occur, and this only for certain initial spacings. (As will be discussed in Sec. 6.7, this ΔV can be absorbed in a manner which avoids passenger injury.) For the more probable, yet still rare, cases of a pushable failure unreportable by the vehicle, ΔV's would not exceed about 5 ft/sec.

Again, however, we should like to remind the reader that with the careful selection of components, an ample use of redundancy, and a rigorous maintenance program, the possibility is extremely remote that simultaneous failures could lead to inadvertent deceleration and at the same time the inability of the failing vehicle to communicate. By using wayside sensors as a further "back-up," false alarms will be introduced which will lead to unnecessary stopping of traffic. The final decision on using a wayside sensor back-up for any particular system design must rest on detailed analysis of cost and of the frequency of both types of events — false alarms as well as the true cases of a rapidly decelerating uncommunicative vehicle.

6.5 VEHICLE IN MOTION — COMMAND LINKS FAIL OR COMMAND NOT PROPERLY EXECUTED

In a PRT network operating under quasi-synchronous control, communications are generally between the local control computers and the vehicles within their control zones. Two-way communications are needed so that, for example, maneuver commands can be issued to the vehicles and the vehicles may report the onset of inadvertent decelerations. For normal operations communications could occur at predefined points on the guideway; e.g., just upstream of maneuver regions and at the beginning of constant speed segments of the guideway. Emergency considerations, however, demand that communications to or from the vehicle can take place at any position on the guideway.

As stated previously, it is desirable that there be redundant paths for communications between the local computer and the vehicles to minimize the probability of being unable to send commands or receive status messages. Still there is a finite probability of being unable to send commands to a vehicle in motion either due to failure of communications receivers aboard a particular vehicle or failure of wayside equipment (which would mean the inability to command a number of vehicles).

It seems appropriate to require each vehicle to repeat commands which are addressed to it and have been received. Such a procedure would verify reception and allow a command with a random transmission error to be corrected. It would also facilitate discrimination between failures of vehicle-borne communications equipment (only one vehicle would not be repeating or would be erroneously repeating commands addressed to it) and failures in wayside equipment or communications channels (many vehicles would not be repeating commands).

The inability to command a vehicle in motion is particularly critical at certain points of a network; namely, those points where vehicles might normally receive maneuver, acceleration, or deceleration commands. The following subsections will identify these critical situations and will discuss appropriate design and procedural responses.

Equally serious is the case where a vehicle receives a command, repeats it properly, but then fails to execute the command or executes the wrong maneuver. These situations will also be dealt with in the following subsections.

6.5.1 Inability to Command Intersection or Merge Maneuvers for a Single Vehicle

The inability to command a vehicle to maneuver in an intersection or merge maneuver zone (or the improper execution by a vehicle of a properly commanded maneuver) would cause that vehicle to be in a slot other than that required. There are two general subcases.

In the first, the subject vehicle is essentially alone on its line but should maneuver to make room for a vehicle merging into its space on the line. Failure to do so could cause a merge collision. To preclude such an eventuality, guideway-mounted vehicle sensors could be placed at the end of the maneuver region on the one line and at a corresponding distance measured upstream from the merge point along the merging line. Simultaneous passage of both of the sensors by the two vehicles would indicate a potential merge collision. If this occurs, a stop command is sent to the vehicle in conflict with the improperly functioning vehicle, and the uncommandable (or misbehaving) vehicle is allowed to proceed for subsequent routing to and stopping on an emergency siding.[5]

---

[5] The uncommandable vehicle would be given no slot slipping or advancing maneuvers on the way to the emergency siding; conflicting vehicles would maneuver to make way for it. Routing can be accomplished without commands to the vehicle since switches are under the direct control of the local computer. Stopping would be handled by the methods discussed in Sec. 6.5.3.

In the second situation, the improperly functioning vehicle could be in the vicinity of other vehicles on the same line which were maneuvering towards it. Since the subject vehicle would not be maneuvering properly, the neighboring vehicles could bump it. This in and of itself is not a severe situation since the relative velocity at time of bumping could be absorbed. Of concern, however, is the possibility that the malfunctioning vehicle will preclude adjacent vehicles from maneuvering to make room for a vehicle about to merge onto the line. Should this be the case, however, the vehicle sensors at the end of the maneuver zone and on the merging line would detect an impending merge collision in time to stop the conflicting vehicle.

6.5.2   Inability to Command Any Maneuvers at Intersection or Merge

This situation would be caused by failure of guideway-mounted command transmitters or communication links. In the case of inter-section operations, the inability to issue any maneuver commands must be countered by denial of any line transfers at that intersection. Since a local computer would be controlling the switches at the intersection, then, upon detection of the fact that no vehicles were repeating commands which supposedly had been sent, both inter-section switches could be set and maintained in the straight-through position. Should a similar occurrence take place at the maneuver region just upstream of a merge point, traffic on one of the merging lines would have to be stopped, probably the lesser used one.

6.5.3   Inability to Command a Vehicle to Decelerate

The inability to command a vehicle to decelerate could be due to a failure in the command link or to the lack of response to a properly received command. This could occur when a vehicle was entering a station or emergency siding or when a vehicle was to decelerate from a higher line speed to a lower one.

When entering a station or emergency siding, the subject vehicle must be stopped by emergency means or else it could run into a vehicle stopped ahead of it. Vehicles following the subject vehicle must, of course, be stopped in sufficient time. Since the subject vehicle cannot be commanded, some other means of activating a braking system is required.

For a vehicle that fails to decelerate from one line speed to a lower one, it would not be necessary to impose an emergency stop if there were some means of imposing the proper deceleration on a vehicle incapable of receiving communications messages. Because we have not been able to discover such a means, we must recommend that such a vehicle also be brought to a stop.

One concept for stopping a vehicle that cannot be commanded involves the use of guideway-mounted vehicle-sensors within or just beyond deceleration zones to determine if the vehicle properly decelerated. If it did not, then a guideway-mounted triggering device would be used to activate the vehicle's braking system.

In earlier sections the concept of a primary braking system independent of traction (achievable through use of a linear electric motor) was suggested. It should be noted, however, that if this concept were employed, a backup mechanical (e.g., disc) braking system should still be incorporated into the design for added safety. The mechanical brake would be applied during normal braking when the speed is reduced to about 2 or 3 mi/hr to ensure a complete stop, since the linear electric motor braking, if applied alone and for too long a time, could actually start the vehicle moving backward. In addition, the mechanical brake would be used as a parking brake to hold the vehicle stationary on a grade or in the presence of a wind, and it would require no power. For the failure situation being discussed, the guideway-mounted triggering device could activate the backup mechanical braking system.

6.5.4   Inability to Command a Vehicle to Accelerate

This situation could occur when a vehicle was to accelerate out of a station siding (prior to merging onto the through line), or in going from a lower to a higher line speed. Again the subject vehicle and those following it must be stopped, particularly since such acceleration zones will often be followed by merge points (e.g., the merge of a station siding line onto the through line). If a vehicle were not up to proper speed and in the proper slot position at the merge point, a merge collision could result, and this is to be avoided. As in the prior situation discussed (Sec. 6.5.3), vehicle sensors could determine that the vehicle was not accelerating and a guideway-mounted triggering device could activate the vehicle's braking system.

6.6   COMPUTER FAILURES AND SWITCH FAILURES

In a PRT network operating under quasi-synchronous control, small microcomputers perform computations and develop vehicle-maneuver and switch-control commands associated with traffic management functions at intersections, merges, speed transition points, and station sidings. In addition, there is a central computer, not involved in the tactical control of vehicles, a primary function of which is to compute and issue revised routing and empty-vehicle dispatching instructions to the local computers when necessary as a result of changes in O-D demand patterns or emergency situations. The central computer might also be involved in managing a "station reservation" or "station delay warning" system, if used; in making certain that each vehicle goes through cleaning, checkout, and preventive maintenance according to predefined schedules; and in such administrative functions as credit checks and customer billing.

6.6.1 Failure of Local Computers

Should a local computer fail to compute or should it erroneously compute maneuver commands or switch control commands, merge collisions could result. As previously discussed, such collisions can be made more improbable by vehicle sensors located in both lines approaching a merge point to check for correlated slot occupancy. Still, the net effect of such a computer failure would be some amount of service disruption.

To avoid this, some level of redundancy must be designed into the local computing function.

Consider an intersection operation. Two computers, given the same input data, could simultaneously generate maneuver and switch-control commands. Before issuance, these commands could be compared. Any disagreement would be an indication that one of the computers had failed. Since there might not be a basis for determining which one had failed, a safe response would be to issue no commands. This would keep both switches at the intersection set in the straight-through direction, thus precluding line transfers and any possibility of collision or stoppage. Traffic would be kept moving, though vehicles which should have transferred lines at that intersection would have to be rerouted at subsequent intersections, perhaps taking longer paths to their destination.

An alternative approach might be to have three separate computers determining maneuver and switch-control commands with the requirement that there be agreement in the commands generated by at least two of the computers. The assumption here is that it is extremely improbable that two or more of the three computers would fail and still produce identical command streams. With this approach the intersection would still be fully operational even if one of the three computers failed. The failure of two of the computers would result in disallowance of line transfers at that intersection, as previously discussed.

In the case of station control computers, the use of only two redundant computers would probably be insufficient, since the response to failure of either one would have to be a cessation of operations at that station siding. As a minimum, the three-computer redundant setup would be necessary so that the interruption of operations at a particular station could only occur if two computers had simultaneously failed. The possibility of this happening can be made extremely remote if a failed computer is repaired or replaced promptly.

Thus, with appropriate redundancy for local computer functions, the probability of service disruptions can be made quite small, and the probability of merge collisions (which would require yet another simultaneous failure) would be small indeed.

6.6.2   Failure of the Central Computer

Failure of the central computer would not introduce safety hazards or cause a disruption in system operations since the central computer is not involved in the tactical control of traffic management operations. Admittedly, the absence of a central computer function would cause service on the PRT network to gradually degrade, since routing and empty-vehicle dispatching instructions in the local computers would not be properly updated. It is desirable that the central computer be backed up with a standby unit.

6.6.3   Switch Failures

The inability to command switches could result from either a failure in the local computers determining the switch-control commands or from failures in the communication links between the computers and switch mechanisms. Fail-operational redundancy concepts for minimizing the impact of local computer failures have already been discussed, as have the desirability of making communication paths redundant.

Switch-control design concepts should be predicated on the assumption that the switch will always be set in the straight-through position in the absence of any positive command to change to the other direction. At intersections this would mean that line transfers would be denied if there was an inability to command the switches — a fail-safe and fail-operational approach. At station sidings this would mean that divergences onto the station siding would be denied.

PRT guideways and switches must be designed in a manner that ensures that the vehicle will always be positively constrained to the guideway while in switch sections. This will be further discussed in Chapter 7. Should the switch mechanism fail (e.g., at an intersection) and a vehicle take the wrong path, the vehicle sensors upstream of the forthcoming merge point would detect an impending merge collision and cause the vehicle(s) to be brought to a stop.

6.7   VEHICLE COLLISION

The design and procedural concepts thus far discussed will ensure that no single-point failure will result in a vehicle collision. A planned soft-engagement for purposes of car-pushing, with a relative velocity at engagement of up to 10 ft/sec, is herein not considered a collision. However, there is the very remote possibility that simultaneous multiple failures could result in collisions. This possibility introduces the question of how to provide for passenger safety — more specifically, how to reduce the probability of passenger injury to an essentially negligible value.

In this section we will show how certain design approaches will ensure passenger safety when there is a collision between two vehicles. (In Sec. 6.8 we will show that these same approaches are also effective against the more severe hazard encountered when a vehicle strikes a large obstacle on the guideway, such as a fallen tree.)

Vehicle collisions can occur either between in-line vehicles or between vehicles which come together side-to-side at a merge point. Both of these cases will now be discussed.

Several characteristics of PRT systems facilitate the application of crash-survivability design concepts to provide passenger safety. First, all of the PRT vehicles on a network would be of substantially the same weight — there is no Volkswagen versus truck situation. Second, all of the passengers are seated, which allows the use of passenger restraint devices that permit high g levels in the passenger compartment during collision. Were standees permitted, collisions would almost assuredly result in passenger injuries and perhaps fatalities. Third, the passengers in the vehicle are truly passengers, not drivers. If, for example, an air bag were to be used as a passenger restraint device, there need be no concern about the consequences of an inadvertent deployment of the air bag as there might be if such an inadvertent deployment interfered with a driver. Fourth, the vehicles are constrained to the guideway. There need be no concern of swerving into an adjacent lane after an initial collision only to be struck by another vehicle, as often happens in automobile accidents. Fifth, because the network is grade-separated at intersections, there need be no concern about a broadside (nose-to-side) collision.[6]

6.7.1 Crash Survivability Concepts and Criteria

Crash-survivability design approaches are basically predicated on the concept of designing the passenger compartment so that it will not deform as impact forces are absorbed by energy-absorption devices, such as bumpers or crushable structures, which are appropriately positioned on the outside of the passenger compartment. Of course, the passenger compartment could be subjected to high deceleration forces during the energy absorption, and passengers must be restrained if they are not to be thrown about inside the

[6] This is generally true except for the CVS system, which employs some single-level intersections.

compartment and perhaps injured or killed.

Various types of restraining devices might be used, such as seat belts, seat belts in combination with shoulder straps, and air bags. There is also the concept of making passenger seats rearward facing, though this, in and of itself, would not afford any protection to a passenger whose vehicle was struck from behind.

It is suggested that it may be imprudent to rely on passengers affixing seat belts or shoulder harnesses when riding on a public transit system. Furthermore, it would be impractical to use an interlock system to preclude vehicle motion until such belts or harnesses were fastened, since failure to do so by some passengers would inconvenience not only them but also other passengers in succeeding vehicles. Such an interlock system would, in effect, give passengers an override control on the system operation, an unacceptable result.

The most logical type of restraining device would be a passive restraint requiring no action on the part of the passenger. Deployment of such a device (e.g., an air bag) could be effected when some threshold deceleration or acceleration level is sensed within the passenger compartment.

Clearly the action of the energy-absorption devices must produce acceptable levels of deceleration of the passenger compartment, consistent with the type of passenger restraint devices employed. Figure 6-12, compiled with data from a number of sources, indicates the general levels of deceleration tolerance for various types of passenger restraint devices. Of particular interest is the right-hand bar of Fig. 6-12 which applies when air bags are being used. It indicates that the passenger will suffer no injuries up to about 60-g deceleration for very short durations.

6.7.2 In-Line Collisions

In order to illustrate crash-survivability design potentials for PRT vehicles, consider the design concept illustrated in Fig. 6-13 which shows a vehicle incorporating the following features:

a. a structurally rigid passenger compartment;

b. an air bag passenger restraint system;

c. forward mounted long-stroke bumpers, perhaps in concert with some crushable-structure fairings; and

d. a rigid rear bumper pad affixed to the passenger compartment structure.

When one vehicle is back-ended by another, it is just as well protected by the compressibility of the front bumper on the striking vehicle as it would be by having its own rear bumper compressible

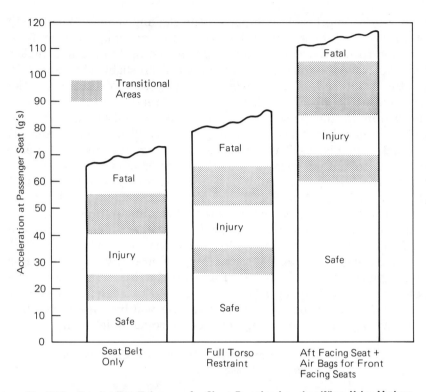

Fig. 6-12. Deceleration Tolerances for Short Duration Impulses When Using Various Body Restraint Systems

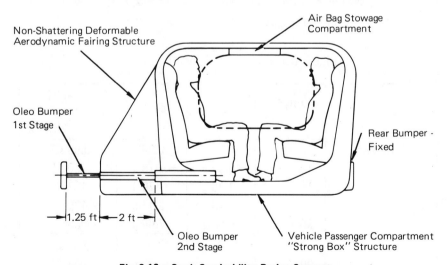

Fig. 6-13. Crash-Survivability Design Concept

with a noncompressible bumper on the striking vehicle. What really matters is the total stroke of the two contacting bumpers. Therefore, for any specified total vehicle length including bumpers, it makes sense to place the long-stroke bumpers and crushable structure only on the front end of each vehicle (as opposed to distributing the available stroke distance half front and half rear) to afford maximum protection to the passenger in the event of collision with a large object which has fallen on the guideway. The bumper concept illustrated in Fig. 6-13 is a two-stage bumper, the first stage being designed to absorb relative velocities associated with soft engagements and "brick-wall" collisions at velocities up to 30 ft/sec, and the second stage designed to absorb higher velocity "brick-wall" collisions of up to 90 ft/sec. (Note that the configuration is not to be construed as a recommended design, but rather as a point of departure for facilitating discussion of crash-survivability design ideas.)

Calculations of decelerations experienced by the passenger compartment are presented in Table 6-1 for the case of a vehicle colliding with a stopped rollable vehicle. In this case, the resultant change in velocity of the colliding vehicle will be one-half the line velocity, V_o, since (assuming vehicles of equal weight) the instant

Table 6-1. Passenger Compartment Deceleration Rates Upon Collision with Stopped Rollable Vehicle

Bumper Stroke 1st Stage	=	1.25 ft
Stroke Efficiency* 1st Stage	=	0.8
Bumper Stroke 2nd Stage	=	2.0 ft
Stroke Efficiency 2nd Stage	=	0.7

$$\text{*Stroke Efficiency} = \frac{1}{L_s} \int_0^{L_s} F \, dx / F_{max} = \frac{F_{avg}}{F_{max}}$$

	LINE VELOCITY	a_{avg}	a_{max}	BUMPER COMPRESSION TIME $\approx 2L_s/V_0$
1st Stage Bumper	5 ft/sec	0.16 g	0.20 g	.500 sec
	10 "	0.62 g	.78 g	.250 "
	15 "	1.40 g	1.75 g	.167 "
	20 "	2.49 g	3.11 g	.125 "
	30 "	5.60 g	7.00 g	.083 "
2nd Stage Bumper	60 ft/sec	14.0 g	20.0 g	.067 sec
	90 "	31.5 g	45.0 g	.044 "

after the collision both vehicles will be moving down the guideway at a final velocity $V_f = 1/2\ V_o$. The kinetic energy to be absorbed, $\Delta(KE)$, is

$$\Delta(KE) = \frac{1}{2} m_1\ V_o{}^2 - \frac{1}{2}(m_1 + m_2)\ V_f{}^2. \qquad (6.3)$$

Since $m_1 = m_2$ and $V_f = \frac{1}{2} V_o$, Eq. (6.3) becomes

$$\Delta(KE) = \frac{1}{4} m_1\ V_o{}^2 = \frac{1}{2}(KE \text{ of striking vehicle}). \qquad (6.4)$$

The energy absorbed by the bumper is $\int_0^{L_s} F\ dx$, where F is the braking force of the bumper as it compresses and L_s is the stroke. This may also be written as $L_s F_{ave}$ or $L_s m_1 a_{ave}$, where F_{ave} is the distance average (not time average) of the bumper force and a_{ave} is the distance average of the deceleration. Thus,

$$Lm_1 a_{ave} = \Delta(KE) = \frac{1}{4} m_1\ V_o{}^2. \qquad (6.5)$$

The calculations which resulted in Table 6-1 are based on the following simplifying assumptions about the operation of this two-stage bumper:

a. For collisions in which the kinetic energy to be absorbed by bumper compression is equal to or less than the vehicle's kinetic energy at a velocity of 30 ft/sec, only the first stage of the bumper is compressed.

b. For collisions in which a higher amount of kinetic energy is to be absorbed, the second stage of the bumper operates, with the first stage assumed to absorb none of the energy.

The above assumptions correspond to saying that the first stage of the bumper operates for collisions of up to 30 ft/sec into "brick walls" or 42.4 ft/sec into stopped rollable vehicles.

Table 6-1 indicates that for collisions up to 90 ft/sec with stopped rollable vehicles, the g levels encountered are well within the no-injury deceleration tolerance indicated in Fig. 6-12 for passengers restrained by an air bag.

6.7.3 Merge Collisions

While the side-to-side collision of two vehicles approaching a merge point would require a number of simultaneous equipment failures, and is thus a very low probability occurrence, such a collision is still, however, conceivable. Obviously both vehicles involved in the collision will come to a stop as they wedge together approaching the merge point.

Perhaps the sides of the vehicle can be designed so that a small amount of crushing of the side structure will allow absorption of the vehicle's kinetic energy. Alternatively, or in addition, the body might be hinged to the vehicle's undercarriage so that it could move laterally by crushing a structure or compressing an oleo strut between the body and the undercarriage. Further, the guideway platform approaching a merge point could be such that a significant amount of forward distance, from the point where the vehicles would just touch side to side, is involved in closing the total lateral displacement (twice that for each vehicle) associated with the energy-absorbing side crush already suggested. Over this distance, the vehicles would completely lose their forward velocity, and this would determine the longitudinal deceleration rate of the passenger compartment.

Let us consider, for example, the mirror image of the geometry of Fig. 3-2, as an exit section from a station siding. Assume that each vehicle can be crushed 0.5 ft on each side. It will be noted that, starting at the "vehicle clearance point," there is about 1 ft of closure (total side crush) in 8 ft of longitudinal motion. Thus, at 30 ft/sec (the case represented by the figure), the vehicles would advance 8 ft in coming to rest. The average longitudinal deceleration during this time would be 1.75 g.

A siding exit section designed for 60 ft/sec, to keep the same time history of lateral acceleration during normal operation, would be designed with all longitudinal dimensions doubled. Thus, the vehicles would stop from 60 ft/sec in 16 ft and the average longitudinal deceleration would be 3.50 g. At 90 ft/sec, the deceleration would be 5.25 g. With the use of air bags, these decelerations are indeed quite tolerable.

There are obviously design parameters that must be determined relative to the specific amount of side crushability (how many inches of crush are required to absorb the kinetic energy) and the specific forward travel distance to be allowed during the crush. Furthermore, the vehicle-chassis and the guideway configuration must be designed so that the vehicles will be constrained to the guideway during such a merge collision. However, proper guideway merge planform design in concert with the use of side crushability can protect the passengers from injury in the event of a merge collision.

6.8   FOREIGN OBSTACLES ON GUIDEWAYS

6.8.1   Small Objects

It is quite conceivable that small objects could accidentally fall onto or intentionally be placed on the guideway; objects such as rocks, beer cans, etc. Several design concepts can be considered to cope with small foreign objects on the guideway. One approach is to design the bottom surface of the guideway with many openings (except within the area comprising the running surface for the wheels) so that small objects will fall or can be swept by brushes on each vehicle through the openings and possibly into a catch pan.[7]

6.8.2 Large Objects

While not a probable occurrence, large foreign objects could conceivably fall or be placed upon PRT guideways and be struck by PRT vehicles. To minimize the probability of such occurrences and to protect the curious from high voltage and other hazards, it is important that the system design not provide easy access to the guideway. Additionally, where guideways are to be emplaced along tree-lined streets, it may be desirable to have some sort of protective structure to preclude falling tree limbs from intruding into the vehicle running space.

Consider, however, the direst of possible cases; namely, collision with a large "immovable" object which has fallen on a guideway. Table 6-2 presents the calculated passenger compartment deceleration rates for various line velocities associated with a collision with such an obstacle. The calculations are based on the two-stage bumper concept shown in Fig. 6-13. In this case, deceleration rates

Table 6-2. Passenger Compartment Deceleration Rates Upon Collision with Immovable Object

Bumper Stroke 1st Stage	= 1.25 ft
Stroke Efficiency* 1st Stage	= 0.8
Bumper Stroke 2nd Stage	= 2.0 ft
Stroke Efficiency 2nd Stage	= 0.7

$$*Stroke\ Efficiency = \frac{1}{L_s} \int_0^{L_s} F\, dx / F_{max} = \frac{F_{avg}}{F_{max}}$$

	LINE VELOCITY	a_{avg}	a_{max}	BUMPER COMPRESSION TIME $\approx 2L_s/V_0$
1st Stage Bumper	30 ft/sec	11.2 g	14.0 g	.083 sec
2nd Stage Bumper	60 ft/sec	28.0 g	40.0 g	.067 sec
	75 "	43.7 g	62.4 g	.053 "
	90 "	63.0 g	90.0 g	.044 "

---

[7] See, for example, the intercostal structure illustrated in Fig. 7-13.

for line velocities up to about 75 ft/sec are within the safe tolerance range of Fig. 6-12 for passengers restrained by air bags. For a line velocity of 90 ft/sec the average deceleration rate indicated in Table 6-2 is at the edge of the safe region, though the instantaneous maximum could cause serious injuries. At best this can be defined as a marginal situation from a passenger safety viewpoint.

One approach might be to limit line speeds to 75 ft/sec (approximately 50 mi/hr). Alternatively, the situation could be alleviated by a different bumper configuration. For example, if a single-stage bumper having a physical stroke of 3.25 ft and a stroke efficiency of 0.7 were used, then a_{avg} = 38.7 g and a_{max} = 55.3 g for a 90-ft/sec collision into an immovable object. Both the average and instantaneous-maximum values now fall within the safe region. Corresponding reduction in passenger compartment deceleration rates would be realized for all types of collisions by use of such a single-stage bumper. However, the full-stroke length would be used even at low collision velocities, possibly making it difficult to integrate bumper and aerodynamic fairing designs in a manner which would not cause fairing damage during low-velocity collisions or during the soft engagements associated with the car-pushing strategy.

It should be noted that even if operations at 90 ft/sec were permitted with the two-stage bumper design previously described, only the passengers in the vehicle that strikes the immovable object need be in possible danger of injury if separations were lengthened in accordance with the headway policy illustrated in Figs. 4-1 and 4-2.

We have, of course, been considering an "immovable" object, though in reality even a large tree across the guideway might move a foot or two when struck at 90 ft/sec. This distance is, in effect, an addition to the bumper stroke and serves to reduce peak deceleration below the injury level of Fig. 6-12.

6.9 POWER OUTAGE

Another type of emergency situation to be considered is that of a power outage on all or a part of a PRT network. If the power outage is confined to a section of the network, computers controlling adjacent network sections would have to be notified so that traffic which would normally be routed into the affected area can be rerouted or, if necessary, brought to a stop until a rerouting can be effected.

Consider, however, a prolonged power outage that affects a major portion or all of the network, and, worse yet, one that occurs during very cold and windy winter weather on a system in a northern city. If the PRT network is a large one, thousands or tens of thousands of vehicles could be stalled on the guideways. With vehicle heating inoperative, the temperature of the passenger compartments could drop precipitously, with the danger of passenger injury or death from prolonged exposure to the cold.

In this dire, yet conceivable scenario, it probably would be impractical to consider using street-driven emergency equipment to effect passenger egress from the PRT vehicles because of the large number of vehicles and the possibility that the streets might be impassable as a result of heavy snows.

Aerospace examined this scenario from the viewpoint of how passenger safety could be ensured. Obviously, some way of getting the passengers out of the PRT vehicles and into sheltered and warm areas is necessary. In examining this issue, several criteria were developed and utilized in the assessment of alternative approaches. These decreed that the escape method:

a.   must be usable by all passengers including the young, the old, and the infirm;

b.   should not put the passengers in a situation of potential danger should power be restored during the escape period;

c.   should not expose the passengers to possible injury resulting from the adverse weather conditions (e.g., strong winds, icing); and

d.   should not, during normal periods, provide easy access to the guideway to vandals or saboteurs.

The first of these criteria tends to eliminate consideration of escape devices such as telescoping ladders, rope ladders, ropes, or inflatable chutes which could be incorporated aboard the vehicles. The remaining criteria eliminate the possibility of having the passengers get out of the vehicles and walk along the guideway (or adjoining catwalks) to a nearby station or to ladders on guideway support columns.

A more reasonable solution emerged from the analysis. This necessitates sufficient backup wayside power to keep the control computers, the switches, and the communications operational (a very small fraction of that required for vehicle propulsion), and sufficient battery power aboard each vehicle to propel the vehicle at reduced speed for a distance of a few miles — sufficient to get the vehicle into the nearest station for unloading and then back out onto the line to make room for succeeding vehicles. Analyses have indicated that approximately 90 lb of battery aboard each vehicle would suffice. Passengers could then deboard at station platforms, as they normally do, and then proceed to street level and into nearby buildings for shelter.

6.10 SAFETY SUMMARY

For a passenger to sustain injury in a PRT system, three occurrences are necessary. First, there must be equipment failures that lead to an operational failure or there must be a hazardous situation caused by other than an equipment failure. Second, this situation must result in a collision — either vehicle-to-vehicle or vehicle-to-obstacle. Third, the collision must subject the passenger to high g-forces.

In Chapter 8 it will be shown that the probability of operational failure can be made extremely small through: (1) adoption of a stringent preventive maintenance program which will avoid wear-out type failures, and (2) extensive use of redundancy in combination with frequent (e.g., daily) checkout of the redundant components to minimize the occurrence of operational failures resulting from component failures. Of course, hazardous situations could result from large obstacles which fall or are placed upon guideways by people bent on disrupting the system's operations. The probability of such occurrences can be minimized by: (1) protecting the guideways when they are located along tree-lined streets, and (2) designing the system in a manner that denies easy access to the guideway and other system equipment.

As regards vehicle-to-vehicle collisions, this chapter has shown that when single-point operational failures are detected and reported, they can be responded to in manners that avoid vehicle-to-vehicle collisions and serious service disruptions. Vehicle-to-vehicle collisions would result only if an operational failure went undetected or unreported, thus precluding the ability to implement appropriate response strategies (e.g., car-pushing, car-stopping, car-rerouting, turn or merge denial, etc.). Since detection and reporting subsystems could also be designed with appropriate redundancies and associated checkout procedures, the probability of a vehicle-to-vehicle collision, given the already unlikely occurrence of an operational failure, could be made extremely small, almost negligible. Vehicles could, of course, collide with obstacles that had fallen or were placed on the guideway[8] and, depending on line speeds and traffic densities, these vehicles might be struck by succeeding vehicles. Again let us emphasize that care must be taken in system design and installation to minimize the probability of such obstacles.

To result in injury, the collision must cause very high-level deceleration or acceleration forces to be felt at the passenger's loca-

---

[8] This is true in any type of automated guideway system, not just a close-headway PRT system.

tion, or to cause buffeting about of the passenger(s) within the passenger compartment. This chapter has shown that the incorporation of energy-absorption devices (long-stroke bumpers and crushable structures) and passenger restraint devices (e.g., air bags) generally can avoid injurious levels of acceleration or deceleration at the passenger's seat location, and can preclude the passenger's being thrown about. It might be noted that, in the unlikely event of a collision, PRT passengers would be better protected than auto passengers or passengers of other transit modes. As opposed to the auto, a PRT vehicle's motion is guideway-constrained. Since collisions would not be occurring at arbitrary angles, the problems of energy-absorption device designs are greatly eased. Also, a collision could not result in the vehicle swerving into an adjacent lane and being struck by yet another vehicle. As opposed to many other public transit modes, there are no standees on a PRT system. This facilitates the incorporation of passive passenger restraint devices. Finally, all PRT vehicles would be of approximately the same weight — the subcompact car versus truck type of accident is not a concern in a PRT system.

From the foregoing, it can be concluded that the number of passenger injuries on a PRT system can be kept extremely small — probably several orders of magnitude below present experience with auto travel and well below other transit modes. However, realistic quantitative assessments to support this belief would, at this juncture, be premature. Such assessments would better await the evolution of a specific system design which can then be subjected to reliability, failure-modes-and-effects, and hazards analyses.

Assuming the proper incorporation into the system design of redundancy, checkout, and preventive maintenance, and a well-structured engineering test program to identify and correct design or procedural deficiencies, equipment malfunctions should be an almost negligible source of safety problems. Of greater concern will likely be hazards created by events other than equipment failure, such as obstacles which have fallen on guideways or attempts to sabotage the system.

Chapter 7
DESIGN CONSIDERATIONS
C. L. Olson

This chapter discusses the alternative design approaches studied by Aerospace for implementing a personal rapid transit system. We compared the approaches in the context of a PRT system which could be deployed over a broad urban area and which could meet the overall performance criteria previously described. Additionally, the specific technologies studied were compatible with quasi-synchronous control and with traffic management concepts (normal and emergency) described in prior chapters.

It is recognized that the particular design approaches developed by Aerospace, and later demonstrated in a 1/10-scale operating model, are not a unique solution to PRT implementation. The objective of the work, at the time it was conducted, was to establish PRT technical feasibility by identifying and demonstrating one set of solutions for the various system elements. It is believed that the particular PRT design concepts evolved and demonstrated do, however, have considerable merit, and reasons for focusing on particular design approaches will be given.

First we summarize the requirements and goals for the PRT vehicle. Then we discuss critical vehicle subsystems and their interaction with the guideway and guideway-mounted components. These subsystems include propulsion, braking, suspension, and switching. [Longitudinal control was covered in Sec. 4.6.7. Passenger protective devices, including long-stroke compressible bumpers (oleo-bumpers), crushable structure, and air bags, were covered in Chapter 6.] We then consider the design of fixed facilities, including guideways, guideway electrification, and ancillary facilities for vehicle parking and vehicle maintenance. Design considerations for stations were discussed in Sec. 3.3 and will not be repeated here.

Many, but not all, of the design concepts were tested in our 1/10-scale operating model. Appendix B describes this model and how various elements were scaled to give as realistic a confirmation of design principles as can be achieved at such a small scale.

7.1 GENERAL REQUIREMENTS AND GOALS

The PRT vehicles should be capable of comfortably seating four adults and would desirably have space for some luggage. (This is a nominal size; actual size for any specified city might range from a seating capacity of three to six, depending upon the need.) Sufficient door width and floor space should be provided to accommodate a wheel chair, possibly with two seats folded away. Alternatively, this would provide room for a shopping cart or baby carriage. Provisions for storage of, say, two bicycles on racks on the outside of the vehicle would also be a desirable feature if conveniently attainable. The vehicles should be as light as practicable to lessen vehicle costs, as well as structural (guideway) costs. With properly designed bumpers and passenger restraints, they should be capable of protecting passengers from injury in the event of a collision resulting from system malfunctions or foreign obstacles on the guideway. We have estimated empty vehicle weight to be 1,800 lb (Table 7-1). As a goal, it would be desirable if vehicle costs of not more than $10,000 (1973 dollars) were attainable, assuming production quantities of 10,000 vehicles (see Sec. 9.2.2).

The vehicle subsystems (passenger protection, propulsion, braking, longitudinal control, switching, suspension, environmental

Table 7-1. PRT Vehicle Weight Estimate

ITEM	WEIGHT lb	PERCENT
Body (incl. Environmental Systems)	500	27.8
Trim	120	6.7
Glass	60	3.3
Propulsion—Dual Primary	350	19.4
Suspension	150	8.3
Wheels	70	3.9
Brakes	30	1.7
Electronics	30	1.7
Safety Equipment	130	7.2
Electrical System (incl. Batteries)	180	10.0
Passenger Amenities	20	1.1
Predicted Weight	1640	91.1
Contingency (approx. 10% predicted wt)	160	8.9
TOTAL	1800	100.0

conditioning, passenger-operated controls, doors, etc.) must have features and performance capabilities compatible with a broad range of requirements emanating from the previously discussed system concept description and issues of passenger and system security, vehicle management, headway requirements, and emergency strategies. For example, the vehicle subsystems must allow operation at fractional-second headways in a manner compatible with quasi-synchronous network control. The subsystems must allow for execution of normal and emergency maneuvers, including the rapid development of high-level deceleration. The vehicle subsystems should allow the provision of a comfortable ride in a pleasantly controlled environment (e.g., lighting, heating, air conditioning), and should provide for those passenger-control options discussed in Sec. 1.7.1 under Passenger Security.

The vehicles should be quiet in operation. They should be designed for easy cleaning, most likely via an automated cleaning process, and to facilitate rapid subsystem checkout and modular replacement of failed equipment. These latter points are important in achieving high levels of reliability, safety, and service dependability.

7.2   PROPULSION SUBSYSTEM

The main propulsion subsystem requirements are perceived to be: high energy efficiency; no exhaust emissions; no on-board fuels (to avoid a requirement for refueling operations); minimum noise and vibration; positive controllability; independence from environmental conditions; and thrust capable of accelerating a 2,400 lb vehicle at a maximum level of 0.25 g up to a speed of 90 ft/sec (about 61.3 mi/hr) up a 5% grade into a 67 mi/hr headwind with 30% gusts.

The above requirements militate against the use of on-board internal combustion engines or fuel cells (to power electric motors) since either would require on-board fuel and associated refueling operations, and the internal combustion engine would result in exhaust emissions. On-board batteries as the primary power source are likewise eliminated. Their limited energy-storage capacity would require relatively frequent battery recharging. Therefore, it was concluded that the vehicles would be electrically powered, with power supplied from the wayside.

Rotary electric motors with drive through the wheels were eliminated as a potential propulsion approach, but not just on the basis of the above requirements. First, it was reasoned that their use would generally limit braking decelerations to those attainable via traction, and this was considered insufficient for coping with an inadvertent locked-wheel deceleration of the vehicle ahead.[1] Second, a rotary motor is subject to wear, whereas a linear electric motor has no moving parts. Therefore a linear electric motor approach for the propulsion subsystem was selected.

At the time this work was being done, there was already much progress in the field of linear synchronous motors and linear induction motors. Siemens AG of the Federal Republic of Germany uses a linear synchronous motor in their H-Bahn system, a GRT system recently developed. The Cabintaxi system uses a linear induction motor. However, we felt that each of these linear motors fell somewhat short of what was needed.

When using a linear synchronous motor, the vehicle speed is directly proportional to the frequency of the applied current (providing there is no slippage). Acceleration is accomplished by gradually increasing the frequency of the a.c. power fed to the motor. Therefore, the linear synchronous motor is well adapted to a system where, at any specified point on the guideway, all vehicles have the same speed. But, when quasi-synchronous control is used, then in the maneuver regions of intersections different vehicles will have different speeds. Thus, the linear synchronous motor is not well adapted[2] to quasi-synchronous control, nor would it be to asynchronous control.

A linear induction motor has less energy efficiency than desirable. Moreover, we were concerned that a linear induction motor would not provide sufficient braking force.

Investigation of possible alternatives led to a propulsion system design which uses a double-sided pulsed d.c. primary mounted on the vehicle, interacting with guideway-mounted magnets. The guideway magnets could be permanent, electromagnetic, or induced, but the configuration illustrated in Fig. 7-1 was considered most

---

[1] The reader will recall (Sec. 6.3.2) that if two vehicles are separated by 5 ft and the first vehicle locks its wheels and skids, the following vehicle can avoid contact if it applies brakes within 0.2 sec and uses a braking deceleration about 15% larger than the deceleration rate of the failed vehicle. This, of course, precludes the use of traction brakes. In Sec. 4.2 it was pointed out that with traction brakes which provide a braking deceleration equal to that of the failed vehicle the collision velocity would be no higher than 4.5 ft/sec. However, it was also pointed out that if, due to worn tires, the second vehicle could not match the deceleration of the failed vehicle, and if the initial separation was around 30 ft, the collision velocity could be 3 to 4 times higher.

[2] It would be possible to use a linear synchronous motor with frequency set for the characteristic line speed. Then an on-board phase shifter (e.g., a selsyn) could be rotated to cause slot slipping or advancing. This is somewhat complex and there would be energy lost in the phase shifter. Moreover, this still does not provide the flexibility for maneuvers within stations or for emergency maneuvers such as car pushing or line clearing.

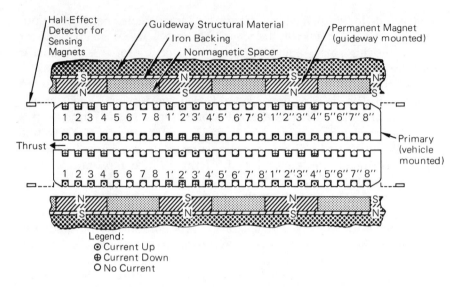

Fig. 7-1. Pulsed D.C. Linear Motor Configuration (Plan View)

practical since permanent magnetic materials, such as barium or strontium ferrite, are becoming commercially available at a reasonable cost, and the guideway-mounted permanent magnets eliminate the need for an on-board secondary field that would be required for induced magnets. As shown in the figure, the magnets alternate between north pole and south pole facing the vehicle-mounted primary. There is a continuous iron strip backing the ceramic magnets. The magnetic flux path is from one north pole face, across the gap, through the iron core of the primary, across the gaps to the neighboring south pole faces, and is completed through the guideway-mounted iron backing.

The iron backing strip is embedded into the guideway structure, and magnets are attached to the surface and separated by blocks of nonmagnetic material.[3] The use of nonmagnetic spacers makes the guideway easier to maintain and, in particular, facilitates sweeping away magnetic debris which may be clinging to the magnets. Magnets are installed in a demagnetized state and later magnetized by bringing up a strong electromagnet.

Coils on the primary are energized with d.c. pulses when they are spatially located opposite a guideway magnet, the direction of the current being up or down, consistent with the magnet polarity (see Fig. 7-1). To reduce the total number of independent circuits the coils labeled 1, 1', and 1'' are in series, but 1' is wound in the

---

[3] On the Aerospace 1/10-scale model the space between magnets was not filled.

opposite direction from 1 and 1″ so when the current is down in 1 and 1″, it is up in 1′. It is also possible to include coils 1, 1′, and 1″ of the other primary in the same series circuit. Thus the figure shows 8 independent circuits, each consisting of 6 coils.

Because the coils only carry current when they are opposite a pole piece, no energy is wasted on coils unable to produce thrust. This leads to relatively high efficiencies which we have estimated to be about 88% for a full-scale motor. This compares very favorably with linear induction motors, which in this size range are usually less than 70% efficient.

Thrust in the motor is varied by controlling the current level in each coil through the use of a pulse-width-modulation chopper composed of solid-state components. The current level is controlled by a closed-loop system discussed in Sec. 4.6.7 (Fig. 4-11). Each primary coil is position-indexed to the permanent magnets through the use of Hall-effect detectors mounted on the vehicle chassis. These small devices provide a commutating function for the coils as they approach the edge of a magnet, since they exhibit a sharp and repetitive output in the presence of a magnetic field. The detectors also sense the magnet polarity so that the current can be applied to the coil in the appropriate direction. The "on" signal to each coil includes a compensating lead time, consistent with the inductive time constant of the coil and with vehicle speed, to permit the field to build up to its full value as it reaches the leading edge of each magnet. This motor thus avoids the need for on-board frequency conversion equipment, as it operates in a self-commutating mode over its entire speed range. Virtually all of the electronic components used in the motor are solid state, which enhances reliability, conserves space, and minimizes vehicle weight and maintenance.

A number of factors were considered in arriving at a nominal arrangement of the guideway-mounted permanent magnets and the length of the interfacing motor primary. The primary must be physically short enough to traverse the minimum radius guideway turns without touching the magnets. In addition, in order to produce constant thrust, the primary and permanent magnets must be arranged in a configuration that will result in a nearly constant flux linkage in the magnetic circuit formed by their interaction. Because of the spatially periodic nature of the magnetic field and the finite length of the primary core, there will be longitudinal forces acting on the iron core (even with no current in the coils) which will tend to draw it into one of its stable points of equilibrium. This we refer to as detent. When the vehicle is moving this has the effect of causing an undesirable longitudinal variation in thrust, or cogging effect. This may be virtually eliminated by careful design.

Configurations containing two-, three-, and four-pole magnetic circuits were considered. The three-pole embrace illustrated in Fig. 7-1 was selected, since it was the minimum-length primary that would provide nearly constant flux linkage. Variable gap pole pieces are used at each end of the primary to accommodate fringing and to avoid the development of undesirable magnetic detent. Skewing of coil slots may also minimize this cogging effect.

The most effective winding configuration for a linear motor with magnets on each side is a single primary core so that the downward path of current opposite a north pole on one side will continue to an upward path opposite a north pole on the other side of the guideway. One turn would then have two working sides. This scheme was considered less practical from a mechanical standpoint. Instead, the primary was split into two halves, independently spring-mounted, with each half maintaining air gap independently of the other and with the lateral compliance required for negotiating turns.

Aerospace has performed the preliminary design of a pulsed d.c. linear motor for a full-sized vehicle (4 passengers, 2,400 lb). The motor performance requirements and size specifications are shown in Fig. 7-2. The motor is calculated to weigh approximately 338 lb,

Motor Thrust & Power Requirements (Prototype)

Maximum*   1260 lb Thrust, 201 hp at 60 mi/hr
Rated   300 lb Thrust, 48 hp at 60 mi/hr
Cruise (level {100 lb Thrust, 18 hp at 60 mi/hr
no wind)   {30 lb Thrust, 2 hp at 20 mi/hr
Emergency Braking 2000 lb Reverse Thrust

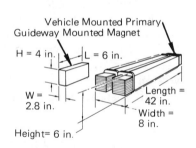

Vehicle Mounted Primary
Guideway Mounted Magnet

H = 4 in.   L = 6 in.

W = 2.8 in.

Length = 42 in.

Width = 8 in.

Height= 6 in.

*Maximum Power Requirements Assume:

Velocity	88 ft/sec
Acceleration	0.25 g
Grade	5%
Wind	67 mi/hr & 30% Gust
Rolling Resistance	Main Support & Guide Wheels
Gross Weight	2400 lb

Electrical & Magnetic Characteristics

E = 1000 Volts (dc)
I = 20 Amps (nominal)
B = 22,000 Lines/in.^{2}
Air Gap ~ 0.25 in.
Spacing Between Magnets = 6 in.
Weight ≃ 338 lb

Fig. 7-2. Pulsed d.c. Motor Sizing

and measures 42 inches in length by 6 inches in height by 8 inches in width. Rated thrust is 300 lb at a vehicle speed of 60 mi/hr. The motor supply voltage, baselined at 1,000 volts d.c., is fed through the pulse-width-modulation chopper to the primary coils. There are a total of 48 coil slots, 24 on each side of the split primary. These coils are connected so that 6 coils (3 in each split primary) are in series in a set, with a total of 8 sets being required. This propulsion configuration thus inherently incorporates redundancy due to the 8 independent windings.

The permanent magnets to be used with this primary were selected to be either barium or strontium ferrite with a flux density of approximately 3,000 gauss. The total magnetic pole face area for the entire primary was estimated to be approximately 150 sq. inches. Therefore, the magnets were sized at 4 inches in height, 6 inches in length and were spaced on 1-ft centers, three on each side of the motor primary.

It is seen in Fig. 7-2 that the magnets are 2.8 inches thick. The indicated thickness was chosen to tolerate extreme subzero conditions. If the magnets are too thin, they will demagnetize in very cold weather.

An important characteristic of most electric motors is that they can be run at several times their continuous horsepower rating provided the periods of overload are short. Typical values are three times rated load for 1 minute, five times for 20 sec and up to eight times for 5 sec. The linear motor is no exception to this overload capability. The cooling system establishes the duration that these overloads can be sustained without overheating the motor. The linear motor is more easily cooled by convection and conduction than its rotational counterpart because of the open ends and the fact that the primary (rotor) does not move relative to its mount. Thus, the pulsed d.c. motor described above is considered capable of producing an extreme overload thrust of 2,400 lb for up to 10 sec.

Electrical power would be obtained from the guideway through sliding shoes, and thus selection of the pulsed d.c. baseline propulsion system requires the guideway beam to support both the copper conductors and the ferrite magnet secondary.

7.3 BRAKING SUBSYSTEM

The principal braking subsystem requirements are perceived to be low wear rate, fast response time, 0.8 g deceleration thrust,[4] little or no dependence of available thrust on environmental conditions, and positive control.

---

[4] It will be recalled that a level of 0.8 g braking deceleration was based on avoiding a collision with the vehicle ahead when it locks its wheels and skids with a 0.7 g deceleration. If smooth guideways are used and the tires are designed for low traction, then the locked-wheel deceleration rate can be substantially less than 0.7 g and the maximum emergency braking level might be correspondingly decreased. In the rare event, however, when one vehicle has struck a large "immovable" object like a massive tree, the additional braking capability will allow the following vehicle to further reduce its speed before hitting the first.

The pulsed d.c. propulsion concept described in Sec. 7.2 fulfills all of the requirements listed above, having the capability to generate reverse (braking) thrust through reversing the direction of the coil current. For the case of infinite jerk rate and deceleration at 0.8 g from the maximum postulated speed of 90 ft/sec, the emergency braking time would be 3.5 sec. The prototype motor described in Sec. 7.2 can be shown capable of producing up to 2,000 lb of thrust for well over twice this time without overstressing the motor components. Emergency thrust build-up time is estimated to be less than 0.002 sec. Thus, the selected baseline for service and emergency braking is the pulsed d.c. motor.

A mechanical braking system which is functionally independent should be provided when the primary propulsion and braking system is a linear electric motor. It would have three uses: (1) to provide the final increment of braking in a normal controlled or coasting stop, (2) to serve as a parking brake when the primary system is not energized, and (3) to be activated by a guideway-mounted triggering device in case of any deceleration command failure (Sec. 6.5.3).

The mechanical braking system could be either a conventional disk brake or the clamping of a linear metal blade imbedded in the guideway with clamping pucks mounted to the vehicle. The use of a clamping brake allows high braking forces to be developed without depending on wheel/guideway friction forces.

7.4 SUSPENSION SUBSYSTEM

In order to avoid the inefficient and objectionably wide flat-roadbed type of guideway which is typically used to support standard four-wheeled vehicles, Aerospace studied the relatively narrow monorail types of guideway which use either an overriding or an underhung suspension concept. These are illustrated in Fig. 7-3. Each of these approaches uses a slender and compact U-shaped beam to minimize visual impact and to permit efficient utilization of structural material.

Because the underhung suspension utilizes an inverted-U shaped beam, it has the advantage of being easier to protect from snow and ice build-up. However, it has some inherent disadvantages as well. One of these was discussed in Sec. 2.2.3 where it was pointed out that to clear street traffic the beam would have to be 5 or 6 ft higher than the beam of an overriding suspension. This would require its supporting columns to be at least 8 to 9 ft higher, since the columns for an underhung design must be attached to the top of the beam. By contrast, in the overriding design the beam is supported from below. In addition, the beam support for an underhung suspension must be cantilevered, which further increases the column thickness.

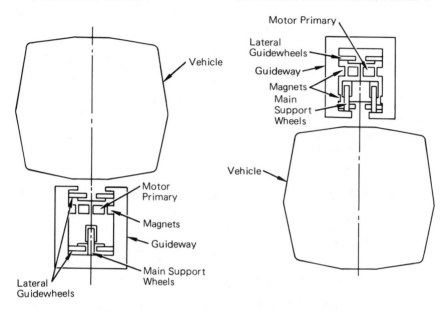

Fig. 7-3. Narrow Monorail-Type Guideway Concepts

The extra height and thickness of columns lead to higher costs as well as greater visual intrusion.

Another equally important consideration is the added mechanical complexity of the underhung suspension. Where the overriding configuration uses only two tandemly arranged main support wheels, the underhung suspension requires four. Another complexity affecting the underhung approach arises where guideways branch or merge. In such regions the guideway widens and the gap through which the vehicle support passes also must widen. As a result, when the vehicle is switching to the left (or is coming from the left branch of a merge), the right main support wheels have no support under them. In such regions there must be some other means of restraining the vehicle from overturning. Should such means fail, the unsupported wheels would fall through the gap, unless, of course, there was functional redundancy in the means for preventing the vehicle from overturning.

Because of the greater mechanical simplicity of the overriding concept, its inherently greater safety, and the lower cost and improved aesthetics of the guideway, we chose this concept for more detailed study. Mitigation of the potential snow and ice problem is discussed in Sec. 7.6.5. The baseline suspension design of Fig. 7-4 was developed from trade-off studies that considered the interaction

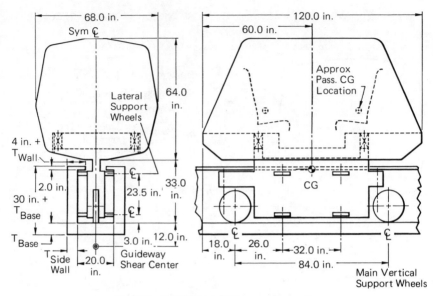

Fig. 7-4. PRT Vehicle/Guideway Geometry

of guideway geometry; vertical and lateral support wheels and vibration isolation devices; propulsion motor configuration and guideway-mounted magnets; switching backup devices; and power, communication, and control-sensor equipment.

Vehicle vertical support is obtained through two tandem main wheels as illustrated in Fig. 7-5. The main wheels are mounted on

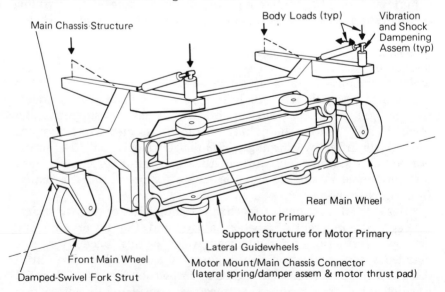

Fig. 7-5. Vehicle Suspension Concept

damped-swivel fork struts which permit motion through switches and curved guideway sections. These wheels are attached, unsprung, to the main chassis spine structure in order to permit close vertical alignment of the chassis with the guideway magnets, electric power, and signal contact equipment. Vertical vibration would be minimal due to the relatively smooth surface of the guideway, and any vertical motion induced by guideway joints would be mitigated by body vibration dampers and seat cushioning construction.

Lateral support and guidance is furnished by eight side wheels — four fixed to each of the two motor primary structures, as illustrated in Figs. 7-4 and 7-5. These wheel sets furnish lateral guidance and primary air gap maintenance as well as overturn stability. The motor primary structures are attached to the chassis spine by spring and damper arrangements which permits partial "buck-out" of the attractive loads between the primaries and the guideway-mounted magnets.

7.5 SWITCHING

The principal switching subsystem requirements are perceived to be: switch cycle time no greater than 1/6 sec (based on 15-ft slots and a maximum line speed of 90 ft/sec); switch-throw time no greater than 1/30 sec (based on a nominal 5-ft vehicle separation distance with a maximum position control error of ±1 ft); continuous and positive lateral support and guidance throughout the switch section; and functionally redundant backup switch subsystem operable after a power failure.

The fast-switching requirement, stemming from short-headway operations, eliminates consideration of movable guideway sections. Mechanical devices considered feasible are arms located on the vehicle which are extended to engage fixed portions of a passive track, or guideway-mounted levers or cams which engage the vehicle. (The guideway-mounted units may be marginal in providing the fast operating times demanded by close-headway systems.) All of these mechanical systems require moving parts which have an inherent response-time lag. If the devices are located on the vehicle, the switch-throw time becomes inconsequential because the on-board switch can be deployed well in advance of the vehicle coming to the branch point. However, moving parts are susceptible to adverse environmental conditions and their design may become mechanically complex, causing poor reliability. Furthermore, devices of this type would require frequent surveillance for wear, replacement, and lubrication in order to meet the stringent safety requirements inherent in automated transit vehicles.

Electromagnetic switching, on the other hand, can provide extremely rapid and readily controllable means of switching vehicles. In this approach, electromagnets would be mounted at switch points in the vertical sides of the channel guideways. These magnets, when activated on the desired side of the guideway, would interact with ferrous material on the vehicle to produce the necessary lateral forces to draw the vehicle into the proper channel. This type of switching has no moving parts and can be actuated by a wayside switch control system. With appropriate switch control system circuit design (e.g., redundancies) this approach can be made highly reliable. The activation time of such devices is limited only by the inductive time constant of the coil winding. An electromagnetic switching system would be relatively insensitive to weather extremes, and would require minimum surveillance and maintenance to ensure safety.

As noted in Sec. 7.2, the baseline propulsion concept developed by Aerospace for close-headway PRT vehicles operations utilizes a pulsed d.c. linear electric motor with vehicle-borne primaries having soft iron cores. This permits integrating the propulsion and switching concepts, with electromagnets replacing permanent magnets in the vicinity of a switch. Only electromagnets on one side of the guideway would be turned on and these would produce the lateral forces required for switching by attracting the motor primary on that side. The electromagnets would also provide the magnetic field necessary for thrust production as the primary coils aboard the vehicle are energized.

The flux density available in the electromagnets would be chosen to be approximately double that of the permanent magnets. This provides the necessary attractive force through its interaction with the armature iron to maintain vehicle stability, and the increased flux density doubles the thrust produced by the linear motor which, of course, is operating effectively on only one side during its travel through the switch. Thus, the switching and propulsion designs are integrated.

The electromagnets also provide lateral support to the vehicle when it is within the widened section associated with guideway branching or merging.[5] The magnets must be strong enough to hold the vehicle firmly against one wall of the widened guideway, since the lateral wheels on the other side are no longer in contact with the other wall. Switch electromagnet sizing is illustrated in Fig. 7-6 for combined adverse wind and centrifugal acceleration loads. The

---

[5] Note that the electromagnets are needed not only at switches but at merges as well.

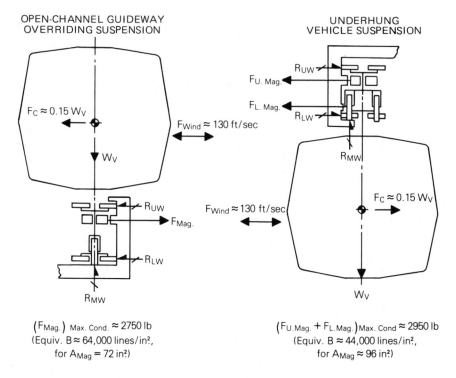

OPEN-CHANNEL GUIDEWAY
OVERRIDING SUSPENSION

UNDERHUNG
VEHICLE SUSPENSION

$(F_{Mag.})$ Max. Cond. $\approx$ 2750 lb
(Equiv. B $\approx$ 64,000 lines/in²,
for A_{Mag} = 72 in²)

$(F_{U.Mag.} + F_{L.Mag.})$ Max. Cond $\approx$ 2950 lb
(Equiv. B $\approx$ 44,000 lines/in²,
for $A_{Mag} \approx$ 96 in²)

Fig. 7-6. Switch Electromagnet Flux Density Requirements for Vehicle Stability

resulting electromagnets are of a very practical dimension and field strength. (For comparison, the figure on the right shows how electromagnets may be used to stabilize the vehicle from overturning when an underhung suspension is being used. It will be noted that two sets of magnets are needed.)

An important consideration in designing the electromagnetic switch is that of maintaining lateral control of the vehicle in the switch "frog" area should a complete power failure to the electromagnets be experienced. Such a failure, however remote, will require the application of "fail-safe" backup measures in the vehicle system.

Such measures could consist of vehicle-borne lock systems, energized in the vicinity of the guideway electromagnetic switch. One of several lock operating concepts investigated by Aerospace is depicted and explained in Fig. 7-7. As the vehicle approaches the switch, there will be a section where there are permanent magnets on the through side of the guideway and electromagnets on the turn side. If the turn-side electromagnets are "On," locking rollers will be extended to lock the vehicle into the turn. If the turn-side electromagnets are "Off," either because the vehicle is scheduled to go

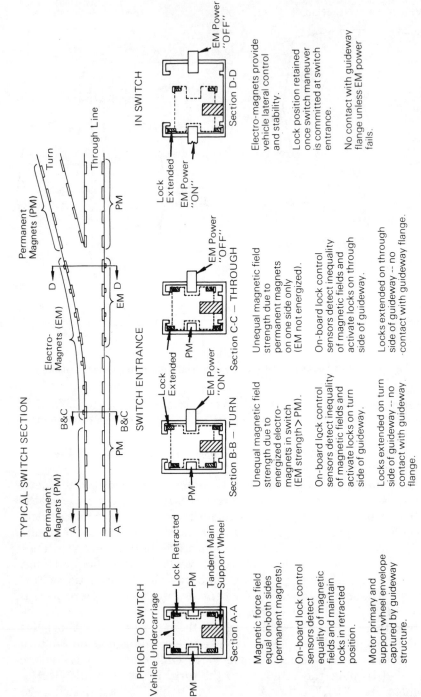

Fig. 7-7. Lock Operating Concept

straight (the through-side electromagnets would be "On") or because the vehicle was approaching the switch during a power failure (when no electromagnets would be "On"), rollers will be extended to lock the vehicle into the straight-through guideway. The locking rollers are normally separated from the guideway flange by about 1/2 inch. Under normal switching operations, as the vehicle approaches the frog where the guideway has widened, the vehicle is held firmly against one side of the guideway by the lateral force of the electromagnets on that side pulling on the soft iron core aboard the vehicle. But, should the electromagnet power fail at any time while the vehicle is in the switch section, there may be a tendency for the vehicle to tip away from the guideway wall and this will cause the locking rollers to engage the guideway flange and constrain the motion. After the vehicle passes through the switch section, the locks would be returned to their neutral position by cam action of a guideway-mounted protrusion. The locking rollers would undergo little or no wear since only rarely, if at all, would they be in contact with the guideway.

7.6 GUIDEWAYS

Stating the design requirements in a general way, guideways should: be narrow beams of high ductility (capable of bending without rupture), be dynamically stable, have beam surface irregularity and stiffness consistent with passenger comfort, have provisions for nulling the effects of earth settlement, and be protected from ice, snow, and lightning. Detailed design criteria are discussed in the following subsections.

As noted in Sec. 7.4, the selection of a baseline guideway beam section is closely dependent upon the selected vehicle suspension geometry. The U-shaped guideway section illustrated in Figs. 7-3 and 7-4 has inherent capability to meet all of the requirements noted above, and this beam shape was selected for further study.

Execution of the guideway beam in pre- and post-tensioned reinforced concrete form is attractive from the standpoint of architectural expression, and indeed represents a viable alternative for straight guideway sections. However, for the long sweeping curves required at intersections, pre- or post-tensioning may lead to buckling, and without such tensioning it is difficult to obtain sufficient strength in long-span concrete beams. Therefore, we have predicated our design and costing studies on the use of a simple steel-plate beam of the type illustrated in Fig. 7-8. It will be understood, however, that for the straight sections of guideway, this could be replaced by the pre- or post-tensioned concrete beam.

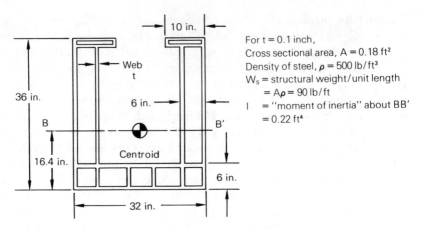

For t = 0.1 inch,
Cross sectional area, A = 0.18 ft²
Density of steel, ρ = 500 lb/ft³
W_s = structural weight/unit length
    = $A\rho$ = 90 lb/ft
I   = "moment of inertia" about BB'
    = 0.22 ft⁴

Fig. 7-8. Typical Cross Section for a Steel Beam

7.6.1 Static and Dynamic Design Criteria

Current practice for contemporary elevated guideway design is to base requirements and criteria on AASHO (American Association of State Highway Officials), and AISC (American Institute of Steel Construction) documents. Unfortunately, these data are aimed at massive bridge-like structure, and do not account for the effects on passenger comfort of vehicle suspension interaction with flexible guideway beams. Structural criteria specifically related to the emerging field of small vehicle/slender elevated guideway design technology are needed, and some of the effects of various criteria on beam and column design will be discussed here.

There are four important structural criteria which must be satisfied by the guideway beam. The first is related to guideway resilience, the second to guideway strength, the third to guideway stiffness, and the fourth and most stringent to dynamic stability. These criteria may be formulated as follows:

A. *Resilience Criterion*

A guideway span shall suffer no permanent deformation as the result of having fully occupied vehicles stalled nose-to-tail along the guideway span. If there were deformation, it would be necessary to replace the beam, and this would be costly. Technically, this criterion requires that the maximum local stress be less than the beam material yield stress.

B. *Column-Out Strength Criterion*

If a column has been removed (e.g., by having been struck by a massive truck), the resulting double-length span shall not rupture when loaded with fully-occupied vehicles nose-to-tail. This requires that the maximum local bending stress be less than the beam material ultimate stress. In the worst case there might be a permanent set, requiring the two neighboring spans to be replaced when the column is replaced.

An alternative is to widen each column at its base into a strong abutment capable of warding off heavy trucks. In that event this column-out criterion can be waived.

C. *Stiffness/Comfort Criterion*

The maximum static deflection of the beam shall be constrained to limit the vertical motion experienced by passengers to that prescribed by comfort standards. For example, if the columns are 60 ft apart, and the line speed is somewhere in the range of 30 ft/sec to 90 ft/sec, the frequency of the vertical motion will be between 0.5 Hz and 1.5 Hz. In this frequency range, established comfort criteria (Fig. 7-9) stipulate that the vertical RMS (root mean square) acceleration be limited to about 0.1 g (or 3.2 ft/sec^2).

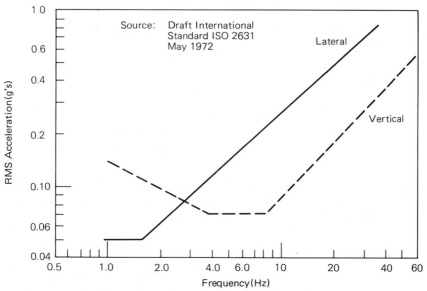

Fig. 7-9. Acceleration Comfort Boundaries (16 minute exposure)

The guideway height (measured from the mean height) at a distance x from a column may be approximated by

$$y = \frac{\Delta}{2} \cos \frac{2\pi x}{L}, \qquad (7.1)$$

where L is the beam span and Δ is the total beam deflection.

If we measure time t from the time that a given vehicle passes a column, then its longitudinal position at time t is given by

$$x(t) = Vt. \tag{7.2}$$

Substituting this into Eq. (7.1), the height of the vehicle at time t is

$$y(t) = \frac{\Delta}{2} \cos \frac{2\pi Vt}{L}. \tag{7.3}$$

Differentiating twice, one obtains the vertical acceleration at the time t,

$$\ddot{y}(t) = -\frac{\Delta}{2} \left(\frac{2\pi V}{L} \right)^2 \cos \frac{2\pi Vt}{L}. \tag{7.4}$$

The RMS vertical acceleration a_v is then given by

$$a_v = \frac{\Delta}{2\sqrt{2}} \left(\frac{2\pi V}{L} \right)^2 \tag{7.5}$$

Taking $a_v \leqslant 3.2$ ft/sec^2, Table 7-2 gives for various line speeds the maximum allowed value of Δ/L^2.

Table 7-2. Beam Stiffness Requirement to Meet Comfort Criterion

V	$(\Delta/L^2)_{max}$
30 ft/sec	25.5×10^{-5} ft^{-1}
60 ft/sec	6.37×10^{-5} ft^{-1}
90 ft/sec	2.83×10^{-5} ft^{-1}

This criterion provides a far more rational approach to specifying beam stiffness than the time-honored approach of limiting the ratio Δ/L to some arbitrarily specified value like 1/800 or 1/1000.

D. *Dynamic Stability Criterion*

The periodic entry of closely spaced vehicles onto a beam shall not excite any resonant frequencies in that beam. If a resonant frequency were excited, the amplitude of oscillation could build up until rupture occurred. This would be a modern-day counterpart of the bridge that collapsed because of resonance set up by marching soldiers. To avoid this catastrophe the fundamental frequency for vertical vibration should be about 1.5 times the maximum frequency of the exciting force (i.e., the frequency of vehicles entering the span).[6] The fundamental frequency could not be lower than the frequency of closely spaced vehicles entering, for then it would be excited by a uniform stream of vehicles of less than the maximum line density.

Assuming vehicles in 15-ft slots, the Table 7-3 provides for various line speeds V, the minimum headway H, and the minimum allowable fundamental frequency f_{min}, assuming that it must be a factor of 1.5 times the frequency of excitation f_e.

Table 7-3. Minimum Fundamental Beam Frequencies

V	Headway, H	Exciting Frequency, f_e	f_{min} (= 1.5 f_e)
30 ft/sec	0.50 sec	2.0 Hz	3.0
45 ft/sec	0.33 sec	3.0 Hz	4.5
60 ft/sec	0.25 sec	4.0 Hz	6.0
75 ft/sec	0.20 sec	5.0 Hz	7.5
90 ft/sec	0.17 sec	6.0 Hz	9.0

Of the four criteria just defined, the last one is the most stringent except at very low speeds. Consequently, we shall consider it first. To understand the nature of the problem we first consider a single beam of constant cross section which is supported at its ends by columns but not attached or, alternatively, is attached by pins. Either alternative will leave it free to assume any slope at its ends. With this kind of support there is no way for a bending moment to be transmitted to the columns. The beam will undergo a static deflection as a result of its average load, but superimposed thereon will be a complex motion which may be regarded as superposition of a number of "normal modes" of vibration. The frequency of the nth mode is

$$f_n = \frac{1}{2\pi} \left(\frac{n\pi}{L}\right)^2 \sqrt{\frac{EIg}{W}} \, , \tag{7.6}$$

where

L = beam span (ft),

E = Young's modulus for steel

$= 30 \times 10^6$ lb/in.^{2} = 4.3×10^9 lb/ft^2,

I = cross-section moment of inertia (ft^4),

W = total weight per unit length (lb/ft).

---

[6] Snyder, J.E., Warmley, D.N., and Richardson, H.H., "Personal Rapid Transit System, Vehicle-Elevated Guideway Dynamics: Multiple Vehicle Single Span Systems," Cambridge MA, MIT Report EPL-81608-1, October 1975.

It should be understood that W must include the structural and non-structural guideway weights as well as the distributed weight of the vehicles. Although precambering will reduce the static deflection it has no impact on the vibrations, since the frequency is dependent on the total mass to be moved vertically.

The worst case occurs, i.e., the lowest frequencies occur, when there are fully occupied vehicles in every slot. Assuming occupied vehicle weights of 2,400 lb every 15 ft, the vehicles contribute 160 lb/ft to W. If we consider the beam to be of the form shown in Fig. 7-8, the structural weight is 90 lb/ft. In Chapter 9 we cost the beam on the assumption that the structural material will not be fully effective and 40% is added to the weight, bringing the structural weight up to 126 lb/ft. The nonstructural equipment mounted to the guideway adds another estimated 84 lb. Thus, the total value of W is 370 lb/ft (160 + 126 + 84). The value of I, as shown in Fig. 7-8, is 0.22 ft^4 since the additional 40% structural weight is assumed to be ineffective in carrying load.

If we assume a beam span of 60 ft, we may now evaluate the fundamental frequency (i.e., $n = 1$) from Eq. (7.6). The result is

$$f_1 = \frac{\pi}{2 \times 60^2} \sqrt{\frac{4.3 \times 10^9 \times 0.22 \times 32.2}{370}} = 3.96 \text{ Hz} \quad (7.7)$$

Comparing with Table 7-3 we see that the guideway would be dynamically stable at 30 ft/sec (about 20 mi/hr) but might even be a problem at 45 ft/sec (about 30 mi/hr).

Before discussing what can be done about this problem, it should be noted that if we had been content to achieve a minimum headway of 0.5 sec, then the maximum excitation frequency would be 2 Hz and the fundamental would be approximately double this. (At higher speeds the vehicles would be more spaced out, which would decrease the distributed weight W and increase the fundamental frequency.) Thus, with a minimum headway of 0.5 sec and 60 ft spans there is no dynamic stability problem. With a 1.0 sec minimum headway, there would be no dynamic stability problem with spans up to 90 ft, or perhaps 100 ft (although the other criteria might not be satisfied without increasing the beam depth).

Since we feel it very important for many urban applications to achieve minimum headways substantially less than 0.5 sec, let us see what can be done to cope with this dynamic stability problem. One possibility is to increase the depth of the beam. If, for example, the 3-ft depth in Fig. 7-8 were changed to 4 ft but no other dimensions were changed, then for a 0.1 inch web thickness the moment of inertia I would increase to 0.45 ft^4. At the same time, however, there would be a partial offset due to W increasing by 23 lb/ft (including the 40% factor for non-load-bearing structure). The effect of these changes is to raise the fundamental frequency to 5.49 Hz, a 39% increase which might extend operation up to about 38 mi/hr.

A more effective gain in fundamental frequency could be achieved by reducing the beam span, since the frequency is inversely proportional to L^2. For example, reducing L from 60 ft to 40 ft will multiply the frequency by 2.25. Thus, with the original beam depth (3 ft), the fundamental frequency could be raised to 8.91 Hz which should be effective up to 60 mi/hr.

Unfortunately the use of shorter beam spans may be aesthetically objectionable and may pose some serious traffic interference problems when the guideway is bridging city streets.

A far more attractive approach is to use a different type of guideway support. It is known that if a beam is "clamped" at its ends to ensure that it is horizontal there, the static deflection is decreased by a factor of 5 (assuming uniform loading) and the fundamental frequency is increased by a factor[7] of 2.2669. Thus, with a 60 ft beam span and 3 ft depth (as shown in Fig. 7-8), the fundamental frequency will be raised to 8.98 Hz which will ensure stability up to about 60 mi/hr. If there are locations on high-speed lines where spans of greater than 60 ft are required, then in addition to clamping it will be necessary to use a beam deeper than 3 ft and possibly with thicker plates for the top and bottom horizontal surfaces. We shall return to clamping later after we have discarded another possibility.

If the beam were continuous over the columns, but not clamped to the columns, the slope would be continuous from one side of the column to the other. With equal loading on two neighboring beam sections, it is apparent from considerations of symmetry that the beam would be horizontal at its point of support. Thus, as with a clamped beam, the beam sections are horizontal at their ends and the static deflection will be the same as that of a clamped beam: i.e., one-fifth of the deflection of an independent beam section which is supported at its ends but not continuous with the neighboring sections. Since the static deflection for the continuous beam is the same as that of a clamped beam, one might hope that the fundamental frequency of vibration is also the same. Unfortunately, this is not the case because the slope is not constrained to be horizontal at the columns. While one section is raised above its static position, its neighbor is depressed below its static position in a type of teeter-totter mode of vibration with the columnar support acting as the

[7] The nth mode frequency is actually increased by a factor $\alpha_n{}^2/n^2$ where is the nth positive solution for α in the equation

$$\cosh(\alpha\pi)\cos(\alpha\pi) = 1 \qquad (7.8)$$

fulcrum. The fundamental frequency of this oscillation is exactly equal to that given by Eq. (7.6). Thus, nothing is gained in dynamic stability.

One might wonder whether this kind of oscillation could not be eliminated by varying columnar spacings but keeping the same average spacing. For example, instead of using 60 ft spacing of columns one might alternate between 50 ft and 70 ft. The effect is that there will still be a teeter-totter vibration mode but the frequency will correspond to that for some intermediate length.[8] The net effect is actually a degradation. One may see this easily in the limiting case as one span goes to zero and the other approaches 120 ft. The existence of the very short span actually ensures that the beam is horizontal in that region. Thus, in effect, the 120 ft span is clamped (horizontal) at both ends. The clamping, as discussed earlier, raises the fundamental frequency by a factor of 2.2669. However, going from a 60 ft span to a 120 ft span lowers the frequency by a factor of 4. (The principle of clamping by supporting on two closely placed columns is illustrated in the architectural model in Fig. 2-6).

Let us again consider a beam which is clamped firmly to very stiff columns at its two ends. There will be two flex points, locations of zero curvature where there is no bending moment. These points will be a distance defined as L_F from the closest column. For a uniformly loaded beam, $L_F = 0.211\,L$, where L is the distance between columns (not the distance between centers). Since the beam carries no moment at the flex points, they are good locations for dividing the beam, as illustrated in Fig. 7-10.

[8] If every other span is L_1 and the alternate ones are L_2, then the frequency of the nth normal mode is

$$f_n = \frac{1}{2\pi} \gamma_n^2 \sqrt{\frac{EIg}{W}}\,, \qquad (7.9)$$

where γ_n is the nth positive solution for γ in the equation:

$$\coth \gamma L_1 + \coth \gamma L_2 - \cot \gamma L_1 - \cot \gamma L_2$$
$$= \pm \left[\operatorname{csch} \gamma L_1 + \operatorname{csch} \gamma L_2 - \csc \gamma L_1 - \csc \gamma L_2 \right]. \qquad (7.10)$$

The minus sign is to be used for odd values of n (including the fundamental) and the plus sign for even values.

The reader may verify two special cases:

(i) When $L_1 = L_2 = L$, the solution is $\gamma_n = n\pi/L$, which brings the above equation for f_n into agreement with Eq. (7.6).

(ii) As $L_1 \to 0$, $(\coth \gamma L_1 - \cot \gamma L_1) \to 0$ and $(\operatorname{csch} \gamma L_1 - \csc \gamma L_1) \to 0$.
Therefore, the above equation for γ becomes
$$\coth \gamma L_2 - \cot \gamma L_2 = \pm \left[\operatorname{csch} \gamma L_2 - \csc \gamma L_2 \right].$$

Squaring and simplifying, this may be written
$$\cosh \gamma L_2 \cos \gamma L_2 = 1.$$

Replacing γ by $\alpha\pi/L_2$, this equation becomes identical to the equation of footnote 7. Thus, the beam span L_2 behaves as though it were clamped.

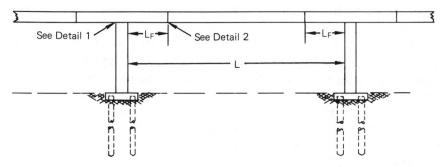

DETAIL 1 — BEAM/COLUMN MOMENT-CARRYING JOINT CONCEPTS

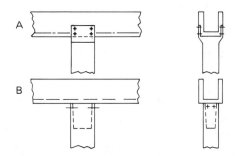

DETAIL 2 — BEAM INFLECTION/EXPANSION JOINT CONCEPT

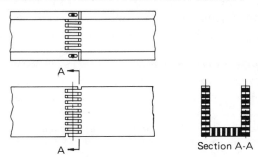

Section A-A

Fig. 7-10. Clamped Beam with Segments Joined at Flex Points

Short beams of length equal to the column thickness plus $2L_F$ are firmly clamped at their midpoints to the end plates of columns. If the columns were post-tensioned reinforced concrete, these would be the end plates to which the column's reinforcing tensioned cables would be attached. One means of attachment would be to have the endplate turned up into a U-shape channel into which the beam could be set, as illustrated in Detail 1 of Fig. 7-10. (The two options shown differ only in how the beam is set into the U-shaped end plate.) The column and beam could then be joined by bolts and shear pins to ensure that any bending moment in the beam would be transmitted to the column and finally to the buried caissons at the foot of the column.

Between each pair of clamped beams there would be a connecting beam of an approximate length $L/\sqrt{3} = 0.577L$. The connecting beam might be pinned (with a transverse horizontal pin) to one of the two clamped beams, and it might have a sliding expansion joint with the other to accommodate thermal expansion or differential earth settlement in the two columns. There is, of course, no need to carry moment across these joints. Detail 2 of Fig. 7-10 illustrates one possibility for the expansion joint.

Although the joints between the clamped beams and the connecting beams should be placed close to the locations where flex points would have appeared on a continuous beam, no serious problems are introduced if the joints are somewhat removed from the flex points. If they are removed, there will still be zero moment at the end of each of the adjoining segments, but there will be a slight discontinuity in slope. For example, for a 60-ft separation between columns the joints nominally would occur 12.7 ft from columns, but if they were anywhere in the range of 10 to 15 ft from a column, the change in slope at the joints would be less than 0.3 milliradians (1 angular minute). With any reasonable secondary suspension system, this would be unnoticeable.

With the joints at the nominal positions the fundamental frequency differs from that of the ideally clamped beam for two reasons. The first is that in a continuous beam with uniform loading the flex points for the fundamental mode of vibration are slightly displaced from the flex points for static deflection. As a result, the fundamental frequency is about 1/2% lower than the fundamental frequency for a continuous clamped beam.[9] A more important

---

[9] More generally, if the joints between clamped beams and connecting beams are a distance L_J from the closest column, the fundamental frequency will be

$$f_1 = \frac{1}{2\pi}\left(\frac{\beta\pi}{L}\right)^2 \sqrt{\frac{EIg}{W}}, \qquad (7.11)$$

where L is the distance between columns (not center-to-center) and β is the smallest positive number which satisfies the equation:

$$\frac{1}{2}\tan\left[\beta\left(\frac{1}{2}-\frac{L_J}{L}\right)\right] + \frac{1}{2}\tanh\left[\beta\left(\frac{1}{2}-\frac{L_J}{L}\right)\right]$$

$$= \frac{\sec\left(\beta\frac{L_J}{L}\right)\,\text{sech}\left(\beta\frac{L_J}{L}\right) + 1}{\tan\left(\beta\frac{L_J}{L}\right) - \tanh\left(\beta\frac{L_J}{L}\right)} \qquad (7.12)$$

Taking $L_J = L_F = 0.211L$, the value of β^2 is 2.2542 which is about 1/2% smaller than the factor 2.2669 for a continuous clamped beam.

effect is associated with the fact that the columns are not infinitely stiff. Because the columns will bend, the beam will not be kept absolutely level. We have not computed this effect, but it should have no major influence on the fundamental frequency because the column is so much shorter than a beam span and hence much stiffer than the beams.

With the beam clamped firmly to the columns, the question arises as to whether the beam will break if a massive truck strikes a column. To avoid such an occurrence, we recommend that the column be widened at its base into a strong protective abutment capable of warding off heavy trucks. Then, of course, the column-out strength criterion (B) can be waived.

An ancillary advantage of the clamped beam design discussed here is its low static deflection. The beam members would, of course, be precambered so that under some "normal load" they would be straight. Then with a uniformly distributed maximum load, δW lb/ft greater than the normal load, the deflection in the middle of the beam would be[10]

$$\Delta = \frac{1}{384} \frac{\delta W}{EI} L^4. \tag{7.13}$$

If precambering is for two vehicles per span, then δW is the distributed weight for two others: i.e., 80 lb/ft. Evaluating Eq. (7.13) for a 60-ft span and for the cross-section shown in Fig. 7-8, we obtain $\Delta = 0.0029$ ft and $\Delta/L^2 = 8.0 \times 10^{-7}$ ft^{-1}. Comparing with Table 7-1, we see that this is about a factor of 35 less than the deflection required for comfort at 90 ft/sec.

In a similar way, because the static deflection of a clamped beam is so small, the resilience criterion (A) is easily satisfied. In addition, even though the column-out criterion (B) has been waived, it would have been easily satisfied.

The above discussion related to the static and dynamic criteria which must be satisfied in beam design. We now consider briefly the criteria which apply to columns and foundations.

---

[10] Equation (7.13) assumes that the joints between the clamped and connecting beams of Fig. 7-10 are placed at the flex points. More generally the static deflection would be multiplied by the factor:

$$1 + 4 \left(1 - 4 \frac{L_J}{L}\right) \left(1 - 6 \frac{L_J}{L} + 6 \frac{L_J^2}{L^2}\right) \tag{7.14}$$

where L_J is the distance between the joints and the closest column and L is the distance between columns. The reader may easily verify that the last term vanishes when

$$L_J/L = (1 - 1/\sqrt{3})/2$$

and the factor becomes 1. For $L_J = 0$, the factor is 5, which is the well-known result for a supported (but not clamped) beam.

We have already pointed out that in those parts of a PRT network where vehicle headways might be substantially less than 0.5 sec, it probably will be desirable to clamp beams to columns in order to avoid using very short spans or deep beams. When this is done, it probably is advisable to broaden the column at its base into an abutment capable of warding off heavy trucks. In other parts of the network, or on whole PRT systems, where headways are greater than 0.5 sec, clamping is not required and columns need not be capable of warding off a heavy truck as long as the column-out criterion (B) is met.

Another criterion which must be met by columns and their foundations is that they be able to withstand the loads induced by simultaneous emergency braking of all vehicles on the line. In some localities it would be prudent to consider additional side-loading resulting from heavy winds acting on the guideway and vehicles. Other than these considerations it is very difficult to draw generalizations about columns and foundations because of their site peculiarities.

7.6.2 Guideway Surface Irregularities

It is important to limit guideway surface irregularities to ensure the passenger a comfortable ride. The comfort criteria of Fig. 7-9 specify as a function of frequency the RMS vertical and lateral accelerations to which the passenger may be subjected.

To see what this implies on surface irregularity, let us consider by way of example the vertical motion. We imagine a sinusoidal surface having wavelength λ and amplitude Δ.

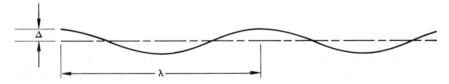

Then for a vehicle which passes the peak at time $t = 0$ and at line speed V, the height[11] of the wheel contact is

$$y_w = \Delta \cos\left(\frac{2\pi Vt}{\lambda}\right). \tag{7.15}$$

This may also be written

$$y_w = \Delta \cos(2\pi ft). \tag{7.16}$$

where $f = V/\lambda$ is the frequency of the disturbance.

---

[11] We assume the wavelength λ is long compared to the distance between tandem wheels. Thus, we assume both wheels at the same height. Therefore, we also ignore pitching motion in this simple analysis.

The vertical acceleration felt by the passenger will depend, of course, on the type of secondary suspension system. To obtain useful insight into permissible surface irregularities let us consider a simple spring suspension with the motion viscously damped. The result of the analysis is that the RMS vertical acceleration felt by the passenger is

$$a_v = \frac{\Delta}{\sqrt{2}} \ (2\pi f)^2 \left[\frac{1 + (2bf/f_n)^2}{(1 - f^2/f_n^2)^2 + (2bf/f_n)^2} \right]^{\frac{1}{2}} \tag{7.17}$$

where

f_n = natural frequency of undamped spring/mass suspension system, and

b = damping ratio (ratio of viscous-damping constant to critical damping constant).

For any frequency f, Fig. 7-9 may be used to find the allowable RMS vertical acceleration a_v. Then, with the values of f_n and b specified, Eq. (7.17) may be used to find Δ_{max}, the maximum allowable value of Δ. Typical results are plotted in Fig. 7-11 for a suspension natural frequency f_n of 1.6 Hz and a damping ratio b of 0.25. The figure plots Δ_{max} for vertical irregularities versus the reciprocal of f; i.e., versus the period of oscillation, T. The reason for plotting against T rather than f will soon be apparent. The figure also plots allowable lateral irregularities as a function of T, assuming that the body is isolated from the lateral guidance wheels by a suspension system with a natural frequency of 1.2 Hz and a damping ratio of 0.50.

Because the wavelength λ is proportional to T (i.e., $\lambda = V/f = VT$), Fig. 7-11 also carries wavelength scales along its abscissa for line speeds V of 30 ft/sec and 90 ft/sec. By comparing Δ_{max} for the same wavelength at the two different speeds, the reader will see that for vertical motion the problem always becomes more severe at higher speeds but that this is not always so for the lateral motion.

The Aerospace Corporation has not made a detailed study of fabrication techniques for guideway beams although we believe the roughness criteria of Fig. 7-11 can be met. An interesting report[12] analyzing guideway irregularity, based on the Dulles Transpo 72 Program, details surface acceptance measurement techniques and concludes that at least one of the Transpo contractors could have met a specification of the type illustrated in Fig. 7-11.

---

[12] Caywood, W.C., and Rubinstein, N., "Ride Quality & Guideway Roughness Measurements of the Transpo '72 PRT Systems," *High Speed Ground Transportation Journal*, Vol. 8, No. 3 (1974).

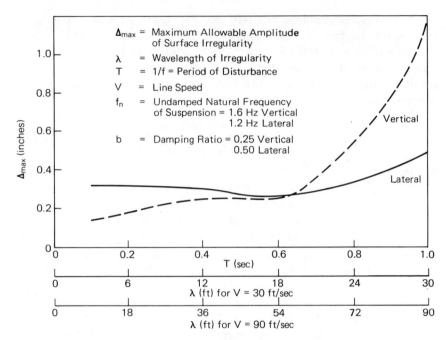

Fig. 7-11. Typical Requirement on Surface Irregularity

The requirements on surface irregularity could be further relaxed by using softer suspensions (lower natural frequencies) than those assumed in Fig. 7-11. However, the body motion would then be less responsive to intentional changes in guideway direction, and on curved portions of the guideway the body would be further displaced from the undercarriage. For example, consider the lateral motion when going around a curve with a centripetal acceleration of 0.15 g. With the 1.2 Hz natural frequency assumed in Fig. 7-11, the body would be displaced by approximately 1 inch. Had we used 0.8 Hz, the surface irregularities could be almost twice as large, but in going around the 0.15-g curve the body displacement would increase to 2-1/4 inches. This would not require widening the guideway if the supporting springs were above the guideway, but there clearly is a practical limit on how much displacement can be tolerated.

Guideway irregularities generated by differential earth settlements probably could be controlled through utilization of adjustable column mounting plates. Such design features have been successfully incorporated in the emplacement of large freeway signs in the Los Angeles area.

It is evident that the whole trade-off area of guideway/suspension interaction is a major one, deserving of high priority for systematic and detailed study in the future.

7.6.3 Intersection Structures

Treatment of a typical two-in, two-out guideway intersection, as illustrated by the plan view in Fig. 7-12, represents one of the most difficult structural and aesthetic problems facing the guideway system designer. Here the requirement is to furnish support for four guideway spans in such a manner as to minimize impact on surface street traffic. Examination of various concepts, including individual column supports and tower-mounted suspension cables, led to selection of the continuous, rigid-frame truss support structure illustrated in the frontispiece as the preferred approach. No structural technique exhibiting lesser visual impact was found, and a further advantage of this configuration is that it tends to feature a mutually balancing set of external loads.

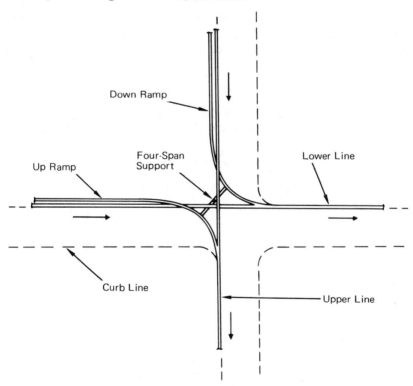

Fig. 7-12. Guideway Intersection for Los Angeles Montage Layout (see Frontispiece)

7.6.4 Guideway Aesthetics

The whole subjective area of aesthetic acceptability of elevated guideways continues to be one of the most controversial aspects of PRT system evaluation. The view was taken early in studies at

Aerospace that an acceptable guideway configuration must minimize visual intrusiveness and light blockage, and the whole slender guideway rationale related earlier in this chapter was evolved in response to such goals. Short of day-to-day experience with an operating PRT installation, however, utilization of realistic photomontage techniques and detailed scaled architectural models appear to offer the most promising guides to perception. The photomontage shown in the frontispiece and the 1/160-scale architectural model photos shown in Figs. 2-3 through 2-6 (see Chapter 2), all of which are based on a downtown Los Angeles setting, illustrate that the guideway and station structures appear small and unobtrusive in comparison to their urban surroundings, and that guideway shadowing does not appear to create a problem. These photographs have been widely viewed in the United States and abroad. Response has indeed demonstrated that "beauty is in the eye of the beholder," although most persons who consciously weighed the PRT system service benefits against the potential visual impacts concluded that the former were predominate over the latter.

7.6.5 Protection from Ice and Snow

Figure 7-13 illustrates some conceptual design features examined at Aerospace which could be developed to protect both the guideway

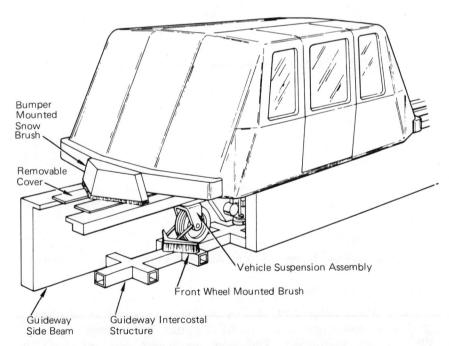

Bumper
Mounted
Snow
Brush

Removable
Cover

Guideway
Side Beam

Guideway Intercostal
Structure

Front Wheel Mounted Brush

Vehicle Suspension Assembly

Fig. 7-13. Guideway Protection from Snow Accumulation

and the vehicles from the accumulation of ice and snow. The light-weight removable cover shown at the upper guideway surface could limit snow ingress to a fairly narrow slot, and the upper surface could be continually swept clean by simple brushes mounted on the vehicle frontal surfaces. Snow which passed through the upper slot could be quickly removed through interstices in the lower guideway surface through the action of a small brush mounted near the front wheels. It should also be noted that the guideway interior surface would tend to run warm for many hours of each operating day, since the pulsed d.c. linear motor primaries, discussed earlier, would dissipate about 10% of the input power in the form of heat. Thus, there would be a built-in heating effect which could be significant for a short-headway system.

7.6.6 Protection from Lightning

Two distinct approaches to protection from lightning are currently in successful use and these have been termed "remedial protection" and "preventive protection." The remedial concept assumes that lightning *will* strike, and seeks to minimize the effects by channeling energy to earth with well-grounded conductors and wire shields. Such conventional protection features lightning rods, which are assumed to furnish protection within a cone of basal radius equal to the rod height. Large steel buildings and structures which have lightning grounding paths will serve as "natural" lightning arrestors for PRT installations in typical urban activity center settings. Application of this protection concept in the lower profile suburban areas could take the form of lightning rods extending above each guideway column to a height of slightly more than one-half span length and having a metallic path of adequate cross section to ground. It is conservatively estimated that a typical installation consisting of a set of dual 1-sq-in. copper cables extending from the top of a 32-ft rod to ground under an 18-ft-high guideway beam would cost about $1,000 per column, including ground and current-flow checkout, or a little over 2% of the nominal system per-mile capital cost.

The preventive protection concept, on the other hand, offers a method of continually discharging the potential energy between cloud and ground in small amounts over a relatively long period so electrostatic pressures required for a lightning stroke are never reached. This amounts to short circuiting the air gap with many low-resistance paths using contacts with specially designed sharp points which promote flow of current into the air. A proprietary dissipation array design technique is reported[13] to have been used

---

[13] Anon., "Multi-Point Dissipator: Lightning Won't Touch It," *Electric Light and Power, T/D Edition*, Cahners Publishing Company, Inc., October 1974.

in a variety of configurations with such success that a bonded warranty against lightning strike losses is included in the installation cost. Installed cost of dissipation-type protection published by one company came to about $1,000 per acre, from which it can be deduced that costs for a linear protective array for a PRT guideway might be attractive.

In summary, it appears that PRT guideways emplaced in urban centers will have built-in lightning protection through the arresting effect of adjacent buildings. Furthermore, there are at least two effective and well established techniques for limiting lightning damage in the more exposed suburban network segments which are available at acceptable costs. These latter approaches would require consideration only for system installations in areas of the country exhibiting high keraunic levels.

7.6.7 Electrification Considerations

It was assumed that the interface between the PRT electrical distribution system and the municipal or commercial power source would be at the subtransmission level: i.e., typically at 35 kV. Figure 7-14 illustrates an assumed configuration for a PRT network electrical substation in which a.c. is rectified to d.c. for guideway distribution. The 35 kV circuit is fed to the 2500 kVA substation transformer through a 3-phase protective circuit breaker. If d.c. is used for guideway distribution, the substation transformer is assumed to be 3-phase to 6-phase to improve the quality of the d.c. output. The 6-phase 1 kV transformer output is fed through a power rectifier and protective circuit breaker to the substation 1 kV d.c. bus. The guideway conductors are assumed fed in four directions from each intersection for a typical network link length of 1/2 mi, and the guideway distribution system was considered to be redundant (installed on both inner walls of the guideway) and connected to adjoining substations in a network to provide a parallel redundant supply, as illustrated in Fig. 7-15.

The configuration of Fig. 7-15 can be considered no more than a typical example, since the distance between intersections may vary and the maximum vehicle density will also vary from one part of a network to another. The network designer will have to find locations for each substation (not necessarily at intersections) so that each can handle its normal load and an assigned fraction of the load of a neighboring substation that is down.

The selection of ≈ 1 kV as the guideway distribution voltage was arrived at by considering $I^2 R$ losses in the conductors, the operating requirements of the propulsion system, and guideway sizing to provide adequate electrical isolation for the conductors. Higher

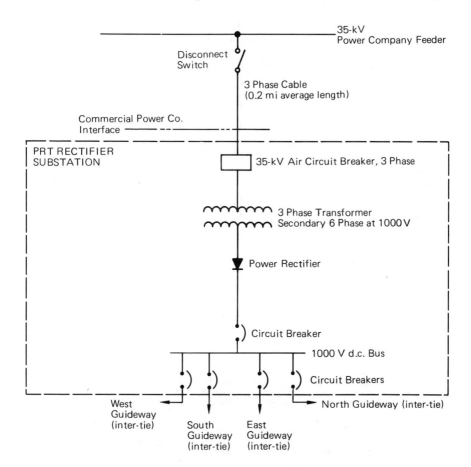

Fig. 7-14. Typical PRT Electrical Substation

voltages would, of course, reduce line currents and therefore reduce I^2R losses. However, as voltages increase, the guideway sidewall height also increases, thereby adding to the guideway costs. Also taken into account was the necessity to maintain input voltage at a suitable level to ensure a proper margin above the counter-emf generated within the motor.

The choice between a.c. or d.c. distribution systems is based on cost considerations. The electrical substation costs for the a.c. over the d.c. option are reduced by approximately the cost of the power rectifier. However, the guideway costs for the a.c. option are increased due to the increased number of conductors (to provide 3-phase, 4-wire). In addition, the a.c. option increases the cost of each vehicle, requiring addition of 4 pick-up shoes and a full-wave rectifier sufficient to handle a 50 hp motor. Operation with 8 pick-up shoes on

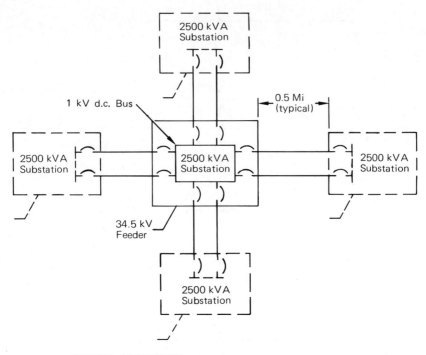

NORMAL OPERATION:
  Each Substation Provides ½ Power to 2 Mi of Guideway.
  At 200 Vehicles/Mi (60% Line Density),
  Power = ½ (400 Vehicles x 10 kVA/vehicle) = 2000 kVA

EMERGENCY OPERATION:
  With Outage of Adjoining Substation
  Power = Normal Power + ¼ Power of Down Substation
        = 2500 kVA

Fig. 7-15. Typical PRT Electrical Network

the vehicle, rather than 4, would also have a negative influence on vehicle reliability and maintenance cost.

Direct current distribution was selected for the Aerospace baseline system concept, since the a.c. alternative was estimated to cost about $160,000 (1975) per mile more than d.c., and to entail additional preventive maintenance costs without commensurate benefits.

7.7 ANCILLARY FACILITIES

7.7.1 Vehicle Storage and Cleaning Facility

During off-peak hours it will be necessary to store most of the vehicles in storage facilities. The vehicles cannot be allowed to cruise and consume power and there is only room for a small fraction of them at stations. It may also be desirable to have each vehicle cleaned automatically every day, to have it inspected, and to have it undergo a subsystem checkout procedure, especially for electronic subsystems. For these reasons we have predicated a sheltered multi-functional facility for storage, cleaning, and checkout.

A sketch depicting a typical vehicle cleaning and storage facility is shown in Fig. 7-16, illustrating areas equipped for internal/external cleaning and vehicle status checkout. The vehicles upon leaving the checkout station either would be diverted to the storage area, during low system utilization periods, or would be dispatched to service operation or to maintenance facilities.

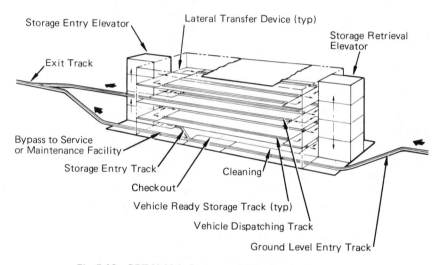

Fig. 7-16. PRT Vehicle Storage and Cleaning Facility Concept

Vehicles entering storage would be lifted from the ground level to other storage levels by elevator. At each level, the vehicles would be directed to storage tracks by lateral transfer devices, would be removed by similar devices at the far end of the track, and again moved vertically by an elevator to place the vehicles on a dispatching track where they would be on call by the system control center.

The activities associated with cleaning and checkout would be semi-automatic, utilizing operators only to monitor and perform certain random discretionary functions, such as removing personal effects left in vehicles and aiding in the use of diagnostic equipments applied to the vehicle at the checkout station. There would be a visual inspection to determine whether there had been any vandalism of the vehicle. If so, the record of passenger ID's would be preserved (Sec. 1.7.2); if not, the record would be erased. The vehicle storage function would be fully automatic.

A conservative requirement that 85% of the system fleet could be stored at one time was adopted for baseline system sizing and cost estimation purposes. The facilities were individually sized for storage of 170 vehicles and were assumed to be located uniformly throughout the network at 2 mi intervals. Each site would involve approximately 5,000 sq ft of surface area for facility construction.

7.7.2 Vehicle Maintenance Facility

As described above, and analyzed in Chapter 9, there would be a daily checkout of critical subsystems in each vehicle to determine its operating status. Should malfunction of any element be discovered, the vehicle would be routed to a maintenance facility for repair.

In considering the basic types of preventive maintenance actions to be performed on various vehicle subsystems, timeline estimates were developed which lead to an overall monthly average for preventive vehicle servicing. These analyses, along with considerations of centralization and attendant congestion, led to the conclusion that a facility capable of servicing up to 250 vehicles/weekday, each taking 2.2 hr (average), would be appropriate. The facility was sized on the assumption of two 8-hr shifts. Such a facility could provide one scheduled service each month for at least 5,000 vehicles.

A typical general arrangement of a PRT vehicle maintenance facility is shown in Fig. 7-17. The facility would be a two-story structure, with the upper story devoted to areas for diagnostics, maintenance order preparation, unscheduled maintenance, and scheduled maintenance activities. All work stations would employ

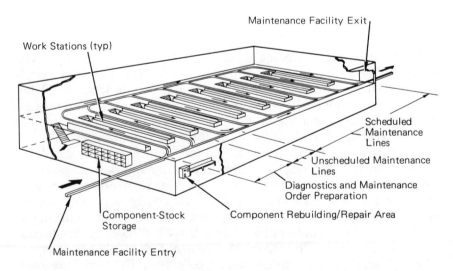

Fig. 7-17. PRT Maintenance Facility Concept

automated servicing equipments and techniques to the fullest extent possible. The ground floor would be for component refurbishment/ repair processing and component stock storage. Each facility would require approximately 14,500 sq ft of surface area.

Chapter 8

RELIABILITY AND
SERVICE DEPENDABILITY

C. L. Olson

8.1 THE MAJOR PROBLEMS OF UNRELIABILITY IN SHORT-HEADWAY PRT SYSTEM CONCEPTS

A commonly accepted definition for reliability is the probability that a system will perform satisfactorily for at least a stated period of time when used under stated conditions. From the viewpoint of the transportation system patron, "reliability" is the chance of completing a trip without an unacceptable delay, and we will call this "dependability." While the acceptability of delay is obviously a most subjective matter, we think that random delays on the order of one minute would be accepted by most system users.

The major problem generated by unreliability in large fleets of automated vehicles operating at short headways on fixed guideway networks is the possibility of a disabled vehicle holding up all upstream traffic on at least one link of the network. Provision of adequate communication links, command systems, service and emergency braking equipment, and vehicle-borne energy absorption and passenger constraint devices, as discussed in Chapter 6, will ensure that passenger safety will not be a primary issue. Instead, system reliability requirements must be aimed at limiting passenger delays to acceptable levels.

A number of concepts for mitigating potential passenger delays upstream of a disabled vehicle have been studied at Aerospace. Chapter 6 discussed concepts for *coping* with disablements which do occur. This chapter discusses means for achieving the goal of minimizing the frequency of disablements at the outset by employing design techniques and operating methodologies which permit attainment of very high reliabilities.

8.2 STATUS OF RELIABILITY DESIGN TECHNOLOGY

Fortunately, the space system developments of the past two decades have made available advanced design techniques, high quality electronic parts, and operating methodologies which can be applied directly to the PRT reliability problem. Some of the results of that experience are illustrated in Fig. 8-1 which summarizes the design-life goals which were set for 12 communications-type satellites with which The Aerospace Corporation has been associated over the past decade.

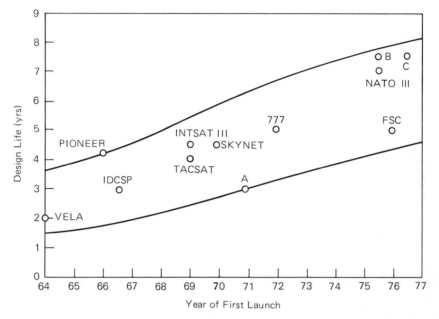

Fig. 8-1. Design Life Trend

It is clear from this figure that the designer's confidence in attainment of high reliability has been growing over the years. It is noteworthy that all of the systems which have, at the time of writing, been in orbit long enough to demonstrate their longevities, have equaled or exceeded their design-life goals.

These increasing reliability goals have been attained in the face of increasing system complexity, which is approaching 100,000 parts for recent vehicles, as illustrated in Fig. 8-2. In contrast, the number of parts in a typical PRT longitudinal control system is nearly two orders of magnitude smaller, which supports the outlook that high reliability PRT systems can be attained with a balanced utilization of current technology.

8.3 RELIABILITY GOALS FOR PRT

In the absence of extensive PRT operating experience, it seems reasonable to utilize the history of the most nearly applicable personal transit system, the automobile. Disability (not accident) rates on the order of 1,000 incidents per 100 million vehicle miles have been

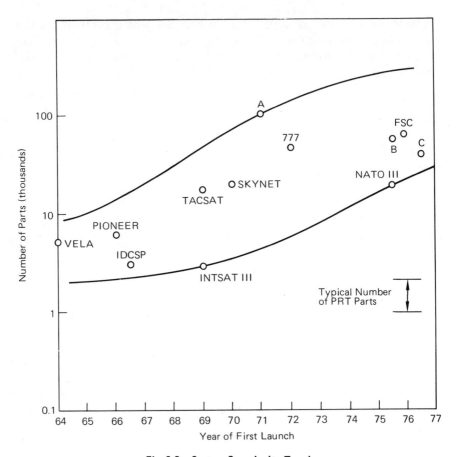

Fig. 8-2. System Complexity Trend

reported for automobiles operating on a wide variety of roadways.[1]

Removal of the driver from the control loop and from the responsibility for maintenance, the relative simplicity of the PRT vehicle, and the use of the design and maintenance philosophy described in the following section would all appear to favor a PRT disability rate goal between 1% and 10% that of the automobile. Thus, disability rate ceilings between 10 and 100 disabilities per 100 million vehicle miles are projected as realistic design criteria, with the range being suggested to accommodate trade-offs between related passenger delays, design techniques, operating strategies, and system capital and operating costs. Some of these trade-offs are quantified later in this chapter.

[1] Wm. F. Hamilton, II, *Automation Performance Requirements for Advanced Urban Transportation Systems,* Carnegie-Mellon University (1970).

8.4 ATTAINMENT OF PRT RELIABILITY/DEPENDABILITY

The approach to attainment of high reliability considers the two generic classes into which all failures can be grouped: failures due to wear-out, which are highly predictable and which tend to be associated with mechanical equipment; and random failures, which are predictable only in statistical terms and which tend to be identified with electronic devices.

Specifically, the design and maintenance philosophy espoused here is based on the following principles:

(1) *Systematic avoidance of wear-out type failures* through adoption of a stringent preventive maintenance/replacement program.

(2) *Minimization of random failures* through use of redundant components and controlled parts in all vital electronic subsystems. (Redundancy[2] is used here in the sense of providing at least two independent means for accomplishment of a given task, so that if the primary means fails there is a backup means for continued operation. By "controlled parts" is meant electronic parts selected through a screening process which results in failure rates much improved over those of comparable commercial parts.)

(3) *Maintenance of redundant subsystems in a healthy state* through regular checkout actions to reveal component failures prior to subsystem functional disablement. (An alternative, not analyzed in detail by Aerospace, is to accomplish checkout by on-board diagnostics which report to appropriate system controls the failure onset of a redundant component, permitting call-in of the reporting vehicle to a maintenance facility after completion of its current trip.)

Regular replacement times for all wear-out-prone vehicle items, failure of which could lead to a "pushing" or "line-clearing" incident, were determined so that wear-out failures would be categorically avoided[3] for the PRT concept studied at Aerospace. The resulting

[2] The power of redundancy follows from a simple rule of the probability calculus: The probability that two independent events will both occur is the product of their probabilities. Thus, if a device had a probability of failure during a day's operation of one in a thousand, the probability of failure of two such devices operated in parallel for the same period would be only one in a million.

[3] Wear-out of well-designed parts is quite peaked in time and follows an approximately normal distribution. A measure of the peak half-widths is σ, the standard deviation from the mean. If, for example, the maintenance protocol were to replace each wear-out-prone part at a time 6σ before the mean time to failure, only one part in a billion (10^9) will fail before replacement.

vehicle planned maintenance schedule is summarized in Table 8-1. This table is used in Sec. 9.3 to estimate preventive maintenance costs.

Table 8-1. Planned Preventive Maintenance Schedule
(Replacement of Wear-Out-Prone Vehicle Components)

	MAINTENANCE PERIOD (months)	MEAN TIME TO REPAIR (hours)
Propulsion	6	1
Control Electronics*	6	1
Communications*	6	1/2
Body Components	6	1
Emergency Devices	6	1/2
Furnishings	6	1/2
Suspension Components and Lubrication	3	1
Power and Signal Collectors	1	1
Total Preventive Maintenance is 25 hr per Year per Vehicle		

*Electromechanical components, if any.

The remaining failure potential is thus reduced to failures based upon chance only, and we predicate a checkout policy which permits repair or replacement of failed redundant components before the entire redundant subsystem fails. This policy of regular checkout plus unscheduled maintenance as required ensures a significant reduction of system failures from the uninspected case, since it makes certain that each new operating period begins with full redundancy restored and the system back in its original good condition.

The PRT concept studied at Aerospace assumes daily semi-automatic vehicle cleaning and checkout operation on each vehicle. The checkout function could be carried out somewhat like the present Volkswagen automobile checkout, through a plug-in equipment module which flags and identifies any failed redundant components for immediate replacement. The checkout period for this concept could thus be any desired multiple of 24 hr. The 24-hr checkout period was arbitrarily selected for purposes of this study. The most appropriate checkout period of a particular system would be determined through trade-offs of disability rates and costs.

8.5 RELIABILITY MATH MODEL

8.5.1 Reliability and Failure Rate

The reliability, $R(t)$, of a device is defined as the probability that the device can still operate correctly after a time t. Another way of stating this is that of a large population of similar devices operable at time zero a fraction $R(t)$ would still be operable at time t. If, in a short time interval Δt, the value of $R(t)$ drops[4] by $-\Delta R$, then the fractional loss in the then operable population would be $-\Delta R/R(t)$. This fractional loss per unit time at the instant t can be found by dividing by Δt and taking the limit as Δt approaches zero. The result is defined as the failure rate, $\lambda(t)$. Thus,

$$\lambda(t) = \lim_{\Delta t \to 0} - \frac{1}{R(t)} \frac{\Delta R}{\Delta t} = - \frac{1}{R(t)} \frac{dR}{dt} . \qquad (8.1)$$

In other words, $\lambda(t)$ may be regarded as the probability of failure per unit time for devices known to be functional at time t.

Generally, it is known that $\lambda(t)$ may have a peak at $t = 0$. This high "infant mortality" rate is due to faulty manufacturing or defective parts. These failures usually show up during factory testing or acceptance testing and should no longer show up during service operations. For devices having wear-out-prone parts, $\lambda(t)$ will rise again as t approaches the lifetime of such parts. However, most electronic parts are not subject to wear-out, and even mechanical parts will not wear out if there is a policy to replace them well in advance of wear-out.

Once one has disposed of the problems of infant mortality and wear-out, the remaining failures are regarded as "random" failures. Experimentally, it is found that if two parts of different age (not subject to wear-out) are both working at the beginning of an interval, then they have an equal chance of working at the end of the interval; i.e., the probability of failure per unit time, $\lambda(t)$, is a constant independent of age. If λ is constant, then the differential equation (8.1) can be solved for $R(t)$:

$$R(t) = e^{-\lambda t}. \qquad (8.2)$$

The mean time between failures (MTBF) is easily computed to be $1/\lambda$.

Let us define $F(t)$ as the probability of failure before time t. Then,

$$F(t) = 1 - R(t) = 1 - e^{-\lambda t}. \qquad (8.3)$$

For t small compared with the MTBF (i.e., for $\lambda t << 1$), a very accurate approximation for $F(t)$ is

$$F(t) \approx \lambda t \qquad (\lambda t << 1). \qquad (8.4)$$

---

[4] By convention, ΔR means the increase in R. Therefore, the decrease is $-\Delta R$. Since ΔR is negative, $-\Delta R$ will be positive.

8.5.2 Redundancy

Thus far we have been describing a "simplex" device or sub-system — one with no redundancy. Let us now consider two types of redundancy. The first of these is active redundancy where two units normally perform the same function (but not necessarily by the same means). If either should fail, the other can carry on alone. Thus, the probability that there is a complete functional failure is the product of the probabilities that each redundant unit has failed. This may be expressed as

$$F_{active}(t) = F_1(t)\, F_2(t)$$

$$= (1 - e^{-\lambda_1 t})\,(1 - e^{-\lambda_2 t})$$

$$\approx (\lambda_1 t)\,(\lambda_2 t) = \lambda_1 \lambda_2 t^2. \qquad (8.5)$$

The approximation which appears in the last line is, of course, good only when $\lambda_1 t$ and $\lambda_2 t$ both are small compared with 1.

To illustrate the significance of the redundancy, let us assume that the two redundant units each have an MTBF of 24,000 hr and that once every 24 hr each vehicle is inspected and failed units are replaced. What is the probability of a functional failure within the 24-hr period? For a simplex system, according to Eq. (8.4), it is

$$F_{simplex} = \lambda t = \frac{1}{24,000} \times 24 = .001,$$

but for an active redundant system (Eq. (8.5)), it is

$$F_{active} = (\lambda_1 t)\,(\lambda_2 t) = (.001)^2 = 10^{-6},$$

an improvement by a factor of 1000. (This was the illustration used in footnote 2.)

The functional failure rate of the actively redundant subsystem is by the definition in Eq. (8.1)

$$\lambda_{active}(t) = - \frac{1}{R_{active}(t)} \frac{d}{dt} R_{active}(t)$$

$$= \frac{1}{R_{active}(t)} \frac{d}{dt} F_{active}(t). \qquad (8.6)$$

For $\lambda_1 t$ and $\lambda_2 t$ small compared with 1, $R_{active}(t)$ will be very nearly 1. Then, by using (8.5) we see that

$$\lambda_{active}(t) \approx 2\lambda_1 \lambda_2 t. \qquad (8.7)$$

Equation (8.7) shows that even though both the primary and backup units have failure rates (λ_1 and λ_2) independent of time, their redundant combination has a failure rate that grows proportional to time. If inspection (and replacement when necessary) is carried out at intervals T, then the average failure rate during the interval will be

$\lambda_1 \lambda_2 T$ but just before inspection the failure rate will be double this average.

In Fig. 8-3 the reliability and failure rate of a subsystem having active redundancy is compared with that for a simplex subsystem.

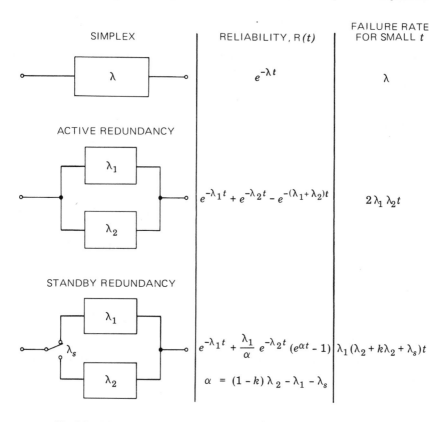

Fig. 8-3. The Effect of Redundancy on Subsystem Functional Failure

The figure also illustrates the other type of redundancy, standby redundancy, where the backup unit is inactive until the primary unit has failed. When the failure occurs it is detected by a failure detection and switching device which substitutes the backup unit for the primary one. Assume that λ_s is the failure rate of the failure detection and switching device. Then $e^{-\lambda_s \tau}$ is the probability that a failure of the primary at time τ is detected and that the standby switch is properly operated. Furthermore, assume that the standby device may have a lower failure rate when standing by quiescently than when operating. Thus, if λ_2 is its failure rate in operation, then $k\lambda_2$ is its failure rate when standing by, where $k \leqslant 1$.

The overall subsystem reliability is

$$R_{standby}(t) = e^{-\lambda_1 t} + \frac{\lambda_1}{\alpha} e^{-\lambda_2 t}(e^{\alpha t} - 1)$$

where $\alpha = (1 - k)\lambda_2 - \lambda_1 - \lambda_s.$ (8.8)

The first term on the right represents the probability that the primary is still operating after a time t. The last term[5] represents the probability that the primary has failed before time t, but that when it failed the failure detection and switching device worked, that the standby unit was then operating, and that it is still operating at time t.

To see how $R_{standby}$ behaves for small t, we can expand the exponentials in Eq. (8.8) into powers of t and keep terms only up to order t^2. The result is:

$$R_{standby}(t) \approx 1 - \frac{\lambda_1}{2}(2\lambda_2 - \lambda_1 - \alpha)t^2$$

$$= 1 - \frac{\lambda_1}{2}(\lambda_2 + k\lambda_2 + \lambda_s)t^2.$$ (8.9)

From Eqs. (8.1) and (8.9), the subsystem functional failure rate is given by the following approximation, valid for small t:

$$\lambda_{standby}(t) \approx \lambda_1(\lambda_2 + k\lambda_2 + \lambda_s)t.$$ (8.10)

When this is compared with Eq. (8.7), we see that a standby system is more reliable than an active system only if

$$k\lambda_2 + \lambda_s < \lambda_2,$$

which is to say only if the quiescent failure rate of the backup unit plus the failure rate of the failure detection and switching device is less than the active failure rate of the backup unit — an intuitively obvious inference.

One more complexity has to be introduced into the model. When a vehicle is not in operation (e.g., when it is parked on a station siding or in a car barn), many of its subsystems can be turned off. In the quiescent state, the failure rate of both the primary units as well

---

[5] The probability that the primary unit fails in an infinitesimal time interval $d\tau$ at time τ is $\lambda_1 e^{-\lambda_1 \tau}\, d\tau$. If this event occurs, the probability that the failure is detected, the switch operates, and the standby unit is then operating is $e^{-\lambda_s \tau} e^{-k\lambda_2 \tau}$. If these events also occur, the probability that the standby unit is still operating at time t is $e^{-\lambda_2(t-\tau)}$. Therefore, the probability of all of these events occurring is the product of the probabilities: i.e.,

$$\lambda_1 e^{-\lambda_2 t} e^{[(1-k)\lambda_2 - \lambda_1 - \lambda_s]\tau}\, d\tau.$$

This may now be integrated over all values of τ less than t to find the total probability of the primary failure before t and the standby unit still in operation at t. The result is the last term in Eq. (8.8).

as the active type backup units will be reduced by a factor k. (The failure rate for a standby backup unit cannot be further reduced while the primary is still operable because it is always in a quiescent state.)

Let us define the function

$$h(t) = \begin{matrix} 1 & \text{when unit is active} \\ = k & \text{when unit is quiescent} \end{matrix} \Bigg\} \qquad (8.11)$$

and define $\bar{h}$ as the time average of h. Thus, for example, if the vehicle operated only 5 hr of each day, then the value of $\bar{h}$ for a day would be

$$\bar{h} = (5 + 19k)/24. \qquad (8.12)$$

For a simplex subsystem there are two failure rates to consider. The first is that which directly influences service dependability as experienced by a passenger. This is the active failure rate λ, expressed as failures per operational hour. The other is the failure rate affecting maintenance costs. For this purpose the weighted average over both active and quiescent periods is the significant quantity. Since the instantaneous failure rate is $\lambda h(t)$, the average over the day is $\bar{\lambda} = \lambda \bar{h}$. To summarize, the results for simplex subsystems are:

$$\lambda_{dependability} = \lambda \text{ failures/opnl hr,} \qquad (8.13a)$$

$$\lambda_{maintenance} = \lambda \bar{h} \text{ failures/hr.} \qquad (8.13b)$$

We now consider the corresponding problem for active redundancy. If we make the simplifying (although incorrect) assumption that the fraction of time that a vehicle is in operation is the same throughout the day, then the probability that unit No. 2 will have failed in time t is $\lambda_2 \bar{h}_2 t$ (for small t). The probability of unit No. 1 then failing per unit of time at time t is $\lambda_1 h_1(t)$, which depends on whether the vehicle is active or not at time t. Thus, the compound probability per unit time of No. 2 having failed and No. 1 failing at time t is

$$\lambda_1 h_1(t) \, \lambda_2 \bar{h}_2 t.$$

Similarly, the probability per unit time of No. 1 having failed and No. 2 failing at time t is

$$\lambda_2 h_2(t) \, \lambda_1 \bar{h}_1 t.$$

Thus, the total probability per unit time of a subsystem failure is

$$\lambda_{active}(t) = \lambda_1 \lambda_2 \, [h_1(t) \, \bar{h}_2 + h_2(t) \, \bar{h}_1] t. \qquad (8.14)$$

Let us consider periodic checkout and replacement at the interval T. From the standpoint of dependability we are only interested in those times when $h_1(t)$ and $h_2(t)$ have the value 1. Averaging over those times within T when the vehicle is in operation, and again assuming that those times are uniformly distributed over the interval

T, we obtain the average "dependability failure rate,"

$$\bar\lambda_{dependability} = \frac{1}{2}\lambda_1\lambda_2\,(\bar h_1 + \bar h_2)\,T \text{ failures/opnl hr.} \quad (8.15a)$$

From the standpoint of maintenance the average failure rate during T is found by averaging Eq. (8.14) as it stands. Again, if $h_1(t)$ and $h_2(t)$ vary rapidly compared with t but maintain a constant running average throughout the day, then we may write the average failure rate for maintenance as

$$\bar\lambda_{maintenance} = \lambda_1\lambda_2\bar h_1\bar h_2 T \text{ failures/hr.}$$

$$(8.15b)$$

A similar argument holds for standby redundancy. The counterpart of Eq. (8.14) is

$$\lambda_{standby}(t) = \lambda_1 h_1(t)\,[k\lambda_2 + \lambda_s\bar h_s]\,t + \lambda_2 h_2(t)\lambda_1\bar h_1 t.$$

$$(8.16)$$

The first term on the right is the probability per unit time that the primary fails at time t multiplied by the probability that either the standby unit or the failure detection equipment would have failed before t. The last term is the probability per unit time that the standby unit fails at time t multiplied by the probability that the primary will have failed before t.

The same averaging techniques can be applied to (8.16) as were previously applied to Eq. (8.14). The results for standby redundancy are:

$$\bar\lambda_{dependability} = \frac{1}{2}\lambda_1\,[\lambda_2\,(\bar h_1 + k) + \lambda_s\bar h_s]\,T \text{ failures/opnl hr.}$$

$$(8.17a)$$

$$\bar\lambda_{maintenance} = \frac{1}{2}\lambda_1\bar h_1\,[\lambda_2\,(\bar h_2 + k) + \lambda_s\bar h_s]\,T \text{ failures/hr.}$$

$$(8.17b)$$

These results will now be applied to the control, propulsion, and braking systems of the Aerospace approach to the PRT vehicle.

8.5.3   Application to the PRT Vehicle

During 1971 and 1972, an engineering model of a fractional-second headway PRT system concept was designed and operated at Aerospace. The 1/10-scale model is described in Appendix B, and it suffices to say here that propulsion and braking were effected through a unique pulsed d.c. linear motor, that the active longitudinal control elements were carried onboard the vehicles, and that electromagnetic switching was employed. The development of this experimental scale-model provided a realistic design for detailed reliability modeling. The scaled system was generally designed in nonredundant form because of the limited test objectives and the relatively brief planned operating life, but the reliability math model has been used to analyze the impact of introducing redundancy into the design.

The serially-connected vehicle and fixed-facility control functions which were derived from the scale model program are shown in Fig. 8-4. The serial connections are like links in a chain and are a means of indicating that if any of the subsystems fails, there will be an operational failure. Because of the potentially large number of vehicles comprising a PRT fleet, the vehicle-borne control subsystems represent the limiting factor on system dependability, and analysis was focused on this area.

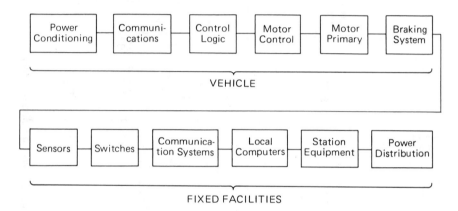

Fig. 8-4. Reliability Model of Functions Requiring Fail-Operational Design

To illustrate the impacts of subsystem configuration on dependability and cost, the vehicle-borne propulsion and control functions were modeled in single-thread nonredundant (simplex) form and in the dual redundant parallel-series connected form shown in Fig. 8-5. Only the motor was left in simplex form because it is already very reliable by virtue of having a high order of internal redundancy. (It will be recalled that there are 8 independent circuits; the motor would be able to produce adequate thrust with any 2 of these circuits nonfunctional.) Those functions for which real-time continuity of information is essential are shown as active parallel redundancies, while switchable standby redundancy was assumed for the remaining subsystems. The subsystem failure rates summarized with the baseline configuration shown in Fig. 8-5 are based upon parts counts generated during the 1/10-scale model development program. However, they have been increased to allow for two changes to the scale-model design: the use of Silicon Controlled Rectifier (SCR) motor drivers rather than the diodes used in the model and the inclusion of diagnostic telemetry in all units. Moreover, the failure

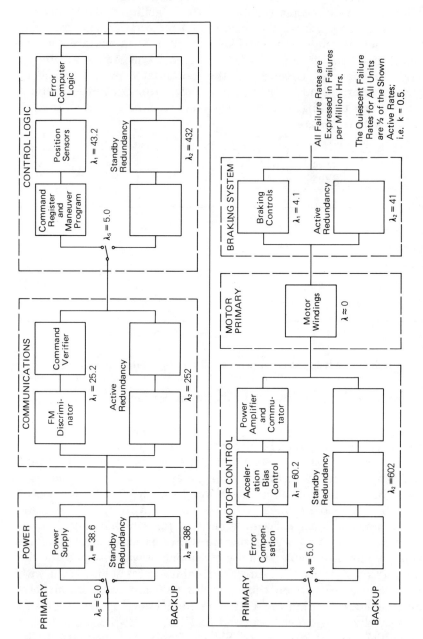

Fig. 8-5. Vehicle-Borne Control System Reliability Model

rates assume use of controlled parts in the primary circuits and commercial parts in the backup components. For comparison purposes, alternative configurations comprised entirely of controlled parts and entirely of commercial parts have also been analyzed.

(It is emphasized that the particular redundancy model illustrated in Fig. 8-5 was selected because it is capable, in a simple way, of illustrating the magnitude of vehicle-borne propulsion/control system reliability enhancement attainable through utilization of redundancy concepts. Many additional redundancy configurations and trade-offs are described by Bazovsky[6] and by Hunter.[7])

8.6   RELIABILITY RESULTS AND CONCLUSIONS

As noted earlier, the complete functional failure of any of the subsystems shown in the dashed-line blocks of Fig. 8-5 would constitute a vehicle operational failure. Therefore, the vehicle failure rate is the sum of the subsystem failure rates. A tabulation of failure rates is presented in Table 8-2 which gives, for each subsystem, both the

Table 8-2. Analysis of Time Averaged Vehicle Failures

SUBSYSTEM	TYPE OF REDUNDANCY	$\lambda_{dependability}$	$\lambda_{maintenance}$
Power	Standby	$.00828T$	$.00500T$
Communications	Active	$.00900T$	$.00544T$
Control Logic	Standby	$.01037T$	$.00626T$
Motor Control	Standby	$.02010T$	$.01214T$
Motor	Active	-0-	-0-
Braking System	Active	$.00010T$	$.00006T$
Total Vehicle System		$.04785T$	$.02890T$

Note: T is the interval in hours between checkout/replacement operations.

$\lambda_{dependability}$ is failure probability per million operational hours.

$\lambda_{maintenance}$ is failure probability per million hours.

It has been assumed that $T \ll$ MTBF's.

failure rate which affects system dependability (from Eqs. (8.15a) and (8.17a)) and that which affects maintenance (from Eqs. (8.15b) and (8.17b)). The table shows each subsystem failure rate proportional

---

[6]   I. Bazovsky, *Reliability Theory and Practice*, Prentice-Hall, Inc. (1961).

[7]   J.R. Hunter, et al., *Preliminary Study of Reliability and Sizing for Automatic Transportation Computer Systems*, Johns Hopkins University Applied Physics Laboratory, Silver Springs, Md. (August 1973).

to T, the interval between checkout/replacement operations. This linear relationship holds only for T small compared with the MTBF of the redundant units.

The resultant average vehicle failure rates (dependability and maintenance) are plotted in Fig. 8-6 versus T. For comparison, the simplex failure rates are also shown. They are based on the use of controlled parts, and it is seen that there are about 172 failures per million operational hours. Although not shown on the figure, the dependability (operational) failure rate for a nonredundant configuration composed of commercial-quality parts is about 10 times as large as the value shown, and the attendant mean time between failures would thus be on the order of 580 hours. This, as might be expected, is similar to the limited experience with contemporary automated transit systems. Failure rates of the nonredundant configurations are, of course, independent of checkout period since their failure mechanics are based on the simple exponential (simplex) reliability law.

The parallel/series redundant configuration, on the other hand, illustrates the dramatic improvement in vehicle system failure rate

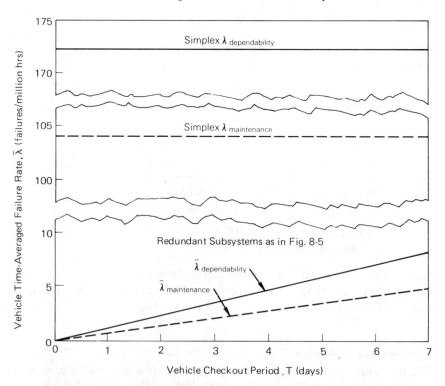

Fig. 8-6. Effect of Checkout Period and Redundancy on Vehicle Failure Rates

which can be attained with the straightforward redundancy model described above and operated with preventive maintenance periods of one week or less. The effect of the redundancy coupled with a weekly checkout is seen to introduce an improvement factor of about 20 over the simplex system with high reliability parts. If a daily checkout is used, the improvement factor is 150. For daily checkout there are only an average of 1.15 failures per million operational hours. The advantage of a daily checkout is clearly to minimize the number of incidents requiring vehicle pushing or line clearing operations. The checkout could be performed in conjunction with vehicle cleaning and inspection.

It is informative to express the failure rate in terms of operational miles traveled between failure incidents. If the average vehicle speed is 30 mi/hr, then there would be 1.15 failures per 30 million operational miles, or one failure per 26 million miles. If a patron traveled 10,000 mi/year on PRT, he could expect to witness a failure in his vehicle each 2,600 years, and the chances are very strong that his vehicle could be pushed by another. On average, during the 2,600 years his vehicle would also be called on once to push another vehicle. Each of these two incidents might consume as much as 5 or 10 minutes of his time.

How many operational failures might occur in a large fleet over a year's time? The estimated operating vehicle disability rate for a typical fleet of 10,000 vehicles per operating year is

$$\frac{1.15}{10^6} \frac{\text{failures/vehicle}}{\text{operating hours}} \times 5 \frac{\text{operating hours}}{\text{operating day}} \times 10^4 \text{ vehicles}$$

$$\times 300 \frac{\text{operating days}}{\text{year}} = 17 \text{ failures/year.}$$

Thus, a fleet of 10,000 vehicles would be expected to experience something on the order of 17 vehicle failures per year necessitating pushing or an emergency stop with subsequent rerouting of traffic, and the vast majority of these disabilities would be of the pushable variety. As noted in Chapter 6, except for the pushee and pusher, all of the following vehicles merely slip slots and are delayed no more than a few seconds. If all the failures were pushable, then 17 "pushee" and 17 "pusher" incidents would be expected per year, and approximately 1/4 to 1/3 of these would involve empty vehicles. Thus, only about 25 perceptible party delays would be anticipated per year for the fleet resulting from vehicle failures. There might, of course, be delays for other reasons, such as a blocked guideway.

Chapter 9
CAPITAL AND OPERATING COSTS

C. L. Olson

The estimates of PRT capital and operating costs summarized here are specifically based upon the Aerospace PRT system concept described in the earlier chapters. The results, however, are thought to be generally representative of any embodiment of the PRT concept, since the concept definition and the related requirements and goals tend to generate systems with many important characteristics in common. Thus, nearly every PRT approach could be expected to predicate small electrically powered vehicles, small off-line station structures, unobtrusive elevated guideways, and mechanization for fully automated operations. The comparisons shown later in Table 9-7 tend to bear out the generality of the cost estimates discussed herein.

9.1 COST ESTIMATING APPROACH AND BASELINE SYSTEM DEFINITION

The general approach used in estimating capital costs was to develop detailed costs for a specific system design-point, which is referred to as the Baseline Design, and to define the variation in system component cost with production quantity. These analyses were then synthesized to produce a mathematical model with the capability to predict system costs in terms of aggregation effects. Detailed cost studies were carried out in the spring of 1973. Therefore, all costs are stated in 1973 dollars unless otherwise indicated.

Specifically not included in the system design-point analysis are right-of-way procurement and utility relocation costs. Also, it is assumed that a prototype development program has been completed and amortized, including the production engineering phase. Thus, no amortization costs for system development are included in the cost estimates.

Based upon an assessment of typical PRT service needs, the following nine Baseline Design characteristics were adopted for design-point cost analysis:

(1) 100 miles of elevated one-way guideway.

(2) 100 vehicles per mile of guideway.

(3) Two intersection turn ramps per mile of guideway — altogether 100 complete intersections.

(4) Two fixed-platform stations per mile of guideway.

(5) One traffic control computer per mile of guideway.

(6) One central control computer per system.

(7) One vehicle maintenance facility per 5,000 vehicles.

(8) One vehicle cleaning, storage, and checkout facility per mile of guideway, sized so that together they can accommodate 85% of system fleet.

(9) Power distribution substations sized to peak power demand of 100 vehicles per mile.

An assessment of capital cost scale effects was made for items amenable to industrial production learning processes, unit module fabrication of structural items, and for large bulk purchases of construction material.

About half of the capital cost of a typical PRT system can be shown to derive from highly repetitive electronic and electro-mechanical items, including electrical substation equipments, vehicles, electronic fare equipments, elevators, automatic cleaning equipments, local computers, vehicle sensors, and electro-magnets. Such items historically exhibit a production "learning factor" of 85%.[1]

The remaining half of the capital cost is derived primarily from fixed civil and structural components, including architectural items subject to modular fabrication, such as guideways and facilities, and construction materials which are subject to cost reductions for large quantity purchase. These items typically show a learning factor of about 95%.

The average of the above values, 90%, is conveniently used in both the tabular and parametric estimates included in this chapter.

9.2 CAPITAL COST ELEMENTS AND BASELINE SYSTEM UNIT COST SUMMARY

Major subsystem capital cost elements are grouped into three general areas:

(1) Costs essentially independent of fleet size — consisting of costs for guideways, stations, computers, software, and the control center complex.

(2) Costs dependent on fleet size — consisting of costs for vehicles, electrical propulsive power, power distribution sub-

---

[1] The meaning here is that with each doubling of production quantity the unit cost is reduced by a factor 0.85.

stations, vehicle maintenance facilities, and vehicle storage, cleaning and checkout facilities.

(3) System engineering and technical management — a line cost item (assumed as 6% of total capital cost) which provides the technical and contract management for system design, construction, and checkout prior to delivery for passenger-carrying operations.

Examples of cost element build-ups are included for guideways and vehicles to illustrate the level of detail upon which all of the cost estimates summarized herein are based.

9.2.1 Guideway Costs

The baseline guideway was configured as a slender, open channel monorail to interface with and support the tandem wheeled (bicycle) vehicle suspension system concept illustrated in Figs. 7-4 and 7-5. The guideway assembly consists of structural and non-structural components.

The structural steel channel design illustrated in Fig. 7-8 was adopted for costing purposes. The beam geometry properties were based on the structural criteria discussed in Sec. 7.6.1, conservatively evaluated for a line speed of 60 mi/hr.

The reinforced concrete support columns and footings were sized in terms of longitudinal load based on the gross weight of one beam span plus the weight of a span full of loaded vehicles, acting in conjunction with a bending moment induced by simultaneous 0.8 g braking of the span full of vehicles. The columns were assumed to be 18 ft in height and spaced nominally at 60 ft.

The required curved sections related to the construction of interchange ramps at intersection guideways were determined through preliminary network geometries analysis which concluded that, on the average, there would be one intersection for each mile of one-way constructed guideway.

The non-structural cost items consist of: power and signal conductors, which are a redundant set of copper bars attached to the interior wall on each side of the guideway; a regularly spaced series of permanent magnets and their iron backing strips located on each side of the guideway interior wall; controllable electromagnet sets at guideway merge and diverge points; and various wayside sensors and communications cable utilized to collect data and communicate with the vehicles operating on the guideway network.

The unit cost estimate for a typical straight section of guideway is shown in Table 9-1. The tabulation consists of material require-ment, labor estimates for fabrication and installation, and equipment

Table 9-1. Guideway Straight Section Unit Cost Estimate
(cost per one-way mile of guideway)

ITEM DESCRIPTION	PER MILE		THOUSANDS OF DOLLARS			
	QTY	UNITS	MATL	LABOR	EQPT	TOTAL
Structural Steel at 90 lb/ft x 1.4 = 126 lb/ft Unload, erect, align, weld, clean, paint, freight	333	Tons	171	65	17	253
Magnets — 2/ft, 2½ in. x 4 in. x 6 in. at .166 lb/in.^{3} = 20 lb/ft Fabricate, install, activate, freight, checkout	53	Tons	106	22	11	139
Soft Iron Backing — ½ in. x 6 in. Continuous both sides = 21 lb/ft Fabricate, install, freight	54	Tons	13	15	2	30
Conductor — Copper 1 in. x 1½ in. continuous — 4 Required = 23 lb/ft	61	Tons	121	15	6	142
Communication Cable	5280	Feet	6	3	1	10
Wayside Sensors	1	Set	25	10	5	40
Total per One-Way Mile			442	130	42	614

needs for each item of guideway construction. A similar analysis was performed for the curved guideway sections used to construct the interconnecting ramps at guideway intersections,[2] and this estimate is shown in Table 9-2.

For comparison purposes, post-tensioned and pre-stressed concrete and aluminum alloy plate were examined as alternate materials for guideway beam construction. It was found that concrete construction costs are comparable to those of steel fabrication and that aluminum alloy plate construction would run about 40% higher.

Unit cost per guideway mile for support column structure is shown on Table 9-3. The tabulation itemizes material requirements,

---

[2] The costs of station sidings are included in the station cost summaries.

Table 9-2. Intersection Turn-Ramp Guideway Unit Cost Estimate
(cost per one-way mile of guideway)

ITEM DESCRIPTION	PER SECTION		THOUSANDS OF DOLLARS			
	QTY	UNITS	MATL	LABOR	EQPT	TOTAL
Additional Steel Structure (126 lb/ft x 440 ft/Ramp)	27.7	Tons	4.5	22.5	2.3	29.3
Magnets — Mat'l, Install, & Activate/Checkout	4.4	Tons	8.8	0.9	0.5	10.2
Soft Iron Backing — Mat'l, Fab & Install	4.6	Tons	1.1	1.3	0.2	2.6
Conductor (copper) — Mat'l, Fab, Install/Check	5.1	Tons	10.1	1.2	—	11.3
Communication Cable — Mat'l and Install	440	Feet	0.5	0.3	0.1	0.9
Wayside Sensors — Mat'l Install, and Check	1	Set	2.0	0.8	0.4	3.2
Electromagnets — Mat'l Install, and Check	4	Sets*	8.0	32.0	—	40.0
Back-Up Switching Auxiliary Power Units	2	Each	4.0	5.0	1.0	10.0
Supporting Structure	4	Cu Yd	0.3	1.7	—	2.0
Total Cost Per Turn Ramp			39.3	65.7	4.5	109.5
Total Cost Per One-Way Mile (2 Turn Ramps per mile)			78.6	131.4	9.0	219.0

*One on each side of guideway, in both diverge and merge regions

labor, and equipment needs for the fabrication and installation of guideway supporting columns and footings.

The total guideway cost per one-way mile includes $614,000 for the straight sections, $219,000 for the intersection guideway assemblies in each one-way mile, and $75,000 per mile for support columns. The overall guideway cost summary shown in Table 9-4 includes overhead, profit, architect fees, and contingency for the construction

Table 9-3. Guideway Support Column Unit Cost Estimate
(cost per one-way mile of guideway)

ITEM DESCRIPTION	QTY PER COLUMN	MATL	LABOR	EQPT	TOTAL
Caissons — 16 in. dia x 10 ft	4	40	260	10	310
Pad — 4 ft x 4 ft x 1-1/2 ft	1	20	40	—	60
Column — 1-1/2 ft x 2 ft x 20 ft	1	40	190	20	250
Column Cap	1	10	20	—	30
Bumper Island	1	20	170	10	200
Total Per Column		130	680	40	850
Total Cost Per Mile of Straight Section (column spacing = 60 ft)	88/mi	11,500	59,900	3,600	75,000

costs of 100 miles of guideway, and indicates a total system cost
(1973 dollars) of $132.3 million for the design-point system, or
about $1.3 million per one-way guideway mile at the Baseline Design
network size.

Table 9-4. Guideway Cost Summary Based on 100 One-Way Mile System
(millions of 1973 dollars)

ITEM DESCRIPTION	COST	OH/PROFIT AND ARCHITECT	CONTINGENCY	TOTAL
Straight Section	61.4	20.0	8.1	89.5
Columns	7.5	2.4	1.0	10.9
Turn Ramps	21.9	7.1	2.9	31.9
Total Cost*	90.8	29.5	12.0	132.3

*Excludes station sidings

9.2.2   Vehicle Costs

The cost analysis performed on the vehicle system consisted of detailed investigation into 11 subsystem areas including body, frame, trim/glass, wheels and tires, brakes and suspension, safety equipment, electronics, motor primary, electrical system, door devices, and heat-air conditioning. The areas of assembly, test, and miscellaneous were not treated in detail but were estimated with cost ratios established in automobile industry practice.

The cost estimating process developed a definitive cost estimate at the 10,000-unit production level, and utilized a 90% production learning factor for extrapolation to other production rates. Cost estimates for production of conventional components were obtained from reference sources like Chilton's Automobile Labor Guide and Parts manual. Electronic controls and pulsed d.c. linear motor costs were based on 1/10-scale operating model detail designs (see Appendix B), with preliminary quotations on price parts at various quantities having been obtained from industrial firms engaged in electronic component production.

A summary of estimated vehicle costs at various production rates is shown in Table 9-5. The underlying cost analysis considered each vehicle subsystem area in terms of engineering drawings, planning, fabrication, finish, inspection, sub-assembly, final assembly, checkout, shipping, and contingency.

The effect on unit cost of production quantities from 100 to 1 million is quite dramatic, as could be expected. The design-point system requirements for a fleet of 10,000 vehicles would lead to a unit cost of $8,800 per vehicle (1973 dollars), if all units were on a single order. It is emphasized that amortization of development engineering or production tooling engineering is not reflected in the summarized vehicle costs.

A preliminary weight estimate for a typical 4-passenger PRT vehicle is shown in Table 7-1. The gross operating weight, less passengers, of 1,800 lb leads to a figure of $4.90 (1973 dollars) per pound for the 10,000-vehicle baseline fleet.

9.2.3   Station Costs

PRT station characteristics were developed for two principal applications: an urban station typical of downtown installations, and a suburban station having operating features similar to the urban station but configured for a much lower patronage demand.

The urban station features a nominal 1,000-sq-ft covered platform, a 480-ft siding from the main through line, 6 fixed vehicle berths along a 66-ft platform, access to platform via an elevator,

Table 9-5. Vehicle Unit Cost Summary for Various Production Quantities

ITEM DESCRIPTION	QUANTITY					
	10	100	1000	10,000	100,000	1,000,000
Body	$ 2,500	$ 1,700	$ 1,200	$ 855	$ 663	$ 505
Frame	1,400	870	750	687	450	250
Trim/Glass	2,900	1,600	1,000	855	600	450
Wheels, Tires	800	560	400	280	200	160
Brakes, Suspension	800	480	320	240	160	120
Safety Equipment	800	480	320	240	160	120
Electronics	3,000	2,200	1,400	1,000	600	400
Motor Primary	2,250	1,600	1,000	750	450	300
Electrical System	1,800	1,350	900	600	450	300
Door Devices	375	300	225	150	112	75
Heat-Air Conditioning	750	600	450	300	225	150
Miscellaneous	750	450	300	187	150	75
Subtotal	$18,125	$12,190	$ 8,365	$6,144	$4,220	$2,905
Subassembly	5,875	3,710	2,735	1,656	1,280	895
Final Assembly/ Inspect	3,000	2,100	1,500	1,000	700	500
Total Cost/Vehicle	$27,000	$18,000	$12,000	$8,800	$6,200	$4,300

NOTE: Costs include parts, labor, contingency, overhead, and profit

outside stairs for emergency use, automatic fare equipment, and patron security and information systems.

The suburban station was assumed to have the same features as the urban station with the exception of a 300-sq-ft covered platform providing only 2 fixed vehicle berths along a 22-ft platform.

The total cost of stations for the 100-mi Baseline System containing 200 stations was estimated at $36.4 million (1973 dollars). This included 40 urban stations at $226,000 each and 160 suburban stations at $171,000 each.

The cost analysis considered the following station items in detail: station structure; station siding guideway; fare, communications, information, and patron security equipments; and support structure for elevated station designs.

9.2.4 Computers and Facilities Costs

System computer requirements were based on a system management concept predicating a large capacity central computer for overall system control functions and smaller computers for control of local traffic flow at guideway intersections and stations. The central computer was assumed to be a "CDC 7600" for cost purposes, and the local computers consisted of redundant sets of "mini" computers for each guideway control zone in the network.

The operations control facility consisted of an office structure completely furnished and equipped to support the operations staff and the integrated system computer complex.

The estimated cost of incremental software was based on 30,000 instructions for a typical city-peculiar application. The cost of basic software program development was assumed to be included in system front-end development costs, and only incremental costs were included in the present estimate. The total cost of the baseline system computers and control operations facilities was estimated at $23.5 million, including $15 million for the central computer, $6 million for 100 sets of redundant intersection "mini" computers, $1.5 million for an operations control facility, and $1 million for the city-peculiar software development.

Vehicle support facilities consist of storage, cleaning and checkout facilities, and maintenance facilities.

The facilities for combined storage, cleaning, and checkout (Sec. 7.7.1) were sized to accommodate 85% of the operational fleet at any one time. This requirement was developed from estimates of the fractions of vehicles operating on the guideways, in stations, in maintenance, and held in reserve as spares. Widespread locations for dispatching of vehicles in the network and limited size of available space in an urbanized area dictated a need for small structures, and facilities of 170-vehicle capacity at an average spacing of two guideway miles were selected for costing.

Vehicle maintenance facilities were provided in the system for all routine preventive maintenance of vehicles on a scheduled basis and for unscheduled repair and overhaul on a demand basis. Each facility was conceptually designed (Sec. 7.7.2) and equipped for production line maintenance procedures and sized to have a daily throughput of 250 vehicles.

The following items were considered in detail for the estimated vehicle storage and cleaning facility costs: basic parking structure, parking guideway, vehicle elevators, automatic moving and control equipment, automatic washing equipment, and electronic checkout equipment. In the maintenance facility cost analysis, the following items were considered in detail: basic garage structure, special mechanical equipment, special electrical equipment, and spare parts storage.

The total cost in 1973 dollars for the baseline system vehicle support facilities was estimated at $39.0 million, including $34.8 million for 50 storage, cleaning, and checkout facilities and $4.2 million for two maintenance facilities.

9.2.5 Power Distribution System Costs

The baseline power distribution system was of the type described in Sec. 7.6.7, consisting of 2500 kVA substations connected to 35,000 volts a.c. municipal or private power generating systems furnishing regulated 1000 volts d.c. power to the system guideway power bus points. Tie-in distance from the substation to its power source was assumed to be approximately one-fifth of a mile.

The substation cost analysis included a 2500 kW capacity rectifier/transformer, bus duct, d.c. switch gear, a 35 kV air circuit breaker, interconnecting cable, enclosures, and miscellaneous equipment.

The unit cost estimate, including overhead, profit, architect fees, and contingency came to $390,000 for each substation installation, and this is typical for an area served by private utility systems. This brings the total 1973 power distribution cost to $33.9 million for the 87 substations required in the baseline system.

9.2.6 Baseline System Capital Cost Summary

The grand total capital cost estimated for the baseline point-design having 100 mi of one-way guideway and 10,000 vehicles consists of the collected sums for fleet-size-dependent and fleet-size-independent costs shown in Table 9-6. The total estimated system cost of $374.3 million (1973 dollars) gives a capital cost per one-way guideway mile of $3.74 million for a PRT system having the baseline characteristics. Assuming an inflation factor of 9% per annum, compounded, the 1978 costs would be about 54% higher, giving a cost per one-way mile of $5.8 million in 1978.

9.2.7 Parametric Capital Cost Model

The baseline design cost data summarized above were utilized along with the 90% learning factor discussed in Sec. 9.1 in development of a mathematical system cost model.

First, consider those parts of the baseline system which are independent of fleet size. Including the 6% addition for system engineering and technical management their cost from Table 9-6 is $203.7 million or $2.037 million/mi. In a system of G_L miles of one-way guideway, the number of doublings of guideway miles relative to the baseline 100 mi system is

$$\alpha = \log_2 \frac{G_L}{100} \tag{9.1}$$

If G_L is less than 100, α is negative and its magnitude represents the number of halvings. The cost per mile (measured in millions of 1973

Table 9-6. Capital Cost Estimate Summary (1973 dollars)*

100 Mile One-Way Guideway/10,000 Vehicle Point Design

	TOTAL COST ($ millions)
Cost Independent of Fleet Size	
Guideways	132.3
Stations (200)	36.4
Computers, Software, and Control Center	23.5
	192.2
Cost Dependent on Fleet Size	
Vehicles	88.0
Power Distribution Substations (peak period 20 kW/car average)	33.9
Vehicle Storage, Cleaning and Checkout Facilities (85% fleet)	34.8
Vehicle Maintenance Facilities	4.2
	160.9
System Engineering and Technical Management (6% of capital cost)	21.2
Total Cost	374.3
Cost per one-way mile	3.74

*Note: Assuming an inflation of 9% per annum, compounded, all figures on this chart should be increased by about 54% to obtain 1978 estimates. Thus the total cost per one-way mile would be about $5.8 million in 1978.

dollars) for fleet independent elements we shall denote as C_I. By virtue of the learning curve,

$$C_I = 2.037 \, (0.9)^\alpha . \qquad (9.2)$$

Now, since $0.9 = 2^{-0.152}$, Eq. (9.2) may be simplified to

$$C_I = 2.037 \times 2^{-0.152\alpha} = 2.037 \times 2^{-\log_2 \, (G_L/100)^{0.152}}$$

$$= 2.037 \times \left(\frac{100}{G_L}\right)^{0.152} = 4.102 \, G_L^{-0.152} . \qquad (9.3)$$

Now we turn to the costs which are dependent on fleet size. For the baseline system, including the 6% system engineering and technical management cost, these costs (Table 9-6) are \$170.6 million or \$1.706 million/mi. Here volume scales as the product of G_L and the number of vehicles/mi, N. Thus the number of doublings of volume relative to the baseline is

$$\beta = \log_2 \frac{G_L N}{10,000} . \qquad (9.4)$$

The unit cost per vehicle scales as $(0.9)^\beta$ but to obtain the cost/mi one must multiply by $N/100$. Thus, the cost per mile (in millions of 1973 dollars) for fleet dependent elements is

$$C_D = 1.706 \, (0.9)^\beta \times \frac{N}{100} = 0.01706N \times 2^{-0.152\beta}$$

$$= 0.01706N \left(\frac{10,000}{G_L N}\right)^{0.152}$$

$$= 0.06918 \, G_L^{-0.152} \, N^{0.848} . \qquad (9.5)$$

The total unit cost/mi is found by adding (9.3) and (9.5):

$$C_U = 4.102 \, G_L^{-0.152} \, [1 + 0.01686 \, N^{0.848}]. \qquad (9.6)$$

This equation is plotted in Fig. 9-1 for a range of typical fleet densities. The cost lines are dashed below about the 10 guideway mile area as a reminder that the related analysis was made under the assumption of independence from development costs. If, for example, a vehicle manufacturer were to recover a substantial part of his development investment over the first 100 to 1000 vehicle sales, the system unit costs would obviously undergo substantial increases in the left-hand regions of the cost plot.

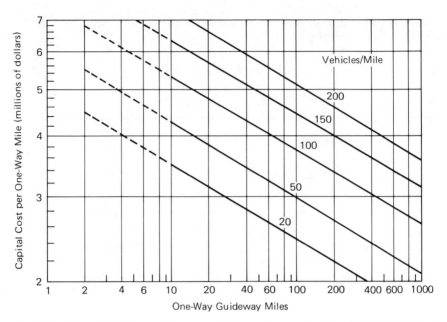

Fig. 9-1. Effect of PRT System Size on Total System Cost per One-Way Mile (1973 dollars)

9.2.8 Comparison with Other System Costs

Table 9-7 contains a comparison of projected PRT system unit costs made by the system developer and by a simple extension of the capital cost equation, Eq. (9.6), to take into account the variation in the number of stations per mile of guideway. Considering the different propulsion and suspension technologies represented by these PRT systems, the unit cost estimates show fairly good agreement, with the overall averages being very well correlated. The significant overestimation of the Transportation Technology unit cost by the Aerospace equation is probably due to the assumption of elevated guideways by Aerospace while the Transportation Technology estimate was based on an at-grade guideway installation. Also, in order to more closely approach the Uniflo estimate, it would be necessary to adjust the cost equation to account for the high complexity of the pneumatic guideway predicated in the Uniflo design.

9.3   OPERATING COST

Operating cost estimates were built up in terms of fixed and variable categories with costs of all labor, materials, and electrical power not related to vehicle fleet size included in the former and all operating costs dependent on fleet size included in the latter. General administration and overhead costs were included as a percentage of total operating costs. Detailed cost analyses were carried out in 1973,

Table 9-7. Comparative Capital Costs of Several PRT Systems (1973 dollars)

PRT SYSTEM	BASIS OF COST ESTIMATE	UNIT COST ESTIMATE BY SYSTEM DEVELOPER ($ million/mile)	UNIT COST ESTIMATE BY AEROSPACE COST MODEL ($ million/mile)
Monocab (A)	Hypothetical 1 Mile, 3 Station, 6 Vehicle System	3.30*	4.74
(B)	Hypothetical 20 Mile, 20 Station, 150 Vehicle System	2.24*	2.63
Transportation Technology Inc.	Hypothetical 2 1/2 Mile, 2 Station, 23 Vehicle System	1.73*	3.60
Uniflo, Inc.	Hypothetical 1 Mile, 2 Station, 20 Vehicle System	6.57*	4.98
Aerial Transit "Palomino" Las Vegas	22 Mile, 300 Vehicle Las Vegas Bid	3.15**	2.72
Rohr "Monocab" Las Vegas (HRRA Estimate)	21 Mile, 150 Vehicle Las Vegas	3.60***	2.59
	Average	3.43	3.54

* DOT-TSC-OST-72-35, Summary Data for Selected New Urban Transportation Systems DOT Nov. 1972 Page 20

** Aerial Transit System of Nevada, Inc., Las Vegas, Nevada, Toward the Future, 1 Feb. 1973, Table 11.

*** Southern California Association of Governments, Regional Transportation Frameworks, Framework 5, Personal Rapid Transit, 30 Jan. 1974 — Pages 2-44.

but these were updated in 1975 because of the significant increase in power costs at that time. All operating costs are quoted in 1975 dollars.

9.3.1 Operating Cost Elements and Operating Cost Summary for Baseline System

The elements within which operating costs have been aggregated are summarized in Table 9-8. The guideway operating costs include automatic spray painting, internal cleaning of magnets and conductors,

Table 9-8. Operating Cost Elements

Fixed Operating Costs (labor, materials and power not related to vehicle fleet size)
 	
    Guideways
        Painting
        Cleaning and Maintenance
 	
    Station Maintenance and Power
        Elevators/Lighting/Doors/Thermal Control
 	
    Electronics (operation and maintenance)
        Computers
        Fare Equipment
        Control Sensors and Instrumentation

Variable Operating Costs (labor, materials and power related to vehicle fleet size)
 	
    Vehicles
        Power
        Maintenance
        Cleaning
 	
    Vehicle Cleaning and Storage Facilities
 	
    Vehicle Maintenance and Overhaul Facilities

General Administration and Overhead Costs (administration personnel, insurance expenses, employee benefits, and other administrative expenses)

and checkout and re-magnetization of the ferrite magnets. Station maintenance and operating costs include cleaning, electrical power for fare equipment, elevators, lights, and air-conditioning, and maintenance of all non-electronic equipments. The electronics operating costs cover inspection and upkeep of station fare equipment, computers, communications links and buffers, and guideway-mounted sensors and instrumentation.

Operating costs for vehicles include electrical power,[3] scheduled

---

[3] Including power for the passenger environmental control units (heating, air conditioning, and lighting), assumed to be 4 kW.

Table 9-9. Annual Operating Cost Summary in 1975 dollars for Baseline
Network (100 one-way miles — 10,000 vehicles)

Fixed Operating Costs (Independent of Fleet Size)	
Guideway	303,000
Stations	827,000
Electronics	1,546,000
Staff Personnel	395,000
	3,071,000
Variable Operating Costs (Scaling with Fleet Size)	
Facilities	
Maintenance (labor & materials)	470,000
Power at 3¢/kWh	170,000
Vehicle	
Maintenance & Cleaning (labor & materials)	5,192,000
Power at 3¢/kWh	4,800,000
	10,632,000
Direct Total	13,703,000
General Administration and Overhead Costs — @15%	
(Administration Personnel, Insurance Expenses, Employee Benefits, and Other Administrative Expenses)	2,056,000
Total Operating Costs	15,759,000
$$\frac{15.759 \times 10^8 \text{ cents per year}}{3 \times 10^8 \text{ occupied vehicle miles per year}}$$	= 5.3¢/ovm

maintenance,[4] daily cleaning, and electronic checkout operations. The facilities' operating costs include cleaning, electrical power, and equipment inspection and maintenance for all vehicle storage and maintenance structures.

The total estimated annual operating costs for the 100-mile Baseline Design system are summarized in Table 9-9 in terms of the elements described above for a 30 mi/hr average operating speed. The fixed component of operating cost is seen to constitute about

[4] Costs for unscheduled maintenance are entirely dependent upon the predicated system maintenance strategy. This trade-off area is discussed in Chapter 8.

22% of the direct total, while the variable component makes up about 78%, which is primarily due to vehicle maintenance and electrical power. The total annual specific operating cost is shown to be about $158,000 (1975) per one-way guideway mile.

At 30 mi/hr average speed, each vehicle in the fleet of 10,000 would be expected to generate about 30,000 revenue miles per year,[5] and on this basis, a break-even fare of 5.3 cents (1975) per occupied vehicle mile is predicted, as shown in Table 9-9. (Assuming 9% per annum escalation, this would be a break-even fare of 6.9 cents per occupied vehicle mile in 1978.) If round-the-clock station attendants were to be assumed, the break-even fare would be increased by about 2 1/2¢ per revenue mile.

9.3.2 Parametric Summary of Operating Cost

The variation of operating cost per revenue mile (the specific operating cost) with average vehicle speed and with number of vehicles per guideway mile (the vehicle density) is shown in Fig. 9-2

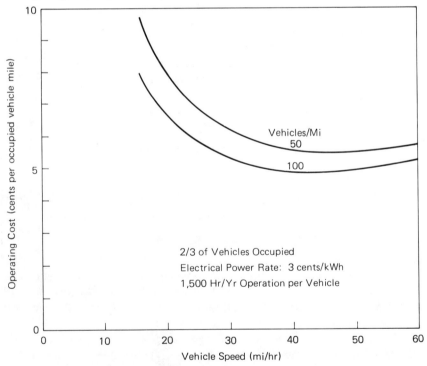

Fig. 9-2. Operating Cost Parametric Summary (1975 dollars)

[5] Assumes 300 weekday equivalents per year, 5 hours travel time per weekday, and two-thirds of the miles logged to be revenue miles (remaining one-third empty).

for a typical case in which 2/3 of all vehicle miles are occupied, vehicles operate 1,500 hr/year, and electrical power cost is 3¢/kWh. For any given speed, the specific operating cost is seen to rise as the vehicle density decreases, reflecting the attendant reduction in revenue miles over which the fixed portion of the operating costs may be spread.

For speeds greater than about 45 mi/hr, the electrical power costs become dominant even though the costs are spread over large annual revenue mileages. It is also evident that break-even fares increase rapidly with diminishing operating speeds (decreasing annual revenue miles), and in the typical case of 100 vehicles/mi, the increase is over 30% when operating speed is lowered from 40 mi/hr to 20 mi/hr. Operating costs are minimized for speeds near 45 mi/hr, and the costs are seen to be nearly constant over the speed range from 30 mi/hr to 60 mi/hr. Although the lower end of this speed range might be satisfactory from the standpoint of service, the upper end will somewhat reduce fleet size (and thus capital cost) because each vehicle can make more revenue trips during the peak hours. Moreover, there would also be an improved modal split with the faster speeds.

Chapter 10
PATRONAGE ESTIMATION

Jon Buyan

The first section of this chapter discusses general techniques for patronage estimation. It reviews some of the traditional approaches to modal-split and demand analysis and pinpoints their deficiencies. It then introduces the simulation approach to modal-split analysis and discusses the benefits of such an approach. It compares the data requirements for using this simulation approach with traditional approaches and concludes with an overview of how the modal-split simulation approach is applied to a specific application.

The second section discusses how an early version of the modal-split simulation was applied to analyze the potential of a limited PRT network in the city of Tucson. It discusses the motivation and constraints of the study, outlines the inputs for and the characteristics of the modal-split model which was used, and presents how this model was used to optimize the PRT network.

The final section discusses an improved patronage estimation package which includes a more sophisticated modal-split simulation model as well as several preprocessors and postprocessors to the modal-split simulation. This package models a city more accurately and handles much larger networks. The structure of the entire package is briefly discussed. It was recently applied to Los Angeles to demonstrate PRT analysis and planning techniques as part of a contract performed for the Urban Mass Transportation Administration of the U.S. Department of Transportation.

10.1 PATRONAGE ESTIMATION TECHNIQUES

10.1.1 Independent Mode Demand versus Modal Split of Total Demand

There are generally two different ways to estimate the demand for a specific travel mode. One is to develop a model which directly yields the total patronage of that mode. This can be called an independent mode demand model since it explicitly calculates the demand only for the mode of interest. A second technique is to develop a model which yields the modal-split fraction captured by each of the modes. These fractions are then multiplied by the total travel demand (which is determined separately) to get the demand for each mode. This can be called a modal split of total demand model.

Although independent mode demand has the apparent advantage that it determines overall demand for the mode of interest in a single step, it has some disadvantages which are difficult to overcome. The first of these difficulties is that it does not explicitly treat the phenomenon of modal shift. Most increased (induced) demand for a mode is caused not by new travelers taking that mode but by travelers shifting from one mode to another. This is particularly true in an urban environment where the automobile already provides a generally available means for urban travel. Therefore the introduction of a new mode, especially a vastly improved mode, is much more likely to shift travelers out of their automobiles than it is to induce new people to travel who did not have an opportunity to do so before. This is true even though one of the prime purposes of the development of the new mode may be to give mobility to people who could not be mobile in an automobile-dominated environment.

Another problem with independent mode demand is that of constraining the total demand. This problem often arises where extreme values of the mode parameters used in the model cause a large loss or generation of demand for that mode, without appropriate consideration of the impact of the modal shift on other modes. Attempts to overcome this by using perceived cost ratios of the various modes or excess cost differentials meet with only limited success.

In the approach of determining the modal split first and then multiplying by total demand, mode shift is considered explicitly. That is, the fraction of travelers taking each mode is determined by considering an entire set of factors affecting mode choice. Of course, mode improvements or deterioration will result in some change in total demand. Usually the extent of such demand inducement or reduction can be estimated on the basis of historic data. Later we shall point out the possibility of estimating induced demand using a simulation approach to modal-split analysis.

10.1.2 The Regression Approach to Modal-Split Analysis

The traditional approach to modal-split analysis has been regression. Regression is a technique whereby parameters of interest which influence a traveler's mode choice are incorporated into an equation to determine the modal-split fraction for that mode. This equation usually contains coefficients and exponents for each of the terms in the equation. The model is calibrated (i.e., the coefficients and exponents are determined) by fitting the equation to historic modal-split data for some chosen year or years to give close agreement between the model's estimation of the modal share and the historic modal-split survey data for the chosen year(s). Typical of the independent variables which are used to compute modal split in the regression equation are travel time, travel cost, mode access time, and perhaps certain ratios or differences which relate the performance of the several modes with regard to these variables.

The limitations of the regression approach to modal-split analysis are numerous. Most of them revolve around the requirement to use mean or median values of traveler attributes or mode performance, rather than the distributions which exist in the real world. For instance, traveler's income or time value and his location relative to a point of access to the mode being considered has to be modeled as an average value over the whole system or over some relatively large part of the system. In the real world some travelers have close access to the mode while others may be very distant. An average distance or time value does not suffice to model these travelers, particularly when the emphasis is on a minor mode where success may be measured by getting only a few percent of the total demand.

Regression techniques have particular difficulty when new modes are being modeled because there are no historic data with which to calibrate the model; i.e., to determine the value of coefficients and exponents. The values are also difficult to estimate because the underlying relationships between these coefficients and exponents and the service parameters of the transportation mode (timelines, cost, etc.) are not readily discernible. Even if a mode is already established but changes are being considered which affect only part of the system (such as adding new lines, relocating stations, or improving the service at some critical stations), a regression approach has difficulty in consistently modeling such limited changes. It usually reverts to changing the average value, whereas in the real world some travelers see significant improvements in service while others are completely unaffected.

An additional difficulty is with evolutionary changes within the city, such as residents moving to the surburban areas and the development of new centers of activity. Again, only some of the potential patrons are affected by such changes; regression is forced to treat such evolution in only an average or general manner.

Regression models usually also suffer in their output because they can report only gross statistics about the changes, since they are sensitive only to average values, and it is difficult to develop them to give specific information about what is happening in a small part of the network which is under analysis.

One of the greatest difficulties with regression from the modeler's point of view is that there is no direct relationship between specific changes in the real world and specific inputs in the model. This makes it difficult for the average planner or systems designer to see how the inputs to the model should be changed when a small improvement is made to a specific part of the network under study.

One of the trends in making regression a more accurate prediction tool is to move in the direction of stratifying the model into several or many different models, each of which is calibrated and applies to a specific part of the city. The approach being suggested in this chapter of using simulation to determine modal split carries this stratification to its logical limit.

10.1.3 Simulation Approach to Modal-Split Analysis

In the simulation approach to modal-split analysis the model can be made as disaggregate as desired. The keystone of the model is to create an individual traveler whose attributes are drawn from distributions which describe travelers residing in various parts of the city. The city itself is modeled on an individual area basis. Areas are selected so as to be relatively homogeneous with regard to trip generation density within the area and income distribution of the traveler. The city can be made appropriately disaggregate until this goal is achieved. Trips are modeled for a specific time period, such as rush hour, midday, or evening, and the traveler's characteristics reflect this time period of interest. Station location and transit service are explicitly modeled and a table of travel times between each pair of stations is an explicit input. Access is also treated explicitly. Travelers evaluate each access mode available from their door location to the station under consideration and do this for the return trip as well. Furthermore, the traveler does not restrict his evaluation to the closest station but considers several stations in the vicinity of each trip end.

The simulated traveler uses a perceived cost function to decide which mode and which path within that mode he will take, and what form of local access he will use. This perceived cost includes out-of-pocket cost, such as the PRT fare, the cost of station access, the operating cost of an automobile, and parking cost. It also includes the value-of-time cost associated with driving, walking, riding, waiting, and any processing which is involved. The time-to-cost conversion factor for the home-to-work trip is generally taken by most investigators to be about 25 to 50 percent of the traveler's income rate. This parameter can be easily varied in the simulation. Additional time penalties can be invoked for particularly discomforting time losses such as for waiting. Finally, the model takes into account how the traveler's personal preferences affect his choice in taking each of the modes — considerations which are independent of time and cost (see Sec. 10.1.6).

10.1.4 Benefits of the Simulation Approach to Modal-Split Analysis

The simulation approach overcomes the deficiencies associated with regression analysis. Since the traveler, the city, and the transit system being studied are modeled in great detail, limited only by the desired fidelity and data availability, mean values are not required for parameters which are important to the traveler. Instead, draws can be made from appropriate distributions, so that different types of travelers can be adequately represented even if they are in the minority. This is an especially important feature when minor modes are being analyzed.

The simulation model can naturally be built up to the desired level of fidelity without starting from scratch each time. That is, as certain system characteristics are realized as being important to the traveler, a new program module can be added, which increases the fidelity in modeling that aspect of travel, without having to change any of the other modules which describe other parts of the trip or the mode decision process.

The simulation approach readily permits sensitivity studies, since all of the traveler attributes and system characteristics are modeled explicitly. Small changes can be made to the simulated travelers, to the system, or to the environment in which the system is operating, and the effect of such variations can be studied in great detail. If certain of these changes apply to only a small part of the system, then only a small part of the input data must be changed.

Perhaps, one of the greatest advantages of a simulation approach is that, in generating simulated travelers, it is possible to determine not only how many travelers take a certain mode, but what types of travelers take it and where. In effect, each of the simulated travelers fills out a questionnaire which describes his attributes and contains all of the details of how his mode choice was made, and why it was best for him. Then these individual traveler records can be processed in a report generator package to completely analyze all of the characteristics both of the system and of the travelers. This is impossible to do in a regression approach. Furthermore, the total effective perceived cost, which is the basis for traveler mode choice in the model, can be averaged for all travelers, regardless of mode, to form a measure of the overall quality of the transportation system in the city. By comparing the average effective perceived cost with and without an assumed mode, one can find the total benefit to all travelers in having included it.

It may also be possible to predict induced total demand from the average perceived cost. We have already demonstrated this possibility for intercity trips, using a modal-split simulation model designed for intercity travel. In a recent study performed by Aerospace for the Federal Energy Administration, it was shown by examining data taken over a number of years that the average effective perceived cost could be used to predict induced intercity travel demand as the quality of the transportation system changed. Similar approaches might be possible in urban arenas.

Finally, since data can be gathered both with regard to revenue and system operations required to serve the travel demand, it is very easy to perform an economic analysis of the system being modeled after the modal-split analysis is complete.

10.1.5 Data Requirements for the Simulation Approach

The data requirements for the simulation approach to modal-split analysis are quite flexible. Actual distribution data are not necessarily required to feed such a model. Often by knowing the mean or median value of a distribution it is possible to use common sense or related distributions to form the shape of the distribution. And although certain data such as income distribution shape may not be available for a specific city, it is usually easy to obtain typical values from other sources on either a county or regional basis. The distributions that are used can be of a textbook variety, such as a normal, a lognormal, or an exponential distribution. However, the distributions can also be tabular, and formed by specifying certain values of the function at specific values of the independent variable, and allowing the computer program to interpolate intermediate values. The use of either a tabular or a textbook type of distribution significantly increases the simulation fidelity relative to using only the mean or median value.

Data requirements are often determined by the scope of the study and, in particular, by the desired fidelity and the study schedule. The general approach is to build a high fidelity model, and then for certain studies, limit the amount of data used to feed the model to be consistent with the particular application. The simulation can be developed so that it uses data in a manner which reduces the cost of the simulation execution as the data input is simplified.

10.1.6 Calibration and Preference Factor Determination

The preference factors for the modes are intended to represent all of the noneconomic or unmodeled factors affecting mode choice; that is, all the factors which are not expressed in units of cost or time. Since they represent the intangibles, the preference factor distributions are the calibration parameters of the simulation model. They are the quantities that are adjusted to achieve consistency between model predictions and mode-use surveys for some past year in which the necessary data base exists. In the simulation, that portion of the traveler's time and cost which is spent on the mode is multiplied by his preference factor for that mode (as drawn from the lognormal preference factor distribution determined during calibration). Preference factors, therefore, represent the degree to which a traveler will go against pure economics in choosing a travel mode.

With new modes such as PRT there is obviously no data base with which one can determine preference factors. However, one can still attempt to estimate preference factor distributions either by comparing the new mode to similar existing modes and making modifications for the differences, or by attempting to assess all the subjective features which make up a preference factor. The latter method often belongs to the realm of psychological scaling theory using paired comparisons.

However, preference factor determination is not a necessary prerequisite for the operation of this modal-split model. For example, all modes can be assigned a preference factor of unity, implying no mode bias on the part of the traveler. This is a very valuable aspect when there are no calibration data available. On the other hand, the data necessary for calibration are minimal compared to the needs of the traditional modal-split models, many of which rely exclusively on calibration data. While other models often require data on stratified groups, often in a particular section of a particular city, the simulated traveler approach requires prior modal-split data on a mode basis only. A major benefit is that the mode preference factor distributions so obtained tend to have a greater range of applicability.

10.1.7 Model Overview

Figure 10-1 presents an overview of how a Monte Carlo modal-split simulation is used to analyze the patronage of a PRT system. One type of input to the simulation model is interzonal data consisting of the number of trips from each origin zone to each destination zone, and distances and travel times by auto between the centroids of the zones. A second type is specific data about each zone required to specify its location and shape (often stylized), the income distribution of travelers originating from the zone, and parking costs for travelers whose destination is within the zone. The third basic type of input relates to characteristics of the PRT system, such as where the stations are located, the travel times between stations, the fare structure for the PRT network, data regarding station access, and

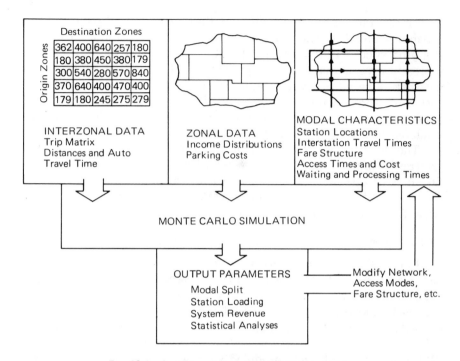

Fig. 10-1. Overview of Basic Modal-Split Simulation

waiting and processing times. These three types of inputs feed the Monte Carlo modal-split simulation program. The program outputs include modal-split, average demand at and revenue from individual stations, and statistical analyses of which travelers take PRT, which do not, and what factors affect their choices.

Since one objective of a patronage estimation process is usually to optimize the demand for a particular mode subject to various constraints, the next step is to modify the network, fare structure, line speeds, or other service parameters, in a manner indicated by analysis of the output data, so as to improve patronage or economic measures of system performance. Having modified the PRT network and/or service parameters, the simulation process is repeated. This process can be reiterated until no substantial further improvement can be achieved.

The next section will discuss how such a basic model was applied to the analysis of a proposed PRT system for the City of Tucson.

10.2 APPLICATION OF THE MODAL-SPLIT SIMULATION TO THE CITY OF TUCSON

10.2.1 Motivation and Scope

This study was conducted during 1970-71 using corporate funds to demonstrate both the viability of PRT on a limited scale and the capability and flexibility of the modal-split simulation approach in studying such a PRT network. The City of Tucson was chosen as a representative arena for the application of a limited PRT system network. The city is automobile oriented with some congestion on east-west thoroughfares, especially during peak hour traffic. A large amount of social, economic, and origin-destination data was available and could be easily used in the modal-split model.

The PRT network being analyzed for the City of Tucson was arbitrarily limited in extent to the order of 60 stations with 50 to 60 miles of one-way guideway. It was of particular interest to do an analysis of the peak hour travel with primary emphasis on work trips, for which a data base was available.

10.2.2 Characteristics of the Modal-Split Model and Input Data

For this particular application the model was sized to accommodate up to 70 PRT stations and 300 different Traffic Analysis Zones (TAZ's) within the city. The primary modes studied were PRT, drive and park, and being chauffeured all the way to the destination with the automobile being returned to the origin and with a similar trip being made for pickup at the end of the day. The access modes to PRT stations which were modeled were walking, park-and-ride, and kiss-and-ride. For this particular study it was assumed that no local bus service was available. The existing bus services are largely in the area which was postulated for PRT service.

Considerable data for input to the modal-split simulation were obtained from the Tucson Area Transportation Planning Agency (TATPA), including an origin-destination tape containing 1980 projections of vehicle trips between TAZ pairs, TAZ coordinates and dimensions, and distributions of automobile parking costs and walking time from parking locations. Census data were used to obtain income information and special survey data were available on automobile ownership. Other characteristics required to describe the PRT system, such as processing time, waiting time, and parking at PRT stations, were created consistent with the PRT system being envisioned.

10.2.3 Initial PRT Configuration

Figure 10-2 presents the initial PRT network configuration chosen for analysis. This particular configuration was selected to serve areas of specific interest. The central business district is located in the northwest corner of the network. The network serves the University of Arizona, with 25,000 students, and South Tucson, which is the low income area directly south of the central business

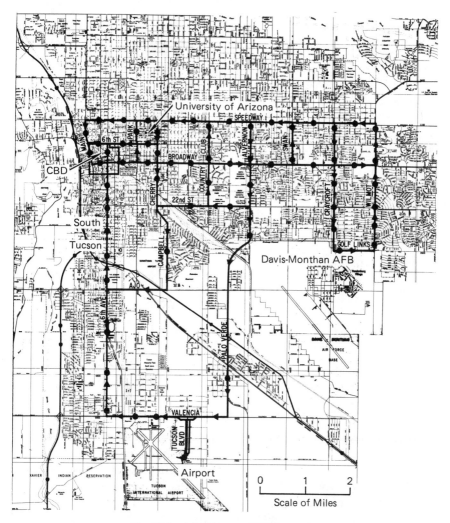

Fig. 10-2. Initial Tucson PRT Network

district. A line runs to the Tucson International Airport at the southern extreme of the network. Davis-Monthan Air Force Base, an area of considerable employment, is served by the western loop of the network. The commercial corridor along Speedway and Broadway is very heavily congested during peak auto traffic. The network consisted of 65 stations and 55 route miles, with only walking access to PRT stations considered.

Figure 10-3 presents some of the results which were obtained from this initial PRT network analysis. Figure 10-3a shows the sensitivity of patronage to PRT fares. Figure 10-3b develops the peak

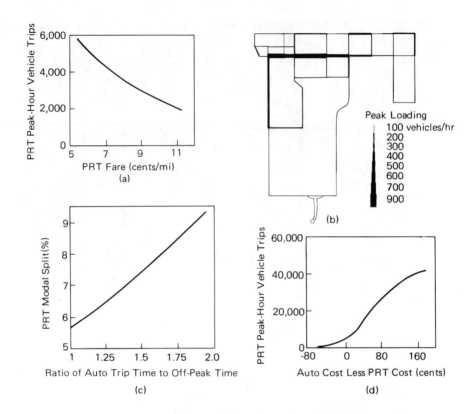

Fig. 10-3. Sample Results for Initial Tucson Network

hour loading over the entire network. Figure 10-3c shows the modal split as a function of an increase in auto congestion, in which the trip times by auto for the entire system are uniformly increased from 25 to 100 percent over off-peak hour values. The curve of Fig. 10-3d is one of the most significant in the output of the modal-split program capability. Since the modal-split technique models the decision of each traveler, it can keep track not only of which mode the traveler takes, but how much difference in cost would cause that traveler to switch modes. Thus, a curve can be generated showing the number of trips as a function of the cost difference between the two modes. Then, without any additional runs, it is possible to predict to a first approximation the change in ridership as a function of the change in the cost of either mode.

These initial results showed a very low patronage for the PRT system. The time-cost of walking turned out to be the major deterrent to increased patronage. Also, much of the network was inefficient in that the round-trip routes for PRT passengers were considerably longer than the equivalent rectangular automobile route.

10.2.4 Intermediate PRT Network Configurations

Several other PRT network configurations were modeled to determine their impact on patronage. These configurations are shown in Fig. 10-4. The second network added lines in the area of the central business district and the University of Arizona. These lines picked up additional trips but they did not significantly increase the total patronage.

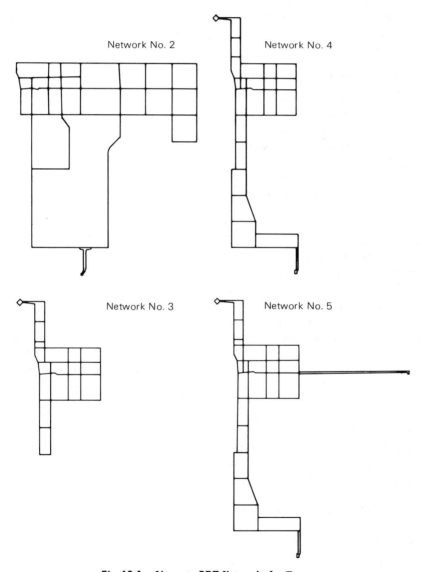

Fig. 10-4. Alternate PRT Networks for Tucson

In the third network, a more compact system was developed to serve the CBD and the University of Arizona plus an additional hotel and shopping area in the north part of the city called the Miracle Mile. However, because long trips were eliminated, such as to the airport and in the vicinity of the Air Force Base, the net patronage was quite low.

The fourth network provided for longer trips and included service to the airport. Also at this time alternative park-and-ride and kiss-and-ride access modes were added, which improved the patronage considerably and thus provided greater revenue with only a small increase in the capital costs.

10.2.5 Final Network Configuration

The fifth network, as shown in Fig. 10-4, kept the improved access modes but also added an extension to provide essentially a line-haul service to the residential areas in the eastern part of the city. This technique of using a spur to an area without providing an entire network proved useful, since 47% of the patronage for this final configuration used park-and-ride as the access mode. This configuration had 57 stations, 54 route miles, and PRT parking lots at 15 of the stations. For an assumed parking cost of 25¢ at the PRT parking lots, and depending on assumed PRT fares and perceived automobile driving costs, the fifth network attracted between 50% and 100% more patronage than the first network, which relied entirely on walking access.

This evolution of a proposed network indicates the value of a high fidelity modal-split model, because many of the changes which resulted in improved performance affected only a fraction of the travelers, yet it was possible to determine what direction the evolution of the network should take based on the detailed modal-split simulation outputs. This capability to perform sensitivity studies as well as to predict what would happen if certain changes were made is a significant benefit of a modal-split simulation model. The model also indicated that well-traveled streets are not necessarily good candidates for PRT lines. PRT lines should be near high-demand areas so that stations can be placed within easy reach of the patrons. Areas adjoining high-density streets are not necessarily areas having a large number of trip ends.

10.3 ENHANCED PATRONAGE ESTIMATION PACKAGE

10.3.1 Motivation and New Capabilities

The basic modal-split simulation model which was discussed in the context of the Tucson application has certain limitations which are overcome in Aerospace's enhanced patronage estimation package. This package is made up of an improved modal-split simulation, combined with several preprocessor and postprocessor programs. The improved capabilities were primarily motivated by the desire to be able to study large networks in very large cities. The enhanced program is currently scaled to handle a city having up to 1,300 zones and a PRT network with up to 1,000 stations.

In addition, since many cities have access modes other than walking, park-and-ride, and kiss-and-ride, the program includes the capability to model dial-a-ride access (see footnote 10, Sec. 1.6) as well as conventional bus networks. The fidelity of modeling the city was improved by the capability of converting the zones of the city to stylized polygons having many sides rather than the stylized rectangles which were used to model the cities in the earlier model.

In a large city many more travelers have to be modeled in order to get an adequate statistical sample over a large network. To handle large numbers of simulated travelers the efficiency of traveler processing required improvement in order to reduce simulation costs.

Finally, since the model was to accommodate large PRT networks, additional aids for network design were desired. These aids would provide information on the location of trip ends within the city which would assist the designer in laying out a network to accommodate these trips.

10.3.2 Description of Presimulation Programs

Figure 10-5 presents a flow diagram of the processes performed prior to modal-split simulation. The principal motivation in having a preprocessing capability separate from the modal-split simulation is to be able to generate a permanently storable traveler file. This file can then be used over and over as the network, fare structure, access modes, or system characteristics are changed. This approach avoids the need to generate travelers for each simulation, and because each simulation uses the same set of simulated travelers, run-to-run comparisons are fair and the results are repeatable.

Cities usually provide the location and shape of their traffic analysis zones (TAZ's) in the form of maps. These maps are converted by the mapping programs to digital data consisting of the vertex coordinates of many-sided polygons representing the TAZ's. The digitizing is achieved using a device called the Rand Tablet (GRAFACON 1010A). Coordinates of TAZ vertices are recorded by having the operator press a button when the stylus has been moved over a vertex.

These mapping programs also include means for updating and correcting the TAZ information in the data base. Furthermore, the capability to join many different sectional maps of the city into a

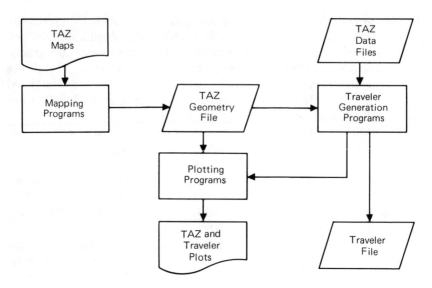

Fig. 10-5. Modal-Split Preprocessing Flow Diagram

composite data base is provided. Finally, the mapping programs sort the data base so that its output, the TAZ geometry file, which for each TAZ contains the TAZ identification and the coordinates of all of its vertices, is ordered according to increasing TAZ identification number.

The plotting programs allow a selection of TAZ's, which may only represent a part of the city, to be plotted to a specified scale. This capability allows for visual checking of the fidelity of the digitizing process. A sample plot is shown in Fig. 10-6 for the Twin Cities, Minneapolis and St. Paul, Minnesota.

In addition to the boundaries of the TAZ's the plotting program can optionally plot each traveler origin and destination trip end (using data from the traveler-generation programs discussed below), as well as the numerical ID for each TAZ. Such a plot is very useful for analyzing trip densities and helping to locate PRT lines and stations as well as establishing the need for various types of access modes to PRT.

The TAZ data files (Fig. 10-5) are external files, since the data contained in them must usually come from sources associated with the city being modeled. The number and nature of these external files will vary from city to city; hence, the programs that accept these files may require slight front-end modifications to accommodate the data for a particular city.

The TAZ data files contain the demand matrix, which is the matrix of trips between origin and destination zones, the coordinates

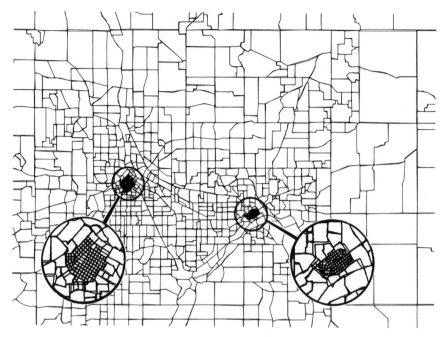

Fig. 10-6. Plot of Portion of Traffic Analysis Zone Map of Twin Cities

of the TAZ centroids, and the peak and off-peak auto distance and auto driving times between these TAZ centroids. It contains the median household income, the nominal local automobile travel speed within the TAZ, and the probability that households in the TAZ own zero, one, or two or more automobiles.

The traveler-generation programs combine all of the various external TAZ data files that separately contain TAZ or TAZ pair information, with the ultimate objective of creating a file containing a complete description of simulated travelers to the extent required to make modal choice decisions.

These programs first allow for the filtering of trips by origin and/or destination TAZ in order to constrain the analysis to certain parts of the city, and allow for scaling of the demand matrix data, so that a different number of trips than that contained in the origin-destination matrix can be simulated. Then the traveler-generation programs take the resultant demand matrix, and the TAZ polygon vertices from the TAZ geometry file, and locate traveler's trip ends within the TAZ polygons in a random fashion consistent with the demand associated with each of these zones.

The individual traveler may have a longer or shorter driving distance and time (peak or off-peak) than would be indicated by merely using the driving distance and time between TAZ centroids.

The program calculates a corrected peak and off-peak driving distance and time for his trip, taking into consideration the offsets of his exact origin and destination from the TAZ centroids.

Finally, an exact household income for the traveler is determined by a random draw using the lognormal income distribution for his resident TAZ. Thus the traveler tape contains, for each simulated traveler:

    a.   traveler ID number

    b.   origin TAZ ID

    c.   x and y coordinates of exact origin

    d.   destination TAZ ID

    e.   x and y coordinates of exact destination

    f.   peak and off-peak automobile driving distance

    g.   peak and off-peak automobile driving times

    h.   household income

    i.   number of automobiles owned by the household

For a large city, typical traveler tapes might include a sample of 100,000 travelers.

10.3.3 Description of Modal-Split Program Inputs

In addition to the traveler file discussed above, the modal-split program has two other types of input files — the parameter file and the PRT/TAZ files. The parameter file is on punched cards and contains system data and that portion of the mode data which is likely to vary from scenario to scenario. The PRT/TAZ files, on disk or tape, contain PRT station data, PRT travel times, certain TAZ data, and a list of PRT stations most accessible from each TAZ.

Specifically, the system data on the parameter file include the time value factor (usually of the order of 0.25 to 0.5) which is used to convert earning rate to time value, and a scale factor to determine how large a sample from the traveler file should be used in the simulation. If this scale factor is less than unity, then only the specified fraction of travelers on the traveler file will be selected for simulation.

Automobile data in the parameter file consist of:

    a.   Driving preference factor distribution parameters.

    b.   A congestion factor to combine peak and off-peak data provided on the traveler file in order to select the appropriate level of traffic congestion for the time of day simulated and for the degree of street offloading anticipated by virtue of the existence of the competing PRT service.

c. A number of parking cost and parking time tables, each of which describes a different cost and time distribution associated with parking in the various destination areas of the city. (The PRT/TAZ files discussed below will indicate for each destination TAZ which of these parking tables should be used.)

d. A set of perceived per-mile auto costs as a function of the number of automobiles owned in the household.

Perceived automobile costs for commuting to work vary considerably from household to household. The crucial factor in such automobile costing is whether the traveler perceives only the immediate direct operating costs (gasoline and consumed oil), total direct operating costs (with additional items such as tires, battery, shock absorbers, oil changes, tune-ups), or total costs (including insurance, license, and depreciation). The differences in cost can range from below 5 cents per mile for immediate direct costs to the order of 15 to 30 cents per mile for total costs.

Objectively, this perception should depend on whether the auto used for commuting would be kept if the work trip is made using public transit instead. For single-auto households it is extremely likely to be kept. For multiple-auto households it depends on the number of autos owned relative to the number of licensed drivers, and whether other than work trip requirements are served by the extra vehicle(s) (such as in the case of recreational or other special-purpose vehicles). Furthermore, for many households the question of reduced auto ownership to reflect use of public transit won't be addressed until the time comes to replace an auto or to face a major repair or maintenance bill.

The model allows for several different perceived cost values, depending on the number of autos owned by the household. The model could be easily modified to make the perceived cost a function of resident zone, household income, number of licensed drivers, number of household members employed full time, or some combination of the above.

The PRT data on the parameter file include PRT ride-preference-factor distribution parameters, the maximum number of PRT stations which will be considered by the traveler for access at each end, and a fare formula specified as a flat charge, a per-mile charge, or any combination of the two. One input is a "wait factor" (usually between 2 and 3) which is used to scale the actual waiting time to a larger perceived time to reflect traveler's dissatisfaction with having to wait for PRT.

One of the most important types of data which is input on the parameter file is access mode data.

Walking access is allowed to all stations. It is characterized by a walking speed and a walk factor which converts actual walking time to a perceived walking time. Walking time is normally charged at a higher rate than riding time, usually by a factor between 1 and 2.

Kiss-and-ride and park-and-ride access are permitted only at the residential end of the trip. Kiss-and-ride access characterization includes kiss-and-ride preference factor distribution parameters, a time value factor which converts the chauffeur's time to effective cost, and a kiss-and-ride unavailability factor which specifies the fraction of travelers who do not have kiss-and-ride as a viable access mode because they have no one to drive them to the station.

The parameter file also includes a number of parking tables used for modeling park-and-ride access. These tables, which describe the fraction of travelers who are to be assigned any specified cost and time, are used to reflect the fact that the ease and cost of parking at or near a residential station varies from one station to another.

These parking tables differ from those previously discussed; the present tables characterize parking at or near stations accessible from residential TAZ's while the earlier tables referred to general parking in a destination TAZ, whether or not near a station. For example, there may be parking facilities at certain residential PRT stations with free or reduced-cost parking for PRT patrons but not for the general public.

Dial-a-ride access is characterized by both system characteristics and individual service area characteristics. System characteristics include preference factor distribution parameters for dial-a-ride, a waiting factor to convert the time spent waiting for the dail-a-ride vehicle to perceived time, and a fare formula which allows a per-mile charge, or a flat fee, or some combination of the two. An individual dial-a-ride service area is specified by a pie-shaped wedge where the apex of the wedge is located at a PRT station. Other characteristics associated with an individual dial-a-ride sector are the maximum expected waiting time, and the speed in progressing through the sector radially toward the PRT station.

Conventional bus access also is characterized by both system characteristics and individual route characteristics. The system characteristics include the preference factor distribution for bus access, a wait factor to convert actual waiting time for the bus to perceived waiting time, and a fare formula which allows the bus cost to be determined on a per-mile basis or a flat-fee basis, or some combination of the two. Individual route characteristics include route location, the headway and speed of the bus along its route, and the interstop distance on the route (which determines how far the traveler has to walk to a bus stop).

The PRT/TAZ files contain, for each station, the station ID, its x and y coordinates, and the average processing and waiting times at that station. In addition, they specify for each station which access mode information from the parameter file shall apply for that station. More particularly, they specify which of the parking cost and time tables and which descriptors of dial-a-ride and conventional bus service should be used.

The PRT/TAZ files also contain the PRT travel times between all possible station pairs. These PRT travel times are produced by Program ROUTE which was described in Sec. 5.4.

The PRT/TAZ files also provide certain types of TAZ data. These TAZ data assign for each TAZ which table of destination-parking cost and time should be used for those who drive to a destination within that TAZ. Another input is the peak and off-peak intra-TAZ speeds to be used to determine driving times between the traveler's residence and stations in close proximity. For TAZ's not in close proximity to the PRT network, driving distances and times to the candidate stations are calculated using the same procedure as was used to compute distance and time between origin and destination for the auto-only trip.

The file also provides for association of up to 10 PRT stations with each TAZ. A station is associated with a TAZ if it is accessible from the TAZ by any of the access modes and is likely to be used by any travelers whose trips start or end in the TAZ.

10.3.4 Description of the Modal-Split Program Operation

The modal-split program operation begins by obtaining a traveler and his trip data from the traveler file. The total perceived cost for the traveler to drive an automobile to his destination is determined. This includes auto driving cost and time, and parking cost and time. The times are converted to dollars to get total cost. If being chauffeured all the way to the destination is available, the total cost of that mode also is determined, including the chauffeur's time value and the return trip cost. The cost of the cheaper of these two modes is then determined and retained.

Next the perceived cost of the traveler riding PRT to his destination is determined. This is an involved process, as it requires selecting the optimum PRT station as well as selecting the optimum access mode at each station. The total cost of riding PRT is the sum of the access and ride costs. First the program compares, for *each* station associated with the *residential* TAZ, the cost of getting to that station by the various possible modes of access, and chooses for that station the access mode with the least cost. Access modes could include walk, drive-and-park, kiss-and-ride, dial-a-ride, and conventional bus. Then, for *each* station in the *destination* TAZ, the program finds the lowest cost access mode to that station. However, neither park-and-ride nor kiss-and-ride is allowed as a destination access mode.

Walking is an access mode available to every station. However, before computing the access cost for any other access mode, the program checks to see if the mode is available to the station. For example, the station must have a bus line or dial-a-ride sector associated with it in order to allow consideration of that type of access.

The program then separately sorts all the candidate origin and destination stations, ordering them by access cost. In determining the optimum station pair, the program considers only the n cheapest access-cost origin stations and the n cheapest access-cost destination stations (where n, the maximum number of stations to be considered at each trip end, is one of the inputs on the parameter file). For each of the n^2 station pairs still under consideration, the program computes the total perceived door-to-door PRT costs, and selects the station pair with the minimum cost. Although the program simulates round trips it does not require that the two one-way segments use the same stations, except when drive-and-park is used and the return trip must terminate at the original residential departure station.

Next, the cost of traveling by auto is compared with the cost of traveling by PRT. The traveler is assigned to the mode which is cheaper for him and a record containing information concerning this traveler is written on an output tape. The entire process is then repeated by reading another record from the traveler file. Processing continues until all selected travelers have been simulated.

10.3.5 MDS Program Outputs

There are basically three types of output provided by the MDS program itself: a standard printed output, a traveler record file on tape or disk, and a station-to-station O-D trip matrix file on tape or disk used for routing and empty-vehicle dispatching (see Sec. 5.2).

The printed file contains all of the parameter file input data, an optional listing of the PRT/TAZ files, and timing data for measuring simulation efficiency.

The traveler record file contains all of the information about each traveler, including the elements of his mode choice decision. This file can be processed by the report generator, which is a separate module within the MDS program package.

The report generator is organized to give two types of reports. There are six standard reports plus specially generated reports which can be virtually unlimited in both number and complexity.

The first standard report gives the modal-split summary and the average trip cost and time by primary mode. The second one gives the modal-split summary and the average cost and time for PRT trips by each access mode. The third gives the cost of an average trip by both auto and PRT broken down into the individual cost elements of the trip. The fourth gives the distribution of cost differences between auto and PRT for 40 preselected cost increments. The fifth standard system report gives, for each station in the system, the number of arrivals and departures for that station by each of the possible access modes. The final standard report is the TAZ report which gives for each TAZ the modal split between auto and PRT for trips by residents of the TAZ and trips by visitors to the TAZ.

The approach taken in generating special reports with the report generator emphasizes extreme flexibility. The report generator features a SELECT option whereby only certain elements such as TAZ's or stations may be specified and reports given for just those elements of the simulation, or all of the elements within a certain numerical range may be specified and a report provided for that set of specific elements. The report generator has the flexibility of allowing the user to request the printing of a statistical report which gives the mean, the standard deviation, and the maximum and minimum of a particular data set, or the printing of a data distribution.

The report generator also has a LIST capability which provides for the printing of any traveler's record which meets the qualifications specified by SELECT statements which precede it. Thus, any traveler meeting certain criteria of interest will have his complete traveler record printed for detailed off-line analysis.

10.3.6 Iterating with the Demand-Estimation Package

Clearly, the demand-estimation package which has just been described is not self-optimizing and iterative techniques must be used. Optimization usually means maximizing PRT demand subject to certain constraints involving fare rates, capital costs, service to selected areas, or other such considerations.

Three general types of iterations can be identified using this package. These are parameter file variations, PRT network variations, and external file variations. Parameter modifications involve changes in fare structure, modification of automobile costs or congestion factor, changes in the access to the PRT system and improvements in the PRT system having to do with waiting, station processing, and such overall system parameters. These iterations can be achieved by changing just a few cards in the parameter file.

The second type of iteration involves modifications to the PRT network, such as numbers of stations and their location, line location, or line speeds. These kinds of changes involve generating new PRT files.

The final type of iteration involves changing the traveler file. This includes modifications to the highway plan or the extent of the city being modeled.

Because of the flexibility of the report generator it is possible to get considerable insight regarding what would happen if many of these variations were attempted. That is, an estimate of the new PRT patronage and even certain information about where the change would take place can be obtained by requesting the right type of report generator output for the initial run. Thus, the impact of many policy questions can be estimated without actually having to rerun the modal-split simulation. Again, this is one of the great advantages of simulating individual travelers and maintaining a record of the elements involved in their mode-choice decision.

Chapter 11
PRT ECONOMICS AND BENEFITS

Harry Bernstein

The prior chapters have discussed the PRT service concept, operating strategies, technological considerations, and PRT costs. In this chapter we shall attempt to look at PRT from two viewpoints: namely, its economics and its benefits. More specifically, the following questions will be addressed:

Can the revenue derived from PRT operation cover the operating and maintenance costs (not including capital cost amortization) such that the system will not require any operating subsidy?

To what extent might PRT revenues cover capital cost amortization?

How are PRT economics affected by considerations of modular network buildup?

What benefits are derived from PRT which might tend to offset those costs not directly borne by its patrons?

11.1 OPERATING ECONOMICS

As discussed in Sec. 9.3 on PRT operating costs, a part of the operating and maintenance cost (variable part) scales essentially linearly with system utilization (e.g., power for vehicles, maintenance of vehicles) and another part (fixed part) tends to be relatively independent of utilization (e.g., power for station lighting, maintenance of guideway). These costs, using 1975 dollars, are detailed in Table 9-9. The administrative and overhead costs are estimated at 15% in the table and may be attributed proportionately to both the fixed and variable costs. Thus, the variable costs, when burdened with 15% overhead, are $12.2 million/yr for the baseline system. Dividing by 3×10^8 occupied vehicle mi/yr for the system leads to a variable cost of 4.1¢/occupied vehicle mile.

Assume the fare charged per occupied vehicle mile is more than sufficient to offset the variable part of the operating cost. The question then becomes whether the part of the fare in excess of that required to offset variable operating costs can offset the fixed operating costs.

To a first order, the fixed part of the operating and maintenance (O&M) costs are proportional to the number of guideway miles in the network. If these costs are to be offset, then:

$$(C_{OF})\,(N_{GM}) = (\Delta F)\,(N_{OVM/YR}), \qquad (11.1)$$

where:

C_{OF} = annual fixed O&M costs, \$/one-way guideway mile,

N_{GM} = number of one-way guideway miles in the network,

ΔF = part of fare in excess of that required to cover variable O&M costs (\$/occupied vehicle mile),

$N_{OVM/YR}$ = patronage in terms of number of occupied vehicle miles per year.

It is obvious from the above relationship that the ability to offset the fixed part of the operating costs will be, for any given ΔF, dependent upon the patronage realized.

Let us now consider a somewhat idealized case in which all points in a hypothetical city are served by a PRT network. The patronage can now be expressed as:

$$N_{OVM/YR} = (\rho)\,(A)\,(W)\,(M_s)\,\Big(\frac{K_1}{K_2}\Big)\,(m)\,(D), \qquad (11.2)$$

where

ρ = population density,

A = city area,

W = fraction workers = 0.33,

M_s = modal-split fraction of passenger miles traveled,

$K_1 = \dfrac{\text{daily total passenger miles}}{\text{daily home-to-work passenger miles}}$ =1.25,

K_2 = average party size = 1.3,

m = miles per day per worker (round trip),

D = workday equivalents per year = 300.

The number of guideway miles is a function of the average network grid density and the area of the city; i.e.,

$$N_{GM} = (N_{GM/A})\,(A),$$

where

$N_{GM/A}$ = guideway miles per square mile.

Combining the above relationships yields:

$$(C_{OF}) (N_{GM/A}) = (\Delta F) (\rho) (W) (M_s) (\frac{K_1}{K_2}) (m) (D). \qquad (11.3)$$

The round-trip miles per day per worker (m) varies city-to-city; for an area such as Los Angeles, this term is of the order of 20 miles/worker/day on average. The modal-split fraction is a function of the PRT system characteristics, including the network grid fineness, as well as the performance available via competitive modes, including driving.

To quantize the modal-split fraction, a highly stylized version of Aerospace's modal-split simulation program, discussed in Chapter 10, was used. The previously stated assumption of complete network coverage obviated the necessity for considering specific trip patterns. Therefore, the simulation was concerned only with a trip from a representative residential zone to an employment center, where the trip distance was varied in accordance with the distribution data (derived from Los Angeles travel patterns) of Fig. 11-1(a). Comparative travel times for PRT and auto (again corresponding to Los Angeles experience) were input to the simulation as a function of the trip distance (see Fig. 11-1(b)). To the PRT trip times indicated in Fig. 11-1(b), walking times for station access were added for both ends of the trip, and, in fact, were multiplied by a factor of 2.0 to reflect a general dispreference for time spent walking as opposed to riding. Walking times were computed assuming 0.5-mile station spacing at the residential end, and 0.25-mile station spacing at the employment-center end of the trip. Such spacing can be provided with approximately three miles of one-way guideway per square mile $(N_{GM/A})$ if it is assumed that the employment center areas are a small part of the total urban area.

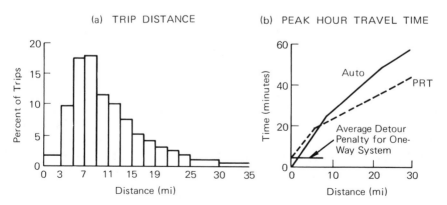

Fig. 11-1. Simulation Input Functions

Two minutes were also added to the PRT time to account for station processing time. Auto parking times of 2 minutes and 4 minutes were used for 80% and 20%, respectively, of the auto trips. It was assumed that 80% of the autos parked free, that 10% cost 50 cents, and that 10% cost one dollar. The traveler's time value was assumed to be 25% of his hourly wage.

The resultant modal-split fraction is seen from Fig. 11-2 to be quite sensitive to the relationship between fares and perceived auto costs. The dashed line in Fig. 11-2 corresponds to the condition where PRT fares and perceived auto costs are assumed to be equal.

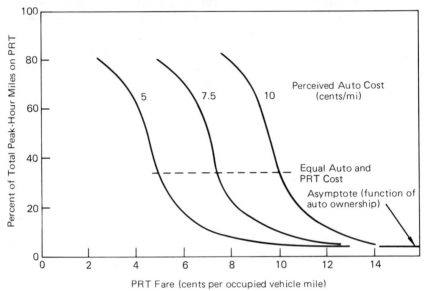

Fig. 11-2. Effect of Relative Fare Costs on Modal Split

In this case, the comparative total trip time is the predominant factor in determining modal split. For this case the PRT system can be expected to capture 34% of the peak-hour miles (which corresponds to 27% of the peak-hour travelers). Thus, we take the modal-split mileage fraction (M_s), appearing in Eq. (11.3), as 0.34.

From the 1975 operational cost data of Table 9-9, the value of C_{OF} is \$35,300/yr/guideway mile (including the 15% overhead burden). A curve of break-even population density vs. PRT fare can now be developed from Eq. (11.3). Such a curve is plotted in Fig. 11-3 (Case I), and shows that for fares of 6-1/2 and 8¢ per occupied vehicle mile [1] the PRT system would operate at a break-even point in

---

[1] These fare levels are believed to be in reasonable accord with people's perceptions of the incremental costs of auto operation; total cost including depreciation and insurance is in the 15 to 30¢ per mile range.

areas having average population densities of 6,800 and 4,200 persons per square mile, respectively. These results indicate that mature PRT networks have the potential for operating without subsidy in cities of moderate population density. For example, the Los Angeles area has an average population density of approximately 6,500 persons per square mile when the total land area of the basin is considered; the areas which might logically be within a PRT network are even more densely populated, with some parts, such as the Wilshire Corridor, having densities in the range of ten to fifteen thousand persons per square mile.

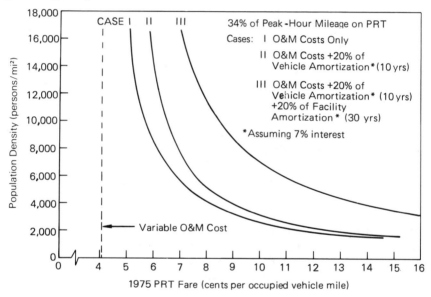

Fig. 11-3. Break-Even Population Densities

11.2 CAPITAL COSTS

In Chapter 9 capital cost estimates for PRT systems were developed. These cost estimates assumed no amortization of development or production tooling costs. For a large network, costs ranging from approximately $2.5 million to $5.0 million per one-way guideway mile (1973 dollars) were indicated, depending upon the number of vehicles per guideway mile and the total number of guideway miles in the network being built (see Fig. 9-1).

These costs are quite low, on a per-mile basis, when compared with those of urban train systems. Capital costs for urban train systems in the same time period range from about $13 million to $30 million per one-way mile depending upon whether the train system is elevated or underground. (These numbers must be doubled to find the cost per two-way route mile.) The lower unit costs associated with PRT emanate from the following considerations:

> PRT is installed elevated;
>
> PRT guideways are light in scale;
>
> PRT guideways are amenable to factory fabrication and on-site erection;
>
> PRT guideways can be installed rapidly, with minimum disruption to normal street activities; and
>
> PRT vehicles are required in relatively large numbers for reasonable network sizes, and hence are amenable to quantity production techniques.

In a PRT network, area coverage and accessibility increase rapidly as the number of one-way guideway miles increases, since lines in the opposite direction are usually spaced 1/2 to 1 mile apart rather than being colocated as in a train system. This factor, in combination with the lower unit costs, results in some rather dramatic service vs. cost comparisons between PRT and urban trains. For example, a detailed comparison was made between a PRT system and an urban train system for Los Angeles. Figure 11-4 is a map showing consultant recommendations for a rail/bus system as presented to the Southern California Rapid Transit District (SCRTD) in July 1973. The solid black lines represent 116 route-miles of rail system and the dashed black lines represent 24 route-miles of elevated busway. The rail/busway system has 61 stations, five stations being located within the Los Angeles central business district. As indicated on Fig. 11-4, the SCRTD's consultants estimated the cost for this system at $3.4 billion in 1973 dollars, and $6.6 billion with the inclusion of a 9% cost escalation factor through the construction period. The consultants also indicated that the relatively thin coverage afforded by the rail system would necessitate a significant expansion in SCRTD's bus fleet to provide for local service and to serve as a feeder for the rail system.

Patronage was estimated at 1,000,000 daily riders on the rail system and another 900,000 riders on the buses — mostly buses for local service and collection/distribution. (Note: the patronage accounting methods used by the consultants counted a single individual taking the bus and then the train on a single trip as one train rider and one bus rider.) The consultants estimated an annual operating deficit of $275 million in the year of completion of the system (1986), with possible escalation of that operating deficit in succeeding years.

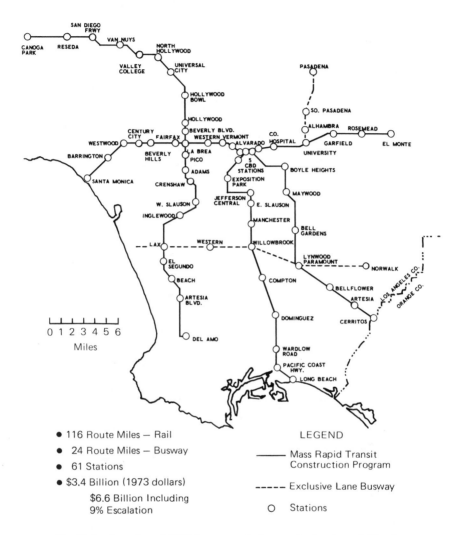

- 116 Route Miles — Rail
- 24 Route Miles — Busway
- 61 Stations
- $3.4 Billion (1973 dollars)
    $6.6 Billion Including
    9% Escalation

LEGEND

——— Mass Rapid Transit
Construction Program

----- Exclusive Lane Busway

O   Stations

**Fig. 11-4.   Consultants' 1973 Recommendations to the Southern California
Rapid Transit District**

In attempting to illustrate the potentials of PRT for Los Angeles, Aerospace developed a conceptual PRT network layout, but one which could be built for approximately half the capital cost of the train/bus system. This layout is shown in Fig. 11-5. As can be seen by comparing Figs. 11-4 and 11-5, the PRT network provides service along all of the corridors served by the train system, and in addition includes service along the San Diego Freeway corridor from the San Fernando Valley to the Los Angeles International Airport area. The coverage within these corridors is, moreover, on an area-wide

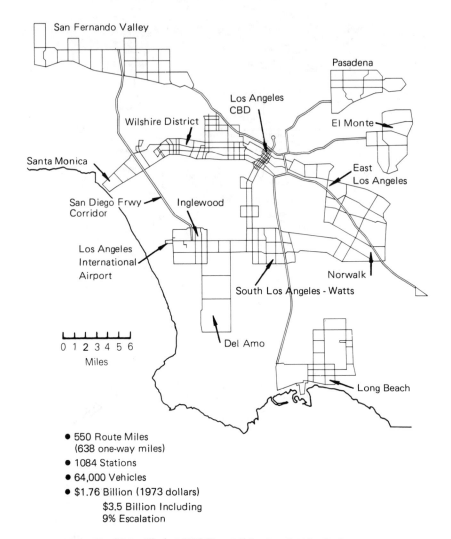

- 550 Route Miles
  (638 one-way miles)
- 1084 Stations
- 64,000 Vehicles
- $1.76 Billion (1973 dollars)
  $3.5 Billion Including
  9% Escalation

Fig. 11-5. Typical PRT Network for Los Angeles Region

basis, with considerable networking for collection, distribution, and local service.

The network illustrated includes 638 one-way guideway miles[2] and 1084 stations. The large number of stations, when contrasted with the 61 stations on the train system, is indicative of the broad and more accessible coverage afforded by PRT — at a much lower

[2] The network is predominantly a one-way network, except where the double stripes are shown to indicate two-way service along those particular lines. There are 462 miles of one-way guideway and 88 miles of two-way guideway for a total of 550 route miles and 638 one-way miles.

capital cost. It should be noted that the particular Los Angeles PRT layout, illustrated herein, is not to be construed as a recommended layout, as Aerospace did not perform analyses to determine the most desirable route placements. Rather, this layout was developed solely to facilitate comparison of the area coverage available for a particular level of capital investment.

In estimating the costs for the PRT network, Aerospace assumed a nominal 100 vehicles per guideway-mile for the fleet size. This number is, of course, a function of the anticipated system patronage. The 64,000-vehicle fleet would probably be adequate to handle the 1,000,000 daily riders estimated by SCRTD's consultants for the train system, though it is believed that the PRT patronage, in view of the coverage and level of service provided, would more likely be higher, perhaps on the order of 1,500,000 daily riders. Should this be true, the required vehicle fleet size would be in the vicinity of 100,000 vehicles. This would increase the costs (in 1973 dollars) from the $1.76 billion indicated on Fig. 11-5 to about $2.14 billion.

If we assume that the PRT network attracts the 1,000,000 passengers per day estimated for the rail system (and no more) and that these passengers travel in a party size of 1.3 on the average, then there would be about 770,000 occupied vehicle trips per day. If the average trip is 8 miles in length,[3] then these would account for 6.16 million occupied vehicle miles per day. With the fleet size of 64,000 vehicles, this would mean about 96 revenue miles per vehicle per day, which (assuming a 300 "weekday equivalent" year) agrees well with the 30,000 revenue miles per year per vehicle value used in computing operating costs. For such a patronage level, a fare of 5.3¢ per occupied vehicle mile (1975 dollars) would allow the network to break even on all O&M costs, as indicated in Table 9-9. Should a higher patronage be realized, the break-even fare would be reduced slightly from 5.3¢, since the fixed portion of the operating costs could be spread over a greater number of trips.

The foregoing comparison serves to indicate the vastly more desirable level of coverage, and hence service, which can be provided by PRT when compared on a per-dollar-of-capital-investment basis with urban trains. Furthermore, it again indicates the potential of PRT revenues derived from reasonable fares to pay for all operating and maintenance costs. Another issue, however, is the extent, if any, to which PRT capital costs might be paid for by fare-box revenues. More specifically, how much additional fare would be required to cover all or a part of the capital costs?

---

[3] The home-to-work and work-to-home trips may be longer, but the average will include a number of shorter trips during the off-peak hours.

Let us consider two parts of the capital cost: first that part associated with the vehicles, and then the remainder. Since each vehicle is assumed to deliver about 30,000 revenue miles per year, the fleet size is a direct function of patronage. Therefore, each vehicle must earn, in 30,000 annual revenue miles, an amount sufficient to amortize its cost plus interest in an appropriate number of years. Assume an incremental fare for purposes of paying off a 10-year, 7% bond indebtedness on the vehicle purchase price. The capital recovery factor for 10 years at 7% is 0.1425. If a vehicle costs[4] about $8,000 (in 1975 dollars), then the fare increment $\Delta F'$ (in $/occupied vehicle mile) to cover vehicle capital costs would equal (8,000) (0.1425) ÷ (30,000), or, when converted from dollars to cents, 3.8¢/occupied vehicle mile. Thus, an incremental 1975 fare of 3.8¢/occupied vehicle mile would pay for the fleet and its financing at 7%.

Now assume that the remainder of the capital costs are to be paid for over a 30-year period, including interest at 7%. If the network has three guideway miles per square mile, this will be a capital cost[5] of about $7.8 million per square mile (1975 dollars) not including vehicles, assuming that the total extent of the network is about 600 one-way guideway miles. The capital recovery factor for 30 years at 7% is 0.0806. Therefore, the system must produce an additional $629,000 per square mile per year in revenues to cover this part of the capital cost. The incremental fare $\Delta F''$ (in $/occupied vehicle mile) may now be computed:

$$\$629{,}000 = (\Delta F'') \, (\rho) \, (W) \, (M_s) \, \frac{K_1}{K_2} \, (m) \, (D), \qquad (11.4)$$

or $\qquad\qquad\qquad (\Delta F'') \, (\rho) \approx 972 \qquad\qquad\qquad (11.5)$

For a population density of 6,500 persons/per square mile, $\Delta F'' = 0.150$ or 15.0¢/occupied vehicle mile. At this population density, and for the assumed modal-split fraction of 0.34, complete recovery of all costs, O&M plus capital, would necessitate a (1975) fare of:

Fare =   4.1   +   2.5   +   3.8   +   15.0
      variable   fixed   vehicle   facility
      operating   operating amortization amortization

= 25.4¢/occupied vehicle mile

---

[4] Table 9-6 shows that in lots of 10,000 the 1973 cost of a vehicle is $8,800. The cost, of course, will be lower for larger lots. For example, if 60,000 vehicles are purchased, the 1973 unit cost would be $6,700. Applying a 9% inflation factor the 1975 unit cost is about $8,000.

[5] According to Table 9-6, the remaining costs (after subtracting cost of vehicles) are $2.86 million (1973) per one-way mile for a 100-mile system. For a 600-mile network, this would reduce to $2.18 million/mile. Adding 9% inflation, the 1975 figure is $2.59 million/mile.

Such a fare is obviously beyond what is reasonable for the users. Furthermore, the indicated break-even fare is not really valid, since the modal-split of approximately 34% is no longer valid. It was based on PRT fares equal to perceived costs of auto operation, and 25.4¢/ occupied vehicle mile is well beyond people's perceptions of auto costs. If, however, the amortization of only 20% of the capital costs were contemplated (with the other 80% assumed to be covered by an UMTA capital grant), the fare, again assuming a population density of 6,500 persons per square mile, would have to be 10.4¢/occupied vehicle mile. While still high, such a fare might be perceived equal to auto costs, particularly if an individual were making the trade-off between PRT use and second car ownership. This consideration is, however, not prevalent in most cases. Unless population densities are much higher, a more prudent conclusion is that fare-box revenues will most likely only cover O&M costs.[6] (Curves of break-even population densities for cases in which 20% of the vehicle costs are to be recovered, and in which 20% of the total capital costs are to be recovered, are also presented in Fig. 11-3.)

11.3 PRT NETWORK IMPLEMENTATION THROUGH MODULAR GROWTH

PRT networks can be modularly built up to the broad network planned for a given locale. Desirably, the planning process will define the broad network to be ultimately realized, and then will define a series of logical modular steps to its realization. Thus each step will be in conformance with the long-range goal.

Obviously it would be desirable if the network, in each of its stages of growth, could be self-sustaining in terms of revenues covering O&M costs. This would avoid accumulation of sizeable operating deficits during the period when the network was being built up to accommodate all the O-D trip ends ultimately planned.

Consider an initial network segment which covers 1/4 of the area ultimately planned for coverage. Further assume that the patronage estimated for the ultimate network just results in a break-even

---

[6] As this book reached its final stage of preparation, The Aerospace Corporation was completing a study in support of the Urban Mass Transportation Administration's Automated Guideway Transit Technology Program. In that study, the patronage and economics of a specific PRT network serving a high-employment-density portion of the Los Angeles region were investigated using Aerospace's modal-split simulation and arena travel data supplied by CalTrans. The results of this new study support the contention that a PRT network's revenues can cover its O&M costs and, in fact, were somewhat more optimistic with respect to the ability of those revenues to pay for a portion of the network's capital cost amortization. However, general conclusions should not be drawn from the study of a single case. The reader is encouraged to acquire and review the report on this study.

situation on O&M costs. If both the residential density and employment density were uniform throughout the entire urban area, then
the probability of an individual from the initial network area also
working within that area is 0.25; this is an effective multiplier on the
population density as regards potential for patronage on the initial
network. Clearly its operating economics will be poor, since the
patronage will be down by a factor of 4 from that required to break
even on O&M costs.

If, however, the area chosen had an employment density twice
the average for the entire area, then the probability of an individual
who lives in the initial network area also working within that area
would be 0.5. In addition, if the residential population density is also
twice that for the entire area, then there will be no decrease in trips
generated per square mile over what is expected for the entire network
when completed. Should this be true, the revenues will cover O&M
costs for the initial network as they have been assumed to do for the
full network. It is clear that initial network segments covering areas
of high residential and employment densities are highly desirable
from an operating economics viewpoint, though this likely will
not be the only decision factor on placement.

Should such desirable locations of initial network segments not
be available or possible, operating deficits will be incurred until the
network approaches its mature configurations. The cumulative value
of these deficits could be considered an equivalent to an increase in
the systems capital cost, though it would likely have to be financed
from local sources. A properly conducted PRT planning process can
identify the magnitude of such deficits, if any, so that financial
implementation plans may be soundly structured. It will, however,
be a new experience to realize that as the network grows to maturity,
the operating deficits will likely disappear. With contemporary transit
modes (buses and trains), such operating deficits are never-ending,
and in fact, tend to increase due to inflation. This avoidance of
operating deficits could very well be one of the most significant
factors in support of PRT implementation.

11.4 PRT BENEFITS

While it is highly likely that a PRT network will not require an
operating subsidy (an unheard of thing for contemporary transit
systems), it is also clear that except under unusual circumstances the
capital costs cannot be amortized using fare-box revenues. There are,
however, many benefits associated with PRT which might be viewed
as offsetting the capital investment required. Let us consider PRT
benefits from a few different perspectives.

(a) *Benefits to Non-Drivers*

To those who don't own or cannot operate an automobile — the poor, the young, the elderly, and the infirm — PRT will afford a convenient and high level of mobility. These people will no longer be captives to their immediate neighborhoods, or dependent on infrequent and slow transit services. They will have a new and ready access to jobs, public services, health care, recreation, shopping, etc. The impact on their lifestyles will be most dramatic. Additionally, it should be noted that many drivers who have served to provide these people with some degree of mobility (e.g., mothers who are essentially chauffeurs for their children) will be relieved of much of that responsibility.

(b) *Benefits to Drivers Choosing to Use PRT*

The worker who chooses to use PRT will save money. The PRT fare will most likely be substantially less than the total cost of driving an automobile. Moreover, the availability of PRT will allow him to avoid second-car ownership. He will be likely to save some time in his home-to-work travel since the PRT trip will likely be quicker, and he will be relieved from the rigors of peak-hour driving. The time he spends traveling can be put to beneficial use: e.g., reading, writing, sleeping. Furthermore, he is less likely to be injured or killed while on his trip than if he were driving.

(c) *Benefits to Auto Drivers Who Still Choose to Drive*

The shift to PRT by many who might otherwise drive will benefit those still choosing to drive. Streets and freeways will be less congested, meaning quicker trips for the auto users. The smoother flow of auto traffic will likely result in some improvement in fuel economy.

(d) *Benefits to the Community*

The ubiquity of PRT and the ability to control network fineness in various areas will facilitate better control of land utilization in consonance with land-use objectives and goals. Significant reduction in auto traffic, which might be most pronounced in the high-density employment and residential areas, will provide a chance to greatly improve the urban environment through the creation of malls and parks on some of the space heretofore devoted to auto travel or parking. Building owners will benefit, since less provision for auto parking will have to be made in their buildings. A significant shift to PRT will also assist air pollution abatement.

The presence of PRT in urban areas previously lacking effective area-wide public transit will also facilitate new initiatives in the provision of education, health care, and social services. For example, specialty schools available for enrollment on a city-wide basis might be contemplated, in the manner of New York's High School of Music and Art or Brooklyn Technical High School. District schools might be combined into larger units which can more readily afford such special equipment as electronic teaching aids, laboratories, and shops.

Additionally, there is the possibility of shipping many classes of containerized urban freight over the PRT guideways using vehicles specially designed for such purposes. (The Japanese CVS Project presently incorporates the testing of such vehicles in concert with automated loading and unloading equipment.) Such shipments could be at off-peak hours or at night; i.e., generally on a non-interference basis with the passenger traffic. City streets would be less congested with truck traffic and less subjected to their noise and pollutant emissions. Costs of freight shipment could be reduced, while simultaneously enhancing the economics of the PRT system.

Finally there is the matter of energy conservation, which will benefit the area and the nation. PRT vehicles would be lighter than most autos and would operate essentially in a cruise mode (as opposed to the stop-and-go nature of urban auto driving). The average energy consumption versus speed for a typical PRT vehicle is summarized in Fig. 11-6. The energy consumption includes a 4.0-kW load for air conditioning, heating, and lighting. In the usual speed range of 30 mi/hr to 40 mi/hr, the PRT energy consumption is seen to be the

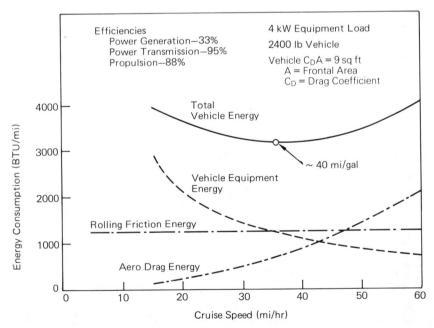

Fig. 11-6. PRT Vehicle Energy Consumption

equivalent of about 40 miles per gallon of gasoline. Assuming that the vehicles are empty during 1/4 to 1/3 of the miles traveled, the total energy consumed (including energy for empty vehicles) per mile of occupied vehicle travel is equivalent to about 27 to 30 miles per gallon of gasoline. Therefore, the energy consumption per occupied vehicle mile on PRT is about 50% to 60% that of city driving for most contemporary automobiles, although this difference will be substantially reduced as automobiles become lighter and more efficient. Because PRT is likely to have a significantly larger patronage than conventional transit modes, any energy savings per passenger trip will affect many more trips. However, even if future energy savings were not significant, it is important to realize that the electrical energy for PRT need not be based on petroleum as is present automotive energy.

Appendix A
ELEMENTARY KINEMATICS
Jack H. Irving

In this appendix we shall derive a few kinematical formulas associated with elementary vehicle maneuvers.

A.1 SPEED CHANGE

Consider a vehicle increasing speed from V_1 to V_2, with maximum allowable acceleration a_{max} and maximum allowable jerk J. Assume that the negative jerk is $-J$; i.e., that it has the same magnitude as the allowed positive jerk.

First we consider the case illustrated in Fig. A-1 where the needed change in speed is so small that there is no time to get the acceleration up to a_{max}. Let t_m be time to the midpoint of the maneuver. The acceleration at that time is Jt_m, which for this case must be less than a_{max}. The speed gained in the time t_m is $Jt_m{}^2/2$, and by symmetry it is seen that the speed gained in the total maneuver is twice this amount; i.e.,

$$\Delta V = V_2 - V_1 = Jt_m{}^2 \qquad \text{for } Jt_m \leqslant a_{max}. \qquad (A.1)$$

Solving for t_m, the inequality may be expressed as $\sqrt{J \Delta V} \leqslant a_{max}$.

The distance L traversed during the maneuver is the time of the complete maneuver, $2t_m$, multiplied by $\frac{1}{2}(V_1 + V_2)$, the average speed, or

$$
\begin{aligned}
L &= (V_1 + V_2)t_m \\
&= (V_1 + V_2)\sqrt{\frac{\Delta V}{J}} \qquad \text{for} \quad \sqrt{J \Delta V} \leqslant a_{max}. \qquad (A.2)
\end{aligned}
$$

For $\sqrt{J \Delta V} > a_{max}$, the acceleration reaches a_{max} and must be limited there, as illustrated in Fig. A-2. The two jerk periods will each last t_J seconds, where

$$t_J = a_{max}/J. \qquad (A.3)$$

During the first (or second) jerk period the average acceleration is $a_{max}/2$ and the speed gained will be $a_{max} t_J/2$. Define t_a as the

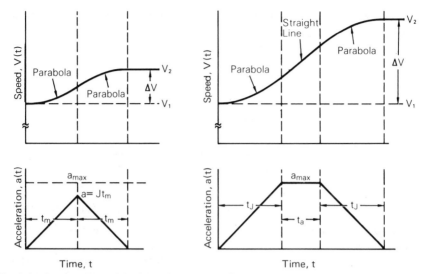

Fig. A-1. Acceleration and Speed vs Time when Maximum Allowable Acceleration (a_{max}) Not Reached

Fig. A-2. Acceleration and Speed vs Time when a_{max} Held for a Time t_a

duration of the constant acceleration period. The total speed change will be

$$\Delta V = \frac{1}{2}a_{max}t_J + a_{max}t_a + \frac{1}{2}a_{max}t_J$$

$$= a_{max}(t_a + t_J). \tag{A.4}$$

The distance L traversed is the total maneuver time $t_a + 2t_J$ multiplied by the average speed; i.e.,

$$L = \frac{V_1 + V_2}{2}(t_a + 2t_J). \tag{A.5}$$

Solving for $t_a + t_J$ from (A.4) and substituting into (A.5),

$$L = \frac{V_1 + V_2}{2}\left[\frac{\Delta V}{a_{max}} + t_J\right] \qquad \text{for } \sqrt{J\Delta V} \geqslant a_{max}. \tag{A.6}$$

The reader should note that $\Delta V/a_{max}$ is the time the maneuver would have taken with infinite jerk rates. The total time is merely this quantity augmented by t_J, and the distance traversed is this total time multiplied by the average speed. It is instructive to rewrite the inequality of (A.6) in terms of t_J. Squaring it and substituting a_{max} from (A.3), $J\Delta V \geqslant a_{max}^2 = a_{max}Jt_J$, or on dividing,

$$\frac{\Delta V}{a_{max}t_J} \geqslant 1.$$

We may now summarize this section by writing the distance traversed, L, in a speed change ΔV as

$$L = (V_1 + V_2)\sqrt{\frac{\Delta V}{J}}$$

$$= (V_1 + V_2)t_J \sqrt{\frac{\Delta V}{a_{max}t_J}} \qquad \text{for } \frac{\Delta V}{a_{max}t_J} \leqslant 1 \qquad \text{(A.7a)}$$

$$L = (V_1 + V_2)t_J\frac{1}{2}\left[\frac{\Delta V}{a_{max}t_J} + 1\right] \qquad \text{for } \frac{\Delta V}{a_{max}t_J} \geqslant 1 \qquad \text{(A.7b)}$$

Although these equations were derived for a speed increase, they apply as well to a decrease, providing a_{max} is interpreted as the maximum allowable deceleration and ΔV as the magnitude of the speed decrease.

For a numerical example, consider stopping from a speed of ~ 0 ft/sec, using a braking deceleration of 0.25 g $= 8.05$ ft/sec^2 and a jerk that lasts 1.0 sec. Then, from (A.7b), the stopping distance, L, is 70.9 ft.

A.2 SLOT SLIPPING OR ADVANCING

We may now apply the equations just derived to slot advancing or slipping, where the speed is changed from V_1 to V_2 and then immediately changed back to V_1. Here again we run into two cases, depending on whether $\dfrac{|V_2 - V_1|}{a_{max}t_J}$ is less than or greater than 1. The distance traversed during the maneuver, D, is double that given by Eq. (A.7).

$$D = 2(V_1 + V_2)t_J \sqrt{\frac{|V_2 - V_1|}{a_{max}t_J}} \quad \text{for} \frac{|V_2 - V_1|}{a_{max}t_J} \leqslant 1. \qquad \text{(A.8a)}$$

$$D = (V_1 + V_2)t_J\left[\frac{|V_2 - V_1|}{a_{max}t_J} + 1\right] \quad \text{for } \frac{|V_2 - V_1|}{a_{max}t_J} \geqslant 1. \qquad \text{(A.8b)}$$

The total time of the maneuver, T, is the distance D divided by the average speed $(V_1 + V_2)/2$.

$$T = 4t_J \sqrt{\frac{|V_2 - V_1|}{a_{max}t_J}} \qquad \text{for} \frac{|V_2 - V_1|}{a_{max}t_J} \leqslant 1. \qquad \text{(A.9a)}$$

$$T = 2t_J\left[\frac{|V_2 - V_1|}{a_{max}t_J} + 1\right] \qquad \text{for } \frac{|V_2 - V_1|}{a_{max}t_J} \geqslant 1. \qquad \text{(A.9b)}$$

The average increment of the instantaneous speed over the initial speed is

$$\frac{V_1 + V_2}{2} - V_1 = \frac{V_2 - V_1}{2}$$

This, multiplied by T, gives the distance advanced relative to the stream traveling at speed V_1.

$$Advance \quad = \quad (V_2 - V_1)2t_J \sqrt{\frac{|V_2 - V_1|}{a_{max} t_J}}$$

$$\text{for} \frac{|V_2 - V_1|}{a_{max} t_J} \leqslant 1, \qquad (A.10a)$$

$$= \quad (V_2 - V_1)t_J \left[\frac{|V_2 - V_1|}{a_{max} t_J} + 1 \right]$$

$$\text{for} \frac{|V_2 - V_1|}{a_{max} t_J} \geqslant 1. \qquad (A.10b)$$

If $V_2 < V_1$, a negative value results, and the magnitude should be interpreted as a slip.

From either (A.10a) or (A.10b), when $|V_2 - V_1| = a_{max} t_J$, $Advance = (V_2 - V_1)2t_J$. Solving for $|V_2 - V_1|$ and substituting, the inequality can be written as $\frac{|Advance|}{2a_{max} t_J{}^2} \leqslant 1$ for the "a" equations and $\geqslant 1$ for the "b" equations. Solving for $|V_2 - V_1|$ from (A.10a) and (A.10b), we have

$$|V_2 - V_1| = \left[\frac{a_{max}}{4t_J} (Advance)^2 \right]^{\frac{1}{3}}$$

$$\text{for } |Advance| \leqslant 2a_{max} t_J{}^2. \qquad (A.11a)$$

$$|V_2 - V_1| = -\frac{a_{max} t_J}{2} + \sqrt{a_{max} |Advance| + \frac{(a_{max} t_J)^2}{4}}$$

$$\text{for } |Advance| \geqslant 2a_{max} t_J{}^2. \qquad (A.11b)$$

When $|V_2 - V_1|$ from these equations is substituted into (A.9a) and (A.9b), the total maneuver time T may be expressed as

$$T = 4t_J \left[\frac{|Advance|}{2a_{max}t_J^2} \right]^{\frac{1}{3}}$$

$$\text{for } |Advance| \leqslant 2a_{max}t_J^2. \qquad \text{(A.12a)}$$

$$T = t_J \left[1 + \sqrt{1 + 8\frac{|Advance|}{2a_{max}t_J^2}} \right]$$

$$\text{for } |Advance| \geqslant 2a_{max}t_J^2. \qquad \text{(A.12b)}$$

Note that the time only depends on the magnitude of *"Advance"* and therefore is the same for slot advancing and slot slipping, depending only on the number of slots to be advanced or slipped.

For slot advancing the total distance traversed during the maneuver may be written as

$$D = V_1 T + Advance, \qquad \text{(A.13a)}$$

and for slot slipping,

$$D = V_1 T - Slip. \qquad \text{(A.13b)}$$

A.3 LATERAL TRANSLATION AT A SWITCH

There is no reason why the above equations should not apply to lateral or vertical motion, as well as longitudinal motion. A vehicle entering a switch section to a siding is accelerated laterally and then again decelerated to arrest further lateral motion, assuming the siding to be parallel with the main guideway.

Typically, the siding would be separated from the main guideway by about 7 or 8 ft to allow about 2 ft clearance between vehicles for aerodynamic disturbances. In the lateral direction the vehicle is initially at rest, and consequently the distance it translates over may be taken as the value of *"Advance."* The values of a_{max} and t_J must be selected on the basis of comfort criteria. Then (A.12a) and (A.12b) may be used to compute the time T of the lateral movement. The results are displayed in Fig. A-3 for two values of a_{max}. After determining the value of T, one need only multiply by the longitudinal speed to find the length of guideway over which the lateral translation occurs.

Let us examine the detailed dynamics for a lateral movement of 7.5 ft as might occur if 2.0 ft clearance is desired for vehicles 5.5 ft

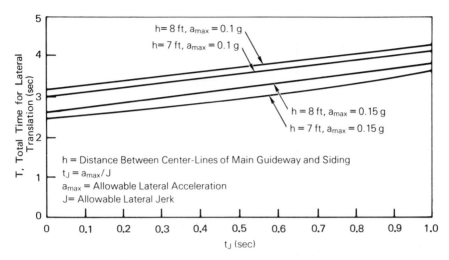

Fig. A-3. Total Time for Lateral Motion of a Vehicle Entering a Siding

wide. Assume a very conservative design,[1] one using 4 sec to complete the lateral movement. Let us further assume that $t_J = 1.0$ sec, so that we are dealing with the transitional case where the maximum acceleration is just reached, i.e., where

$$Advance = 7.5 \text{ ft} = 2a_{max}t_J{}^2.$$

Then, $a_{max} = 3.75 \text{ ft/sec}^2 = 0.116 \text{ g},$

and $J = 3.75 \text{ ft/sec}^3 = 0.116 \text{ g/sec.}$

Figure A-4 plots the lateral jerk, acceleration, velocity, and displacement as a function of time. It is seen that after 2.5 sec (more precisely 2.486 sec), the displacement is 5.5 ft and the vehicle is clear of vehicles on the through line. This result is independent of line speed.

The entrance section to a station must be long enough to allow a vehicle to come to a stop in the closest input queue slot. Assume for such a vehicle that braking starts 1.8 sec after the tail of the vehicle has entered the entrance section, i.e., 1.8 sec after it has passed the point where the guideway begins to widen. Let the longitudinal jerk rate be 0.25 g/sec = 8.05 ft/sec³. In the next 0.7 sec the vehicle will have dropped back, relative to where it would have been with no braking, only 0.46 ft, since $8.05 \times (0.7)^3/6 = 0.46$ ft. At this time (2.5 sec after the start of the lateral motion), the tail of the vehicle will be clear of vehicles on the through line. Thus, when the vehicle entering the siding has laterally cleared vehicles on the through line,

---

[1] Probably 3.5 sec or even 3.0 sec is quite comfortable, as can be verified by the reader by changing lanes in his automobile in this time.

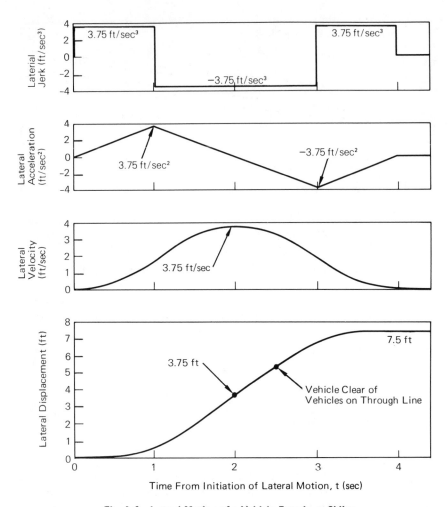

Fig. A-4. Lateral Motion of a Vehicle Entering a Siding

it will have dropped back by less than 0.5 ft, which presents no hazard.

Since the above argument is independent of the line speed,[2] the entrance section length may be found by computing the stopping distance from (A.7b) and adding 1.8 sec (the time in the entrance

---

[2] The time taken as 0.7 sec, more precisely should be taken as 0.7014 sec for a line speed of 30 ft/sec or 0.6935 sec for a line speed of 60 ft/sec, meaning that the clearance point is passed at 2.5014 sec or 2.4935 sec, respectively. Recalling that for a nonbraking vehicle the clearance point is passed at 2.486 sec into the section, the extra small fraction of a second allows the vehicle to reach the clearance point in spite of its speed reduction brought on by braking. Thus, the dependence on speed is so slight as to be completely ignored.

section prior to applying brakes) multiplied by the line speed. The result, with a minor correction, is

$$Entrance\ Length = \frac{V}{2}\left(\frac{V}{a_{braking}} + t_{J-braking}\right) + 1.8V - 0.5, \quad (A.14)$$

where V is the line speed, $a_{braking}$ is the normal braking deceleration, and $t_{J-braking}$ is the duration of the longitudinal jerk used for normal braking. Using the first two terms of (A.14) would bring the vehicle to rest with its tail at the end of the entrance section, but the tail should be 0.5 ft beyond there if a 10-ft vehicle is to be centered in an 11-ft input queue slot; hence 0.5 ft has been subtracted in Eq. (A.14).

By symmetry arguments, assuming vehicle acceleration is equal in magnitude to the braking deceleration, the length of an exit section from a station siding is also given by Eq. (A.14). Using Eq. (A.14) with $a_{braking} = 0.25\ g = 8.05\ ft/sec^2$ and $t_{J-braking} = 1.0$ sec, we find that at a line speed of 30 ft/sec the entrance (or exit) section is 124.4 ft long and at a line speed of 60 ft/sec it is 361.1 ft. A sketch of the 30 ft/sec entrance section is shown in Fig. 3-2 of Chapter 3, and a plot of entrance (exit) length versus line speed is given in Fig. 3-3.

Appendix B
THE AEROSPACE ONE-TENTH SCALE MODEL PROJECT

C. L. Olson

B.1 SCALE MODEL PROJECT DESCRIPTION

The Aerospace Corporation, during 1971 and 1972, constructed and operated a scaled physical model facility to further investigate the characteristics of the integrated propulsion, control, and switching concept. The specific objectives of the scaled model project were to (1) demonstrate the operation of the pulsed d.c. linear electric motor for both propulsion and braking, (2) demonstrate and test the operation of the vehicle digital control subsystem, (3) verify the feasibility of several command transmission techniques, (4) verify electromagnetic switching concepts, and (5) derive engineering data useful for the design of full-scale subsystems.

The scaled model facility consisted of an oval guideway measuring 45 ft by 14 ft with a single siding and electromagnetic switches. Three scaled PRT vehicles (1-ft long), containing double-sided pulsed d.c. linear motors and on-board control systems, were successfully operated on this guideway simultaneously. The guideway was sized to permit the demonstration of constant speed operation, slot-slipping and slot-advancing maneuvers, merging, switching, and emergency stops. The nominal operating velocity for the scaled vehicles was 3 ft/sec, representing a full-scale velocity of 30 ft/sec. All of the key propulsion subsystem elements, such as the guideway magnets, motor primary shape and dimensions, and primary slot configuration and size, were scaled to 1/10 full size. The important features of the model system are illustrated in Figs. B-1 and B-2.

The guideway installation was outdoors and was connected to an indoor control room through underground conduit. The control room contained the d.c. power supplies, and it contained a control panel and paper-tape sequencer for commanding the individual vehicles. The power and command circuits were connected to conductors mounted on both sides of the guideway (redundant) and were linked to the vehicles through sliding contacts.

Fig. B-1. PRT Scaled-Model Test Facility

B.2   MODEL DESIGN AND SIMULATION

Choice of the scale factor for model length was bounded by available installation space and miniaturization problems, including packaging of control electronics. A scale length factor of 1/10 was selected as a reasonable compromise within these constraints. It was felt that there were practical and psychological advantages to the use of real time, and unity was hence selected as the scale time factor. Since vehicle dynamics are not scalable, vehicle mass was chosen so as to permit scaled accelerations to result from application of scaled thrust forces.

The design approach taken on the model was to create a vehicle which faithfully scaled the thrust-producing elements of a full-sized vehicle, and at the same time permitted the investigation of command data techniques and vehicle maneuver characteristics. Since only three vehicles were included in the model system, use of a command

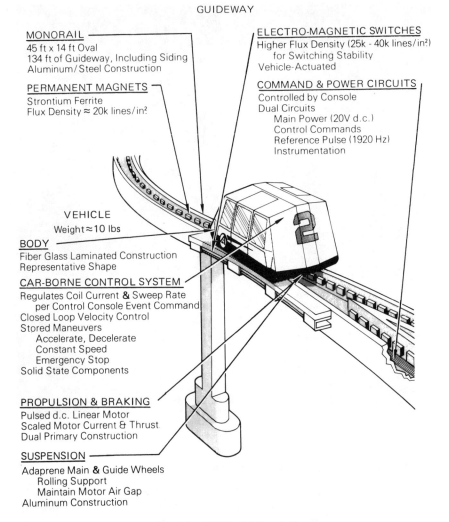

GUIDEWAY

MONORAIL
45 ft x 14 ft Oval
134 ft of Guideway, Including Siding
Aluminum/Steel Construction

PERMANENT MAGNETS
Strontium Ferrite
Flux Density ≈ 20k lines/in?

ELECTRO-MAGNETIC SWITCHES
Higher Flux Density (25k - 40k lines/in?)
    for Switching Stability
Vehicle-Actuated

COMMAND & POWER CIRCUITS
Controlled by Console
Dual Circuits
    Main Power (20V d.c.)
    Control Commands
    Reference Pulse (1920 Hz)
    Instrumentation

VEHICLE
Weight ≈ 10 lbs

BODY
Fiber Glass Laminated Construction
Representative Shape

CAR-BORNE CONTROL SYSTEM
Regulates Coil Current & Sweep Rate
    per Control Console Event Command
Closed Loop Velocity Control
Stored Maneuvers
    Accelerate, Decelerate
    Constant Speed
    Emergency Stop
Solid State Components

PROPULSION & BRAKING
Pulsed d.c. Linear Motor
Scaled Motor Current & Thrust
Dual Primary Construction

SUSPENSION
Adaprene Main & Guide Wheels
    Rolling Support
    Maintain Motor Air Gap
Aluminum Construction

Fig. B-2. PRT Model Description

computer was not necessary. Thus, the model vehicles were configured to accept commands from a wayside console for execution of some 12 maneuver profiles, using only the on-board control system for position verification.

Both computer simulation and mechanical dynamic simulation techniques were used in the design of the model elements. The vehicle control subsystem was simulated on a hybrid digital/analog computer to verify the design of the error computation and logic circuits. Logic components on the computer were used to generate simulated Hall-effect detector pulses, control the error generation, and time the maneuvers. The vehicle dynamics and motor servo compensation circuits were also simulated with analog components. This technique proved useful in verifying the choice of servo gains and in investigating transients during startup and maneuvering.

A track simulator test fixture was designed to provide the capability of performance evaluation of the linear motor and control electronics with a stationary vehicle. The simulator consisted of an endless steel band mounted on a pair of free-wheeling pulleys with permanent magnets bonded to the band at the 1.2-inch pole pitch spacing, as illustrated in Fig. B-3. The band and magnets were guided

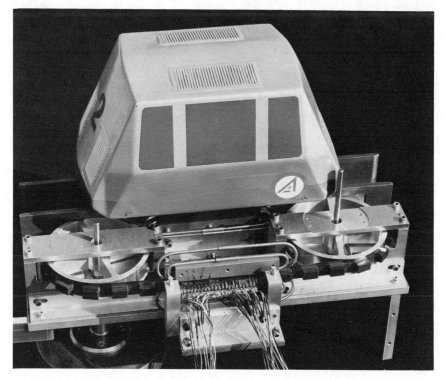

Fig. B-3. Stationary Vehicle Undergoing Motor Tests on Track-Simulator Test Fixture

past one side of the motor armature by linear ball bushings to maintain the working air gap of 0.030 inch, and to minimize friction between the band and the back iron provided to complete the field magnetic circuit. A rotary d.c. torque motor attached to one pulley shaft provided a controlled torque for either loading or unloading the linear motor. Inertia was coupled to the pulley shaft to obtain dynamic conditions equivalent to the linear operation of the vehicle on a fixed guideway.

The propulsion system for the scaled model followed the configuration established by analysis for the full-sized motor (Sec. 7.2). The motor primary (Fig. B-4) was designed with a split core containing a total of 48 coil slots.

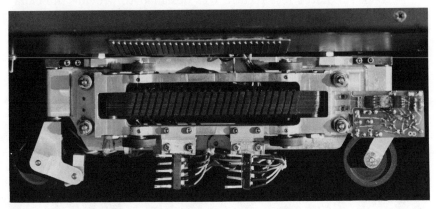

Fig. B-4. Motor Primary and Vehicle Suspension

B.3   MODEL SYSTEM CONTROL

The vehicle-borne control loop utilized in the model was functionally similar to that illustrated in Fig. 4-11, except for the following variations: The model substituted a preprogrammed paper-tape unit for the local wayside computer; maneuver profiles were stored and not computed; initialization was obtained manually; circuits were not redundant; there was no on-board accelerometer; and emergency stop control was provided by a pressure-sensitive switch on the front of each vehicle. When an obstacle was encountered, the pressure switch commanded full braking force from all vehicles on the guideway.

Since it was anticipated that microcomputer techniques would be used in a full-scale vehicle and since they were also used in the model vehicles, the control system was, of course, full-scale, and has served as the basis for the extensive reliability studies described in Chapter 8, where the effects of adding redundancy are evaluated.

Coded command information was transmitted from the wayside console either in a manual or automatic (paper tape) mode. The scaled vehicles contained solid state circuitry to receive and decode digital commands and to process and interpret commands for propulsion control. Transmittal of command data was implemented in two ways: (1) frequency modulated (FM) signals in the 300-600 kHz range were hard-wired to track conductors, and the data entered the car through contact brushes, and (2) data were transmitted via an amplitude modulated (AM) waveform at radio frequencies (25-30

MHz) to vehicle-borne receivers. Twelve individual car commands were stored in each car and were executed upon receipt of the appropriate command signal from the console. A block diagram of the model command system, using the FM mode, is shown in Fig. B-5.

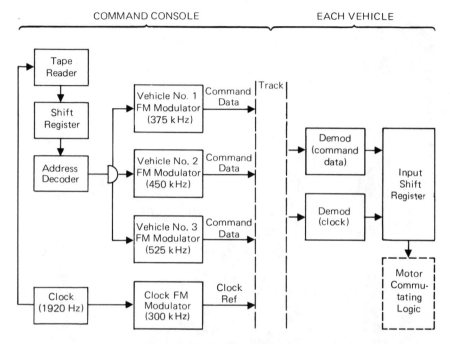

Fig. B-5. Model Command System

B.4 GUIDEWAY, VEHICLE SUSPENSION, AND SWITCHING

The open-channel monorail model guideway shown in Fig. B-1 was constructed at a height of approximately 21 inches, representing 1/10 of the normal urban installation height. Outer walls and bottom were made of aluminum; the inner walls were soft iron to provide a good path for the magnetic circuit. The permanent magnets, made of strontium ferrite, were bonded to the iron inner wall at carefully indexed locations at 1.2-inch intervals. At the switches, slots were provided in the guideway sidewalls to permit installation of the electromagnet pole faces. Five conductors were mounted on each upstanding flange for transfer of power and information to the vehicles through sliding contacts.

The vehicle suspension was designed to provide vehicle stability and lateral guidance, as well as to maintain a nominal primary/magnet air gap of 0.030 inch. All vertical loads were carried by the two main support wheels, and side loads on the split core primary were picked up by four lateral wheels on each side, as shown in Fig. B-4. The suspension was designed to permit a variation in buck-out of the magnetic attractive side loads on the lateral wheels.

The model guideway had two switch locations at which electro-magnetic switches were installed, as shown in Fig. B-6. Permanent

Fig. B-6. Electromagnetic Switch Installation

magnets at those locations were replaced by soft-iron pole pieces wound with coils containing 2,300 turns each. The pole pieces were inserted through slots milled in the guideway sidewall. The switch command energized an infrared light source on the vehicle, and the light was sensed by a receiver mounted in the guideway to trigger the switch mode. In this mode a group of eight poles were de-energized on the straight section and the opposite set of eight poles on the divergent section were energized. This condition was maintained sufficiently long to cause the turning vehicle to diverge. The process was then reversed so that the straight section was energized again before the following vehicle approached.

B.5   MODEL OPERATIONS

Initial scaled-model vehicle operations were devoted to checkout of the guideway/vehicle interface and to the initial testing of the pulsed d.c. linear motor and electromagnetic switching equipment. These test operations permitted the refinement of design details in the guideway power and control circuits, vehicle electrical pickups, electromagnetic switching sensor placement, and vehicle suspension settings. Vehicle power demands and general motor operations were also verified, and tests of the command data transmission system were also successfully conducted.

With development of the full complement of three closed-loop controlled vehicles, a complete series of typical PRT operations was conducted. Multiple-car operations were demonstrated in which all three vehicles were started, accelerated, and run at line speed while maintaining a constant 1/2-sec headway. Successful demonstrations were made of various vehicle maneuvers, such as merging and diverging at full speed, slot-slipping, slot-advancing, and multiple-car switching. Emergency operations were demonstrated by placing a specially designed decelerator (barrier) on the guideway which was calibrated to produce settable decelerations simulating decelerations between 0.25 g and 0.75 g. The lead vehicle, upon impacting the barrier, transmitted a command to the other vehicles through a voltage level applied to one of the track conductors, and all three vehicles executed an emergency stop.

A 16-mm color film covering all phases of the model operations was completed and is available for loan, in voice-annotated form, from The Aerospace Corporation.

GLOSSARY

ACT Automatically Controlled Transportation, a shuttle system developed by Ford Motor Company and installed in a Dearborn, Michigan shopping center.

Advanced Group Rapid Transit (AGRT) A system being developed under the sponsorship of UMTA which will employ 12-passenger vehicles (all passengers seated) separated by a 3-second headway. Two designs will be tested on test tracks at Pueblo, Colorado Proving Grounds. Candidates are a wheel-supported vehicle system developed by Boeing Aircraft Company (a variant of the Morgantown GRT), an air-suspension design by Otis Elevator, and a magnetic-suspension design (ROMAG) developed by Rohr and currently owned by Boeing.

AGRT *See* Advanced Group Rapid Transit

AGT *See* Automated Guideway Transit

AIRTRANS A 40-passenger GRT, developed by LTV, operating at the Dallas-Fort Worth Airport.

ARAMIS A line-haul variant of PRT developed by Engin Matra with the support of the French Government. A test track has operated at Orly, France. Four-passenger vehicles are separated by 30 centimeters, in platoons or "trains." The platoons are separated by approximately a one-minute headway.

Asynchronous Control A car-following control scheme in which each vehicle measures the distance to the vehicle ahead of it and adjusts its speed accordingly. At merges and intersections there must also be some measurement of the location of merging vehicles to resolve conflicts. Routing can either be preplanned or under computer control, taking into account line densities and speeds.

Automated Guideway Transit (AGT) Any transit system in which completely automated vehicles travel on fixed guideways along an exclusive right-of-way, grade-separated from street and pedestrian traffic. Vehicles may be operated as single units or in trains. Three major categories of AGT are: Shuttle-Loop Transit (SLT), Group Rapid Transit (GRT), and Personal Rapid Transit (PRT).

Berth The location on a station platform where a vehicle will stop. The berth length is the length of the vehicle plus the distance between vehicles stopped at the platform. Usually there will be a gate near the midpoint of the berth, through which the passenger will enter the vehicle.

Cabintaxi A system of small PRT vehicles operating under asynchronous control, developed by DEMAG and Messerschmitt-Bölkow-Blohm with the support of the Federal Republic of Germany. A test track is operating at Hagen. A 12-passenger GRT variant (with all passengers seated) is currently being constructed in Hamburg with the first section to be operational in 1979.

Car Follower Any control system, such as a traditional asynchronous control system, in which an attempt is made to position the vehicle relative to the vehicle ahead. *See also* Point Follower

CBD Central Business District

Computer-controlled Vehicle System A PRT system developed and tested in Japan by a consortium of eight companies under the leadership of the University of Tokyo and the sponsorship of the Japan Society for the Promotion of Machine Industry. The system had both passenger and freight vehicles. The project was completed in 1976, and follow-on activities are still uncertain.

CVS See Computer-controlled Vehicle System

Docking Station A fixed-platform station using a guideway and vehicle suspension design capable of moving vehicles sideways so that a vehicle entering the station can pass by parked vehicles and move directly to a prescribed platform berth.

Group Rapid Transit (GRT) A category of AGT system which employs vehicles or vehicle trains shared by strangers. GRT systems generally have off-line stations so that vehicles need not stop at every station. There are several service concepts which can be used on GRT, depending upon the network layout, the protocol for route assignment, and the protocol for making station stops. (These concepts are discussed in Section 1.2.2.)

GRT See Group Rapid Transit

Headway Interval of time between the passage of successive vehicles. More precisely, the headway between two vehicles is the interval of time between the instant when the first vehicle's nose (forward-most point) passes a particular point on the guideway, and the instant when the nose of the second passes the same point.

Line-Haul Transportation Transportation along a corridor, without substantial branching for collection or distribution of passengers.

Loop Transit A system of automated vehicles or vehicle trains circulating on a guideway loop, utilizing on-line stations and long headways. There is some question as to whether a two-way line-haul system, utilizing arcs at the ends for vehicle turn-around, should or should not be regarded as a flattened loop, and therefore be classified as loop transit.

Modal Split The fraction of travelers going by each of the available modes of transportation. A modal split model is a means of predicting these fractions. Generally it does not take into account the effect that the availability of a new mode might have on inducing more travel.

Morgantown GRT A GRT operating on the campus of the University of West Virginia. The development was sponsored by UMTA, with Boeing Aircraft as the prime contractor.

Off-Line Station A station in which loading/unloading platforms are in juxtaposition to a siding off the through guideway, so that vehicles may bypass the station and thus avoid waiting for predecessor vehicles making a station stop. Such off-line stations are required when automated transit vehicles are to be operated at very short headways, since these headways, perhaps as low as fractions of a second, are much shorter than the time required for a station stop.

On-Line Station A station where loading/unloading platforms are in juxtaposition to the through guideway. When a vehicle stops at the station, all vehicles behind it must wait until the stopped vehicle has unloaded and/or loaded passengers and cleared the station. Consequently, headways generally have to be 60 seconds or greater.

Personal Rapid Transit The most advanced category of AGT system. A traveler and his companions would be assigned a private vehicle, not shared with strangers, to take them on a nonstop no-transfers trip from their origin station to their destination station. Typical vehicle capacity would be three to six passengers, all seated. Stations would be off-line and networks usually would include extensive branching. Normally, empty vehicles would be queued at the departure station so that no waiting would be required. Depending on the type of control and safety features, headway could be down to 0.25 second.

Point Follower Any vehicle control scheme, such as synchronous or quasi-synchronous control, in which the vehicle attempts to move along with an imaginary moving point. Staying in the middle of a moving slot is equivalent to following a moving point. *See also* Car Follower

PRT *See* Personal Rapid Transit

Quasi-synchronous Control A control system which, like synchronous control, employs the concept of synchronized imaginary moving slots. However, in contrast to synchronous control, no slot reservations are made. The vehicle may leave the departure station whenever it is boarded and is able to merge onto the through line. As the vehicle approaches each intersection, a local computer controlling the traffic at that intersection will look up the best route to the destination station from that point and determine whether it is desirable for the vehicle to turn. The local computer will also resolve conflicts at the intersection by ordering vehicles to advance or slip slots. (*See* Single-Stream and Split-Stream intersections.) The system is designed so that each intersection computer is autonomous (except following certain types of failure), and is not permitted to impinge upon the autonomy of its upstream neighbor by ordering slot-slipping maneuvers that cannot be carried out within its area of jurisdiction. As a result, it may be necessary for the computer to deny a turn for a vehicle wishing to enter a crowded line. The vehicle thus waved on will take an alternate route to its destination. Generally, denials will be given to those vehicles that will suffer the least penalty in taking the alternate route.

Shuttle-Loop Transit (SLT) A compound category of AGT systems, including shuttle transit and loop transit. These are technically the simplest of the AGT systems since they use on-line stations and long headways. *See* Shuttle Transit; Loop Transit

Shuttle Transit The simplest form of shuttle transit is the horizontal equivalent of an automatic elevator where a single vehicle or train of vehicles moves back and forth on a single guideway. There can be on-line stations at the ends of the guideway or at intermediate stops. A more complex version uses two or more vehicles or trains with bypasses so that oppositely directed vehicles can bypass each other.

Single-Stream Intersection An intersection configuration and control scheme utilized in quasi-synchronous control. Conflicts are resolved by the local computer requesting slot-changing maneuvers in the two streams of vehicles approaching the intersection (assuming a one-way network); such maneuvers to be completed *before* vehicles have arrived at the branch points leading to the turn ramps. *See also* Split-Stream Intersection

Slot Size The longitudinal distance along the guideway allocated to each vehicle when operating at minimum headway under synchronous or quasi-synchronous control. Slot size is thus the length of the vehicle plus the minimum separation between the vehicles. Dividing slot size by the line speed gives the minimum headway.

SLT *See* Shuttle-Loop Transit

Split-Stream Intersection An intersection configuration and control scheme utilized in quasi-synchronous control. Conflicts are resolved by the local computer requesting slot-changing maneuvers in the two streams of vehicles approaching the intersection (assuming a one-way network); such maneuvers to be completed *after* vehicles have passed the branch points leading to the turn ramps. This requires that the branch points be farther from the point of guideway crossing than is necessary in the single-stream intersection, but it "decouples" the turning vehicles from those going straight, and thereby reduces the percentage of vehicles that must be denied turns.

Synchronous Control A control system based on the concept of imaginary moving "slots" or "blocks," each either empty or occupied by a vehicle centered in it. For each line there is a prescribed speed for slot movement and the slot alignment is such that where two guideways merge, the incoming slots will exactly coincide. Before a vehicle leaves a station, reservations are made for slots that it will occupy throughout its travel, and a time of arrival is reserved at the destination station. The departure time is delayed until all reservations are confirmed. Variations allow a certain amount of preplanned slot changing en route by temporarily increasing or decreasing the vehicle's speed.

UMTA Urban Mass Transportation Administration of the United States Department of Transportation

INDEX